MODERN CAR
# TECHNOLOGY

# MODERN CAR
# TECHNOLOGY

**JEFF DANIELS** LOOKS UNDER THE SKIN OF TODAY'S CARS

**Haynes Publishing**

For *Modern Car Technology*, Jeff Daniels was awarded the 2002 Renault UK Journalist of the Year Award. This prize is presented to the Guild of Motoring Writers member judged to have made the most outstanding journalistic effort in any medium (newspaper, magazine, book, radio or television), with particular emphasis upon initiative and endeavour.

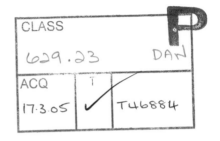
First published in October 2001
Reprinted December 2002

A catalogue record for this book is available from the British Library.

ISBN 1 85960 811 6

Library of Congress catalog card no. 2001132561

Published by Haynes Publishing, Sparkford,
Yeovil, Somerset BA22 7JJ, UK
Tel: 01963 442030 Fax: 01963 440001
Int. tel: +44 1963 442030 Fax: +44 1963 440001
E-mail: sales@haynes-manuals.co.uk
Web site: www.haynes.co.uk

Haynes North America Inc., 861 Lawrence Drive, Newbury Park, California 91320, USA

Printed and bound in Britain by J.H. Haynes & Co. Ltd., Sparkford

# Contents

# Introduction

The motor car is central to most of our lives, yet many of us take it entirely on trust, without understanding what happens under the bonnet or anywhere else. Fair enough; the car manufacturers have lived with that attitude for a long time now and have sought to make their products as foolproof as possible, with technology 'transparent' to the uninterested owner-driver. Yet the technology is there, and many car drivers are interested in it to some degree.

Being interested in it, and actually understanding it can be two different things. In the last 15 years or so, the amount of technology in our motor cars has increased in the most dramatic way. In the late 1980s, you could still buy a new petrol-engined car with a carburettor, and the kind of simple exhaust system which dated back almost a hundred years. Now, you get multipoint fuel injection and a catalytic-converter system without the option. In the late 1980s, the airbag was unheard of in Europe: today, it is difficult to find a car which doesn't have a driver airbag, and some models carry as many as eight separate bags (driver and passenger front, side, and head-protecting 'curtain'). Alongside these very obvious developments have come others. Anti-lock brakes are now almost standard, traction control is becoming more common, and a cunning combination of the two has given us 'electronic stability enhancement'. Air conditioning and even automatic transmission are becoming more common in European cars, having long been taken for granted in the USA and (mainly) in Japan.

There are good reasons for all these developments. Cars have become very much cleaner, safer, more comfortable and easier to drive as a result. And there is more to come. If you think the last 15 years have seen dramatic technical developments, just wait for the next decade and a half. In the next few years we shall begin to experience cars which warn us of trouble ahead and advise us how to find a way round it, which will maintain a safe distance from the vehicle ahead and automatically stay in the middle of a motorway lane. Engineers are looking eagerly at the improvements they can achieve by replacing mechanical links to the engine, the brakes and the steering with electric 'by wire' systems. We are likely to see a switch from our familiar 12-volt electrical systems to more powerful, more efficient 36-volt ones. Engines and transmissions themselves will become even cleaner and more fuel-efficient – and

we shall see a new generation first of electric 'hybrids' and eventually of fuel-cell-powered cars to make the world a cleaner place and to make redundant the threat of exhausted crude oil reserves. The materials of which cars are made, and the way in which they are manufactured, are likely to change. And so on, and so on …

But how is the interested car-owning, car-driving observer to understand, to keep up with and anticipate all these developments? For some time it has seemed to me – and, it emerged, to my editors at Haynes – that there was a gap in the market, so to speak. There are books on the technology of the motor car which start by assuming you know nothing and which try to avoid using words of more than two syllables. There are plenty of others which are written by highly qualified experts, for experts, making no concession at all to any lack of technical or mathematical qualification on the part of the reader. There is precious little in between.

The purpose of this book is to fill the gap. It doesn't waste time or space explaining things from first principles, except in a few cases where the first principles are well worth going back to because some people seem to have lost sight of them. Otherwise, I have assumed a level of reader knowledge which would qualify you as at least a moderate motoring enthusiast, and started from there. At the same time, I have avoided 'deep' technology. There are no mathematical formulae here. I still believe the principles, the purpose and the benefits of most technical features can be explained to an intelligent reader in carefully chosen words. One thing I have been careful to do, as far as possible, is to explain for-and-against; most engineering decisions are the result of an argument in which one approach is judged to have more advantages (or fewer disadvantages) than another. Very few things in this business are ever completely clear-cut, especially when extra cost is taken into account.

This book might be described as a distillation of the process by which I gain my own understanding of how the world of vehicle engineering is evolving. I do it by wading through masses of published papers and manufacturer press releases, and travelling the world to look at, to be briefed on and to evaluate new vehicle technologies. It is at least a full-time task. In fact the spread is now so wide that even I have to be selective. For example, I can afford to pay relatively little attention to the world of heavy commercial vehicles, of trucks and buses, fascinating though they are. I simply don't have the time. The writing of this book was done in the intervals between visits to various factories, test tracks and research centres, and several times I returned with new information which made me rewrite various existing chapter sections.

This is an endless situation, of course. There will be more visits, and more reading, and eventually there will be a need for an updated edition of this book. But I have tried to anticipate. Often enough, the trends are clear long before the car manufacturers reveal the detailed engineering of the way forward. I have tried to identify the trends as far as I can, and to suggest how they might be brought to reality. All I can hope is that the result is informative and interesting.

Jeff Daniels
London SW20
October 2001

# Acknowledgements

I started life as an aeronautical engineer, fell into motoring journalism almost by accident, and have learned something from almost every senior motor industry engineer with whom I have talked since 1967. Inevitably, some of them are no longer with us, while others have retired or moved into fresh fields. To name them all would take a couple of pages and a lot of diary research. Purely off the top of my head, in roughly chronological order and with no disrespect to any missing name, the engineers I remember meeting and learning from with particular pleasure include; Sir Alec Issigonis of BMC; Rudolf Uhlenhaut of Mercedes; Harry Mundy and Bob Knight of Jaguar; Peter Wilks and Gordon Bashford of Rover; Harry Webster and Spen King of Triumph; Ulrich Sieffert and Peter Waltzer of Volkswagen; Nobuhiko Kawamoto of Honda; Jim Randle of Jaguar; Philippe Ventre of Renault; Don Runkle of GM and later of Delphi; Akihiro Wada of Toyota; and Richard Parry-Jones of Ford. Also three very special designers: David Bache of Rover, Wayne Cherry of GM and Patrick le Quement of Renault. And finally, one non-engineer with a valued insight into what makes the motor industry tick – Professor Garel Rhys of Cardiff University Business School. To them – or, where sadly appropriate, to their memories – my special gratitude.

# **1** **Engine** general **principles**

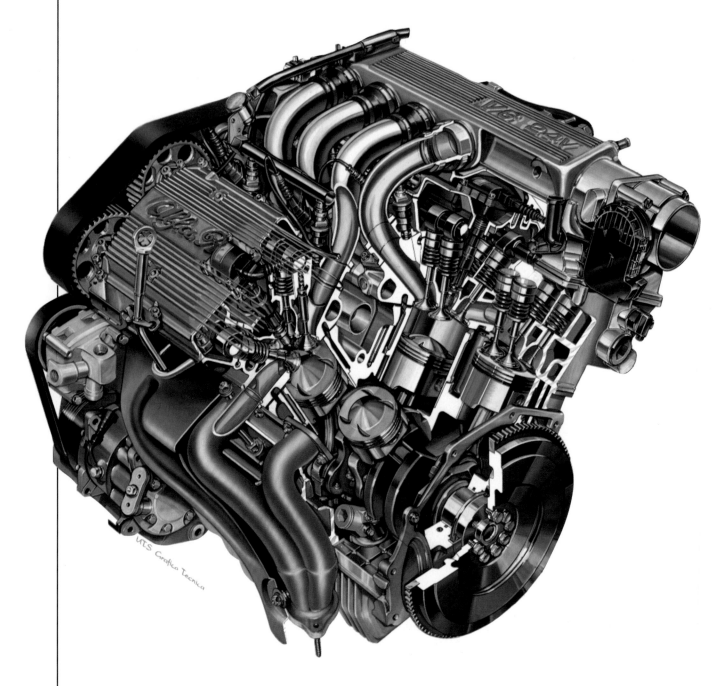

Inventors, especially amateur inventors, can be determined beyond all reason in their belief that there must be a better way. One of the best examples of this attitude is seen in engines for motor vehicles. For the last hundred years, the vast majority of road-going vehicles have been powered by internal-combustion engines with reciprocating pistons and poppet valves. For all of those hundred years, inventors have suggested thousands of alternative concepts – everything from new forms of valve gear, through internal-combustion engines that did away with the pistons and connecting rods, gas turbines, and external-combustion engines (such as steam engines); not forgetting the electric car, of course. Most of those ideas never got off the drawing board. The ones that did were either pushed along by enthusiastic sponsors, or had enough just merit to be worth a closer look – if not actually to succeed. Steam and electric cars did well in the early 20th century, but eventually could not offer the performance or the convenience of their conventional rivals. A handful of experimental prototype cars have run with gas turbine engines. Possibly the nearest any 'new concept' came to real success was the Wankel rotary engine which reached production in the 1960s. In the end, however, all these alternatives failed to oust the engine we know so well, and we have to ask ourselves why this should be.

The job of any engine used to power a vehicle is a simple one. It must take stored energy and convert it into mechanical work. The energy can be stored in a whole variety of ways; from electricity in batteries, to air compressed in cylinders, to twisted rubber bands, but one of the main reasons for the success of the combustion engine is that by far the lightest and easiest form of storage is to carry a tank of fuel which releases its chemical energy through burning. It happens that a number of such fuels are readily available in convenient liquid form, making them easy to transport and to dispense into individual vehicles. Among them are petrol and diesel oil, although there are several alternatives.

If you take an engine which works on the principle of burning a fuel, then you need enough air to provide the required (and considerable) amount of oxygen. So the task of the engine becomes one of drawing in air, mixing it with the fuel, burning the mixture, converting the resulting pressure into mechanical movement, and expelling the burned gases afterwards. So long as an engine does this with efficiency – converting as much of the chemical energy as possible into mechanical work – then the lighter, simpler, cheaper and easier it is to make, the better. This is where most of the inventors come to grief: they are so keen to overcome some particular drawback of existing engines as they see them, that they produce something which in other respects is heavier, more complicated, more expensive, and (usually) less efficient.

Today we are on the threshold of a new age which will almost certainly see the internal-combustion engine replaced by the fuel cell and the electric motor. The fuel cell converts the stored chemical energy of hydrogen and, using oxygen taken from the air, converts it directly to electric power with water as the only by-product. The fuel cell is important enough to be dealt with separately in Chapter 8, but at this stage it is worth noting that the fuel cell in itself is not an engine. You need a fuel cell plus an electric motor to achieve what the familiar piston engine achieves – the conversion of chemical energy into mechanical motive power.

# From external to internal combustion

People have always pondered the best way of converting the energy of burning into motive power. In the 18th century, there appeared the first truly practical method, the steam engine. The principle of the steam engine is that water is heated to form steam under pressure, and that pressure is then fed through a valve and into a cylinder to drive a piston. By the time the piston has moved from its highest to its lowest compression position, the steam has cooled down and lost most of its pressure. As the piston moves up again, it simply expels the 'spent' steam through another valve – unless water is in short supply, in which case you can condense it and feed it back to the boiler in a closed circuit.

The steam engine is an external-combustion engine. That is, it burns fuel continuously but outside the actual engine, and uses steam as the 'working fluid' which carries the energy of burning into the engine to make it work. There have been many projects for external-combustion engines using a closed circuit containing something other than steam as the working fluid. Steam was the obvious choice in the 18th century, because water in any required quantity was free, because the only available fuel was coal, which could

*Opposite: One of the most admired V6 engines, the Alfa Romeo unit dates back to the late 1970s as a basic design but has been constantly upgraded, not least with the move to four valves per cylinder, creating the unit now fitted in the 156. Points of special interest include the distinctly domed piston crowns for high compression ratio, with cut-outs for valve clearance. The long-curved inlet tracts from the massive plenum chamber are also worth noting. As can be seen, camshaft drive is by toothed belt. (Alfa Romeo)*

only be burned in an external boiler, and because the temperatures involved could be easily handled by the crude materials with which engineers had to work. A modern external-combustion engine might work better with a fluid that boiled at a higher temperature than 100°C. That way, you would achieve much better efficiency than a steam engine (steam railway locomotives are around 5 per cent efficient). But you would still have an engine which consisted of a boiler unit and a conversion-to-mechanical-work unit, with the working fluid running around a circuit between the two. The bulk and complexity of the external-combustion engine, and the development of liquid fuels, led many people in the 19th century to wonder whether a practical engine could be developed in which the fuel could actually be burned inside the engine, doing away with the external boiler and all its associated pipework.

## Fuel to burn

We have already come a long way from the days when it was first realised crude oil could be refined to petrol and (later) diesel oil which would burn quickly, cleanly and efficiently in internal-combustion engines. Today our anxiety is partly that these fuels

are still not clean enough, but above all that they will not last for ever. Estimates of how long our crude oil reserves are likely to last run from 40 to 65 years, depending on how optimistic you are about discovering new oil fields. In any case, some time before the oil actually runs out, fuels derived from it will have become too expensive to use. Fortunately, there are readily available alternatives – probably too many of them, since there is a great deal of argument about which one will be the most effective substitute.

In theory, the internal-combustion engine can be modified to run on any gas or liquid that will burn fast enough. Some alternatives are already in fairly widespread use – liquefied petroleum gas (LPG), compressed natural gas (CNG), the alcohols (ethanol and methanol) and other fuels derived, like ethanol, from vegetable matter. Liquid hydrocarbon fuels can also be derived from coal, and coal reserves are far larger than crude oil reserves. All these alternatives have their enthusiastic backers, although methanol lost a good deal of support during the 1990s. At one time it looked the most promising alternative, but fleet trials showed that its use in engines with catalytic converters resulted in the formation of foul-smelling formaldehyde. The current Californian state exhaust emission regulations place a limit on formaldeyde levels as a direct result. The future of methanol is far more likely to be as a source of hydrogen for fuel cells (see Chapter 8).

## The 4-stroke cycle: the most basic principle

By the late 19th century the problem of how to burn fuel in a controlled way inside an engine had been solved with the development of the 4-stroke cycle, now generally called the Otto cycle after one of the leading researchers in the field. It seemed evident at the time that you couldn't have continuous burning in an internal-combustion engine. In fact you can, because the gas turbine is an internal-combustion engine to which fuel is fed in a continuous stream; but a century of steadily evolving steam engine technology had conditioned the 19th century

*This part-cutaway drawing shows the general layout of the complete PSA HDI turbodiesel engine in its original 2-litre, 8-valve form. Among the interesting points is the accessory drive system in which a single poly-vee belt drives the power steering pump, alternator and air-conditioning compressor in a single long, winding loop. Note that with no throttle valve to create low pressure in the inlet manifold, diesel engines also need a vacuum pump to operate the brake servo unit. (PSA)*

researchers to think in terms of an engine in which pistons moved in cylinders and were linked to a crankshaft by connecting rods.

The 4-stroke cycle was such a good concept that the vast majority of modern vehicle engines use it. If we exclude diesel engines for a moment, then in the first stroke of the cycle, the piston sucks in the air and fuel, and the two begin to mix. During the second stroke, the piston compresses the mixture until it is ignited towards the top of the stroke by the carefully timed firing of a spark plug. The third stroke sees the pressure of the rapidly heated gas pushing the piston downwards, while during the fourth stroke the piston pushes the burned gases out of the cylinder, ready for the whole process to begin again. These four strokes are conventionally known as induction, compression, power and exhaust (and less reverently, among engineers, as suck, squeeze, bang and blow). The degree to which the air above the piston is compressed – the ratio of the space above the piston at the top of its travel to the space above it at the bottom of its travel – is the compression ratio. In modern 4-stroke spark-ignition engines the compression ratio is around 10:1.

All the light-duty diesel engines offered in today's passenger cars also use the 4-stroke cycle. The important difference between diesel and petrol engines is that the diesel uses a much higher compression ratio (of around 20:1) which makes the air hot enough to ensure that ignition takes place spontaneously as soon as the fuel is injected. In the petrol engine, the fuel is already there, pre-mixed with the air and is ignited by the firing of the spark

*The essential difference between 4-stroke and 2-stroke engines is that the latter depends on the air/fuel charge being 'squeezed' around a transfer port by downward movement of the piston, while combustion takes place above. Although the 2-stroke is light, compact and mechanically simple, its NOx emissions are unavoidably higher than in the 4-stroke, and its long-term durability remains suspect. (Ford)*

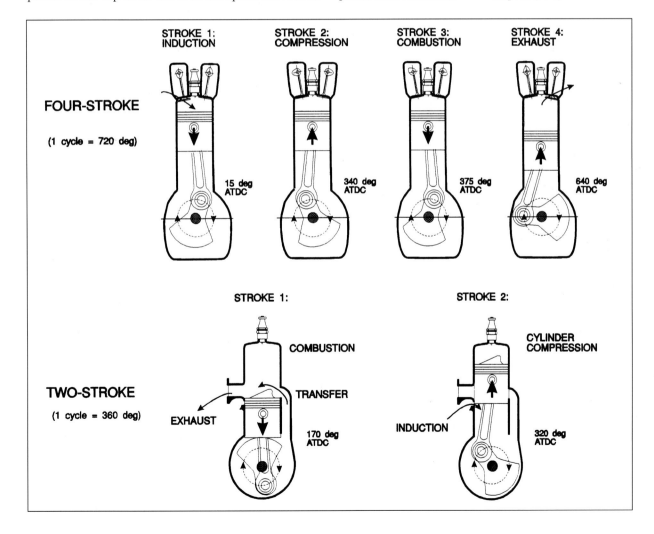

plug; in the diesel, the fuel is injected with careful timing and ignition takes place more or less immediately. While most people talk happily about petrol (or gasoline) and diesel engines, engineers often resort to the shorthand of SI (spark ignition) and CI (compression ignition) when distinguishing between the two.

# The 2-stroke
## – doomed to failure?

An alternative approach to the 4-stroke cycle, however, is offered by the 2-stroke engine. In the 2-stroke, carefully placed ports in the cylinder wall are uncovered by the equally carefully-shaped piston as it moves down and then up again, allowing air and fuel to be admitted at the same time as exhaust gases are being driven out. Thus every piston downstroke is a power plus induction stroke, the induction taking place after the inlet port is uncovered, and every upstroke is an exhaust plus compression stroke, with

most of the compression taking place after the ports have been covered. Since there are no mechanical valves to operate, the 2-stroke can be made simple and compact. Also, because every downstroke (rather than every other one as in a 4-stroke) is a power stroke, the 2-stroke can be powerful in relation to its size and weight.

For these reasons, the 2-stroke engine has been used in millions of motorcycles (and marine outboard engines, lawn mowers, and other powered appliances) and in a good many cars, the most familiar being the Saab 96 of the 1960s, and the Wartburg and Trabant made in the former East Germany before reunification. The two main problems with the 2-stroke in larger sizes are that its fuel consumption is high, and its exhaust emissions well beyond anything which is permitted under the latest European or American legislation; also, because the piston rings have to pass across the ports millions of times in an engine's average life, most engineers have reservations about long-term wear and durability. The fuel consumption and exhaust emission problems arise mainly because it is impossible to prevent some degree of mixing of the incoming mixture and the outgoing exhaust: some 'neat' mixture always escapes via the exhaust, while some exhaust gas always lingers in the cylinder. Consequently, all of today's production car engines operate using the 4-stroke cycle.

# The importance
## of **valves**

Operation of the 4-stroke engine is crucially dependent on valves which open at the right time to let air and fuel in, and exhaust gas out. Many different valve designs have been experimented with, but the mushroom-shaped poppet valve has never been bettered for lightness and simplicity, even though some other types – notably the sleeve-valve which was used in some engines of the 1930s – have promised greater efficiency. The detail design of valves, their operation and their timing (exactly when during the engine's operating cycle they begin to open and finish shutting) has become an important aspect of engine design in its own right, and we shall look at it much more closely in Chapter 4.

*The last serious attempt to make the 2-stroke into a practical proposition for modern car use was made by Ford, working with Orbital. In 1992 Ford demonstrated a version of the Fiesta powered by this advanced 3-cylinder, 2-stroke engine. Overall performance was good, but doubts about emissions performance and durability meant the unit never reached production. (Ford)*

# Alternative engines

Of all the engines invented as alternatives to the piston engine, only two have enjoyed any kind of success: the gas turbine and the Wankel rotary engine, and it is worth looking briefly at why they have never taken over as mainstream vehicle power units.

The gas turbine compresses air, adds and burns fuel – continuously rather than intermittently – and exhausts the gas through a turbine which drives the compressor. The problem then is what to do with the considerable energy left in the exhaust downstream of the turbine. In a jet aeroplane, the answer is easy: you squirt it out of the back, pushing the aeroplane forward. In a vehicle, you must find some way of using that energy to drive the wheels, which means driving a second 'power' turbine to extract the rest of the energy, leaving only a gentle exhaust (from which you remove most of any remaining energy by passing it through a heat exchanger to cool the exhaust and heat the incoming air). The drive from the power turbine may be taken either to a high-speed electric power generator, or, via gears, mechanically to the wheels. The two main drawbacks of the gas turbine for vehicles are first, that it is very difficult to achieve the kind of 'instant' throttle response provided by a piston engine, and second, that it is very expensive to make, even after 60 years of progress in the aerospace industry. Technically practical vehicle gas turbines also look rather strange, because the exhaust/intake heat exchanger, essential to achieve reasonable efficiency, is usually the biggest component of the engine.

The Wankel rotary engine works on the 4-stroke principle, but with combustion chambers which grow larger and smaller in volume as a central rotor, which has a special 'deltoid' shape with three high-points, spins within an 'epitrochoid' housing with two hollows and two high-points. It is the expansion of gas as fuel burns which spins the rotor, which in turn drives the central shaft to which it is geared. For a given power output, the Wankel engine is light, compact and very smooth in operation, and it was installed in several production car models by NSU (now part of the Volkswagen Group) and by Mazda. It suffered early problems with the seals between the tips of the rotor

*Mazda remained faithful to the promise of the Wankel-type rotary engine long after every other car manufacturer had abandoned it. At the 1999 Tokyo Motor Show, the company displayed a new and more advanced version of the engine with side inlet and exhaust ports and revised induction arrangements, claiming 280bhp output (with turbocharging) from two 654cc rotors, and much improved fuel economy. For the 2001 model year, this 'Renesis' engine was fitted to a new version of the RX-7 sports car. (Mazda)*

and the outer housing, but these were overcome with development. The real and insoluble problem was the shape of the combustion chambers, which allowed too much heat loss – so the engine was never as economical as its piston rivals – and insufficient control of airflow during the combustion process, which meant in practice that the exhaust emissions were too high. Promising though it was in some respects, these drawbacks killed the Wankel concept as a vehicle engine, although it survives in some other applications where fuel economy and emissions are less important, and light weight and smoothness more so – such as chainsaws …

# **2 Engine** design **fundamentals**

It is convenient to think of any piston engine in two parts. The lower part is the cylinder block plus the 'rotating assembly' formed by the crankshaft, connecting rods and pistons. The upper part includes the cylinder head, the valves and the system that drives them. The job of the block and the rotating assembly is to turn the pressure created by burning the fuel into a mechanical output, to be passed on to the wheels through the clutch or (in an automatic) the torque converter. The job of the cylinder head and valves is to get air and fuel into the engine, burn it in the right place at the right time, and get rid of the burned gases afterwards.

Put that way, it sounds terribly simple – and to some extent it is. It becomes slightly more complicated when coming to terms with the fact that 'mechanical output' covers two different though related things, power and torque. The relationship between these two is often misunderstood. More accurately (if cynically), most people think they understand power, but all too few of them understand torque, so that may be the best place to begin.

**Torque** is normally defined as the average 'push' provided by the engine. Since the engine delivers its output by turning a shaft, we actually measure the torque as the effect of a force applied at a given distance. The modern unit for doing this is the Newton-metre (Nm) – a force of one Newton (which is defined as the force needed to accelerate a mass of one kilogram at a rate of one metre per second per second) acting on the end of an arm one metre long. The old 'imperial' measurement, still widely quoted, was the pound-foot (lb ft) – a force of one pound weight (in other words, a one-pound *mass* multiplied by the acceleration due to gravity) acting on the end of an arm one foot long. For conversion, if you ever need it, 1lb ft equals 1.356Nm.

The torque depends mainly on the average amount of pressure (the 'brake mean effective pressure' or BMEP) which pushes the piston down during the power stroke, the time for which that pressure is applied, the area of the piston, and the stroke of the crankshaft – the distance through which the piston moves up and down. It also depends more or less directly on the engine's compression ratio. Additionally, it also depends less directly on other things, such as the timing of valve opening and closing, and on the speed at which the engine is running. When the engine is turning at high speed, there is less time for the pressure to develop and exert its full effect, which is why maximum torque in most engines occurs somewhere between one-third to one-half of the engine's maximum safe speed.

**Power** is the rate at which the engine does work. In its most basic terms – familiar to anyone who took maths and mechanics seriously at school – work equals force times distance, and power therefore equals force times distance divided by time. But distance divided by time is speed, so power equals force (in the engine's case, the torque) times speed (its operating speed). So it is the engine's speed which relates power and torque; but why should the two things be considered separately?

One way to approach this question is to begin with units of power. Back in the 18th century, engineers decided a convenient unit for measuring the output of the new steam engines would be the amount of work of which a typical horse was capable – specifically, when hauling coal up a mine shaft by means of a rope running over a pulley. The horse-power was settled at 550lb ft per second; in other words, the average horse could (in theory) haul 550 pounds of coal up a shaft at a speed of one foot per second. In fact, to do this you need a mighty big horse, because 550 pounds is a lot to haul. Lifting 55 pounds at 10 feet per second – which is around 7mph or 11km/h – sounds more reasonable for an average-size horse, yet it calls for the same power output. In this analogy, the load – 550 pounds or 55 pounds – represents the torque, but because the speeds are different, the power output is the same. But the big horse is moving very slowly and steadily, while the smaller one is trotting smartly along.

Incidentally, that very practical figure of 550lb ft per second remained the standard unit of power in the old imperial measure until it gave way to metrication; it was the brake horsepower (bhp), in other words the power measured at the brake, a device which applied an increasing load to the output shaft until the engine speed held steady. The standard metric power output unit is the kilowatt (kW), which is rather more than 1bhp. To convert kW to bhp, multiply by 1.34.

In real-life car terms, maximum power versus aerodynamic drag determines the maximum speed, while torque versus weight (and heavily influenced by the gearing) determines the acceleration. It is strange, therefore, that while most drivers rightly value acceleration more than sheer maximum speed, they carefully study power output figures and pay much less attention to torque.

*Opposite: For such a small company (though now it forms part of General Motors) Saab has a formidable reputation as an engine developer, having been a pioneer of turbocharging, four valves per cylinder and direct coil-over-plug ignition. When GM took over, Saab quickly adapted its new parent's 3-litre V6 engine to its own purposes, as seen here, for use in the top versions of its newest cars. There are many interesting details in this view, not least the front-mounted turbocharger and intercooler installation. (Saab)*

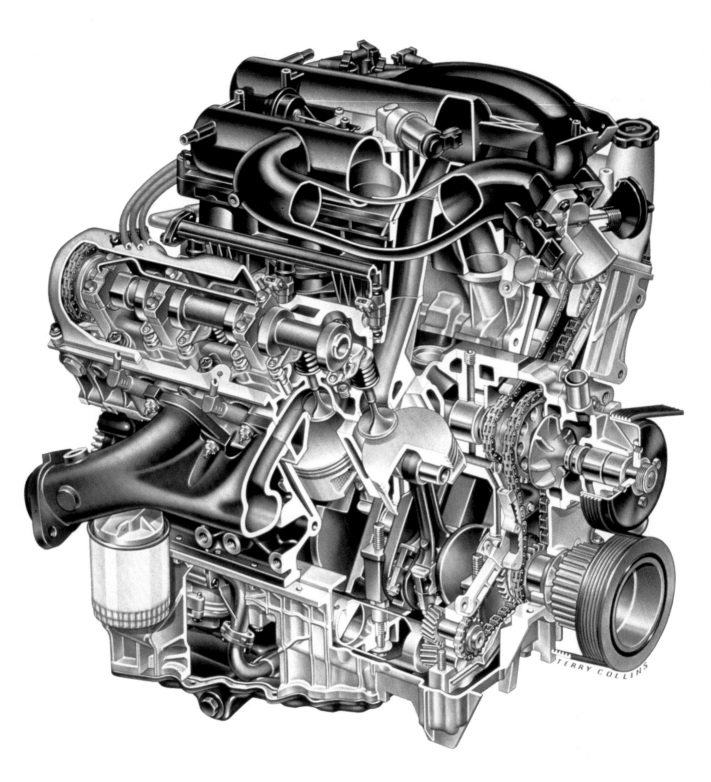

The 4-litre V6 engine which powers the 4WD Ford Explorer is one of the largest 6-cylinder petrol engines in production. Its layout is typically American, with two valves per cylinder, a single overhead camshaft per cylinder bank, and chain-driven camshafts. (Ford)

Balancing torque and power is vitally important in the familiar internal-combustion (IC) piston engine, because it develops very little torque when it is running slowly. Consequently, to start from rest and pull away from low speed, some means has to be provided to allow it to run fast enough to develop high torque, even though this means it will very

ENGINE DESIGN FUNDAMENTALS

quickly reach its maximum safe speed. Somewhere before this point, therefore, it must be slowed down again relative to the speed of the car. This, of course, is the function of the gearbox, to be discussed in full in Part 2. But the distinction between power and torque needs to be borne in mind throughout the whole process of engine design. An engine designed for good torque output, developing maximum torque at relatively low speed – say 2,500rpm compared with a peak *power* speed of 6,000rpm and a maximum safe speed of 7,000rpm – will always be more 'flexible', pulling more willingly from low speed and needing less gearchanging. An engine designed for high power will always provide better vehicle performance – so long as the driver is willing to use the gearbox to keep the engine speed close to peak power. It will be much less willing to 'chug along' in a high gear at low speed, and will certainly not accelerate briskly without changing down one or two gears. Such an engine may have the same 6,000rpm peak power speed (but there will be more power), but it will develop its maximum torque at, perhaps, 4,000rpm. At 2,500rpm it will deliver less torque than the 'flexible' engine.

So here we have a need for engineering compromise – or at least, for designing the engine for a specific purpose, a particular kind of driver. You may design either a highly flexible engine with lots of low-speed torque, or a high-performance engine with relatively weak low-speed performance and a need for lots of gearchanging; or you may opt for a careful balance between the two (one of the nice things about the old-fashioned British imperial units was that in a typical well-balanced engine, the maximum torque in pounds-feet was about the same number as the maximum power in bhp). As we shall see later on, some modern engineering developments have begun to reduce the need for compromise and allow designers to enjoy the best of both worlds, but the basic power-versus-torque distinction remains, along with the basic techniques for adjusting the balance one way or the other.

In practice, however, the balance is mainly adjusted one way, because it is fairly easy to increase the maximum amount of power delivered by an engine, but much more difficult to increase the torque (except by supercharging). This is because the power developed by an engine depends above all on the rate at which it can burn fuel. That in turn depends on how fast it can suck in air and expel exhaust gas, and *that* in turn depends on the speed of the engine and the size of the ducts and valves through which the air and gas pass. In very round terms, Formula 1 racing teams reckon that running an engine 1,000rpm faster is worth another 50bhp – so long as you can persuade the engine to stay in one

piece. The torque, on the other hand, depends on the factors I have already mentioned, and in any given engine most of them are fixed. The only thing which can easily be varied is the BMEP, which can be influenced a little by detail design, slightly more by altering the valve timing or increasing the compression ratio, and a lot more by pumping air into the engine under positive pressure, in other words by supercharging.

Of course, you don't need all that much torque – just enough to ensure the engine delivers the power you need – so long as you have lots of gears and are happy to spend a lot of time shifting between them. But most road-going cars have only five forward speeds, and most road-going drivers quickly tire of needing to change down for every gradient, every bend, and every time they even think about overtaking. For acceptable performance, every car needs a certain torque output (in fact, a certain torque-to-weight ratio). Just what amounts to acceptable performance varies from car to car, but in each case it largely determines the actual engine size – because in any sensibly engineered and naturally aspirated, as distinct from supercharged, modern petrol engine the maximum torque is never going to be far from 100Nm/litre (73.8lb ft/litre).

# Internal losses

It has to be said that the IC engine is not particularly efficient in an overall sense. By the time it has rejected heat into its coolant, and lost a lot more through the exhaust system, a petrol-fuelled spark-ignition engine never turns more than around 38% of the chemical energy in its fuel into useful work to drive the car. Diesels fare a little better, with peak efficiencies of up to 42%. But some engines fall short even of these figures, because of their internal 'parasitic' losses. These losses, which arise from pumping, friction and windage, can be considerable.

Pumping losses occur because in order to burn its fuel, the engine has to draw in air – quite a lot of it, especially at high speed and power output – and then push out the exhaust gases. It takes a good deal of power to do this, and this is power which is lost so far as propelling the car is concerned. So the engine designer is at some pains to make it as easy as possible, through the design of the inlet and exhaust manifolds, and of the the inlet and exhaust ports within the cylinder head itself, for the air and exhaust gas to flow smoothly and with the least possible resistance. Unfortunately, an engine designed with passages which favour easy flow at maximum power may prove very unpleasant to drive at low speed, when trickling along in a traffic jam for example. This is because good behaviour at low speed – strong low-

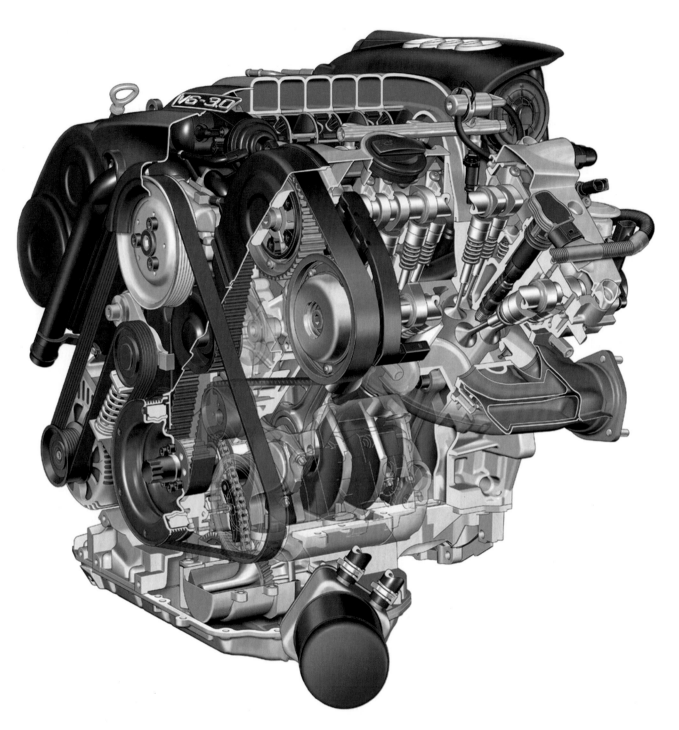

The performance of the Volkswagen-Audi 4-cylinder in-line engines with 5 valves per cylinder was sufficiently impressive to encourage Audi to adapt the same basic cylinder design to its V6 engine, creating a 30-valve unit. Points to note in this drawing include the complex design of the inlet manifold with 'cross-over' tracts feeding each bank of cylinders, the 'direct ignition' coil-over-plug arrangement pioneered by Saab but now widely used, the complicated camshaft needed to drive three inlet valves per cylinder, and the carefully fabricated, double-walled and insulated exhaust manifold which helps to warm the catalytic converter more quickly by absorbing little of the exhaust gas heat itself. Also well worth noting are the two very long drive belts – a toothed belt driving all four camshafts, and an even longer multi-vee 'serpentine' belt driving all the accessories. (Audi)

speed torque, in other words – depends on a fast flow of air into the combustion chamber, and a relative trickle of air passing through a wide inlet port will slow down. Thus in any road-going car, the engine designer has to balance the needs of low-speed 'driveability' and high-speed performance, either by making a compromised choice (so, yet another design compromise), or by adding features which mean the actual size and shape of the passages can be changed according to power output. For example, some engines with two inlet valves per cylinder have an arrangement to shut off one of the inlet ports at low speed, opening it only when the power requirement is high enough.

In the spark-ignition (petrol) engine, the pumping losses at low speed are increased by the part-closing of the throttle valve. When the throttle is nearly closed, the induction stroke of the piston not only sucks in air, but also reduces the air pressure in the whole of the inlet manifold downstream of the throttle, which means the induction stroke itself consumes more power. The closer the throttle valve is to the inlet port, the more severe this effect becomes, which is one reason why modern petrol engines have seemingly complicated inlet manifolds

*This cutaway drawing of the BMW Valvetronic engine, announced in 2001 and built in the company's British engine factory, shows many features of interest including, naturally, the extremely complex valve operating mechanism which employs not only variable timing of both inlet and exhaust valve opening, but also variable lift of the inlet valve from practically nothing to almost 10mm. Also noteworthy is the way in which each pair of exhaust pipes feeds into a separate close-coupled pre-catalyst unit. (BMW)*

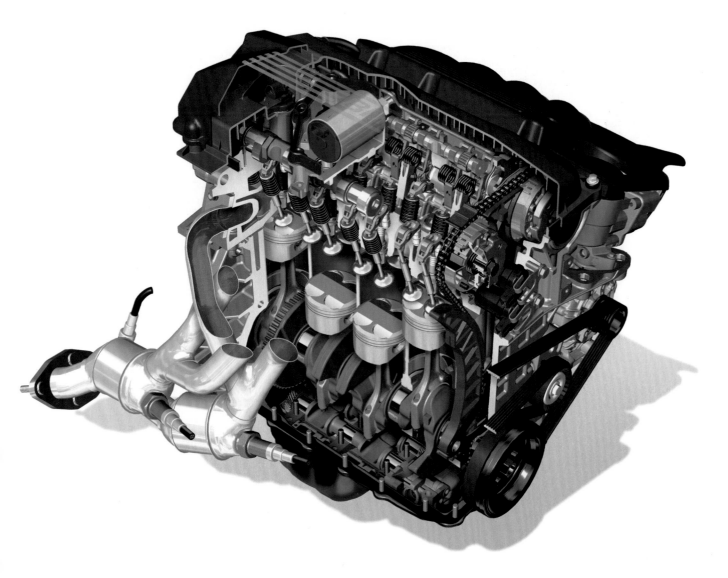

with long air ducts, with the throttle valve installed at the entrance to a 'plenum chamber' some distance away from the inlet valves. Diesel engines don't have throttle valves, so at part-load their pumping losses are less. This is one reason (their higher compression ratio is the other) why diesels are more efficient, and therefore more economical, than conventional petrol engines.

Friction losses are also vitally important. The main friction losses occur between the piston rings and the cylinder walls, and in the crankshaft bearings, both the 'big ends' where the connecting rods are attached to the crankshaft, and the 'main bearings' in which

the crankshaft is carried in the cylinder block. It is worth noting that there is no metal-to-metal contact in any of the crankshaft bearings, or at least there shouldn't be: if it happens, the engine will not last long. Instead, metal-to-metal contact is prevented by the presence of a thin film of oil, and the friction loss arises from overcoming the viscosity of this oil as the metal parts run very close to each other with an often

*Audi's W12 engine, fitted to the A8 during 2001, is surely one of the most complicated-looking units in production –* *although essentially it consists of two of VW's narrow-angle V6 engines sharing the same crankshaft. (Audi)*

ENGINE DESIGN FUNDAMENTALS

considerable difference in speed. In the same way, lubrication is vital to the long life of the piston rings and cylinder bores. But even with proper lubrication, many experiments have shown that the friction losses rise quickly as engine speed is increased, especially beyond around 6,000rpm. Formula 1 and similar engines which run at extremely high speed for the sake of sheer power suffer fearsome internal friction losses, and therefore very poor fuel consumption. In the design of engines for road-going cars, it is also worth bearing in mind that fewer cylinders generally mean lower friction losses, because there are fewer piston rings and fewer (though larger) bearings. In engines of equal size and power output, for example, a 4-cylinder engine is likely always to be slightly more economical than a 6-cylinder. This is one reason why some designers have chosen to make apparently large 4-cylinder engines, of anything up to 3-litre capacity.

In recent years, much more work has been devoted to reducing internal friction losses. Much of the improvement has come from better materials, both engine oils and alloys for bearings and piston rings. The best oils now provide good protection with lower viscosity, while bearings and piston rings are often narrower than they used to be without any sacrifice of strength, but with less surface over which friction losses can occur.

Windage losses occur through internal air movements in the engine other than those which take place in the inlet and exhaust systems and the combustion chamber. For example, when a piston is descending during the induction stroke, what happens to the air *beneath* the piston? It has to transfer to the space beneath one of the other pistons which is ascending in a power or exhaust stroke. The air flows and speeds involved in these transfers can be considerable – and the airflow around the rapidly rotating crankshaft has to be taken into account as well. It is only in the last 20 years or so that the detail design of engines to reduce windage loss – for example, by smoothing and enlarging air passages through and around the crankcase – has been taken really seriously, but the gains have been worthwhile.

As I pointed out to begin with, so long as the engine performs its function with fair efficiency, then the simpler, lighter, and cheaper to make it is, the better. Put more precisely, the engine designer's objective is to provide the power and torque asked for

*Typical of the current generation of engines for medium-sized European cars is this 2-litre 16-valve twin-cam unit for the Ford Mondeo, introduced in 2000. Concern to make the package* *as compact and light as possible has to be balanced against the need for high efficiency, which tends to create a demand for bulky and complicated induction systems. (Ford)*

in the design specification at minimum cost, with maximum economy and minimum exhaust emissions. There are a few other requirements, like durability and what the engineers call 'driveability' – a crisp response and steady pull when it is needed. Any feature which does not contribute to these objectives is a waste of time. Yet modern engines are full of apparently weird and wonderful systems of great complexity; each of them must contribute something worthwhile. But what?

# The **architecture of the** engine

There is a basic layout to any engine – the number of cylinders and the way they are arranged. Even before looking at the various layouts in current use, however, we should define three of the most basic numbers in any engine – the bore, stroke and capacity. The bore is the diameter of each cylinder; the stroke is the distance the piston moves between top and bottom dead centre. The 'swept volume' of each cylinder is the area of the piston times the stroke – so if the bore is B and the stroke is S, the swept volume is $(\pi B^2/4 \times S)$, and the capacity or swept volume of the engine is the individual cylinder capacity times the number of cylinders. Thus an engine of a certain capacity may have a small number of large cylinders, or a larger number of smaller cylinders. In most of the

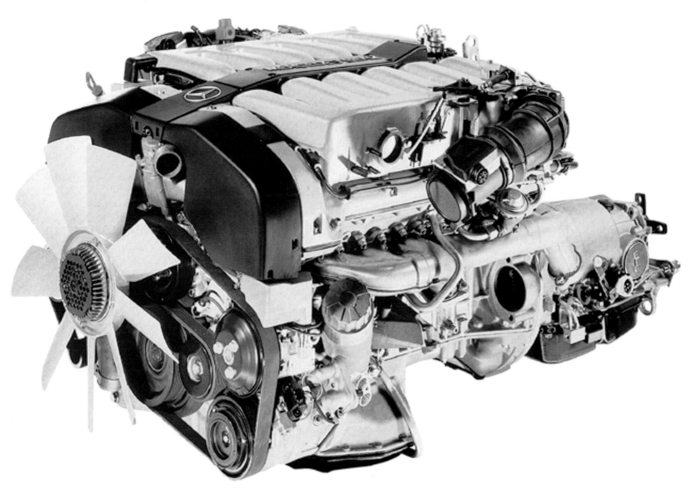

world, the bore and stroke are measured in millimetres and the capacity in cubic centimetres (cc) or in litres. In North America, a lot of people still give engine measurements in inches and cubic inches; one litre is roughly 61 cubic inches.

Today, the bore and stroke of a typical passenger car engine are about equal. High-performance engines designed to run at high speed may have the bore larger than the stroke – dimensions referred to by engineers as 'over-square' – while engines designed with economy and pulling power in mind are more likely to be 'under-square' with the stroke greater than the bore. Over-square engines leave room for large inlet and exhaust valves, which – as we shall see – are important for high power output. Under-square engines are more compact lengthwise, but taller and therefore more difficult to install under a low bonnet. It may be useful to remember that when an engine has 'square' dimensions of 86mm (3.4in) bore and stroke, its capacity is very close to 2-litres (actually 1,998cc) if it has four cylinders, and thus to 3-litres with six cylinders, and 4-litres with eight cylinders.

Today, the vast majority of engines in smaller cars have four cylinders in-line, while many larger cars have six cylinders arranged in a 'vee' with two banks of six cylinders each. But some small cars have

*Despite today's accent on efficiency and economy, the V12 engine is still seen as the ultimate power unit for luxury cars. Although Jaguar no longer offers a V12, such units are offered by BMW, Mercedes and Toyota, while Audi now has a 'W12'. The magnificent Mercedes V12 is shown here, a major engineering achievement even if it is slightly out of tune with the times.* (Mercedes)

engines with two or three cylinders, some medium-sized cars have 5-cylinder engines, and large luxury cars may have V8 or even V12 engines, while V10 engines are not unknown.

Why so many different layouts? There are two main considerations to bear in mind here – the need for smooth power delivery, and the actual size of the cylinders. For smoothness of operation, the more cylinders the better. Because only one of the four strokes of the standard working cycle actually provides any 'push', a single-cylinder engine would push only

*Opposite: Well worth detailed study: the Mercedes M120 engine in the S-class is a 'classic' V12 with 60° between cylinder banks. Note the 'crossed-over' induction system, the duplex chain drive to the four camshafts, the 'siamesed' cylinder bores and the hydraulic tappets immediately beneath the direct-acting cams.* (Mercedes)

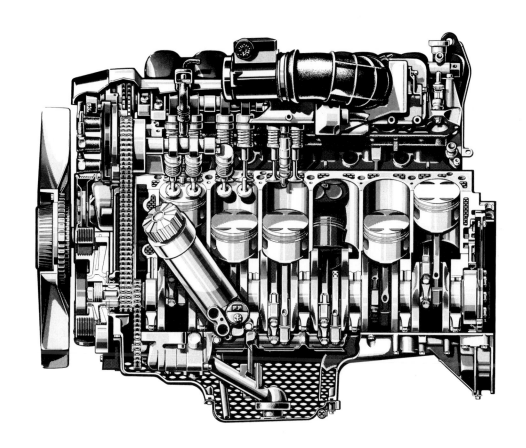

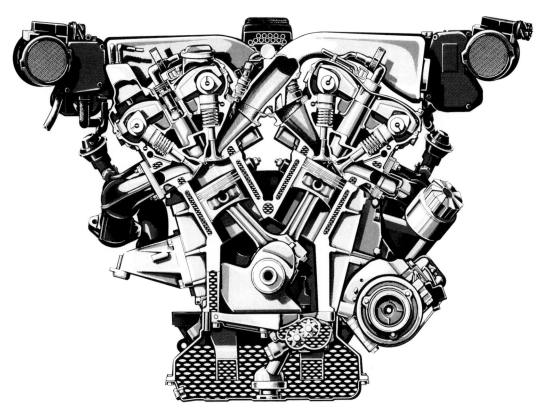

once in every two revolutions. This is no problem in a motor-mower and not much of a problem in a motorcycle (although most motorcycles now have at least two cylinders), but when more power is needed, as in a car, and the cylinder is made larger, the engine's roughness of operation becomes more obvious. The answer is to use multiple cylinders, with their power strokes evenly spaced, so that the flow of power is more nearly continuous. It can never be truly continuous, of course: it will always be formed by a series of pulses, one from each cylinder's power stroke. But the more cylinders there are, the closer the pulses will be, and with 12 cylinders the effect is one of almost perfectly smooth power delivery.

However many cylinders an engine has, the power-pulsing effect is smoothed out by the flywheel, attached to the clutch end of the crankshaft. The flywheel stores energy through its rotation. In effect it absorbs some energy during each power stroke and feeds energy back into the drive to part-fill the 'troughs' between them. The larger and heavier the flywheel, the better it will do this. On the other hand, the engine designer wants his engine – and therefore its flywheel – to be as light and compact as possible. Also, the mass of a heavy flywheel makes the engine slower to accelerate (or decelerate) as the driver operates the accelerator. Apart from making the engine feel more sluggish, this can also (as we shall see later) be a big disadvantage when changing gear. Thus we arrive at the first of the many technical compromises involved in the design of any engine (and any car). A heavy flywheel will make the engine smoother, but it will also make it more sluggish, and will pass on a few problems to the gearbox designer. Significantly, one standard move when converting a road-going engine for serious racing is to lighten the flywheel, because fast response and easy gearchanging then matter far more than ultra-smooth engine operation.

In general, the fewer the number of cylinders in an engine, the heavier the flywheel needs to be to achieve acceptable smoothness. In a 2-cylinder engine (like the old Citroën A-series flat-twin in the 2CV, for example) the flywheel looks huge. In a V12, it can be made small enough to be neatly tucked away, adding very little to the overall bulk of the engine, its size actually determined by the diameter of the clutch or torque converter needed to cope with the engine's torque output.

# The influence of cylinder size

The other major factor in deciding the number of cylinders is individual cylinder capacity. As the capacity is reduced, the cylinder's volume decreases faster than its surface area. This means that more of the available heat from burning the fuel is lost through the walls of the cylinder, into the coolant, instead of helping to expand the gas in the combustion chamber and 'push' the piston. Car engine designers generally feel that an individual capacity of 200cc is the minimum for reasonable efficiency, and 300cc (or more) per cylinder is preferable. At the other end of the scale, a very big cylinder may not give the fuel time to burn completely during the power stroke. Once the spark plug has fired, the 'flame front' moves through the fuel/air mixture at a fairly steady speed. If the cylinder has a bore of much more than around 100mm (4in), the front may not reach the cylinder walls in the very short time it takes the piston to complete the power stroke, leaving some unburned fuel to be swept out into the exhaust. To avoid the danger of this happening, designers look to an upper limit of around 800cc for individual cylinder size.

These cylinder-size criteria mean that for engines below 1-litre capacity, a designer may seriously consider using three cylinders rather than four, while for engines bigger than 4-litre capacity, at least six cylinders are essential. Inevitably, there is a feeling that somewhere between these upper and lower limits there is an 'ideal' cylinder capacity of around 500cc, which automatically leads to the 4-cylinder 2-litre engine, the 6-cylinder 3-litre and the V8 4-litre.

# Mechanical balance

There are, however, a number of engines in volume production with odd numbers of cylinders. General Motors uses a 3-cylinder 1-litre engine in the Opel/Vauxhall Corsa, and some Japanese manufacturers use the same layout. Audi, Fiat, Honda and Volvo all offer, or have offered in-line 5-cylinder engines, and Volkswagen has its oddly configured VR5 engine in the Golf. Chrysler fits its big Viper sports car with a V10 engine, and Porsche recently introduced a V10 of its own. Motor sport enthusiasts know very well that the most successful Formula 1 engines of recent years have been V10s.

To return to basics, however, an engine needs to be mechanically balanced for really smooth operation. A single-cylinder engine suffers not only from the rough-running feel of single power strokes with long intervals between them; because of action and reaction, every time the piston moves up or down, the engine and the end of the car to which it is attached will try to move in the opposite direction. Of course, you can try to overcome this effect by fitting your crankshaft with counterweights, which move up as the piston comes down, and vice versa. However, because the counterweights rotate with the crankshaft, they also in effect move from side to side. Thus in a single-cylinder engine, you can cancel the up-and-down effect but only by introducing a side-to-side shake instead.

If you have two cylinders in-line, things become much easier. Not only do you have one power stroke per engine revolution instead of every other revolution: if you arrange things so that one piston moves up as the other one moves down, the up-and-down effect is cancelled out. Unfortunately, you end up instead with an engine that tries to rock back and forth because the pistons are still out of balance front-to-rear, so to speak. If the front piston is moving down and the rear piston moving up, then the front of the engine will try to move upwards while the rear tries to move down. It won't move very far, of course, because the engine is bolted (on flexible mounts) to the body. Instead, the vibration will be fed

*Once so common in cars like the Volkswagen Beetle and the Alfasud, these days the flat-4 'boxer' engine has become a real rarity, surviving – but successfully – in the medium-sized Subaru models, famous for their rallying exploits. In its latest form the 2-litre Subaru engine uses four valves per cylinder. Boxer engines are more expensive to make but bring the advantages of a lower centre of gravity and a shape which fits into a low nose for good aerodynamics. (Subaru)*

*Lesson in complicated compactness: 24-valve V6 engine packaged for transverse installation in the Jaguar X-type. Interesting points include the size of the carefully engineered induction system compared with that of the 'core' engine,* *and the enormous length of the poly-vee belt which runs in a serpentine path to drive all the main accessories – a practice which may come to an end with the arrival of 36V electrics and compact 'on demand' motor drives to accessory units.* (Jaguar)

into the body and thus to the car's passengers. In a flat-twin engine, with the pistons moving in opposition and a two-throw crankshaft, the cylinders cannot be directly opposite and the out-of-balance causes a rocking motion around the vertical axis – but a relatively small one because the crankshaft throws are closer together than in an in-line twin. The author once part-mischievously suggested a perfectly balanced flat-3 engine in which two small pistons opposed a larger central piston of twice the weight. Flat-4 engines, like those famously used in the original VW Beetle, the Alfa Romeo Alfasud, and many Subarus, are similar in principle but (naturally) smoother in operation, while flat-6 engines (as in the Porsche 911) are smoother still. They also help to keep the car's centre of gravity lower, and when used with front-wheel-drive they make it easier to design a sloping, aerodynamic bonnet; on the other hand, they are expensive to make and create some servicing problems. Checking or changing the spark plugs, for example, is never easy.

Apart from serious primary imbalance, which has to be taken care of in any sensible design for a car engine, there is also the problem of 'secondary' imbalances caused by the fact that the connecting rods don't travel straight up and down, but swing from side to side as the crankshaft rotates and the pistons rise and fall. Thus the piston's 'push' is usually

to one side or other. The effect can be reduced by making the connecting rods longer so that the swing-angle is smaller, but this makes the engine taller and so more difficult to install. Analysing all the out-of-balance forces, especially the secondary effects, needs some fairly complicated mathematics, but the main conclusions are that an in-line 4-cylinder engine is reasonably well balanced, and an in-line 6-cylinder engine can be almost perfectly balanced by playing off the forces created by its pistons and connecting rods against each other so that they cancel out. It follows that a V8 engine – which in effect is two 4-cylinder in-line engines sharing a single crankshaft – is always reasonably well balanced, and a V12 is excellently balanced. The feel and refinement of a V8 depends to some extent on the design of its crankshaft, with the big-end bearings all formed in a single plane, or in two planes at right angles. Also, the 'ideal' angle between the cylinder banks of a V8 engine to minimise the effect of secondary imbalance is 90°, while for a V12 it is 60° (or 120°, but this makes for a wide engine which would be very difficult to install).

While the 6-cylinder in-line engine can be made extremely refined, which is one reason why BMW for example remains faithful to it, there is no denying that a V6 engine is far more compact and easier to install – especially if you need to set the engine transversely in a front-wheel-drive car. In most ways, from a mechanical point of view a V6 can be thought of as half a V12, and the ideal angle between its cylinders is again 60° (or 120°, or 180°, in other words a flat-6 engine of the type made by Porsche). However, there are several V6 engines which have a less than ideal 90° angle between their cylinder banks. Some of them – for example, the V6 engine in the old Citroën-Maserati SM, and the joint-venture 'PRV' V6 which powered some Peugeot, Renault and Volvo models in the 1980s – had started life as V8s and then been 'shrunk' by having two cylinders removed. But other V6s have been quite deliberately designed with a 90° angle, because it makes the engine wider but lower, which can make it easier to install where bonnet height is more restricted than engine compartment width, and because the wider angle leaves more room between the cylinder banks for what may be a complicated and bulky inlet manifold and fuel injection system. The inferior refinement which results from forces no longer being perfectly balanced may be accepted as a necessary penalty, or alternatively it may be restored through the use of a balancer shaft – a shaft driven from the crankshaft, and carrying offset weights whose out-of-balance effect has been calculated to cancel out the engine's basic imbalance.

In practice, twin balancer shafts are usually fitted. To return to our single-cylinder engine with its

ENGINE DESIGN FUNDAMENTALS

crankshaft counterweights cancelling the natural up-and-down shake but instead causing side-to-side shake, this shake could be cancelled out by having a second shaft with deliberately out of balance weights at 180° to those on the crankshaft. This would cancel out the sideways shake – but sadly, would restore the up-and-down shake which the counterweights were fighting in the first place. If, however, you throw away the counterweights and instead fit two balancer shafts rotating in opposite directions, they cancel out each other's sideways shake while together opposing the vertical shake, and you end up with a much smoother engine (in a strictly relative sense, since a single-cylinder engine is never going to feel really smooth).

Such a balancer shaft arrangement may be used to smooth the operation of large in-line 4-cylinder engines. The technique has become far more popular in the last 10 years or so, though it was pioneered by Porsche (in the 944/968 series) some years earlier. To cancel out all the secondary imbalances in a 4-cylinder engine, two balancer shafts are needed. Their position is usually carefully calculated, one on each side of the engine and usually with one shaft higher than the other, although when Cosworth developed a 2.4-litre version of Ford's DOHC 4-cylinder engine, they installed the shafts side by side in the engine sump, with apparently successful results.

*When balancer shafts were first introduced to smooth the operation of large 4-cylinder engines they were usually mounted at carefully calculated heights alongside the cylinder block. Today the trend is to house close-coupled shafts in the sump. This is the balancer shaft assembly for the BMW Valvetronic engine announced in 2001. The offset weights of the shafts (which are chain-driven from the crankshaft and rotate at twice crankshaft speed, in opposite directions) can be seen, together with their bearing arrangements and the way they are geared together. (BMW)*

Balancer shafts are even more essential when odd numbers of cylinders are chosen. We have already seen that there are several reasons why such a choice should be made, for example to avoid having individual cylinders which are too large or too small for efficiency. But there also exist some 'modular' engines in which, for example, a larger capacity in-line 5-cylinder unit was developed by adding another cylinder to a 4-cylinder engine (so that both can be machined and assembled on a single manufacturing line) as a cheaper alternative to developing a V6. Both Fiat and Volvo use in-line 5-cylinder engines which originated in this way, and which have 4-cylinder 'cousins'. The Volvo modular range also extends to an in-line 6-cylinder engine. On the assumption that any

5-cylinder engine will be intended for a fairly up-market car in which refinement is essential, a single balancer shaft to offset the inherent imbalance of the engine itself must be fitted. A shaft may also be used to correct the imbalance of a 3-cylinder engine, but since any such engine is more likely to be small and fitted to a low-priced car, it may be judged worth accepting the extra vibration and avoiding the cost of the shaft, pulleys, and drive belt or chain. With modern engine mounts, which are remarkably good at damping out vibration, and with careful design of each component with features like crankshaft counterweights, the vibration inside the car is unlikely to be severe, and it may well be the rather odd noise made by the engine which betrays the fact that it only has three cylinders.

The V10 engine is likely always to remain an oddity. It has proved a great success in Formula 1 for the most basic of reasons: eight cylinders is too few (the airflow through the engine is too restricted to develop ultimate power) while twelve is too many (higher parasitic losses, especially internal friction). The ideal angle between the banks of a V10 is 72° (360° divided by five) or of course 144°, which nobody has tried in practice. The 72° angle is usefully wider than the 60° of a V12, providing extra space for the inlet manifolds and fuel injection equipment. Even though the engine is less than perfectly balanced, with this many cylinders operation is smooth enough not to need a balancer shaft.

As several 3-cylinder engines show us, it is by no means necessary to achieve perfect balance before an engine feels acceptably smooth. Motoring history, up to the present day, has plenty of other examples of engines which adopted odd-looking layouts for good reasons – usually to achieve compactness and ease of installation. Lancia, for example, built a whole series of V4 engines in which the angle between the banks was extremely narrow, in fact just sufficient to allow the engine to be made usefully shorter, and not much wider than an in-line 4-cylinder engine. The last such Lancia narrow-angle V4 was the 1.6-litre engine used in the Fulvia and Fulvia Coupé, the latter a Monte Carlo Rally winner in the highly competitive 1970s. Lancia also experimented with narrow-angle V6, V8 and V12 engines, examples of which can still be seen in the Lancia museum in Turin.

Around 1990, Volkswagen re-invented the narrow-vee concept, producing an extremely compact V6 engine of 2.8-litre capacity, with a 15° angle between the cylinder banks, for use in the Golf and other models with transverse engine and front-wheel-drive. Even though the angle of exactly 15° looked suspiciously convenient to anyone familiar with Lancia's narrow-vee engines (the carefully calculated 'optimum packing' angle between Lancia's cylinder banks was sometimes measured in degrees, minutes and seconds!) the Volkswagen VR6 proved a success, if not actually outstanding. Even more interesting, however, was the move which came in 1998 with the removal of one cylinder to produce the even more compact VR5 engine of 2.3-litre capacity. This too proved to be quite acceptably smooth when carefully mounted, in the Golf and Passat.

*Opposite: This illustration of the complete rotating assembly, including valve gear and variable-lift mechanism, of the BMW Valvetronic engine includes a number of interesting details, such as the auxiliary chain drive to the balancer shaft assembly in the sump. Note the use of only four counterweights on the crankshaft, which helps to offset the weight of the balancer shafts. Seen like this, the need not only for a tensioner but also for a damper support for the long camshaft drive chain is more obvious. (BMW)*

# **3** **The** engine's **bottom end**

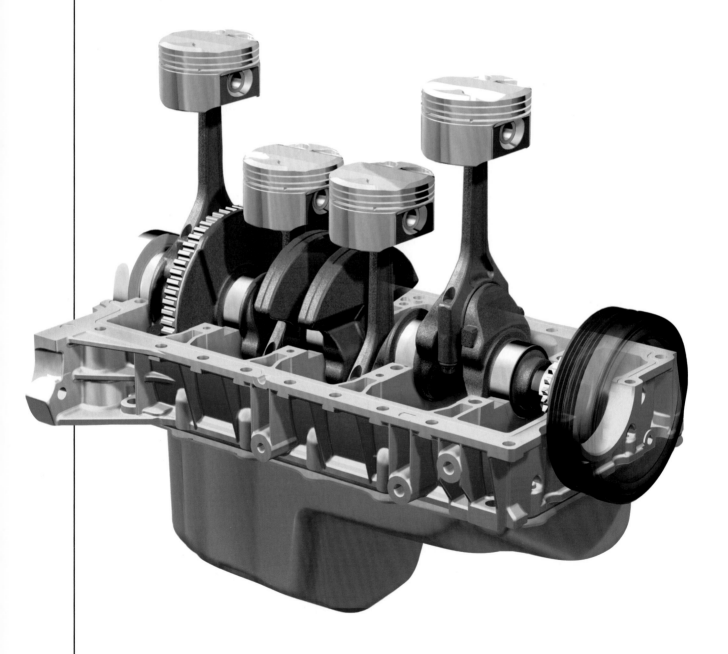

The cylinder block forms the bulk of the engine, yet performs only two tasks. It houses the cylinders (surrounded by cooling passages) and forms the top half of the main bearings in which the crankshaft rotates. The size of the cylinder block is largely determined by the bore of the individual cylinders. Clearly, the centres of the bores must be more than one bore apart; the question is, how much more? If you leave lots of space between the bores, the block will be bigger and heavier. But if you don't leave enough, the engine will have no built-in 'stretch' (many engines see their capacity increased by 'boring-out' in the course of their lives, and often are designed from the outset to offer more than one capacity). You can 'stretch' an engine by enlarging its bore or increasing its stroke, but it is generally much easier to enlarge the bore, which in principle can be done simply by adjusting the production machinery. Changing the stroke means you need a whole new crankshaft – and the space within the crankcase to make sure it has enough clearance as it rotates.

The ideal in cylinder block design used to be to leave a wide enough gap between the cylinders to run a cooling passage between them. However, if the designer was determined to enlarge the bore substantially, it was always possible to do away with the cooling passage and have the cylinder walls touching – a technique in which the bores were said to be 'siamesed' for obvious reasons. With careful design, it was found that this approach had few snags and that the block as a whole could become usefully stiffer, and the blocks of some modern engines are 'siamesed' from the outset.

The one dimension which almost never changes during the life of an engine is the distance between the cylinder bore centres. This is because once the production line has been set up, changing the bore centre measurement involves complete upheaval. The machines which clear and finish the cylinder bores need complete resetting or replacement (if the individual bore measurement is changed, all they need is adjustment to remove slightly more or less metal). At the same time the spacing of the main bearings, which are always in line with the gaps between the cylinders, are shifted and so the engine also needs a completely new crankshaft. By the time all this been done, one might almost as well have a completely new engine taking advantage of the latest technology. There have been many examples of engines which enjoyed long lives in many different versions but always retained the same bore centres. One famous example is the old BMC/Austin-Morris B-series engine, used in everything from the late 1940s Morris Oxford through the MGB to the Austin Princess of the mid-1970s, but which always had a bore centre measurement of 88mm (3.5in).

# **Block** material

All cylinder blocks used to be made from cast iron, but this material has one big disadvantage: it is heavy. Consequently, many cylinder blocks are now made of aluminium alloy; an alloy block can weigh less than half as much as a cast-iron equivalent. Advanced researchers are looking at the still lighter magnesium alloy as a block material. Prototype engines have even been run with metal cylinder liners located in lightweight plastic cylinder blocks, although these engines have always proved horribly noisy.

However, cast iron also has two strong advantages over light alloy – in other words we are back yet again to engineering compromise. Finely machined cast iron forms a perfect surface for the walls of cylinders, with strong resistance to rubbing wear. Thus the earliest engines with alloy blocks, like those used in most of the larger Renaults from the mid-1960s, still used cast-iron cylinder liners. This was a more expensive solution but it combined the advantages of low weight with cast-iron cylinder walls. The cylindrical liners can either be cast in place – inserted into the mould before the light alloy is poured or forced in – or they can be pressed into place afterwards, with suitable sealing arrangements. Also, they can be either 'dry' – in solid contact with the metal of the block – or 'wet', with cooling passages formed between block and liner. This is a neat solution but one which means special care must be taken with sealing, at both the top and bottom of the liner.

*Opposite: Here, the main rotating assembly of the BMW Valvetronic engine sits in place on its ladder frame support, which forms the lower half of each main bearing. The frame is a substantial pressure-casting in its own right, weighing roughly half as much as the block itself and being responsible for a large part of the overall stiffness of the unit. Most aluminium-block engines are now designed in this way. (BMW)*

At the bottom end of the block, the main bearings are always inserted as 'shells' of specially developed alloys, usually of lead, tin and bronze, often with small amounts of more exotic metals, deposited on a strong steel backing plate. These bearings have to combine high resistance to erosion with a degree of 'give' to accommodate the ultra-thin oil film which actually carries the load. The shells are inserted in two halves above and below the crankshaft, and are 'tabbed' to prevent them moving round in their housings. They are held in place by the main bearing caps, made of the same material as the block and bolted to it once the crankshaft and the lower bearing shells have been installed – a task much more easily achieved, on the production line, with the block upside-down.

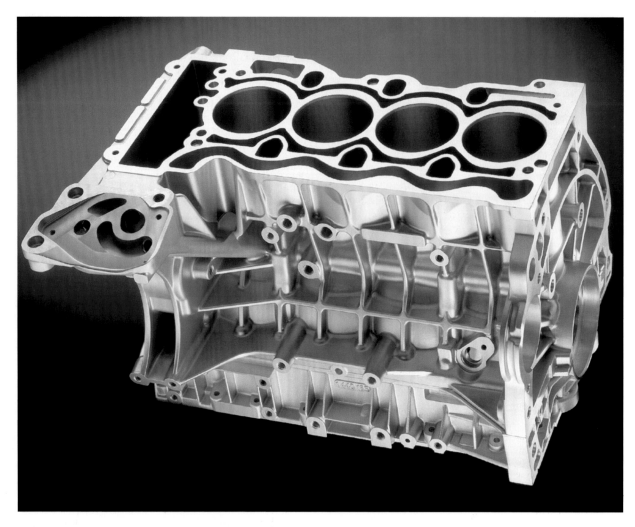

*The cylinder block of the BMW Valvetronic engine is an 'open-deck' design which allows manufacture by pressure die-casting, with the cast-iron cylinder liners pre-positioned in the mould. Note the close spacing of the cylinder bores, which are 'siamesed' with no water passages between them. Such close packing means the engine is more compact as a whole, but also means that any additional capacity will have to be gained by increasing the piston stroke. (BMW)*

# Cast iron versus aluminium

The other advantage of cast iron is that compared with aluminium alloy, it is very stiff. Among other things, this means that an engine with a cast-iron block tends to be quieter than an alloy-block equivalent (a lot of the noise made by an engine radiates from the walls of the block). To overcome this problem, alloy blocks have to be stiffened with extra material and ribs, which means their weight advantage is not quite as great as you might expect. A plain block of cast iron weighs roughly two and a half times as much as the same size block of aluminium (cast iron has a specific gravity of around 7.2, compared with 2.7 for aluminium and 1.8 for magnesium alloy), but as already pointed out, an alloy block is doing well to halve the weight of a cast-iron equivalent.

Because of this better stiffness, cast iron is still the favoured material for diesel engine cylinder blocks, since diesels suffer more of a noise problem. One or two engines in which essentially the same design is used for petrol and diesel versions (like the old Peugeot-Citroën XU/XUD series) use alloy for the petrol block but cast iron for the diesel. A few small diesel engines are now being developed with aluminium blocks, however. The cylinder blocks of vee-configuration engines, especially V6s, are inherently stiff because of their near-cubical dimensions, and these are best of all suited to the use of aluminium alloy.

For production engineers, aluminium alloy has a further advantage in that it can be 'pressure die-cast'. The only way to make a cast-iron block (or any other component) is to prepare a mould with a sand core and then carefully pour the iron into the mould, afterwards shaking the sand out before plugging the openings with 'core plugs'. But because it is lighter and flows easier and faster, aluminium alloy can actually be forced into the mould under pressure. This makes the process faster, and the end product is almost spectacularly 'clean' and accurate. On the other hand you need a very large and expensive machine to pressure-cast something as large as a cylinder block. A number of other methods have been developed, such as the Cosworth process, which permit fast and 'clean' production of alloy blocks and heads without resorting to positive pressure. Meanwhile the cast-iron experts have evolved ways of making their blocks faster, and with thinner walls which means that they are lighter. The contest between the two materials is not over yet, although the argument is certainly moving in aluminium's direction, because of the growing importance of 'greenhouse emissions' and of fuel economy – and lightness means economy.

## Overcoming aluminium's **problems**

It is now possible to treat machined aluminium alloy surfaces chemically, with a deposited layer which is then partially etched away to leave a raised surface basically of silicon, with a network of microscopic channels to hold the lubricating oil in place. It is worth noting that cast-iron blocks and liners are now machined to achieve the same effect; a mirror-smooth, completely scratch-free surface is not the best answer when it comes to preventing cylinder wear. The most familiar aluminium-treatment process is Nicasil, originally developed as a treatment for the interior walls of the Wankel rotary engine, and first used in a production piston engine by Porsche, in the V8 which powered the big 928. Such treatment has become steadily more popular, though still not universal. A good example of its recent use is in the alloy block of the current Jaguar AJ-V8 engine which powers the XJ and S-type saloons. Obviously, it enables the block to be cast 'as one' without needing to worry about cast-iron liners, although the block must instead be passed through the chemical treatment stage.

Aluminium's lack of stiffness compared with cast iron can be countered in other ways besides forming ribs along the sides of the block. It is now normal, in alloy-block engines, to add a solidly cast 'bedplate' beneath the main bearings, bolted to the block itself. This stiffens the whole block and – very importantly – keeps the main bearings in alignment no matter how much stress the block is subjected to, which helps to reduce noise and minimise crankshaft wear. In some engines, the sump is also cast alloy rather than pressed-steel sheet. This makes it more expensive, but again its extra stiffness contributes to that of the block as a whole, and reduces noise radiation.

## The **rotating** assembly

The pistons, connecting rods and crankshaft between them convert the pressure created by the burning of the fuel, into the rotating motion which, via the gearbox and the transmission, drives the wheels. As we have already seen, the principle of linking the pistons to the crankshaft by means of connecting rods, each with a little-end bearing within the piston (and held in place by the gudgeon pin) and a big-end bearing wrapped around the crankshaft throw, seems fairly crude and certainly causes some out-of-balance problems as the bottom end of the rod swings from side to side. Many inventors have offered alternative arrangements to overcome this problem, but the result has always been the same: more joints, more complication, and extra frictional losses through the use of gears. These inventors, like so many others, had lost sight of the fundamental need. So long as the engine does its job of taking fuel in at one end and delivering mechanical output at the other, then the more compact, the lighter, simpler and cheaper it is to make, the better. If you add complication in the expectation of improving performance or efficiency, your idea had better deliver more than enough to pay for itself. That is a lesson to which we shall return, more than once.

## The **piston ...**

Piston design has become a complicated science. The forces acting on a piston are very large, and never constant. During the power stroke, the pressure in the cylinder drives it downwards, but during the other three strokes the pressure is relatively insignificant, and the piston is driven by the crankshaft via its connecting rod. In addition, the piston accelerates and decelerates at an enormous rate. At the top and bottom of its stroke – at Top Dead Centre and Bottom Dead Centre – it is stationary. Somewhere between those two extremes it is travelling very fast indeed, fast enough to travel the length of its stroke well over a hundred times a second, in a high-performance engine at maximum power. It is interesting to put some figures on what is involved. If the engine is turning at 6,000rpm (100

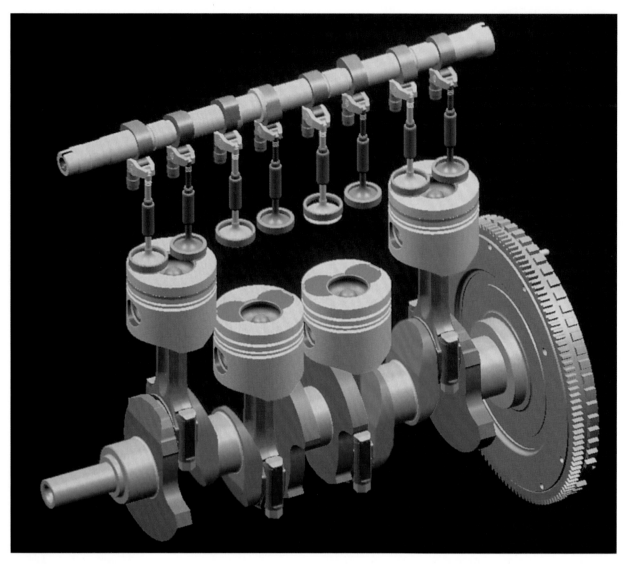

*This diagram shows the layout of the valve gear and complete rotating assembly of the PSA HDI turbodiesel. Among the points worth noting are that the combustion chambers are incorporated in the pistons, and the crankshaft has only four counterweights, two in the centre and one at each end. A fully balanced (eight counterweight) crankshaft would give slightly smoother running but would be heavier as well as more expensive to make. (PSA)*

revs per second) and the piston stroke is 80mm (3.2in), then the piston's average speed works out close to 58km/h (36mph). This may not sound a lot, but it is the average speed: the peak speed is rather more than twice that. And you must bear in mind that the piston accelerates from a standstill to its peak speed, comes to a stop again and then sets off in the opposite direction to complete the cycle, one hundred times a second. To make matters worse, the piston crown is seared by intense heat during the power stroke, but next time round it has to draw in a fresh charge of cool air, so it suffers high thermal stress as well.

The piston must therefore be strong enough to withstand all these forces, but it must also be as light as possible. The more it weighs, the higher the forces generated by the piston itself as it accelerates – and these forces have to be reacted by the crankshaft and the rest of the engine. That is why all modern pistons, even in diesel engines, are made of aluminium alloy rather than steel (although the pistons for some high-performance engines are cast with steel inserts to stiffen them and prevent them expanding too much when they get hot). Beyond that, one of the secrets of making a piston light is to cut away as much of it as you dare. Look at a piston of 50 years ago or more, and it has a deep cylindrical shape, because designers

were desperate to ensure it remained upright in the cylinder bore in all circumstances. Its modern equivalent looks almost unbelievably shallow, with much of the skirt – the section below the gudgeon pin – cut away on each side, leaving only two small sections to prevent the piston tilting around the axis of the pin. And in any case, through careful design, the forces acting on the piston are balanced to keep any tendency to tilt to a minimum.

Tucked into their grooves around the crown of the piston are the piston rings, of specially formulated cast iron. In virtually all of today's passenger car engines, there are three rings, the upper two working together to prevent the combustion pressure from blowing past the piston into the crankcase, and the lowest one a slotted 'scraper' to control the amount of oil on the cylinder wall (the walls are lubricated by oil thrown up from the crankshaft, to form a 'mist'). The oil is essential to prevent ring wear, but excess oil is undesirable. The only practical way to make sure there is enough is in fact to make sure there is too much, and then have the oil control ring scrape away the excess. As part of the process of making modern pistons more compact and lighter, the rings have become narrower, shallower, closer together and higher towards the piston crown, placing even more demands on the materials used to make them and the accuracy of their manufacture.

# The **connecting rods ...**

The connecting rods form the vital link between the pistons and the crankshaft, transmitting the effect of all the combustion pressure but also having to pull the piston downwards during the induction stroke. The

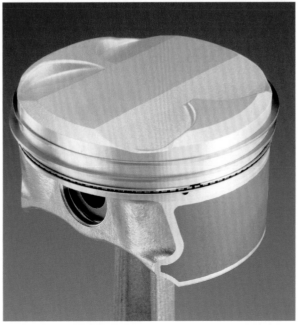

load on each connecting rod therefore alternates between tension and compression, but not in a particularly tidy way. The rod must be strong enough to withstand the maximum tension, but also stiff enough not to bend when it is under compression. To combine stiffness with lightness – since weight is again a very important consideration – all connecting rods have an H-beam cross-section. Steel connecting rods are still the most common, either pressed (cheapest) or forged (stronger), but both sintered (powdered metal, moulded and then solidified) iron and aluminium alloy rods are also found in some recent engines, and there have been experiments with alloy composite rods in which the aluminium is stiffened by ceramic fibres. The highest-performance competition engines generally use titanium connecting rods.

The little-end bearing which connects the rod to the piston is a complete circle with a bearing bush pressed into place, but the big-end bearing must be split to enable assembly around the crankshaft, the two halves of the bearing being bolted together afterwards. With sintered-iron rods, it is now common practice to part the big-end by a controlled fracture rather than by cutting; when the big end is assembled, the fractured faces fit together perfectly, providing excellent location in all directions. Naturally, the big end needs careful bearing design, like that of the main bearings.

# The **crankshaft** ...

Unlike the pistons and connecting rods with their up-and-down movement, the crankshaft has only to rotate. But it is subject to very large and rapidly shifting vertical forces, and it must therefore be stiff and well located by the main bearings within the cylinder block.

Making the crankshaft stiff is by no means easy, because it has to incorporate the 'throws', normally one for each cylinder, to accept the big ends of the connecting rods. In almost all modern engines, there is a main bearing between each cylinder – thus in a 4-cylinder in-line engine, there are five main bearings, three between the cylinders and one at each end. In V-engines there are main bearings between each pair of opposed cylinders, so that a V6 for example has four bearings.

*Crankshaft design varies greatly according to the load imposed by combustion pressures. This is the crankshaft for Ford's Duratorq DI direct-injection turbodiesel, as used in the new Mondeo. This crankshaft is formed by forging, has substantial overlap between the main and big-end bearings, and eight counterweights, two per cylinder throw. In contrast, the far more lightly loaded crankshaft for the Mondeo's 4-cylinder petrol engines is made of cast iron and has only four counterweights, which helps to make the engine significantly lighter.* (Ford)

In older engines, some main bearings were omitted for the sake of low cost and also to reduce frictional losses, to which each extra main bearing adds significantly. Until the 1960s it was usual for 4-cylinder in-line engines to have only three bearings, one at each end and one between cylinders 2 and 3, and the original Austin Seven engine of the 1920s (among others) was notorious for having only two bearings, one at each end. Today it is generally accepted that locating the crankshaft with a 'full set' of well-aligned bearings is a much better option than trying to make a less well-located shaft stiff enough. With today's high compression ratios and loadings, a two-bearing shaft in the manner of the Austin Seven would have to be extremely thick and very heavy, if it could be designed at all without resorting to high-strength materials.

Virtually all crankshafts are made in one piece, but in theory it is possible to fabricate a shaft by welding, shrink-fitting and pinning together a series of smaller components. Fabricated crankshafts, which in the past have been used in some small-capacity car engines, have two advantages: they do away with the need to begin with a complicated and expensive casting, and they allow the big-ends to be made in one piece and slipped over the big-end bearings before assembly, with no splitting and bolting. But they are very difficult to manufacture accurately, and however carefully the joints between the components are made, they eventually tend to shake loose during a long, hard life.

The majority of modern crankshafts are made of special-grade cast iron, although where extra strength is needed, in diesel engines and some high-performance petrol engines, the shaft may be machined from a steel forging. A few 'exotic' engines made in very small numbers have crankshafts machined from solid steel billet, because the extremely high cost of doing so is still less than the cost of setting up a facility to produce iron castings or steel forgings (which still have to be machined, though not to anything like the same extent). In most modern engines, the crankshafts receive further specialised treatment after they have been machined. The bearing surfaces are hardened using heat or chemical treatment, and the radiused edges of the bearings are often 'fillet rolled' to increase their

*Another view of the Ford Duratorq DI crankshaft shows more clearly the shaping of the counterweights and the use of the centre main bearing as a thrust bearing to locate the shaft lengthwise in the cylinder block. The junctions between the crankpins and the webs are the most vulnerable points where stress is concerned, and special techniques are used to treat these areas during manufacture and to make sure there is enough of a radius to avoid the risk of surface cracking leading to fatigue failure. (Ford)*

strength and resistance to fatigue.

Essentially, the crankshaft consists of a series of main bearings and offset big-end bearings, joined by 'webs' which can be extended, in the opposite direction to the big-ends, to form counterweights. A 'fully counterweighted' crankshaft has weights on either side of each big-end bearing throw. The main bearings are generally spaced at the same intervals as the cylinder bore centres. The main bearings are always larger in diameter than the big-ends, and the crankshaft is easier to make stiff if the main and big-end bearings overlap when viewed end-on. Obviously, it is much easier to achieve overlap with a short-stroke, and probably over-square engine.

There is a good deal more to crankshaft design than this. One often overlooked feature is the series of galleries drilled through each bearing and web, carefully joined-up and blanked off as necessary. These galleries have the vital task of supplying oil, under moderate pressure supply from the pump, to the bearings. Without the oil, the engine would quickly seize. Even a few seconds of starvation, if for instance the oil pump intake in the sump is uncovered during hard cornering because the oil level is too low, can cause serious damage. There is no way in which adequate lubrication of the bearings can be achieved through simple 'splashing'; a reliable pressure supply is essential.

Each end of the crankshaft carries further vital components. The aft end carries the flywheel, while the front end can be truly complicated. In every current production engine, the drive to operate the valves is taken – by chain or toothed belt – from a sprocket on the nose of the crankshaft. The oil pump is now usually wrapped around the crankshaft nose (though the alternative of a pump immersed in the oil in the sump, with a gear-driven shaft drive from the crankshaft, is still common). The crankshaft must also provide drives to all the other ancillaries: the water pump, the alternator, the power steering pump, the air conditioning compressor. Today's preferred method of doing this is to wrap a single very long 'polyvee' drive belt in a serpentine route around a pulley on the crankshaft nose, and the drive pulleys of each ancillary unit (with intermediate idlers and

*All versions of the new Ford Mondeo are fitted with a dual-mass flywheel like the one shown here. Splitting the flywheel into two separate masses, with a spring element between them, reduces and damps some of the critical vibrations which would otherwise occur at particular engine speeds and loads. (Ford)*

tensioners where necessary). This tidy solution brings some challenges: all the pulleys must be accurately aligned, and if the belt breaks, everything fails at once. But today's wide, shallow, carefully constructed belts never break, at least not in normal circumstances, unlike the old vee-belts which were much more vulnerable to wear and failure.

# A future without **accessory drives?**

It is likely that in the near future, the need for accessory drives will be much reduced. A start in this direction was made many years ago, when the belt-driven cooling fan behind the radiator was replaced by an electrically driven fan. Not only did this do away with the 'fan belt' – always a nuisance, often noisy and with a high failure rate; it also meant the fan need be driven only when necessary, in other words when the engine was getting too hot. This meant there was a useful energy saving. And, of course, the fan could be placed where it would do most good, without having to worry about how to run the belt and pulleys needed to drive it. Today, engineers are looking hard at extending these advantages to most of the other ancillary drives. Some cars already use electrically driven power-steering pumps (or simply use electric motors to operate their power steering). Air conditioning compressors can be run in the same way, and probably will be. The alternator itself is likely before long to be integrated with the starter motor in a single 'toroidal' unit forming part of the flywheel. The only remaining units driven from the crankshaft (apart from the valve gear) will then be the oil and coolant pumps – and some engineers even think the coolant pump might benefit from electric drive.

As we shall see, there is also a fair chance that the drive to the valve gear may also be done away with, in time. Meanwhile, the toroidal alternator/starter motor itself seems set to create a major upheaval in engineering, opening up all kinds of possibilities. Partly because everyone accepts these new units will work at 42 volts rather than 14 volts (feeding an electrical system set at 36 volts rather than 12 volts), they will be much more efficient and also much more powerful. As starter motors, they will be virtually silent and near-instant in operation, so that 'stop-start' operation in city traffic at last becomes truly practical. With the help of clever electronics, they could also help to smooth out any vibration in the crankshaft or the transmission, and may even provide additional drive power for maximum acceleration or hill-climbing.

# **Taking care** of the crankshaft

Apart from providing all these drives, the crankshaft needs to be accurately located fore-and-aft within the block, and is therefore provided with a thrust bearing as well as its main bearings. The crankshaft must be protected against torsional vibration, in other words the risk that one end of the shaft will vibrate in its rotation, relative to the other end, because it is driven by a succession of power strokes from the connecting rods (visually, it is easiest to imagine the flywheel rotating back and forth while the nose of the shaft is held fixed). Some vibration is inevitable because the shaft cannot be made infinitely stiff; the engineering trick is to ensure the vibration is damped out before it can do any harm. Harm can certainly be done, since it was not unknown for the crankshafts of early engines, designed before the importance of torsional vibration was appreciated, to shear completely because the shaft 'resonated' – at a certain speed, the vibration would become bigger and bigger until failure occurred, usually between a main bearing and a crankshaft web. Modern car crankshafts are usually so stiff that their theoretical resonant speed is far higher than the engine's maximum operating speed, but many engines are equipped with 'torsional vibration dampers' to absorb the energy and keep vibration to an absolute minimum, for the sake of comfort. The most common technique is to split the flywheel – or one of the crankshaft mounted pulleys – into inner and outer sections joined by a thin layer of elastomer which 'swallows' the vibration before it can have any serious mechanical effect.

# 4 The engine's top end

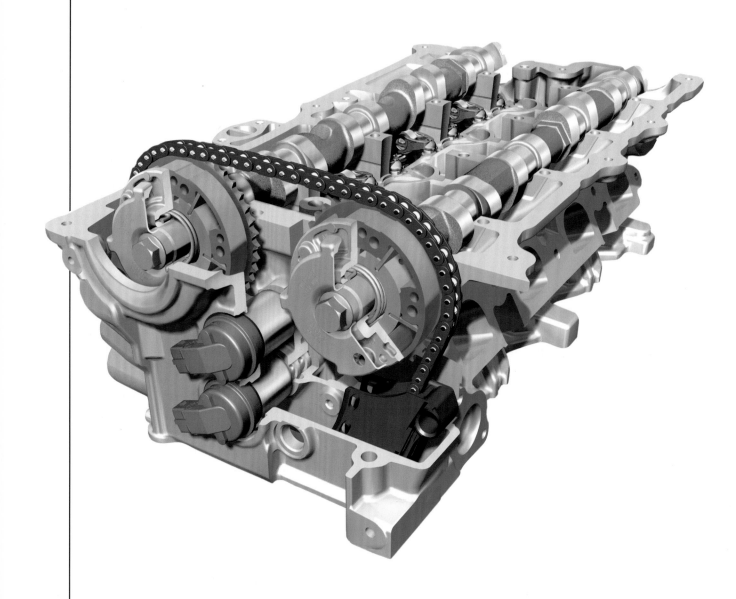

At its simplest, the job of the cylinder head and valves is to get air and fuel into the engine, burn it in the right place at the right time, and get rid of the burned gases afterwards. The burning takes place in the combustion chamber above each piston. At least, that is where it ought to take place, although it sometimes seems all too easy for it to happen partly in the exhaust system. These days, all combustion chambers are directly above the piston crown although in the early days of motoring, some very strange configurations with offset chambers were used for a variety of reasons, but mostly to give the piston an easier time, and to make it easier to operate the valves.

The simplest petrol-engine combustion chamber, whatever its shape and position, has an inlet valve, an exhaust valve, and a spark plug. In simple 4-stroke operation, the mixture of air and fuel vapour is drawn through the inlet valve, which then shuts during the compression stroke. The spark plug fires the mixture at the top of the compression stroke, and the power stroke takes place. Then the exhaust valve opens so that the burned gas can be pumped out of the cylinder into the exhaust manifold and its downstream exhaust system.

# Valves and valve gear

In all modern passenger car engines, the valves are poppet-type – that is, they resemble inverted mushrooms which close against circular seats. The valves are normally held closed by springs, and pushed open ('lifted') when required by tappets at the end of the valve stems. It is also possible to operate the valves through a system which positively opens *and* closes them – the 'desmodromic' principle. This does away with the need for substantial valve springs, but is itself complicated and expensive to make and maintain. Desmodromic valves have been used in some racing engines, notably the all-conquering Mercedes GP cars of the mid-1950s, and also in some high-speed motorcycle engines, but hardly ever in a road-going production car.

Some current GP engines use air pressure rather than springs to close the valves, again saving their weight and the power needed to compress them; but these engines use an air supply from a cylinder pumped up before the race, which is hardly a practical technique for a road car.

In most respects, the larger the valves, the better. Recall that for maximum power, the engine must pass as much air and fuel mixture as possible through itself in the shortest possible time. Clearly, the larger the

valves and the deeper they open, the more mixture can enter the combustion chamber – so long as the rest of the intake system doesn't impede the flow. Note in passing that it isn't the circular area of the valve (as so often suggested) which is the important factor, but its circumference, because the mixture enters the combustion chamber through the circular slot between the valve head and the seat.

This is why so many engines now have two inlet and two exhaust valves. If we look at the simple geometry of a single valve head with a diameter of (say) 40mm (1.6in), then its area is roughly 12.6cm² (2in²) and its circumference is 12.6cm (5in). If we take instead two valves each with a diameter of 20mm (0.8in), then their total area is only 6.3 cm² (1in²) – but their combined circumference is still 12.6cm (5in), so they will be able to pass just as much mixture, if they are opened to the same depth. Generally they can indeed be opened to the same depth, because the maximum valve lift is mainly determined by the available clearance above the cylinder head, and that remains the same however many valves there are.

Why is this important? For at least four reasons. First, in the half-circle of a real combustion chamber, you can actually replace a single valve head with two heads which are significantly more than half its diameter. To put figures on it, in the 86mm (3.4in) bore of a 'square' 4-cylinder, 2-litre engine, you might reasonably have a single inlet valve of 36mm (1.4in) diameter – but in the same half-circular space, there is ample room for two valves each of 30mm (1.2in) diameter, with a combined circumference 67% greater than for the single larger valve, and therefore capable of admitting well over half as much mixture again in a given time. The second factor is weight: because of the square-cube law (area increases as the square of a linear dimension, volume – and therefore weight – as its cube) the two valves together weigh only 16% more than the single valve, assuming they are directly scaled, and valve weight is important as we shall see. The third factor is that assuming the exhaust valves are paired in the same way, then there is space for a spark plug in the very centre of the combustion chamber – the best possible place for it, since the flame front then has the least distance to travel through the mixture. The fourth and last factor is more complicated, and involves the various things

*Opposite: View of the BMW Valvetronic cylinder head from the front end, with the variable-lift mechanism removed, shows a layout typical of many of today's more advanced engines, with twin overhead camshafts, chain-driven in this case, and variable valve timing by means of the vane-type variator units picked out in blue (outer casing, driven from the sprocket) and green (inner core, directly connected to the camshaft nose). (BMW)*

you can do if you have two inlet valves rather than just one. Basically, it gives you the option of making the flow through each of the valves different, normally to suit low-speed and high-speed operation – a subject to which we shall return.

These are the reasons why so many modern engines have four valves (two inlet, two exhaust) per cylinder. As a layout it is not new, since the Peugeot Grand Prix engine of 1912 had four valves per cylinder; but the idea began to be established for road cars only in the 1970s, and has become the European and Japanese standard only in the last few years. Not everybody agrees it is the best solution. For example, many of the latest Mercedes engines have three valves per cylinder – two inlet, one exhaust – with twin spark plugs, one on either side of the single exhaust valve. Some engines from the Volkswagen group, and a few Japanese engines, have five valves per cylinder; a good geometric case can be made for this arrangement, which allows air to enter the cylinder at an even higher rate, but actually operating all the valves efficiently causes a few headaches.

The valves are opened and closed by cams carried on a camshaft – or on two camshafts, one for the inlet valves, the other for the exhaust valves. The camshaft is driven from the crankshaft, either by chain or by toothed belt, or directly by gears in the case of high-performance engines for competition. Since (in basic theory, at least) each valve needs to open only once every two revolutions of the engine, the camshafts are driven at half the crankshaft speed. The cams may act directly on the valve tappets, or may operate them via 'rockers' or 'fingers' – the essential difference between the two being that rockers pivot in the middle with the cam working the opposite end from the valve, while fingers are pivoted at the far end with

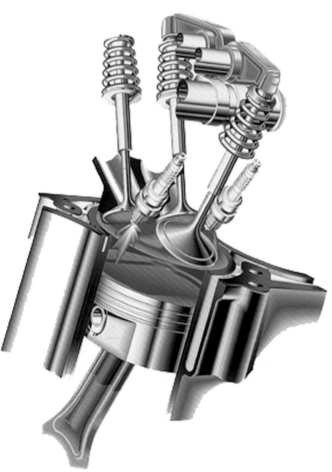

THE ENGINE'S TOP END

*The Volkswagen group has built more engines with 5 valves per cylinder than anyone else, mainly in the 4-cylinder form seen here. Driving three inlet valves per cylinder from a single camshaft gives a less than ideal layout with the central valve pointing further 'away' from the cylinder axis than the valves on either side, but this seems to create no real problem. Features of this engine include a toothed-belt drive to the exhaust camshaft only, with drive transferred to the inlet camshaft by a short chain at the opposite end. Ignition is 'direct', coil-over-plug. The crankshaft is fully counterweighted and the design of the pistons is typical of modern practice.* (Audi)

the cam acting closer to the valve. Rockers may also be operated by pushrods from a camshaft located somewhere else, conveniently closer to the crankshaft. With direct valve operation, the tappet normally takes the form of a tiny 'bucket' sitting over the end of the valve.

Many early car engines had their valves housed alongside the piston, and opening upwards into a 'remote' combustion chamber. This made the engine lower and also meant the flat, shallow and simple cylinder head was easy to remove for decarbonising, a ritual which 1930s motorists had to conduct at regular intervals because of the inferior quality (by modern standards) of the fuels and oils they used. These 'side valves' could conveniently be operated by short pushrods from a single camshaft close to the crankshaft, with a short, simple chain drive. Side-valve engines were in common use until the early 1950s, being fitted for example to the original Morris Minor and to the Ford 100E Anglia/Prefect series. But they were inefficient, because they suffered severe pumping losses as mixture and burned gas shuffled between the cylinder and the combustion chamber, and as the need for easy decarbonising vanished, they gave way to 'overhead valve' (OHV) engines with the valves directly above the piston.

During the 1960s, the typical OHV engine still had its valves operated by pushrods and rockers. In many engines of that time, the inlet and exhaust ports were on the same side of the cylinder head, so that the incoming air could be warmed by the emerging exhaust gas. In such engines, all the valves were set in-line, either vertically or offset to one side, which made machining the head simpler and cheaper. Some engines, however, were 'crossflow', with the inlet

valves and ports on one side, and the exhausts on the other. This arrangement speeded gas flow and favoured higher performance, and many 1960s performance conversion kits consisted essentially of crossflow cylinder heads for bolting on to single-sided engines. But operating opposed valves via pushrods from a single camshaft was never easy, and by degrees car manufacturers took their lead from pioneers like Alfa Romeo, threw away their pushrods and moved their camshafts into the cylinder head to create the modern overhead camshaft (OHC) engine.

The engine may have a single overhead camshaft, which may either operate one set of valves (normally the inlet valves) directly and the other set via rockers, or may sit close to the centre of the head and operate all the valves via fingers or rockers. Alternatively twin

*In some engines with twin overhead camshafts, space is saved by taking the drive to the inlet camshaft only, and transferring the drive to the exhaust camshaft either by a carefully engineered 'scissor' gear drive as seen in this Toyota example, or via a short chain and two small sprockets at the far ends of the shafts, an approach used by Volkswagen among others.* (Toyota)

*This is the valvetrain layout developed by Renault for a 16-valve version of its 1.9-litre common-rail diesel engine – a version which has yet to enter production but which could deliver 140bhp and a great deal of torque, with the help of turbocharging.* (Renault)

to look rather complicated, and partly because the DOHC layout leaves a convenient central space for access to the spark plugs. It also means that where variable valve timing (to be discussed later) is used, the timing of each set of valves can be adjusted independently by relatively simple means. On the other hand, unless the twin camshafts are far enough apart, there can be problems finding the space for their side-by-side drive sprockets, especially with a toothed belt camshaft drive. Some DOHC engines (from Toyota and Volkswagen, notably) drive just one camshaft directly, and then drive the second camshaft by chain or gears from the first. Again, a DOHC layout makes the top end of an engine more bulky, and the whole unit more difficult to install.

The shape of the combustion chamber also contributes to decisions in this area. The most efficient chamber is the most compact – and compactness is best achieved with a narrow angle between the inlet and exhaust valves, and a fairly flat piston crown. For best gas flow, on the other hand, the inlet valves should be more nearly 'opposite' the exhausts, with a wider angle between the valves, and the piston more or less domed to achieve a high enough compression ratio (in either case, the piston crown may need to have recesses to ensure valve

camshafts may be used, one for each set of valves, the engine then becoming double overhead camshaft (DOHC) rather than single (SOHC).

There are arguments in favour of all these layouts, although the modern move towards four valves per cylinder favours DOHC, partly because a single camshaft with 16 cams (in a 4-cylinder engine) begins

*In most respects, this Alfa Romeo 4-cylinder engine from the 156 is typical of modern design with 4 valves per cylinder. It differs in having two sparking plugs per cylinder, one at the centre of the cylinder and the other one towards its outer edge. This arrangement makes less sense than Alfa's original Twin Spark arrangement, in an 8-valve engine, in which the plugs were positioned symmetrically – but 'Twin Spark' had become an Alfa Romeo selling point and the second plug had to be retained even though there was little space for it. Note also the variator on the nose of the inlet camshaft, to vary the valve timing, and the care taken to achieve long inlet tracts with the smoothest possible airflow. The engine mounting arrangements and the oil filter housing design are also interesting.* (Alfa Romeo)

clearance). In practice, modern DOHC engines seem to have divided themselves between 'economy' units with an angle somewhere between 20 and 30° between the inlet and exhaust valves, and 'performance' units with an angle closer to 40–45°.

The valves themselves remain essentially simple, although the materials from which they are made, especially in high-performance engines, are now specially developed alloys. Valves can be cooled by making the stems hollow and inserting a small amount of pure sodium, which effectively transfers heat away from the valve head as it splashes up and down; but this is only cost-effective in high performance engines. The coiled valve springs need careful design to ensure they remain effective up to the maximum rated speed of the engine, yet without being so stiff that it takes a lot of effort to open the valves. Until quite recently, many engines were speed-limited by 'valve bounce' – at a certain speed, the springs would begin to resonate, allowing the valves to open again after they had closed, and the engine would lose power. Today, almost all engines are speed-limited through an electronic setting in their engine management control unit. Designers sometimes reduce the overall spring rate, and guard against the effects of a single resonant speed, by using two concentric springs of different rates.

*View of the underside of the BMW Valvetronic cylinder head shows the 'pent-roof' combustion chamber shape typical of a 4-valve per cylinder layout, with central sparking plug, as well as the layout of coolant passages and holes for the head securing bolts. The large blank slot on the left accepts the valve-gear drive from the crankshaft, which is inserted as a pre-assembled 'cartridge' during manufacture. (BMW)*

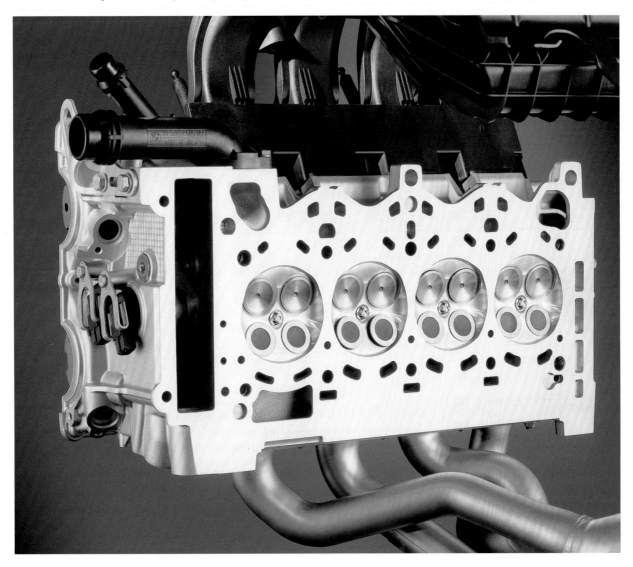

*Modern engines developed for high efficiency tend to be complex in their layout. This illustration shows the cylinder head of the BMW Valvetronic engine with all the moving parts from its valve train separately* *displayed. The four rows of components on the right are those which form the variable-lift inlet-valve mechanism which allows the engine to operate without a conventional throttle valve.* (BMW)

# Chain versus toothed belt

When it comes to driving overhead camshafts, the choice lies between chain and toothed belt, with plus-points on either side. The chain needs lubricating, while the toothed belt is 'dry'; it also needs more careful tensioning and vibration damping, especially on its 'slack' side. On the other hand, the chain is more compact – toothed belts for the valve train are up to 30mm (1.2in) wide – and given good materials and proper lubrication, should last almost indefinitely, while toothed belts usually need replacing after a specified mileage (although this can now be as high as 100,000 miles/161,000km). Toothed belts are (probably) cheaper. Chains have tended to be the automatic choice among the 'prestige' car makers like BMW, Jaguar and Mercedes, but are also used on many smaller engines – but a count of today's production engines would probably show toothed belts in the majority.

Whichever drive is chosen, it needs to be able to transmit substantial power, especially at high engine speeds. What is happening, after all, is that the camshafts are continually lifting the valves against the considerable load of their springs. It has been estimated that operating the 16 valves of a conventional modern 4-cylinder engine at 6,000rpm consumes well over 1kW. That is why engine designers are keen to reduce both the weight of the valve gear and its frictional losses. The friction has a clear and definite effect; there is a modern trend towards fitting cam followers with small rollers, to avoid the friction of sliding contact. This roller arrangement is easiest to build into a system in which the valve is operated by fingers, a technique adopted by Renault in all its recently introduced 16V engines.

The weight of the valve gear is equally important. The heavier each component, the higher will be the stresses in the system as it operates. Part of the appeal of using four valves per cylinder is that it reduces the weight of the valves for a given gas flow rate. One of the reasons for abandoning the pushrod OHV layout was the weight and inertia of the pushrods. The camshafts themselves need to be stiff and yet light; torsional vibration of camshafts, as well as crankshafts, has been known, and in any case, any twisting of the camshaft from end to end will affect valve timing accuracy. Some manufacturers now make the shafts hollow to reduce weight while retaining stiffness.

*Modern engine designers can choose between toothed belt and chain drives for camshafts. In the Ford Duratorq DI diesel seen here, a chain drive is used to the twin overhead camshafts. Chain drives are more compact, and these days are usually 'for life' with no replacement ever needed; but note the need for a chain tensioner (at left) and two high-density nylon dampers to discourage the longer free lengths of chain from vibrating. Note also the presence of a second chain drive behind the immediately visible one, to drive the oil pump which is located in the sump. (Ford)*

# Hydraulic **tappets**

Another ritual once regularly performed by DIY car owners was the setting of tappet clearances – ensuring there was a small but positive clearance between the rocker-end and the tappet when the valve was closed, to make sure it was really closed, because even a small gas leakage past a closed valve seriously reduces engine efficiency and eventually, life. This concern also lay behind the regular regrinding of valve seats. Today, many engines are fitted with hydraulic tappets, tiny but ingenious devices which 'pump up' with engine oil to ensure there is zero clearance but no more, so that the valves are closed when they should be, an added benefit being that noise is reduced (an old-fashioned engine with too much tappet clearance could rattle fiercely). The move towards four valves per cylinder encouraged the use of hydraulic tappets, because checking the clearance on 16 valves in a 4-cylinder engine, let alone 32 valves on a V8, becomes a major chore. The tappets also provide automatic engine speed limiting because beyond a certain rpm, they can no longer exhaust oil fast enough for the valve to shut completely. This is why an early move by anyone modifying an engine with hydraulic tappets for racing is simply to remove the tappets and replace them with 'solid lifters', enabling the engine to run faster.

Hydraulic tappets weigh a good deal more than 'solid' mechanical ones, and cost a great deal more. This is enough to force any designer to wonder if he could do without them. Where hydraulic tappets are not used, it is easy to continue the practice of a century, and build a lock-nut contact into a rocker arm or finger for the purpose of adjusting the tappet clearance. There is more of a problem with valves directly operated by overhead camshafts. In this case clearance is usually set (on the production line) by inserting a small 'biscuit' shim of exactly the right thickness beneath each bucket tappet. Adjusting the clearance in service is an extremely fiddly business, but in most modern engines the need rarely if ever arises. For example, Jaguar said when announcing its AJ-V8 engine that although it had chosen not to use hydraulic tappets, careful design and choice of materials meant that the valve clearances were 'set for life' and would never need adjusting.

# The tricks of **valve timing**

In the theoretical 4-stroke engine, the inlet valve opens at the top of the induction stroke and closes at the bottom, while the exhaust valve opens at the bottom of the exhaust stroke and closes at the top. Although an engine would fairly happily run on this basis, it ignores two vital factors. First, the opening and closing of the valve is not an instant event but takes place through half a turn of the camshaft (in other words through a quarter-turn of the crankshaft, or almost half the total piston movement, since the camshaft turns at half the crankshaft speed). So, do you start to open the inlet valve at the top of the intake stroke, knowing it will not be fully open until the piston is well down its travel? Or do you start it a little earlier? Similarly, do you arrange for the exhaust valve finally to close when the piston reaches the top of the exhaust stroke, knowing that it will be nearly closed some time before that, or do you leave the valve slightly open for a short time after the piston reaches top dead centre?

That is one factor – and complicated enough to ensure that the design of cam profiles has become a computer-aided science in itself. You can for example shape the cam so that it opens the valve, and allows it to close, quite quickly, with the cam holding the valve fully open during a substantial part of its contact period. That improves the gas flow, but it also means the valve has to be accelerated very fast in both directions, which means higher loads on the cam and

the camshaft, and a stiffer valve spring (which means even higher loads on the camshaft). A compromise has to be reached, a trade-off between valve opening time (and therefore gas flow) and ease of valve operation. In practice, the cam profiles for a road-going car with a flexible, high-torque engine, and a racing car with everything optimised for maximum power, look astonishingly different.

The other factor, even more important, is that air and gas itself has mass and inertia. Thus for example, if you have a flow of air rushing through the open inlet valve, it will not stop as soon as the piston reaches bottom dead centre in the induction stroke and starts upwards in compression. It will only stop some time later, and if you want the maximum amount of air to enter the engine (which you mostly do), it is best not to close the inlet valve until that happens. In the same way, it is worth starting to open the exhaust valve well before bottom dead centre so that the valve is fully open when the exhaust stroke starts; and once you have the exhaust streaming out, there is some advantage in leaving the valve partly open until after top dead centre.

So the tidy picture of valves opening and closing

exactly when the piston comes to the top or bottom of its travel has to be thrown away. In particular, when the piston reaches the top of its stroke at the end of exhaust and the beginning of induction, there is normally a period of 'valve overlap' in which both inlet and exhaust valves are at least part-open. During this period, the incoming flow of air/fuel mixture helps to flush the remainder of the exhaust gas out of the cylinder, while the early opening of the inlet valve means more mixture can be admitted. The trick is to adjust the timing so that flushing is almost 100% without losing any of the fresh mixture down the exhaust. In some racing engines, the amount of valve overlap (defined as the degrees of crankshaft angle at which the inlet valve begins opening before top dead centre – BTDC – plus the angle at which the exhaust valve closes after top dead centre – ATDC) is considerable, although it can be overdone, especially in a high-compression engine. If the valves are well open as the piston reaches top dead centre, the piston may hit a valve with immediately disastrous consequences. The overlap at bottom dead centre (exhaust opening before, BBDC, plus inlet closing after, ABDC) carries no such danger and the total angle is always greater than at top dead centre and often substantial, especially in engines designed for high-performance.

The overall result is that each engine has a 'timing diagram' setting the four angles, normally set down as inlet opens BTDC/inlet closes ABDC/exhaust opens BBDC/exhaust closes ATDC, each figure in degrees of crankshaft angle. The figures are not always positive, especially these days when strange-seeming measures are needed to minimise exhaust emissions (of which more later). To take two examples from Renault, the little 1.2-litre, 8-valve D-series engine, which powered the 'entry-level' Clio when it was introduced, had valve timing 10/38/32/-6 degrees; the more modern 1.6-litre, 16-valve K-series engine's timing was -1/18/14/4 degrees (minus timing means the event takes place before rather than after, or vice versa). Thus the small engine had an overlap of only 4°, and the K-series (which met a more severe emissions standard) of only 3°, and with valve operation grouped around different points, the first before and the second after top dead centre.

*Opposite: Overhead view of BMW's Valvetronic engine with the cam cover removed shows three 'camshafts' – two operating the valves in the normal way, and one (the most immediately visible one) working through a linkage to vary the inlet valve lift as a substitute for normal throttling. The large unit in the centre of the head is the electric motor which works through a worm-drive to position the variable-lift shaft according to instructions from the engine control unit. (BMW)*

In any event, knowing the valve timing is only half the battle. It tells you little unless you are also shown the cam profile. Contrary to what one might expect, it is the 'gentle' engines which tend to have smoothly rounded profiles, while all-out racing engines often have profiles with very sharp peaks: but the 'gentle' engines have very little valve overlap, while the racing engines have far more. If you are going to have substantial valve overlap and high valve lift, you need to get the valves out of the way fast before the piston arrives, hence the sharp-peaked profiles, which therefore accelerate their valves at the highest rate.

# Varying the **valve timing** and **lift**

Choosing valve timing is yet another engineering compromise. To develop maximum power at high speed, you need positive valve overlap around TDC, because power crucially depends on getting as much mixture as possible into the cylinder in the short time available – and the faster the engine is running, the shorter the time. But at low speed, looking for something less than maximum power, it is better to have zero overlap, or even a short period in which both valves are closed. Small or zero overlap makes an engine much more responsive and 'driveable' in heavy traffic, for example.

Throughout the 1990s, more and more engines were fitted with variable valve timing so that the overlap could be varied according to driving conditions, the speed and load on the engine. The initial approach, confined to DOHC engines, was to install a device in the drive sprocket for the inlet camshaft which used engine oil pressure to make the camshaft rotate relative to the sprocket itself, and therefore to the crankshaft, so that the inlet valves would open and close earlier or later. Changing the timing of the inlet valves had more effect than altering the exhaust valve timing. Early devices simply switched between two positions, providing one valve timing for low-speed, low-load and another for high-speed, high-load. This was quite sufficient to enable engine designers to achieve easier starting and better torque at low and medium speeds without compromising high-speed power output. Eventually, devices were developed which could set the inlet valve timing at any point between the high and low limits, and some manufacturers, such as BMW, began altering exhaust valve timing too, mainly to reduce exhaust emissions even further. Today, variable inlet valve timing (VIVT) is becoming commonplace, and a number of engines are already equipped with fully variable timing.

Varying the valve timing simply shifts the points at which the valve opens and closes.

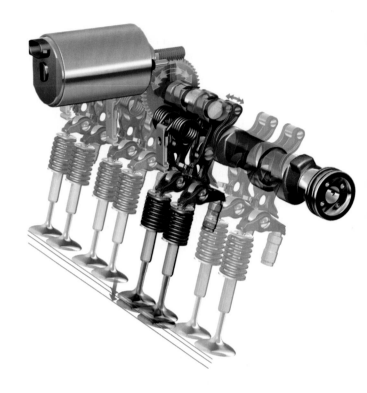

The valve stays open just as long, and is lifted just as high – giving two other factors which people have taken a close look at varying. It is certainly worth the look, because ideally the valve should be open not only at exactly the right time, but also exactly as long and as high as will admit the right amount of mixture. If the valve is open too long and too high, the speed of the mixture past the valve slows down, and it may 'sit' inside the combustion chamber itself rather than maintaining a motion which keeps the mixture even and helps the flame front to spread faster. A complex but interesting mechanism is used in the MG-Rover 1.8-litre K-series VVT engine, shortening the time for

which the valve stays open (and thus also altering the valve overlap), but most of the devices which have reached production simply de-activate one of the inlet valves in each cylinder. This is the approach used by Honda in its high-performance CVT engines, which are also notable for their high efficiency. Honda does not completely de-activate the valve, but arranges for it to lift by a tiny amount to avoid the danger of it sticking. Honda also combines variable valve timing with this dual-lift mechanism in some of its engines, and has most recently combined all of these techniques with 'conventional' variable valve timing using a variator.

An alternative approach, first adopted by Toyota and now quite widely used in engines with two inlet valves per cylinder, is simply to shut off one of the inlet ports by means of an automatically operated flap. Generally, the two inlet ports have different shapes: the one which is always open has a profile which 'twists' the air/fuel mixture into the combustion chamber, to maintain a strong swirling flow, while the one which is opened only at higher speed and load is 'straight-through', allowing mixture to pass through it at the highest possible rate.

# Doing away with **valve gear?**

Experimental engines have already been run in which the valves are operated not by camshafts, but by individual actuators using hydraulic power, or electric power applied through solenoids. Using such techniques, the opening and closing of each valve can be individually controlled. With such a system, clearly the valve timing can be altered in any way at all, not only providing the best timing for maximum power or maximum torque (or very slow and economical idling) but creating some theoretical possibilities which engine designers find very exciting. It would, for example, be possible to shut off some cylinders completely at low load, so that the others work more efficiently; or the engine could be turned into an air compressor to reduce the load on the brakes and perhaps recover some energy when running downhill. But the main appeal of the system is that it enables valve timing and lift to be precisely matched to the needs of the engine at any moment, depending on operating conditions. It has been estimated by engineers who have already run experimental units that efficiency could be increased (that is, fuel consumption could be reduced) by up to 20% using this technique. In addition, the mechanical design of the engine would be simplified because the conventional valve gear – the chain or toothed belt, the tensioner mechanism, the sprocket wheels and the camshafts – would be eliminated.

The one real problem with this technique, given that electronics have made the task of control relatively simple, is the power needed by the actuators, and their sheer size. It seems generally agreed that electric actuators, passing a high current through a solenoid, is a better solution than hydraulics, simply because hydraulic actuators are likely always to be very expensive. But a solenoid which develops the power needed to accelerate a valve as fast as the cam on a camshaft would do is big and heavy. At least, it is when it is supplied from a 12-volt electrical system. However, for many good reasons, the car manufacturers are now close to adopting a 36-volt standard, with the alternator delivering 42 volts (just as today's alternators deliver

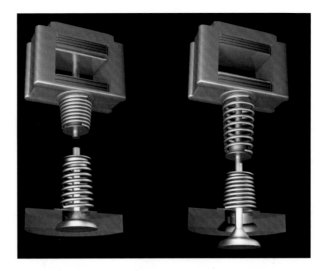

A 'camless' valve system will not necessarily do away with valve springs. In the system developed by Renault, the camshaft has indeed vanished but a pair of springs remains for each valve. Electrical power is saved because the operating system need only top-up the energy lost as the valve shuttles from the 'open' to the 'closed' spring, under electronic control. (Renault)

14 volts to supply a 12-volt system). With three times the voltage, the current needed to provide valve-driving power is much less, and the solenoids can be very much smaller – probably small enough not to take up any more space than a conventional system of twin overhead camshafts and valve springs.

Even so, the amount of power needed is considerable – of the order of 2kW with a 4-cylinder, 16-valve engine running at high speed – and would overload any existing electrical system. The new 36-volt systems will provide far more power for this and other purposes, though, so that difficulty is avoided. Renault has studied a slightly different approach in which the valve 'bounces' between two springs, with the solenoids dictating the timing of their operation but needing to supply only as much power as is needed to make up for the mechanical losses. Renault estimates the power requirement for its system could be as little as 300W when the engine is idling or running at low speed.

There seems widespread agreement that the question is when, rather than if the 'camless' engine will become a production reality. As soon as 36-volt electrical systems are established, the major hurdle will have been overcome, and the advantages are then too great to ignore. Renault's team suggests such engines may be in service by 2010 at the latest.

# **5** **Air, fuel** and **combustion**

Complex though the whole theory of valve operation may be, the object is simple enough: to get the mixture in, and to get the exhaust gas out of the combustion chamber. But the real key to engine operation is what happens in the chamber itself. It is no good assuming that once the mixture has been compressed, the firing of a spark somewhere near TDC will make everything happen. To begin with, the fire takes some time to light. If you look at the effect of a single spark in a static chamber containing air and petrol vapour, you may see what looks very much like an explosion.

However, an explosion is actually the last thing you want: the instant huge rise in pressure is enough to damage any engine in a short time. All engines have a 'detonation limit' at which the firing of the spark will explode the fuel rather than making it burn smoothly, leading to the phenomenon generally known as knocking or pinking. The higher the compression ratio, the more advanced your ignition, and the lower the octane rating of your petrol, the closer you are to the knock limit. Many modern engines deliberately run close to the limit and are fitted with sensors to warn when knocking is about to happen; the engine control unit then retards the ignition timing to prevent it happening.

Assuming you stay clear of detonation, what you have is a smooth but extremely fast burn, so that the pressure rises quickly – but not too quickly – to a peak, just as the piston reaches TDC. But when you have an engine running at 6,000rpm, with each cylinder firing every second revolution, you have a total time, between the piston starting from BDC of the compression stroke and returning there at the end of the power stroke, of one-fiftieth of a second in which the whole burning process must take place and the resulting pressure must do its work.

Actually you have less than that, because there is clearly no point in firing the spark the moment the inlet valve has closed, and the piston has barely started on its way up. On the other hand, if you wait too long, the piston will be on its way down again before full pressure has been developed, and a lot of energy will be wasted. Thus the timing of the spark is absolutely crucial, and there must be a way of changing the timing – of advancing or retarding the ignition – according to the engine's needs as speed and load vary. The earliest engines left adjustment of timing to the driver, and even some post-1945 cars had an ignition timing advance and retard knob, with push-pull operation, alongside the choke knob on the dashboard. The procedure, nearly enough, was to pull them both out for a cold start, and push them in again as soon as the engine would pull smoothly.

By 1945, though, the distributor had largely taken over the task of adjusting the timing. Beneath the distributor cap with its single high-tension feed from the coil and its series of output leads, one to each spark plug, lay an ingenious mechanism in which a pair of whirling spring-loaded bob-weights would 'pull' the timing forward as the engine speed increased. Additionally, a vacuum capsule was fitted which would adjust the timing according to load (the higher the load, the lower the pressure inside the inlet manifold from which the pressure tapping was taken). Steadily refined in design, the distributor worked remarkably well for half a century, but it was always a weak spot where reliability was concerned ('setting the points' was yet another chore regularly performed by mechanics or DIY owners until the late 1970s). Its end came when it proved incapable of providing the accuracy, or the flexibility of control, demanded by engines in the new age of exhaust emission limits.

Today, the ignition timing – like so much else – is determined within an electronic control unit (of which more later). There is still a coil – or almost as likely, an individual coil for each cylinder, or perhaps for each pair of cylinders – but the triggering of each spark is done with extreme accuracy, and without any moving parts, by an electronic signal. Some units fire not just a single spark, but a series: in many engines, the spark fires not only during the compression stroke but also during the exhaust stroke, partly because it makes design of the system simpler (it means that each plug fires each time the piston approaches the top of the cylinder) but also because it seems to have some small benefit for exhaust emissions, and no perceptible effect on spark plug life.

To outward appearance, the spark plug itself has changed little in the last half-century. That belies the huge effort which has gone into refining the insulating and conducting materials used, and the way plugs are made. The apparently simply task of jumping a spark between two electrodes, one fed by a pulse of very high voltage and the other earthed to the cylinder head, is actually very complicated. Engineers talk of 'hot' and 'cold' plugs – designed to cope with different in-cylinder temperatures – and of 'heat range', the combination of hot and cold rating. They also talk of the need to avoid 'cold fouling' before the engine has warmed up,

*Opposite: The high-point of the combustion process in the Ford Duratec HE engine, as fitted to the Ford Mondeo. Apart from showing the layout of the four valves and the perfectly situated centre spark plug, the illustration shows how the pattern of airflow within the cylinder, created by careful shaping of the inlet ports, has concentrated the fuel towards the centre of the cylinder and kept it away from the walls where there would be some tendency for fuel to condense, increasing HC emissions and reducing combustion efficiency. (Ford)*

'sooting', and of course general erosion of the electrodes. Today, some of the most advanced (and expensive) spark plugs have wire-thin electrodes of almost everlasting platinum or other precious metal, and have service lives of 60,000 miles (96,500km) or more. Technologists are also looking at the idea of using the spark plug electrodes as an ingenious sensor to detect what is happening inside the combustion chamber.

The spark and its timing are only part of the story. The important thing is what happens to the air/fuel mixture after it has entered the combustion chamber, before the firing of the spark and immediately afterwards. The engine designer's basic ideal is to have a perfectly even mixture moving fast but in an orderly and predictable way, because that results in the cleanest burn, the flame lit by the spark travelling quickly to all parts of the combustion chamber. Some years ago, fast movement of the mixture was encouraged by 'squish', the combustion chamber in the cylinder head being smaller in area than the piston crown, so that mixture around the edges of the chamber was 'squeezed' towards the middle as the piston rose. Today squish is out of fashion, mainly because it creates a narrow crevice in which some fuel always lurks unburned, but also because it results in a combustion chamber shape which is less efficient than it might be. A strong squish effect is more difficult to achieve in a 4-valve chamber anyway.

Today's key words are 'swirl' and 'tumble'. Both are created by careful shaping of the inlet ports and the piston crown. In swirl, the mixture in the cylinder spins round its central axis, faster and faster as the piston rises, so there is a small, fairly calm area in the very centre and rapid movement to spread the flame front as it moves outwards. In tumble, the mixture rolls around a horizontal axis (assuming an upright engine!) in the manner of washing in a tumble dryer. Again, the movement is accelerated and tightened as the piston rises. In this case, the spark normally occurs with the mixture passing it at high speed, and the flame front is carried quickly around the 'tumble'. Both flow patterns have their own strong believers among engine designers; the important thing is that both produce a clean and consistent burn. Also, both work best with the central spark plug typical of a 4-valve cylinder head.

## Putting in the **fuel**

Spark-ignition engines normally run on petrol (in the USA, gasoline), which these days is a careful blend of different hydrocarbons plus a number of additives, all designed to fulfil a stringent specification which lays down things like volatility and boiling point. One of the most significant figures in the specification is octane rating (already referred to), which is a measure of the fuel's resistance to detonation – its tendency to explode rather than burning. Although the oil industry often argues there is too much emphasis on octane rating, it is the only number of which motorists are really aware; they simply accept the rest of the specification, including the regular adjustments which are made between 'summer' and 'winter' fuel.

In fact this familiar number, the Research Octane Number (RON), goes hand in hand with the more rarely quoted Motor Octane Number (MON) which is arrived at by a different testing method. In broad terms, RON measures the resistance of the fuel to detonation when accelerating, and MON to the resistance at steady high speed and load. Both RON and MON can be increased through the use of various additives. For many years, lead compounds were used for this purpose, but they have now been banned, not only to remove lead from the atmosphere but also because they 'poison' the catalytic converters used to control exhaust emissions – something to be discussed later. Leaded petrol is now banned in most developed countries. Adequate octane ratings of up to 98RON can be achieved with good formulation and alternative additives.

In the USA, great interest has been shown in 'reformulated gasoline' which has been shown to reduce exhaust emissions to a significant extent. Unfortunately, arguments began during 2000 about the safety of some of the additives used in reformulation, especially the 'oxygenate' (adding oxygen-bearing compounds lowers the burning temperature to the benefit of emissions) methyl tertiary butyl ether, understandably known as MTBE!

Petrol is by no means the only fuel which can be used in spark-ignition engines. There are many alternatives including the alcohols (ethanol and methanol) and a number of hydrocarbon gases, such as liquefied petroleum gas (LPG), a mixture of propane and butane, and natural gas (methane). None of these fuels are 'straight' alternatives, though, and any petrol engine needs to be modified in order to use them.

# Now history:
## the carburettor

Until the introduction of fuel injection, the fuel was added by passing the air through the throat of a carburettor. As the air passed through the narrow throat, it travelled faster, the pressure dropped, and fuel was sucked into the air stream. The faster the engine was running, the more air would be drawn through, and the more fuel would automatically be added. Control of the engine involved only the movement of a butterfly valve – the throttle – which opened or closed the throat. It was a brilliantly simple concept and it worked well for the better part of a century (like the distributor). But the carburettor always needed add-on features to work well at all times. For cold starting, it needed a 'choke' to reduce the air supply, ensuring a richer mixture. Many carburettors also needed small pumps to add extra fuel whenever the driver suddenly opened the throttle, to prevent the engine momentarily dying from fuel starvation – the dreaded 'flat spot'. Eventually, chokes were made automatic, not always with complete success. Various designs were tried to reduce the turbulence which occurred downstream of the throttle valve, adding to pumping losses. The last generation of carburettors became amazingly complicated, with pipes and chambers and jets which sought to compensate for different operating conditions and, especially, for the worst the driver could do. Then, quite quickly, the carburettor vanished from the scene, to be replaced by various forms of fuel injection.

The problem was that the carburettor, like the distributor, simply was not accurate enough, nor could it respond quickly enough to meet the demand for lower exhaust emissions, while fuel injection could. The basic principle of all modern fuel injection is that fuel is held under constant moderate pressure in a gallery which is connected by pipes to the injectors. Fuel is injected under electronic control, by means of a solenoid lifting a needle-valve clear of a seat for a certain time. The crucial factors are the moment at which the injector is opened – the injection *timing* – and the length of time it stays open (which determines the amount of fuel injected; the rate of flow through the injector is not controlled, except indirectly by varying the pressure in the fuel delivery gallery) – the injector *duration*. The amount of fuel injected is carefully calculated to match the amount of air entering the engine at any time.

Some early fuel injection systems were purely mechanical rather than electronic, and some of them – notably those from Bosch – were extremely ingenious and worked well. In the end, though, it proved easier to depend on electronics, which allowed systems to be made more compact, more reliable, and easier to adapt to the requirements of different engines.

In theory, the injectors can be positioned almost anywhere. Some early systems in effect took the carburettor, removed the 'passive' fuel delivery system and added one or two injectors, to create 'throttle-body injection'. But there are advantages in injecting fuel as close to the cylinder as possible. The further the mixture has to travel through an inlet

manifold, the more chance there is that some of the fuel will condense on the walls or get caught in crevices, upsetting the carefully calculated mixture strength. It became standard practice to position the injectors actually within the inlet ports, often spraying fuel on to the backs of the inlet valve seats. This is 'multipoint' as opposed to 'monopoint' injection. In theory the injection could take place at any time, leaving the fuel to be swept into the combustion chamber by the entering air as the inlet valve opened (bear in mind that the time between one injection pulse and the next could be as little as one-fiftieth of a second; it was not as though the fuel sat around for any length of time). With this arrangement, all the injectors could be opened at once, at an appropriate moment in the engine operating cycle, creating the so-called 'simultaneous' injection system. Again, this worked well but there was no escaping the fact that the conditions for fuel injection were not the same for all cylinders. In some, the mixing of air and fuel was more complete, and burning was better.

Eventually, pushed mainly by ever-tighter exhaust emission rules, but also in search of more economy, higher power and better response, the engine designers accepted that each injector had to be opened individually at the best time in relation to its own cylinder. This made control more complicated, because the engine control unit had to deliver four individual injector control signals rather than a single signal which could be sent to all four at once, but the results were worth it. The result is 'sequential' injection, and almost all passenger car petrol engines now in production are equipped with multipoint sequential injection.

# Injecting directly

An obvious question for any layman is why the fuel is injected indirectly into the inlet port, rather than directly into the combustion chamber. The three main reasons are first, because it makes design of the injector easier, second that it gives more time to inject the fuel, and for the fuel to mix with the air, and third, that it makes cylinder head design easier.

The indirect injector lives outside the combustion chamber, protected from everything that happens during and after ignition by the closed inlet valve. An injector sitting in the roof of the combustion chamber has to withstand all the changes of temperature and pressure which take place. At the very least, it will be more expensive as a result. It also has to deliver its fuel faster. When the engine is working at maximum speed and power, in other words when it needs most fuel, the time available for injection is very short in any case. But the indirect injector can deliver fuel throughout most of the cycle if necessary, while the direct injector obviously cannot inject when the exhaust valve is open, because the fuel would vanish straight down the exhaust, to create a monster backfire. The time available to the direct injector is far less, so it must deliver fuel faster when it is open, usually under significantly higher pressure.

Mixing is a potential problem with direct injection. With an indirect injector, the air and fuel begin to mix as they pass through the inlet valve, and throughout the swirling or tumbling movement which continues as the piston first falls, then rises again. The direct injector feeds the centre of the combustion chamber for a short time only, and must do its best to ensure good mixing by 'atomising' the fuel into extremely fine droplets, through a combination of high pressure and small, multiple entry holes.

Again, the engine designer must find room for the direct injector in the cylinder head. Indirect injectors normally form part of the inlet manifold, but the direct injector has to fight for space in the roof of the combustion chamber with the valves and, especially, the spark plug. The ideal position for both is central and upright, but obviously only one of them can be. Access is likely to be more awkward, and there will be less space for coolant passages around vital areas of the head.

Given that indirect injection works extremely well, these seem very good reasons not to bother with direct injection. Yet most of the world's car makers are either working on engines with direct injection, or offer them already; Mitsubishi arrived early in the field with its GDI (Gasoline Direct Injection) principle, and others including Toyota, Renault and Peugeot-Citroën have already followed, with more or less subtle variations to avoid getting into trouble over patents.

The appeal of direct injection is mainly that of better fuel economy – although power output also benefits. The economy comes from the ability of direct injection to overcome one of the weaknesses of indirect. With indirect injection, the fuel is (more or less) evenly mixed with air throughout the combustion chamber. This means that as the mixture becomes weaker – the more air there is in relation to the fuel – the more difficult it becomes to 'light the fire'. When there is just enough air to burn all the fuel, the condition engineers call 'stoichiometric' or 'lambda one', the air weighs around 14 times as much as the fuel (because 80% of the air by weight is nitrogen rather than oxygen), and the ratio of air to fuel is therefore 14:1. By the time air/fuel ratio reaches around 18:1 (otherwise 'lambda 1.3', lambda being an expression of the weakness of the mixture),

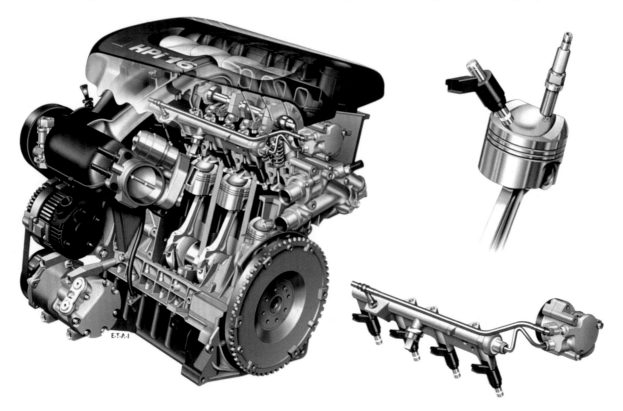

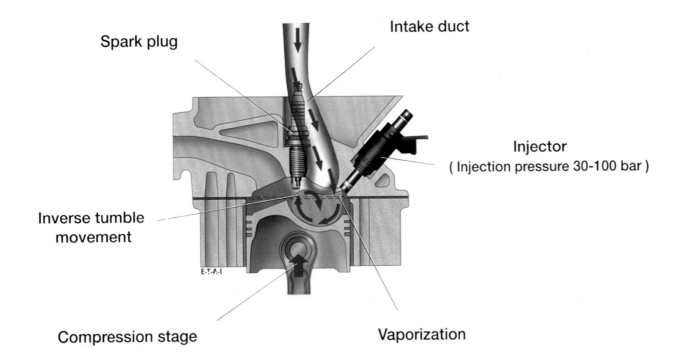

Spark plug

Intake duct

Injector
( Injection pressure 30-100 bar )

Inverse tumble
movement

E·T·A·I

Compression stage

Vaporization

*This detail drawing shows how the inlet airflow is shaped in the PSA HPI direct-injection petrol engine so that, with the careful positioning of the injector, the charge is swept around the piston cavity and as close as possible to the sparking plug, for reliable combustion. (PSA)*

a conventional engine begins to misfire; from time to time the fuel burns incompletely or not at all in the combustion chamber. By around 22:1 (lambda 1.6) it is very difficult to get a conventional engine to run smoothly and with good combustion.

But why would anyone want to run such lean mixtures if they cause problems? For two reasons. First, burning fuel in an excess of air – the condition known as 'lean burn' – means there is more chance of all the fuel being properly burned (so long as the fire can be lit to begin with). Second, if you can burn a very small amount of fuel in a large amount of air, you can leave the throttle wider open even when the engine is running a very light load. This reduces the pumping losses and brings a significant improvement in efficiency and therefore in fuel economy. Note, in passing, that the benefit is only achieved when running at low speed and light load. Nobody in their right mind would design an engine to operate 'lean burn' with the throttle wide open at full power, because it would be needlessly large and heavy.

Direct injection makes extremely lean-burn operation possible because the fuel can be injected precisely into the centre of the rolled-up swirl or tumble flow of air in the cylinder. Even though the mixture averaged through the combustion chamber may be very weak, close to the spark plug it can still be strong enough to light the fire every time, without any danger of misfire. Direct injection engines like the Mitsubishi GDI can run as lean as 40:1 (close to lambda 3) so long as the car is cruising gently.

When peak power is demanded, the direct-injection engine must deliver enough fuel for the engine to operate at lambda 1. This is where it can achieve a moderate power boost, because spraying the pressurised fuel directly into the cylinder drops the temperature, just as an aerosol spray onto your skin always feels cold. This in turn raises the engine's detonation limit, and the designer can take advantage of this by increasing the compression ratio (the Mitsubishi GDI engines run a ratio of around 13:1), increasing power output and enjoying a further small gain in efficiency.

Because fuel economy is now a top priority for all car designers except perhaps in the USA, direct injection is widely seen as the way of the future for petrol engines. Among the European manufacturers, Renault, Peugeot and Citroën already offer them in medium-sized cars, and by 2005 the technology will be well established – although far from universal – and most car manufacturers will offer it in some form. One advanced concept which has been widely studied is that of air-assisted injection, in which pressurised air is blown through a specially modified injector in order to increase fuel flow and improve fuel atomisation in the cylinder.

# 6 Manifolds, supercharging and engine control

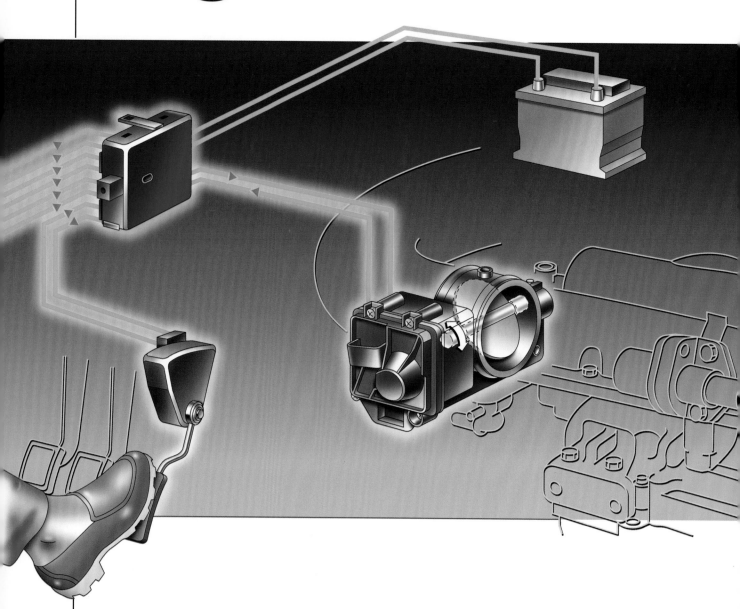

Once upon a time, the inlet manifold was the cheapest possible pipework which could be designed to carry the mixture from the carburettor to the inlet ports in the cylinder head. Today, the carburettor has vanished in favour of injectors which are in effect part of the head. Yet when you open the bonnet of a modern car, the most visible single feature is often a large and complex inlet manifold. Why is it needed?

In the first place, there is still a need to carry air from the intake, through the air filter housing, on through the throttle valve and thus into the cylinders. Engines for top-class motor racing arrange things differently, with simple metal gauze traps to stop the engine ingesting anything that might do mechanical harm, and with an individual throttle valve for each cylinder, joined to it by a single pipe of carefully calculated length. The only road-going cars to have had one throttle per cylinder were a few high-performance models of the 1960s and 1970s – notably from Alfa Romeo – whose 4-cylinder engines were equipped with twin Weber DCOE carburettors, each DCOE being 'two carburettors in one' with twin throttles and air passages, but most of the other components shared.

Today, nobody seriously considers separate throttles as a road-car solution. The standard technique is to place the throttle at the entrance to a large-volume 'plenum chamber' where the air can settle down to a uniform condition before being extracted towards the cylinders. The design of the actual manifold between the plenum chamber and the inlet ports has become ever more crucial as designers have tried to combine high power and efficiency with good low and mid-range torque. The crude inlet manifold designs of the early years suffered from several problems. The path from the throttle to some cylinders was shorter than others, and the closer cylinders got more than their fair share of the mixture. Also, as long as inlet valves were open in adjacent cylinders, one cylinder could 'rob' the other of airflow. Perhaps worst of all, the early designs took no account of the way inlet pipes act rather like organ pipes: without going deep into a complex subject, it is possible to 'pulse tune' them by adjusting their length to improve the airflow.

Eventually, it was accepted that the best way to design an inlet manifold was to ensure that as far as possible, the pipe to each inlet port should be completely separate from the others, and long enough to achieve the desired tuning effect. Thus in a modern manifold, each pipe runs between the plenum chamber (which acts as a 'settling tank') and its own inlet port. The most effective pipe length is far longer than would ever be found in a manifold from, say, the 1950s, and this has led to the design of manifolds, especially noticeable in V6 and V8

engines, whose pipes 'cross over' to feed the ports in the cylinder head which is furthest away.

Such designs are not in themselves enough to achieve high efficiency in all conditions. Like so many aspects of engine design, they are a compromise. Ideally, you need to be able to change the length of the induction pipes to match the engine speed. The higher the engine speed, the higher the induction frequency, and the shorter the ideal pipe length should be. The theoretical ideal would be something like a trombone-slide, but nobody has ever been brave enough to confront the problems of operating such a system, of sealing it and lubricating it in a multi-cylinder engine. Instead, many modern inlet manifolds have simple valve arrangements to change their effective length by opening or closing cross-linking passages between the pipes. Opening the cross-links is rather like moving the plenum chamber closer to the engine: the effect is to shorten the pipe. The pipe length is still not variable, but can be switched between two or three different values, one certainly for maximum high-speed power, the others to increase the mid-range torque. Such 'variable geometry' inlet manifolds are becoming increasingly common, and some ingenious layouts have been devised to prevent them becoming too complicated and therefore expensive.

*Opposite: True 'drive-by-wire' takes signals from the accelerator pedal sensor and uses them as driver-demand signals to the engine management system, which then positions the motorised throttle valve, as seen in this Renault system diagram. (Renault)*

Inlet manifolds are increasingly made out of tough plastic, which saves weight and allows them to be extremely accurately moulded.

# Exhaust manifold

As with inlet manifolds, so exhaust manifold design used to be crude, with the pipes from each cylinder gathered as quickly as possible into a single 'downpipe'. But again, individual pipe length is important. Since the exhaust stream from each cylinder is pressure-pulsed (once every other engine revolution), the ideal point for joining two exhaust pipes is one where the pressures do not 'fight' – where high pressure from one cylinder meets low pressure from another. This has led designers either to keep the pipes completely separate for as long as possible (ultimately leading to the 'bunch of bananas' manifolds seen on most Formula 1 engines), or to the carefully contrived 'four into two into one' layout seen in modern 4-cylinder engines for road cars.

Worries about exhaust emissions have led to two other design trends in the latest manifolds. It has become normal to site a 'pre-catalyst' chamber in the

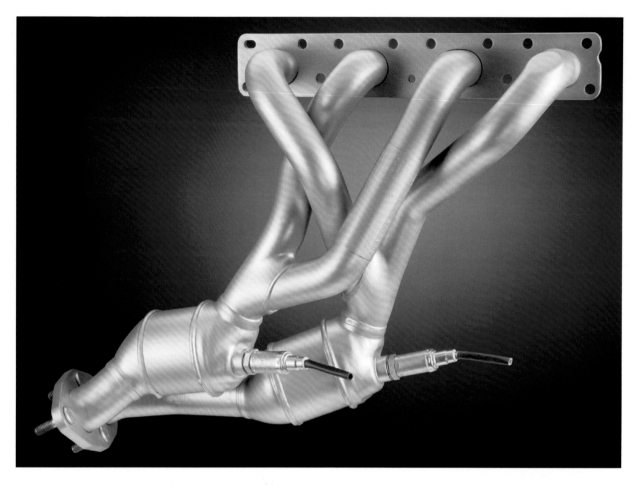

exhaust system as close to the engine as possible, so that it will warm up quickly after a cold start. This limits the length of individual pipe available to designers, unless they use more than one pre-catalyst chamber (most V6 and V8 engines already do).

Also, in order to make sure as much of the engine heat as possible reaches the pre-catalyst, exhaust manifolds themselves are now designed to absorb as little as possible. Almost all manifolds used to be made from cast iron, but more are now being made from steel, with much thinner walls. The exhaust manifolds on the top Mercedes S-class are actually double-walled, insulated stainless steel, to ensure the absolute minimum of heat is absorbed before it reaches the pre-catalyst.

# **Super**charging

All the way through this discussion so far, I have assumed the engine is 'naturally aspirated' – that it needs to suck air in from the atmosphere. But there is an alternative, which is to blow air into the engine under positive pressure. This is supercharging, and it can be accomplished in various ways. By far the most

*The complete exhaust manifold system for the BMW Valvetronic engine shows how carefully the four downpipes have been fabricated and joined as pairs to feed into two close-coupled catalyst pre-converter units before finally joining to form a single passage at the flange which couples to the rest of the exhaust system. Note the twin oxygen content sensors, each directly upstream of a pre-converter housing.* (BMW)

popular is turbocharging, in which a small turbine extracts energy from the exhaust gas and in turn drives a compressor to deliver the pressurised air. Some people think of turbocharging as an alternative to supercharging, but in reality it is just one particular *kind* of supercharging which just happens to have become the best known and most widely used. It is equally possible to drive the compressor mechanically, either directly from the nose of the crankshaft – the favoured layout in 1930s racing cars – or by means of a chain or toothed belt. The question then is what kind of compressor it is best to use.

Any form of supercharging multiplies the engine's BMEP, and therefore its torque, roughly by the amount it multiplies atmospheric pressure, which is

1 bar (or 14.5psi if you were born early enough). So a supercharger which delivers 0.8 bar (around 12psi) boost – which is the kind of figure used by 'blown' road-going petrol engines – increases the BMEP and therefore the maximum torque by around 80%. The maximum power is also increased, although by how much depends on the design of the engine. If air is being forced into the cylinder, the designer can reduce the valve overlap considerably. This increases the mid-range torque even more, but reduces maximum high-speed power. Since today's naturally aspirated road cars generally have quite enough power to reach illegal maximum speeds, but never (it seems) quite enough torque for situations where strong acceleration is needed, it makes more sense to use supercharging mainly to boost the torque, knowing there will be a substantial power increase anyway. In racing cars it is another matter; the turbocharged 1.5-litre Formula 1 cars of the 1980s used very high boost pressures, and suitable valve timing, to achieve outputs eventually well in excess of 1,000bhp in short-lifed 'qualifying' engines.

One problem with supercharging, unless you adopt special measures to prevent it, is that because the boost pressure in effect increases the compression ratio, it also brings the engine closer to its detonation limit. Early turbocharged engines had substantially lower compression ratios than their naturally aspirated counterparts – around 7.5:1 instead of 10:1 – to avoid the risk of detonation and a short but spectacular life.

*To some people, the idea of calling a powerful turbocharged engine an 'ecopower' unit may seem strange, but Saab's 2.3-litre transverse 4-cylinder engine has been carefully optimised, using fairly low turbocharger boost pressure, to achieve high efficiency with very low emissions. Note the array of radiators in this illustration of the complete engine package, in effect ready for installation, with the usual long and complex poly-vee belt drive around a whole series of accessories.* (Saab)

This meant they were less efficient when running 'off boost' at low speeds and loads, but in the 1970s and 1980s turbocharging was all about high performance, and lower efficiency did not matter all that much. At the same time, these engines were also over-fuelled at high speed and load, to prevent them overheating (they were developing more power, so they were creating and rejecting more heat; adding excess fuel is one way of cooling the charge, because of the heat it absorbs as it evaporates). This meant that the early turbo engines suffered from poor economy, but that did not seem to matter either. Then came the much tighter exhaust emission limits of the 1990s, and the technique of adding excess fuel was ruled out because it caused too much emission of unburned hydrocarbons. The turbo engine fell out of favour for several years (in 1990, almost every major car manufacturer offered at least one turbo model). Then gradually it returned, now mostly with more modest boost pressures of around 0.5 bar, and new control strategies to enable it to run with higher compression ratios and greater overall efficiency, to say nothing of better fuel economy and much reduced emissions.

# Turbocharging – the familiar technique

The technique of turbocharging appears to have the appeal of 'something for nothing' – it 'reclaims' energy which would otherwise have vanished out of the exhaust pipe. In practice, very few things in this world are to be had for nothing. Inserting a turbocharger unit in the exhaust system always compromises the design of the system and causes back-pressure which in some degree interferes with the engine's operation. At the very least, the valve timing must be altered to take account of this. Then again, there is the whole question of the cost of the turbocharger, and of protecting vital components in the engine compartment from the very high temperatures involved: at high speed and load, the turbine casing of a turbocharger runs at bright red heat.

The designer also has to consider whether it is worth fitting an intercooler, adding more expense and more pipework. The intercooler overcomes the problem which arises due to the pressurised air delivered by the compressor being quite hot, up to 100°C. This reduces the efficiency of the engine – as we have already seen, cooling the charge increases the amount of air and therefore the amount of fuel that can be burned, while heating it has the opposite effect. The air can be cooled again after it emerges from the compressor by passing it through a small heat exchanger, a kind of mini-radiator where incoming air acts as the coolant. This is the intercooler, which can improve the output (and the fuel economy) of any supercharged engine by up to 20%.

Most turbochargers look remarkably small in relation to the amount of air that passes through them. That is because the centrifugal compressor and radial turbine, carried close together on a single shaft, spin very fast – from around 80,000rpm for a relatively large unit to something approaching 200,000rpm for a really small one. Choosing the right size of turbo for the engine is vitally important. The early turbo engines of the 1970s had to use units available 'off the shelf', and developed for other applications such as big commercial vehicle diesel engines. It was quickly appreciated that a turbo which was oversized in relation to the engine was good for top-end power but bad for mid-range torque and, in particular, engine response.

A large part of the problem was that a big turbo took a second or so to 'spin up' when the throttle was opened at low load, causing a delay before the boost pressure began to build and so increase the engine's output – an effect which became known as 'turbo lag'. The smaller the turbo, the lighter its compressor/turbine assembly and the quicker it would accelerate – apart from which, it would provide some boost at lower speed. But in the 1970s suitably tiny turbos did not exist, at any rate not in production. Today, turbochargers like Garrett's T15 and T20, and their equivalents from the German company KKK and the Japanese IHI, are much better matched to the needs of small and medium-sized road car engines, and turbo lag has become a thing of the past – except in cars for top-level competition, especially World Rally Championship competitors, who still use big turbos for the sake of maximum power, even if it means they are less efficient and more difficult to drive on ordinary roads, away from the special stages. The latest generation of small turbos also use variable geometry to keep the exhaust gas flowing faster at low load, so that the turbine is always spinning at a reasonable speed. Several variable-geometry devices have been invented for this purpose, from turbine inlet guide vanes with a variable angle, to 'iris' shutters which vary the area of the turbine open to the gas flow.

Any turbo needs a control mechanism. Left to itself, it would boost the engine's output, which would deliver more exhaust gas to the turbine, which would boost the engine's output even more, which would .... until something could no longer stand the mechanical strain. So a ceiling is put on the boost pressure by arranging for a pressure-controlled valve – the 'wastegate' – to vent some of the exhaust gas through a bypass and back into the exhaust system downstream of the turbine. In the early days of turbocharged Formula 1, it was common practice to tighten down the wastegate to increase the maximum

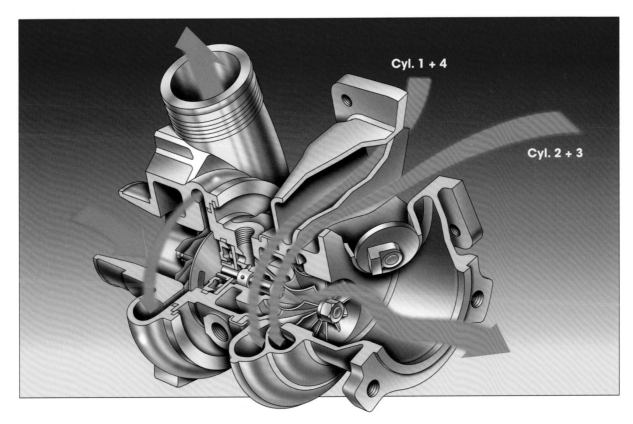

Cyl. 1 + 4

Cyl. 2 + 3

boost pressure as far as the team dared for qualifying; eventually the regulations put a stop to it. In the latest generation of very small turbos, the variable-geometry device can itself be used as a control mechanism, reducing reliance on the wastegate.

Engineering problems in the turbo mainly arise because you have an extremely hot turbine and a fairly cool compressor, sharing a common shaft and very close to each other. Oil is taken from the engine's lubrication system to lubricate the shaft, and turbo units sometimes also have their own cooling circuits, taking coolant from the engine. Some problems were caused in the early days by 'cooking' of the oil in the turbo if the engine was shut down while the turbine and casing were still very hot, but better lubricants and the introduction of turbo cooling now largely prevent this (though it is still a good idea to let a turbo engine run gently for a minute or so before you turn off the ignition).

# Mechanical
# **supercharging**

Although the turbocharger is now the most widely used type of supercharger, it only emerged as a practical engineering solution after the Second World War, during which turbos were developed to enable

*Renault has sought to improve the efficiency of turbocharged engines by developing this 'twin-scroll' unit which prevents interference between exhaust gas flows from paired cylinders by keeping them separate until after they have passed through the turbine and delivered their energy. (Renault)*

piston engines to develop high power for long periods at extreme altitude. By that time the mechanical supercharger had been in use in high-powered cars for 20 years or more, and had been extensively developed for the Grand Prix cars of the 1930s.

The speed of any mechanical supercharger is directly related to that of the engine (by whatever gearing is built into the drive) and so there is no risk of the output spiralling out of control in the same way as a turbocharger. The supercharger air output is proportional to the speed of the engine and therefore matches its demand, so everything stays in balance. No very high temperatures are involved, and there is no risk of turbo lag, so in some ways the mechanical supercharger is an excellent alternative to the turbo; on the other hand there is the need for an extra mechanical drive (these days, almost certainly by toothed belt) in an already crowded engine compartment, and both the drive and the supercharger itself can be noisy. But the advantages have been enough to attract a number of car manufacturers, including Aston Martin, Jaguar and Mercedes, away from turbocharging.

Many different designs exist for machines which simply blow air through themselves, or actually compress it in the process (superchargers may do either). Some of the designs date from the 18th and 19th centuries: for example the Roots blower with its tightly intermeshing twin rotors in a close-fitting casing, the most popular supercharger unit of the 1930s and still widely used, was invented in the USA by the brothers Root in the 1870s. Vane-type blowers are also widely used, and may simply blow or – with an eccentric drive and arrangements to allow the vanes to slide in and out of the rotor – may provide a moderate supercharging effect. With an eccentric-drive Vane-type blower, the more eccentric the drive, the greater the boost pressure (determined by the difference between maximum and minimum chamber volumes) – but also the greater the loads on the vane tips, whose sealing begins to suffer. Vane-type units can't achieve the high boost pressures available from a Roots unit or a centrifugal blower. Other types of interlocking-rotor compressor emerged through the 20th century, some of them based on the hundreds of rotary machine designs proposed by Felix Wankel – whose rotary-piston engine probably came closest to challenging the reciprocating piston type – or interlocking helical rotors, as found in the Lysholm compressor. The choice for the designer is very wide, and depends on exactly what supercharging is meant to achieve – top-end power, mid-range torque, or a blend of the two.

# Advanced thinking: Saab's SVC

The Swedish manufacturer Saab – now part of General Motors – has a strong reputation for innovation in engine design. It was one of the first companies to embrace both turbocharging and 4 valves per cylinder for production road car engines, and most recently has suggested an ingenious way of varying the compression ratio with its SVC (Saab Variable Compression) concept.

The appeal of variable compression is that it enables the engine to be run very close to the knock limit, yet with 'ideal' ignition timing, in all operating conditions. Under light load, for example, the compression can be very high indeed (Saab uses 14:1) and the engine becomes much more efficient. Normally, with such a compression ratio, the engine would suffer severe knocking at high speed and under any significant load, unless the ignition timing was severely retarded (and that alone might not be enough); and retarding the ignition is bad for efficiency anyway. The alternative is to lower the compression ratio as the knock limit is approached – if you can find a neat way of doing it.

The SVC engine splits its block into upper and lower parts, the lower part containing the crankshaft and the upper part the cylinder bores. The two parts are hinged together at one side and joined at the other by a mechanism which can push them apart or pull them closer together. As they are pushed apart, the

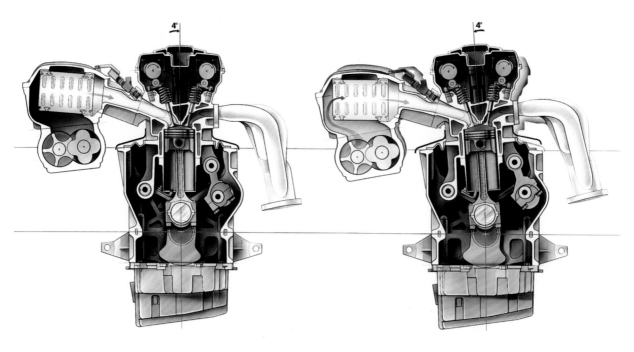

upper block tilts slightly sideways and the piston cannot move quite as far up the bore, so the compression ratio is lowered. A tilt angle of only 4° gives the necessary 3mm (0.1in) change in piston height at TDC which is all it takes to vary the compression between 8:1 and 14:1. Saab is running prototype supercharged, 1.6-litre, 5-cylinder in-line engines with the SVC system, delivering well over 200bhp with excellent overall fuel economy; but noise levels are high and other problems remain to be solved before SVC can enter production. The concept shows, however, that there is still scope for ingenuity in engine design – so long as it remains faithful to a few basic principles.

Other technical teams have studied different ways of achieving variable compression, mainly using adjustable mechanical linkages between the big-end and the piston, instead of a fixed-length connecting rod, but up to the end of 2000 no such engine had been publicly demonstrated.

# Exercising control

There was a time, up to around 1975, when the engine more or less regulated itself. The driver operated the ignition switch and the accelerator, the ignition timing depended on the action of the distributor, and the fuel delivery on the construction of the carburettor, with the automatic choke richening the mixture for cold starting. Some manual adjustments, of the idling speed for instance, could be made under the bonnet, and the most complicated challenge was balancing the airflow through twin carburettors.

That has all changed. I have just discussed the electronic control of fuel injection and of ignition timing, the two basic essentials of 'electronic engine management'. In any modern car, capable of meeting today's exhaust emission requirements, a 'black box' of electronic equipment, the engine control unit (ECU) takes data supplied by many sensors and calculates exactly what the ignition timing, and the fuel injection timing and quantity, should be. The ECU then sends its control signals, cylinder by cylinder, cycle by cycle, to the ignition system and the fuel injectors.

The most essential sensors are those which tell the ECU the angle of the crankshaft (normally taken from a reference marker on the flywheel, which passes the sensor as the Number 1 piston passes through TDC), the engine speed (how many times the reference marker passes in a given time – the ECU has a timebase, of course) and the amount of air entering the engine, which indicates the engine load. Normally, unless it is running lean-burn, a modern engine is supplied with exactly the amount of fuel to keep it at lambda = 1. The timing of ignition and injection is normally carried in a 'map' in the ECU's electronic memory, programmed at the factory. Many times a second, the ECU checks the engine speed and load, looks up the timings for those conditions in its memory, and uses the information to fire the spark plugs and the fuel injectors. In an engine with variable valve timing, the ECU is responsible for controlling the valve timing too, referring to yet another memory-map to determine the correct values. If any of the sensors fails, modern ECUs are programmed to assume a 'sensible' average value for the missing information, and the system is then said to work in 'reversion mode' (sometimes referred to as 'limp-home mode'). The unit also remembers any such fault which has occurred and can pass the information on to specialised garage diagnostic equipment.

Naturally, the ECU is responsible for other things as well. It richens the mixture for a cold start, for which purpose it needs to know the coolant temperature, from yet another sensor (using the same information, it also switches the electric cooling fan on and off). It controls the idling speed. Today, almost always, it also sets a maximum safe engine speed by cutting back the fuel supply as the limit is reached. It receives information from any 'knock sensors' and retards the ignition as the detonation limit is approached. With its power to decide whether the engine will run or not, the ECU can check whether the ignition key has the right security code, and immobilise the engine if it does not. The ECU can provide operating output signals to other devices including the variable-geometry inlet manifold, the turbocharger wastegate, or one feature we have yet to discuss, the exhaust gas recirculation (EGR) valve.

The ECU can equally well control engine output, for instance to provide steady-speed cruise control or to reduce excessive torque to prevent wheelspin, as part of a traction control system (TCS) or vehicle stability augmentation system. These functions are much simpler to build in if the car is fitted with a 'drive-by-wire' throttle linkage rather than an accelerator cable linking the pedal directly with the throttle valve. In drive-by-wire the cable is replaced by electric wiring. Sensors beneath the driver's pedal determine its position, and whether and how fast it is

*Opposite: Saab has demonstrated its SVC (Saab Variable Compression) engine in which the cylinders tilt slightly relative to the lower part of the block containing the crankshaft, as seen here. A tilt angle of only 4° is enough to alter the* *compression ratio from 8:1 to 14:1 for higher efficiency when there is no danger of detonation. The tilt 'hinge' is on the left and the rotary actuator on the right. Note that the engine is mechanically supercharged. (Saab)*

moving. That information may be sent directly to an electric motor which positions the throttle, or increasingly, it may instead be sent to the ECU which in turn provides the output to the throttle. This not only allows the ECU to perform its cruise control and TCS functions more easily, but also means the throttle response can be 'shaped' in a way which would never be possible with a mechanical link. Drive-by-wire first appeared in a production car (the BMW 750) in the late 1980s. It will become the industry standard by 2010 at the latest.

One task the ECU still cannot perform perfectly is completely accurate control when operating conditions are changing fast, such as when the driver suddenly treads on the accelerator pedal (or suddenly lifts off). Although modern units work very fast, they can still be beaten by what engineers call 'transients'. Even the earliest ECUs worked well in steady-state conditions; most subsequent developments have involved adding extra functions as already described, but also getting closer and closer to full engine control in transient conditions. Because information has to be handled in real time, an ECU cannot be directly compared with (say) a desktop PC. By PC standards, the ECU can survive with very little memory. What it needs is the ability to handle information at high speed, and many of the latest units use 32-bit processors to enable them to carry out even more calculations of ignition and fuel settings per second.

# Controlling **emissions**

In theory, the internal-combustion engine burns its hydrocarbon fuel, and the end products are water (from the hydrogen) and carbon dioxide (from the carbon). There is nothing directly harmful about either, although people are now worried about the long-term 'greenhouse effect' of too much carbon dioxide ($CO_2$) on the world's climate. Most researchers seem now to agree the greenhouse effect is a real one, although there is endless debate about how serious it is, how quickly it will have an effect, and whether motor vehicles should take as much of the blame for $CO_2$ levels worldwide as they are getting at the moment.

Aside from the greenhouse question, the emissions situation is in reality much less clean and tidy. There are three main problem areas. First, not all the hydrocarbon (HC) is burned in the engine: some of it always escapes unburned. Second, some of the carbon is not burned completely to carbon dioxide, but only to carbon monoxide (CO), which is extremely poisonous. Third, although the nitrogen which forms 80% of the air we breathe should pass through the engine unchanged – since nitrogen is almost an 'inert' gas – a very small proportion of it is persuaded, under

the temperature and pressure of combustion, to combine with oxygen to form a mixture of the three oxides of nitrogen, generally referred to in vehicle engineering as NOx.

While the threat of CO is obvious, that of HC and NOx is more subtle. Given the right conditions, they lurk in the atmosphere and react, in the presence of sunlight, to create ozone and 'smog', both of which are bad news for air quality and especially for anyone with a breathing problem, such as sufferers from bronchitis or emphysema. This apart, NOx also combines with water in the atmosphere to create 'acid rain' which is said to harm vegetation and to erode some building materials, especially soft stone. Just how bad the situation could become was first seen in Los Angeles from around 1950 onwards: the city not only had a very high car population but also sat in a 'bowl' in the Californian mountains, with onshore winds from the Pacific Ocean which meant that pollution could become trapped, building up for days on end.

Eventually in the late 1960s the state of California, and then the USA as a whole, enacted legislation to limit the amount of HC, CO and NOx which cars were allowed to emit from their exhausts. Japan and Europe eventually followed suit, several years later. Those limits became tighter as time went by, but the most crucial point was reached when petrol engines could no longer meet the limits without the help of catalytic converters. In Europe, catalytic converters have been mandatory on all new petrol-engined cars since the beginning of 1993, which means the majority of cars now on the road have them.

All new cars today have to be certified as complying with the exhaust emission regulations for the markets in which they are sold. One problem for engineers is that the regulations vary from market to market, as do the 'test cycles' to which the cars are subjected in order to obtain certification. The European cycle is a fairly simple combination of acceleration, deceleration and steady-speed periods, while the main American (US Federal) cycles are more like 'recordings' of real-life driving in particular situations, in city traffic and on the open road (the 'highway'). Although most people judge the severity of emission regulations by the amount of HC, CO and NOx permitted, changes to the test cycle can have a huge effect. Recently introduced European and US test cycles, for example, no longer allow any warm-up period before emission measurement starts, and the starting temperature itself will soon be lowered to below freezing point. Both these moves make it much more difficult to meet severe HC and CO limits. Since 1997 the European cycle has had a higher-speed 'extra-urban' phase added to it, which generally makes it more difficult to respect the NOx limit.

Another aspect of exhaust pollution which has not been addressed by conversion is the effect of sulphur which is present in both petrol and diesel fuel as an impurity, in concentrations of up to 500 parts per million (or more, in some low-quality fuels). This sulphur burns to form sulphur dioxide, which then combines with water to form acid rain in the same way as NOx. Sometimes it also reacts with water in catalytic converters to form small amounts of the 'bad egg' gas, hydrogen sulphide. But the worst effect of sulphur is that it 'poisons' some of the more advanced emission control devices, as discussed in the next section. For all these reasons, severe limits are now being introduced on the amount of sulphur permitted in fuel. Most engine designers and emission control experts would like to see no more than 20 parts per million; the ideal would be none at all.

# The working of **the catalyst**

In chemistry, a catalyst is a substance whose presence encourages a reaction to take place, though itself remaining unchanged. Many metals are catalysts for particular reactions, but the ones with the most

*To meet future exhaust emission limits, complex and expensive devices like this electrically heated catalytic converter, which reduces HC emissions after a cold start, will be needed – especially for larger cars. (Siemens)*

'universal' effect are the rare and precious metals platinum, palladium and rhodium. It was quickly shown that when the exhaust gas from an internal-combustion engine was passed over a bed of these metals maintained at a high enough temperature, the oxygen would be taken from the NOx (to leave pure nitrogen) and in effect was used to complete the burning of the HC and CO to produce water vapour and carbon dioxide – a combined process known as 'three-way' catalysation. After that, it took a lot of hard engineering to turn the principle into a catalytic converter which could be fitted into a car exhaust – and to create several new problems.

The two most urgent problems were lead in petrol, and mixture strength. Up to the 1960s, lead compounds were used to increase the octane rating of petrol. But the lead, passing through the engine, applied itself as a kind of topcoat covering the catalyst, and progressively rendering it useless – a process which came to be known as 'poisoning'. The only answer was to restrict catalyst-equipped cars to using lead-free petrol, and eventually (for other good health reasons) to ban petrol containing lead altogether.

The mixture-strength problem came about because it was quickly proved that the three-way catalytic converter only worked properly if the engine was working at an exactly stoichiometric mixture strength – that 14:1 ratio, or lambda = 1, which means there is exactly enough air, no more and no less, to burn all the fuel. If there is too little air (thus too little oxygen) then the HC and CO will not be completely oxidised (burned) to harmless by-products. If there is too much air, the NOx will never be completely reduced to oxygen and nitrogen. So a new generation of engines emerged in which the mixture strength was maintained precisely at lambda = 1 at all times, with the help of so-called 'lambda probes' in the exhaust system which reacted to the presence of too much or too little oxygen, sending a signal to the ECU which would accordingly alter the amount of fuel injected. Indeed, the modern ECU is as much concerned with controlling exhaust emissions as it is with ensuring the correct behaviour of the engine in response to the driver's wishes.

Even though it was expensive, in some ways the catalytic converter was a blessing in disguise. It had been found, especially in the USA, that engines designed to meet severe emission limits without using converters suffered from poor fuel economy and bad 'driveability'. With the converter in place and taking care of emissions problems, the engineer could go back to basics and improve the behaviour of his engine in most respects, although as emission limits became tighter still, the pressure to improve designs became constant.

Logically, one way to improve emissions performance is to prevent, or at least minimise, the formation of emissions at source – in other words in the combustion chamber. Engineers have come a long way in this direction. Lingering HC has been reduced by making 'crevice volumes' such as the narrow slot between the piston and cylinder wall above the top piston ring, and the hollows around the valve seats, as small as possible. Close control of airflow within the cylinder, helped by computer techniques, makes for more complete burning and lower levels of CO. Levels of NOx have been reduced through the use of exhaust gas recirculation (EGR) which bleeds quantities of gas from the exhaust system and adds them to the incoming air. The EGR is pretty well inert, and its presence reduces the formation of fresh NOx. These measures apart, the faster and more precise control of the engine in transient conditions, already referred to, plays its own part in reducing 'pre-catalyst' emissions to a minimum. Any improvement is useful, since no converter is 100% effective; 90% is a good working average, leaving the remaining 10% to emerge from the tailpipe. If emissions from the combustion chamber can themselves be reduced by (say) 20%, then what eventually comes out of the tailpipe will be reduced by a similar proportion.

# Catalytic converter **design**

The typical converter is a stainless steel 'can' forming part of the exhaust system, containing the catalyst spread ultra-thinly over a 'substrate' – either a cylinder of honeycomb ceramic, or carefully-rolled corrugated stainless steel. Either kind of substrate creates a huge surface area – about the area of an average football pitch, according to the manufacturers – in a cylinder barely a foot long and a few inches across, upon which the ounce or so of catalyst is evenly deposited.

As already explained, the catalyst only works properly when the gas flowing into it contains exactly the right amount of oxygen, delivered by the engine which regulates the mixture strength depending on signals from an exhaust stream oxygen sensor (the lambda probe). But it also works properly only when it is hot enough. Emission control experts talk about a 'light-off temperature' of around 300°C at which the catalyst converts 90% of noxious emissions. Care also has to be taken to avoid overheating the converter, since this can seriously damage the substrate, reducing conversion efficiency and causing partial exhaust blockage. Normally, peak temperatures are limited by the design of the can, but a special problem occurs if the engine misfires, allowing relatively large amounts of unburned fuel (we may still only be talking a thimble-full) into the converter, where it burns and sends the temperature soaring. A few minutes of engine misfiring may completely ruin a converter. That is why modern engines and emission control systems are equipped with sensors to detect misfiring, to prevent it happening if possible and to warn the driver if a really serious problem has occurred. Some converters are equipped with a temperature sensor to detect directly if the unit is hot enough to suffer damage – this has been a requirement in the Japanese market for some time.

In the future, emission control systems will also check whether the catalyst is working properly, using extra information from a second oxygen sensor downstream of the converter, and comparing its data with that from the existing upstream sensor. The new systems will keep track of operation and note any faults as they occur, to be downloaded during service, a technique known as on-board diagnosis (OBD).

# Dealing with the cold start problem

One emissions challenge still plagues engineers, and that is what to do about HC and CO emissions after a cold start, before the catalytic converter reaches its light-off temperature. With modern engines and emission control systems, it has been estimated that up to 90% of all the HC emissions in the standard test cycles occur in the first two or three minutes after the cold start which is now required.

One obvious move is to make sure the catalytic converter lights-off as quickly as possible, by mounting it close to the exhaust manifold. The problem is how to do this without it overheating and suffering damage. Almost all modern petrol-engined cars now have two separate converters, one 'close-coupled' to the exhaust manifold, with a substrate and catalyst treatment designed to withstand higher temperatures (palladium is better than platinum for this particular purpose), and another unit in the exhaust system beneath the cabin. The close-coupled converter warms up much faster and deals with the cold-start HC and CO emissions, while the main converter takes care of the full three-way conversion of the exhaust gases in normal, fully-warmed operation.

Other ideas which have been tried include 'adsorbers', beds of special material in the exhaust system close to the manifold, which absorb HC at low temperatures but release it again when they are warmed through, to be dealt with by the main converter. Adsorbers are one of the devices to suffer 'poisoning' by sulphur impurity in petrol. Developers have also looked at methods of speeding the warm-up of the main converter, either using electric power (which causes a big drain on a standard battery, but may become more practical if 36-volt electrical systems become standard) or by deliberately releasing small amounts of fuel into the exhaust system with extra injection pulses, to produce the kind of rapid temperature increase which would be so dangerous when caused by misfiring in fully-warm operation.

# Emissions control with lean-burn

So far, we have looked at emissions control in engines running a mixture strength of exactly lambda = 1, which is what most of them do. If instead of this you run a weak mixture, with excess air, the engine's emissions of HC and CO fall, but the formation of NOx increases. As we have already seen, in this situation the three-way catalytic converter no longer works properly.

Because HC and CO are already low, what is really needed in this case is a converter which can reduce NOx back to nitrogen and oxygen. This is a tough task, because you are trying to make the nitrogen compound give up its oxygen in a gas stream which already has plenty of excess oxygen. One researcher once described it as like trying to dry washing in a rainstorm. This has not stopped people trying, and three main approaches to the problem have emerged. The first is the straightforward one of trying to find a catalyst that works despite all the problems. Some teams have claimed success, mostly using a substrate formed from a porous ceramic material known as zeolite, but the best conversion rates demonstrated have been around 30%, compared with over 90% for a three-way converter. Even so, reducing the NOx emissions by 30% may be enough to bring an engine within the legal limit.

The second approach is a two-stage strategy. First the NOx is trapped in a specially prepared chemical 'bed' – in principle, rather like the adsorber which deals with cold-start HC. Then, when the bed is nearly full, the ECU triggers a small extra injection of fuel which burns in the converter and reduces the NOx as required. This method, which was first used in a production car by Toyota, has proved rather more effective than 'pure' catalytic conversion but obviously causes a slight increase in fuel consumption and calls for some clever sensors and computer software. This type of storage-reduction converter is badly affected by sulphur impurity in petrol, and can only be used where guaranteed low-sulphur fuel is available.

The third approach is completely different, involving the creation of a gas plasma field within the exhaust system. A high proportion of any gas passing through the field is broken down into its component elements. Thus both CO and NOx could be dealt with in this way (but a simple oxidising catalyst would still be needed to deal with HC). NOx is the real target for such systems, which have been demonstrated by the systems specialist Delphi and by a team from the UK Atomic Energy Authority. However, in order to work effectively these systems need considerable amounts of electric power at a high voltage, and so join the list of good ideas waiting for the 36-volt electrical system.

The emission control picture with lean-burn engines is complicated by the fact that they only operate lean-burn under light load and at moderate speed, as previously explained. At full power, all modern petrol engines operate at lambda = 1 and in this condition they need a conventional three-way catalytic converter to control emissions. In effect, therefore, this new generation of engines need two converters combined, one to operate normally, the other to deal with NOx.

# **7**Diesel (compression ignition) **engines**

Once upon a time, almost the only passenger cars with diesel engines were taxis, because although diesel engines were very economical and lasted for ever, they gave poor performance, were rough, noisy and smoky, and diesel fuel pumps on the forecourt were filthy things tucked away on the far side where the lorries went.

Yet in 1999, 25% of the passenger cars sold in Europe had diesel engines. Experts predict that by 2006, that share will have risen to 38%, and in some countries it is already that high. Clearly something has happened to make the diesel much more acceptable to the private car buyer. In fact two things have happened. Fuel has become much more expensive, so the economy of the diesel is more appealing (and in those countries with a high diesel market share, diesel is much cheaper than petrol), and diesel engines themselves have become far cleaner, smoother, and more powerful, without sacrificing any of that precious economy.

As briefly explained in an earlier chapter, the principle of the diesel engine is that of compression ignition. When air is compressed, it gets hotter; think how hot the barrel of a bicycle pump becomes if you work hard pumping up a tyre. If the compression is sufficient, the air becomes so hot that fuel squirted into it ignites at once, without any help from a spark plug. Better still, with modern combustion chamber designs, the fuel ignites almost no matter how weak the mixture, so the engine output can be directly controlled by altering the amount of fuel supplied, with no need for a throttle valve, and therefore no pumping losses. It is this freedom from pumping loss, plus the extra efficiency which results from the far higher compression ratio (up to around 20:1) which makes the diesel so economical. On the other hand, the higher compression also means that stresses in the engine are greater, and the whole bottom end of the engine needs to be stronger. It also means the engine is noisier, because the pressure rise after combustion has such a high peak. The high compression means the combustion chamber is tiny at TDC, so there is no scope at all for any valve overlap, and when developing high power all diesel engines 'strangle' for lack of air, generally before they reach 5,000rpm. And of course in the days when petrol engines could survive with cheap and simple carburettors, diesel engines needed expensive fuel injection systems. It all added up to a lack of interest unless a long and economical life was the main consideration, as in a taxi or a light commercial van.

Because of their high compression ratio, diesels need more powerful starter motors than petrol engines, and are usually equipped with heavy-duty batteries. Starting from cold usually needs the assistance of 'glowplugs' which look rather like spark plugs, but simply provide a high temperature within the cylinder to help ignition to take place when everything is cold. Glowplugs are always operated automatically, cutting out as soon as the engine begins running or shortly afterwards. Modern glowplugs take only a few seconds to warm up, and today's diesels can be started almost immediately (20 years ago, in very cold weather, it could be ten seconds or more before the dashboard warning light showed that the glowplugs were warm enough to assist starting).

Diesel fuel has to be different, because it must ignite as soon as it comes into contact with the hot, compressed air. This is exactly what causes detonation (knocking) in a petrol engine, because in these conditions petrol lights up so quickly that the burn can only be described as an explosion. Diesel fuel must therefore be blended so that it burns on contact, but burns slowly and progressively. This is why diesel fuel is less volatile, feels 'stickier' to the touch and is actually quite a lot denser than petrol (if fuel was sold by the pound rather than by the litre, diesel would not appear nearly as economical). The readiness of diesel fuel to ignite on contact is expressed as a 'cetane number', rather like the octane number of petrol (but the comparison can't be taken too far). Cetane itself is a highly inflammable fuel and represents a cetane number of 100, while another fuel, the very 'unwilling burner' methyl naphthalene, sits at the other end of the scale and is rated at 0. Real-life diesel fuels have a cetane number of 45–50, with the higher number preferred for modern diesel engines.

To put petrol into a diesel-engined car by mistake is to invite two kinds of disaster. The violence with which the petrol burns can quickly cause serious damage, but the engine will almost certainly have stopped sooner than that. This is because diesel fuel is a good lubricant – which is why it feels sticky-slippery to the touch – and diesel fuel pumps are therefore lubricated by the fuel passing through them. Petrol, far from being a lubricant, is a very efficient cleaner, so the pumps in a diesel fuel system seize very quickly if they are fed petrol. In very cold conditions, at air temperatures of minus 20°C and below, diesel fuel sometimes needs to be thinned out to persuade it to flow at all. If so, it is thinned with paraffin, never

*Opposite: The 5-cylinder 2.4JTD common-rail diesel engine as used in the Alfa Romeo 156. Despite its high output – by diesel standards – this engine uses only two valves per cylinder, its breathing helped by high turbocharger boost. Staying with two valves helps to make room for injectors and glowplugs. Points of interest include the 'bowl-in-piston' combustion chambers, the very strong crankshaft and the detailing of the clutch and flywheel assembly which has to transmit very high torque. The 'overhung' radiator at the left is the air-to-air turbo intercooler. (Alfa Romeo)*

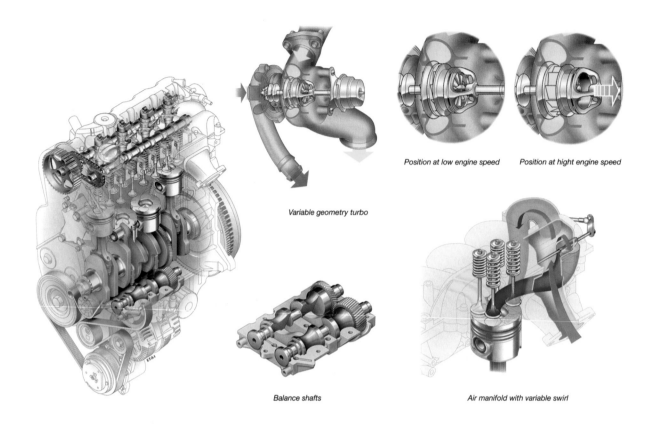

Variable geometry turbo

Position at low engine speed    Position at hight engine speed

Balance shafts

Air manifold with variable swirl

with petrol. Most modern diesels working in Arctic conditions are fitted with fuel heaters to keep the fuel flowing. Great care must also be taken not to allow water into the diesel fuel injection pump, even though water often collects in fuel tanks. Even a small amount of water, sitting in the injection pump when the engine is switched off and left to stand overnight, can be enough to ensure the pump is completely seized by morning. All diesel engines are therefore protected by a water filter which needs checking and emptying from time to time.

Filling a petrol car with diesel fuel is not quite as disastrous. The chances of completely wrecking the engine are more remote, but the engine will deliver very little power and the exhaust will be extremely smoky. The only answer is to completely drain the fuel tank and refill with petrol.

# Injecting enough fuel

Diesel fuel can't be injected into the cylinder over a relatively long period, like the petrol in a direct-injection spark-ignition engine. Because ignition begins within a few microseconds of injection beginning, all the fuel must be injected in the

*Above: One of the most advanced medium-sized diesel engines is the PSA HDI series with common-rail direct injection, here in 2.2-litre 16-valve form for the Citroën C5. Details shown include the twin balancer shafts housed in the sump, the principle of the variable-geometry turbocharger, and the means of controlling the amount of swirl through the inlet ports. (Citroën)*

shortest possible time. Once the piston has started to accelerate down the cylinder, it is really too late to add any more fuel, as there is a great risk of some of the fuel emerging unburned as 'black smoke'. The only way to inject enough fuel in so short a time is to inject at very high pressure.

*Opposite: The essential difference between indirect-injection (IDI) and direct-injection (DI) diesel engines is that in the IDI unit, the fuel is injected into a pre-chamber where ignition begins before expanding into the main combustion chamber above the piston. The pre-chamber means combustion is easier and smoother in its early stages – but efficiency suffers because the charge must be 'squeezed' through the narrow pre-chamber throat. Although not shown, DI diesels need glowplugs too, although they may not be fitted to all cylinders. (Ford)*

## INDIRECT INJECTION COMBUSTION SYSTEM

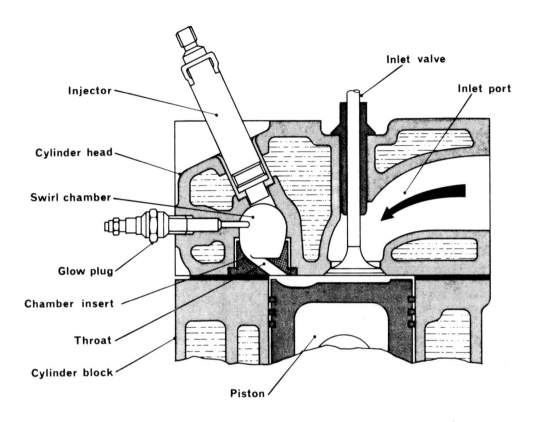

Injector
Inlet valve
Inlet port
Cylinder head
Swirl chamber
Glow plug
Chamber insert
Throat
Cylinder block
Piston

## DIRECT INJECTION COMBUSTION SYSTEM

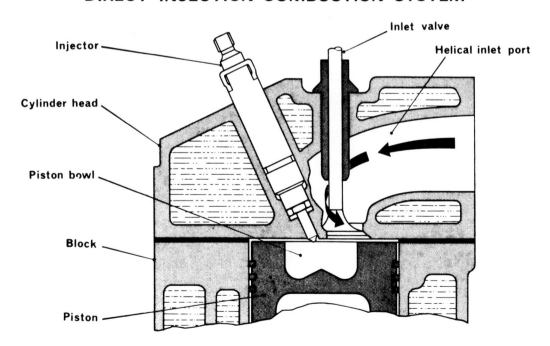

Injector
Inlet valve
Helical inlet port
Cylinder head
Piston bowl
Block
Piston

Early 'light duty' diesel engines used a system of indirect injection into a small 'pre-chamber' in the cylinder head – a system developed by the British pioneer Sir Harry Ricardo. Even when a very small amount of fuel was being injected – and the amount of fuel needed per stroke when the engine is idling would barely dampen a sugar lump – the mixture in the pre-chamber would still be strong enough for reliable combustion, and the flame would spout through a linking passage into the main combustion chamber where burning would continue until finished. Such engines generally needed injection pressures of around 700 bar to work well.

The indirect injection (IDI) engine was eventually developed into a highly satisfactory power unit, the best example of all probably being the 1.9-litre XUD engine series used by Peugeot and Citroën, and built in huge numbers. But the narrow throat linking the pre-chamber with the main combustion chamber was itself a source of pumping losses – air had to be forced into the pre-chamber, and had to spurt out afterwards – and it was clear that engines with direct injection (DI) would be even more efficient and economical. A lot of work was needed before answers were found to the problems of DI – especially ways to ensure that reliable ignition and full burning could be achieved in the much larger space of the main combustion chamber.

*When it was introduced, the Alfa Romeo 156 was a pioneering application for common-rail diesel fuel systems. The layout of the system is shown here, applied to the powerful and impressive 1.9-litre JTD 4-cylinder engine.* (Alfa Romeo)

DIESEL (COMPRESSION IGNITION) ENGINES

The answer, found in all modern light-duty DI diesels, is to form the combustion chamber as a bowl in the crown of the piston, with the fuel injected into its middle, usually striking a 'pip' in the centre of the bowl which helps it disperse. The shaping of the bowl, and of the inlet ports, is also crucial for maintaining the correct pattern of airflow as the piston rises, so that the injected fuel is concentrated in a small volume until it is properly alight. In effect, in a DI diesel the in-cylinder airflow performs the same task as the pre-chamber in an IDI engine.

DI diesels need higher injection pressures than their IDI counterparts because the time available for injection is even shorter – the IDI pre-chamber gave a 'cushioning' effect to the process and injection could begin earlier. At the same time, the new generation of DI diesels are far more powerful, so designers need to inject fuel in larger amounts.

Until quite recently, the standard technique for injecting diesel fuel was to use a low-pressure pump to lift fuel from the tank and supply it to a high-pressure pump, which in turn would deliver pulses of fuel to the injectors. Early high-pressure pumps looked rather like miniature in-line engines. A camshaft, driven from the engine crankshaft and with as many lobes as the engine had cylinders would depress a series of pump-plungers in turn, creating the high-pressure fuel delivery pulses. Such pumps are still in widespread use in large commercial-vehicle diesels, but from the 1960s passenger car diesels moved to rotary injection pumps. The rotary pump can be thought of as a single cam lobe moving around a series of pump-plungers, again as many as there are cylinders in the engine. In some ways these pumps resemble the old-fashioned ignition distributor in a petrol engine, and they are often referred to as distributor pumps. Such pumps are more compact and cheaper to make than the in-line type, and are capable of delivering fuel pressures up to 1,000 bar. Mechanical (and more recently, electronically controlled) devices built into the pump adjust the injection timing, by advancing or retarding the operating cam, and the fuel delivery, by opening spill valves to 'dump' the injection pressure once sufficient fuel has been injected.

*This diagram neatly shows many of the features of the PSA Peugeot-Citroën HDI common-rail diesel engine including the piston with its toroidal 'bowl-in-piston' combustion chamber, the not-quite-upright electronically controlled fuel injector, and the glowplug (right). Also shown are the vertically installed valves operated by a single camshaft whose cams bear on low-friction roller followers set in the middle of 'fingers' with outboard hydraulic lash adjusters. (PSA)*

# Common-rail **systems**

The latest generation of light-duty diesel engines has abandoned the high-pressure distributor pump and switched either to the 'common-rail' system, or to the 'unit injector'. In general appearance, the common-rail system closely resembles a direct injection petrol fuel system. The common rail itself is maintained at constant high pressure by a delivery pump (far simpler than a rotary distributor pump), and the rail in turn is connected to the injectors. Each injector is equipped with a solenoid valve which is opened electronically from a central control unit which sets both the initial opening and the time for which the injector remains open. In other words, in a common-rail engine, control is exercised at the injector rather than at the pump, which is really a more logical way of doing things. The main drawback is that the injectors themselves are more complicated and expensive to make, but this is a small price to pay when set against greater flexibility and precision of control, and in particular the ability to operate at considerably higher injection pressures – today's systems work at around 1,500 bar and development teams are seeking to achieve 2,000 bar. This very high pressure is the most important difference between common-rail diesel systems and the superficially

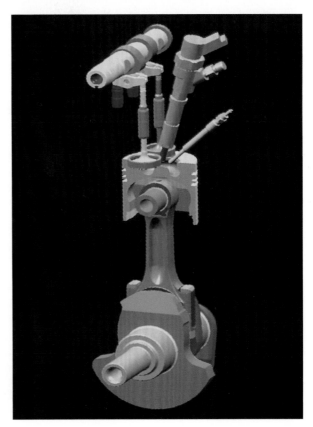

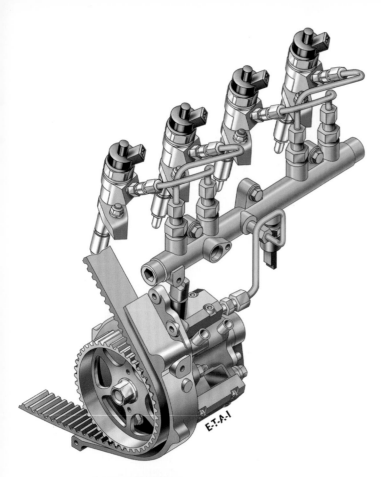

*Left: This illustration shows the common-rail fuel system of the PSA HDI turbodiesel. The common rail itself (in yellow) is pressurised by the pump which is driven by the same toothed belt which turns the camshaft. Individual pipes from the rail feed each injector, which in turn is opened at the right moment, and for the right length of time, by an electronically controlled solenoid. If necessary, this allows more than one injection pulse per engine cycle per cylinder. (PSA)*

similar petrol injection systems, which work at about one-tenth (or less) of diesel pressures. Apart from allowing more fuel to be injected in the short time available, higher pressures also mean that the fuel can be properly atomised while being injected as a very 'tight' cone-shaped spray, which makes it possible to

*Below: This diagram shows in more detail the way in which the common-rail fuel system in the PSA HDI turbodiesel engine is fitted to the cylinder head. The injector heads can be seen, and also the lower halves of the bearings for the single overhead camshaft. This compact 8-valve layout takes up much less space than would be needed with four valves per cylinder and twin overhead camshafts. (PSA)*

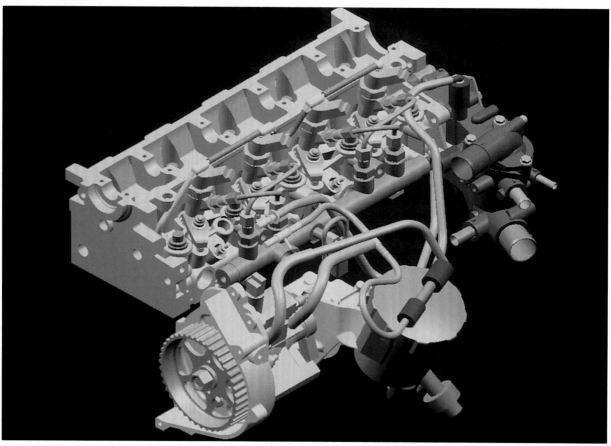

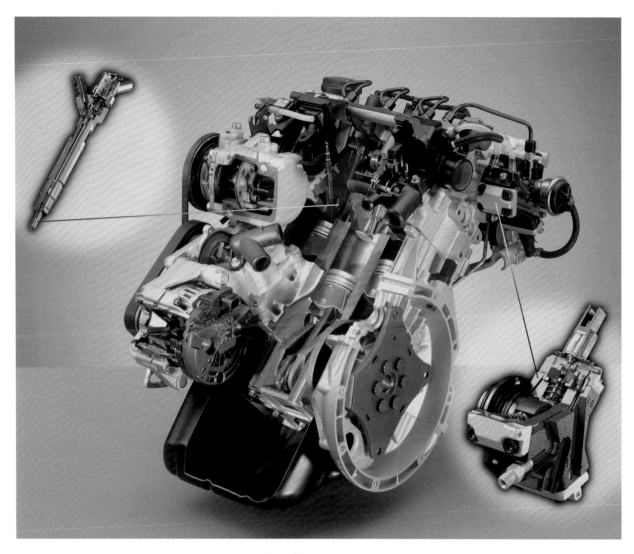

*A great deal of ingenuity has gone into the design of this extremely small diesel engine for the Smart car. The need for reasonable refinement,* *adequate power output and extremely low emissions meant the engine could not afford to be crude in any respect.* (DaimlerChrysler)

use smaller cylinder sizes. Along with all its other advantages, common-rail diesel injection is therefore potentially the key to highly efficient, super-economical 4-cylinder diesels as small as 1.2-litre capacity, and even smaller with three cylinders.

Most of the major car manufacturers are now studying 4-cylinder or 3-cylinder diesel engines of 1.4-litre or smaller capacity, suitable for use in ultra-economical supermini-sized cars. Volkswagen has already launched 1.2-litre diesels for the Lupo, and Fiat has demonstrated a 1.2-litre 4-cylinder engine using an advanced injection control system. Ford and PSA have a joint programme to develop a new small

diesel, and Renault is well advanced with development of a 1,461cc unit, with turbocharging, intercooling and common-rail fuel system, with a power output target of 80bhp (and 185Nm/137 ft lb of torque). In this engine, the common 'rail' is actually a highly pressurised squat cylinder from which the supply lines emerge radially.

# Unit injection: an alternative to common rail

The alternative unit-injector system mounts a single injector above each cylinder and operates it directly via a camshaft. This approach has two clear advantages: it gets rid of all high-pressure piping, since high pressure only exists within the injector itself, and it already allows injection pressures higher than 2,000 bar according to Volkswagen, the first company to

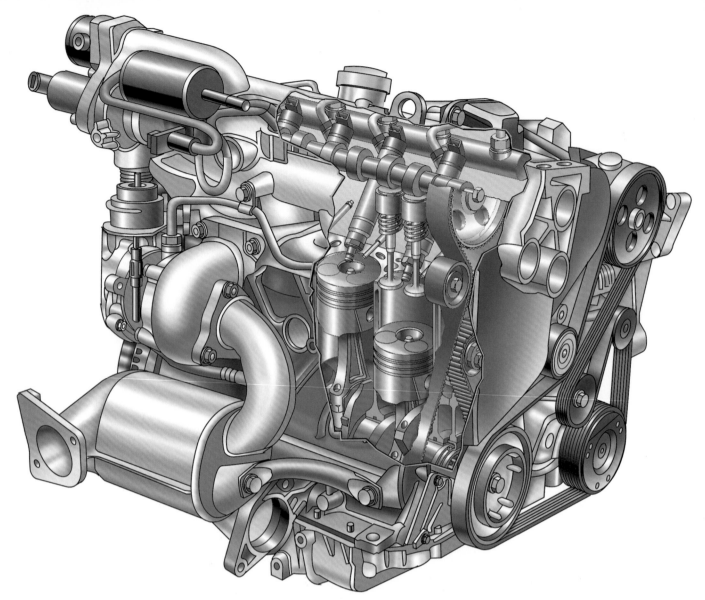

adopt this approach. On the other side of the coin, room has to be found in and above the cylinder head for the relatively bulky injectors and their operating camshaft, and the system wastes some energy at low speed and load because the cam must always operate the injector through its maximum-power stroke, with any excess supply being bled away through spill valves. Mainly for these reasons (or so it seems) the majority of modern light-duty diesels now use the common rail approach. The flexible control made possible by common rail has the further advantage that with advanced electronics, the injection process can be split into a number of separate pulses. It is already common to begin with a 'pilot injection' pulse, a very small amount of fuel being injected ahead of the main charge to make the ignition process less 'sudden'. By avoiding too steep a pressure rise, the characteristic diesel 'rattle' which was especially noticeable in some early DI diesels is greatly reduced. Development teams are also studying 'post-ignition' pulses to help operate advanced emission control systems. Fiat has

developed a common-rail system which it calls Multijet, which also splits the main injection pulse into two or three separate events to make the pressure pulse in the cylinder 'fatter' but with a lower peak. This system, used in the 1.2-litre diesel engine already mentioned, is claimed to benefit both noise levels and exhaust emissions.

Along with changes to the fuel system, modern passenger car diesels have evolved in the same way as their petrol counterparts, especially in the common use of four valves per cylinder, with the injector rather than a spark plug positioned centrally and upright. The greater airflow made possible by increasing the number of valves matches the higher fuel flow of the injection systems, and some modern diesels now deliver power outputs which would have been thought respectable in petrol engines 20 years ago, and with far higher torque. Most diesels still use cast-iron cylinder blocks for the sake of mechanical strength and stiffness, although aluminium alloy is being seriously studied as a weight-saving alternative.

# Turbocharging **diesels**

The majority of modern light-duty diesels are turbocharged. Turbocharging works very well with diesel engines. Diesel exhaust gas tends to be cooler than that produced by petrol engines, which gives the turbocharger an easier time, and the wastegate control is needed only to avoid overstressing the engine (or the transmission). There is no need to avoid detonation, since in effect the diesel depends on the principle of spontaneous ignition to work at all. What is more, given the way gas flow through a naturally aspirated diesel is so limited by valve lift and timing, turbocharging is an excellent way of increasing output. Almost all modern passenger car diesel engines are turbocharged as standard, or exist in turbocharged as well as naturally aspirated versions. Power outputs of 60bhp per litre, which used to be thought good for petrol engines, are now seen in the best turbodiesels. This kind of power output calls for intercooling, since cooling the incoming charge can make a big difference to the amount of gas which can be passed through the diesel engine. Some engines, from Peugeot and Renault for example, are offered with intercooling and in lower-powered but cheaper versions without. Passenger car diesels are now probably the biggest market for small turbochargers, and many of the most advanced developments, such as using variable geometry to maintain exhaust gas speed through the turbine under low load, are aimed at diesels in the first instance.

*Below: At the 1999 Tokyo Motor Show, Mazda showed this 2-litre turbodiesel engine with common-rail direct injection. The supply pump which pressurises the common rail, and the rail itself, can be clearly seen in this side view. Less evident are the 4 valves per cylinder, the carefully shaped inlet ports, the variable-geometry turbocharger and the intercooled exhaust gas recirculation (EGR) system. (Mazda)*

# Advanced diesel thinking

In 1999, Renault provided some indication of how much potential exists in the diesel engine with further technical development. The company took the original (intercooled) dTi version of its 1.9-litre engine, producing 100bhp, as its starting point. The dCi development of this engine, equipped with a common rail fuel system, delivers 110bhp with the advantage of substantially lower exhaust emissions. A later version of this engine with a variable-geometry turbocharger delivers 120bhp, and 270 instead of 250Nm (199 instead 184lb ft) of torque. In its 'ultimate' version, with a 16-valve cylinder head and a higher-pressure second-generation fuel system, the output target is 140bhp and 300Nm (221lb ft), plus the ability to meet the much more severe emission limits being introduced in Europe for 2005.

BMW, which together with Mercedes has produced some of the most powerful diesel engines yet installed in passenger cars, has said that it sees 'variability' as the key to further development. Among other features, the company says it is studying variable-swirl inlet ports, variable valve timing, and advanced injector designs capable of passing fuel at different rates depending on speed and load, so that fuel quantity would no longer depend entirely on the time for which the injector was open. BMW is also looking at variable compression ratio and at two-stage supercharging, and at using extra information such as fuel density and quality to achieve even more precise control of combustion. Looking even further into the future, BMW suggests it might be possible to inject a completely prepared fuel-air charge, rather than just the fuel, into the cylinder at the appropriate moment; one of its engineers even suggests 'changing from intermittent to continuous combustion', which might involve a compound engine (burning some of the fuel to drive a larger turbocharger and using some form of power take-off to recover the energy and feed it back to the crankshaft), or even a concept closer to an external-combustion engine.

# Controlling diesel emissions

Exhaust emissions from diesel engines cannot be controlled in the same way as those from most petrol engines. As already explained, petrol engine emissions can be controlled to a very low level by passing the exhaust through a 'three-way' catalytic converter, so long as the air/fuel mixture strength is held precisely at lambda = 1. But the diesel operates as a lean-burn engine most of the time, except under full load, and the three-way catalyst will have little effect. In fact the diesel resembles the lean-burn petrol engine and shares one of its problems, that while its emissions of HC and CO are inherently low, its emissions of NOx are higher. The diesel also suffers a problem of its own, which is that its different fuel and its very high compression ratio encourage the formation of 'particulates' – very small particles of solid matter which are a by-product of its combustion. A lot of doubt and argument still surrounds the real importance of particulates and whether they are a serious threat to health, but stringent limits are now placed on particulate emissions as part of all exhaust emission regulations.

While HC and CO emissions are low, many passenger car diesels now fit a simple oxidising catalyst unit – one which makes sure the emissions are fully oxidised to water vapour and $CO_2$ – to take care of any remaining amounts. Where the more serious and tricky problem of NOx emissions is concerned, levels of NOx are already reduced as far as possible through the use of exhaust gas recirculation (EGR), which is fitted to many modern diesels. The EGR flow is sometimes passed through its own intercooler (shedding heat to the engine coolant) so as not to affect power output by reducing the charge density in the combustion chamber.

A more complete answer might be the NOx reduction catalyst principle already mentioned when discussing lean-burn petrol emissions. A storage-reduction system, fed by a late injection pulse to supply tiny amounts of extra fuel to the catalyst unit when needed, is one possible answer. Such devices need low-sulphur fuel, already widely available as 'city diesel' in order to avoid any risk of poisoning the storage bed. Another solution might be the plasma treatment approach mentioned earlier. Research teams are also working on systems, such as the Siemens SiNOX principle, which use an additive injected into the exhaust gas, to react with the NOx in a special unit in the exhaust system.

The most obvious answer to the particulate problem is to trap the particles in a filter in the exhaust system. In theory, the nuisance of cleaning or changing the filter at regular intervals can be avoided by making the filter hot enough that the particles – which contain more carbon than anything else – burn gently away to form $CO_2$. Such traps are called 'regenerative' because they clean themselves and need attention only at long intervals. Regenerative traps work well in heavy commercial vehicles, whose engines spend much of their time at fairly high load and therefore with exhaust temperatures high enough to ensure that regeneration takes place. But diesel-engined passenger cars may spend much of their time at low speed and load in city traffic (indeed, these are the conditions where the diesel's advantage over petrol is greatest). An exhaust temperature of around 500°C is needed to ensure regeneration, and a 'school and shopping' diesel car may travel hundreds of miles without its exhaust temperature approaching even 300°C.

To overcome this problem, PSA (Peugeot-Citroën) has introduced a trapping system in which a fuel additive reduces the temperature needed for regeneration, while the injection of extra fuel whenever the trap shows signs of clogging raises its temperature through controlled 'afterburning'. This system, already fitted to diesel versions of the recently introduced Peugeot 607 with plans eventually to extend it across the Peugeot-Citroën range, is claimed to reduce particulate emissions almost to zero – but it has no effect on NOx, which needs to be treated separately.

Renault has proposed an all-embracing system of diesel emission control which depends on using an extremely high proportion of EGR. This technique reduces NOx to very low levels but at the cost of higher particulate formation. In other words, the

Renault approach is to avoid producing NOx as far as possible, and to accept a high level of particulates which is dealt with through exhaust aftertreatment in a regenerative trap. Compared with PSA's trapping system, Renault's has to deal with a higher volume of particulates, and is therefore triggered more often – every 400km (250 miles) in extreme cases. To help the process, it raises the temperature of the trap bed partly by 1.2kW of electrical heating, via a group of four diesel glowplugs in the 'nose' of the canister immediately upstream of the bed itself. Using this strategy, together with second-generation common-rail injection, Renault says it is confident of being able to meet the Euro 2005 emission standard for diesels with something of a margin in hand.

*PSA Peugeot-Citroën was the first group to develop a regenerative particulate filter for diesel passenger cars and put it into production, first for the Peugeot 607 and then for the Citroën C5. Efficient operation of the system, with reliable burning-off of the trapped particles, depends partly on injecting a fuel additive and partly on injecting enough extra fuel to boost the trap temperature if the trap shows signs of clogging. (Citroën)*

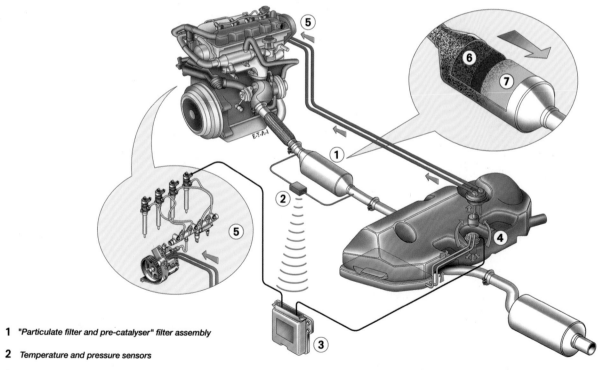

1   *"Particulate filter and pre-catalyser" filter assembly*

2   *Temperature and pressure sensors*

3   *Engine ECU*

4   *Injection of an additive into the fuel in the main tank if necessary*

5   *Specific information sent to the injector head when post-combustion is needed*

6   *Pre-catalyser*

7   *Particulate filter*

# **8** **Electric** and hybrid **propulsion**

A few years ago, many people believed the 'pollution-free electric car' would eventually replace cars with internal-combustion engines and so solve all our problems of exhaust emissions and the risk of liquid fuel running out. The kind of car people had in mind drew its power from batteries, which would be recharged whenever they began to run flat. It was a simple point of view which ignored one factor: the power for recharging has to come from a power station of some kind, and if it burns 'fossil' fuel, the best that happens is that the pollution is transferred from where the car is driven to wherever the power station has been built. Worse still, the late 1990s saw a fairly determined effort by several of the world's larger car manufacturers to establish an electric car market in California. It is now accepted that the effort has failed, partly because of the limited range of all battery electric vehicles (let's call them BEVs) but mainly because the batteries themselves turned out to be very expensive to make, and had too short a life before they needed replacing. Some researchers also questioned the environmental impact of processing (and recycling) the huge amounts of 'unfriendly' metals, such as lead and cadmium, necessary to make all the batteries which would be needed if the majority of the world's vehicles were BEVs.

Does that mean the end of the electric car dream? By no means. It may not even mean the end of the BEV, although it now seems likely to be reserved for special purposes, like making commercial deliveries in city centres. But it is more sensible to think of an electric car as one whose wheels are driven by electric power, and then to divide such vehicles into three classes, the first of which is the simple BEV. The first alternative is a car in which an internal-combustion engine drives a generator, which in turn produces the power to drive the wheels. This is the 'hybrid' electric vehicle or HEV. Finally, there is the vehicle, probably the one with the brightest future ahead of it in the long term, in which the electric power is provided by a fuel cell. We may call such vehicles FCEVs. It seems likely that during the next half-century, the FCEV will gradually take over as the standard type of passenger car, with the HEV helping to smooth the transition, and the internal-combustion engine eventually becoming quaint and old-fashioned, rather in the way we now look at a steam railway engine, while small numbers of BEVs will travel routes which don't take them too far from their recharging depots. To have a clearer understanding of this future, we obviously need to look at the HEV and FCEV in more detail – but first, we need to think about batteries and their possible alternatives, even if the BEV itself has only a limited future.

# The battery: simply energy storage

The only purpose of any battery is to store chemical energy and release it on demand.

Whether the BEV is practical or not, all vehicles need some kind of device to store energy. Even the conventional IC-engined car needs a battery for starting, and for powering all its electrical systems regardless of whether the alternator is generating enough power at that moment. HEVs and FCEVs will probably need a much larger 'energy buffer', either a battery bank or an alternative, to enable their power units to operate at maximum efficiency all the time, with the buffer taking care of troughs and peaks in demand, by absorbing and feeding-back energy. The battery has a certain future in front of it, no matter how vehicle technology develops.

For vehicle propulsion, the battery obviously needs to be rechargeable, rather than the throw-away type we use in portable radios and torches (flashlights). There are many chemical combinations which can be used as the basis for a rechargeable battery. Some store more energy (per weight and size of battery) than others but many of the high-energy combinations depend on expensive and exotic materials, some of which are also potentially dangerous, singly or in combination. The best energy density of all would be achieved by a battery which brought together hydrogen and fluorine, but nobody with any sense of self-preservation would try to create one.

To give some idea of the energy-storage performance gap between petrol and a lead-acid battery, the energy released by burning 1kg (2.2lb) of petrol is equivalent to around 12kWh, of which some 4.5kWh will be converted to mechanical energy by a typically efficient internal-combustion engine. A typical automotive lead-acid battery with a 50Ah rating at 12 volts, for a total stored energy of 0.6kWh, weighs approximately 20 kg (44lb). Thus a lead-acid 'battery bank' with a capacity of 4.8kWh capacity, allowing for a small energy loss during power conversion, weighs about 160kg (352lb). Carefully optimised design of the bank and its associated components may reduce this to perhaps 100kg (220lb). In other words, to store a

*Opposite: Whatever the impression given by diagrams of how its drivetrain works, in the metal the Toyota HV-M4 looks surprisingly conventional. The transverse-mounted front engine is a specially adapted 2.4-litre petrol unit with what Toyota calls a 'high expansion ratio cycle'; the most obviously new features are the rear-mounted electric motor, with drive to the rear wheels, and a battery bank sitting immediately above. Toyota claims twice the fuel economy of a normally powered vehicle of similar size. (Toyota)*

given amount of energy, the battery weighs 100 times as much as the equivalent quantity of petrol – and the vehicle has to carry that weight around with it, with serious effects on its overall efficiency. The most advanced battery concepts being seriously studied may improve on the lead-acid battery by a factor of four, which means that energy-for-energy, they would still weigh 25 times as much as the equivalent petrol in a tank. However, since the emergence of the environmental lobby as a serious force in the 1970s, intense research has been devoted to such advanced batteries.

The results have not been encouraging. One late-1990s review suggested that the number of battery concepts being seriously studied for vehicle use had halved since the late 1970s, leaving only six types with any prospect of use in the foreseeable future. These included the existing and well-proven lead-acid battery and nickel-cadmium battery. The remaining four types were listed as nickel-metal hydride, sodium-nickel chloride, lithium-carbon and lithium-polymer (lithium-ion). While these four battery concepts achieve significantly better energy density than lead/acid, without exception they also cost much more – though it has been argued they may reclaim some of the cost difference by lasting longer in service. In practice, most of the vehicle manufacturers have equipped their demonstrator BEV, HEV and FCEV prototypes with either nickel-metal hydride or lithium-ion batteries. These two types are now technically well developed but still extremely expensive by comparison with lead-acid, and have yet to be manufactured in large volume.

One possible alternative to the battery, with better energy storage density and much better 'power density' (batteries overheat if power is drawn from them too fast) is the condenser. Condensers are most familiar as very small components in electrical circuits, which temporarily store electrical energy instead of letting the current pass. Banks of large-size condensers are able to store a considerable amount of electrical energy. While condensers are unsuitable for long-term storage, they may provide an efficient answer for short-term storage – for instance, for storing energy recovered during braking, before re-using it for acceleration. In 1997 Honda demonstrated a car with a condenser bank which would store enough energy to power a 10kW electric motor for 12 seconds, enough to accelerate along a motorway slip road or complete an overtaking manoeuvre. Several Japanese research teams have suggested using a combination of an advanced battery – nickel-metal hydride or lithium-ion – and a high-energy capacitor to provide a lightweight, flexible and efficient energy buffer store for an HEV.

# Electric motors:
## vitally important

Any kind of electric vehicle needs a traction motor – that is actually our chosen definition of an electric vehicle. As the HEV and FCEV gradually take over from today's internal-combustion-engined cars, more and more traction motors will be needed and their technology will become more important.

One of the problems, though not the most serious one, of early BEVs was that they used fairly crude motors with even cruder control systems which were noisy and gave a jerky response. An electric power unit which is acceptable in a milk float may feel dreadful in a passenger car. During the early 1990s the technical choice between AC and DC motors seemed finely balanced. The AC motor has better basic efficiency, but needs an inverter unit to convert DC power drawn from the battery into AC power for the motor drive. Electric vehicle prototypes which appeared towards 2000, especially in Japan, mainly used synchronous AC motors, although Honda uses a brushless DC motor-generator installed 'sandwich style' between the engine and transmission of its Insight, one of the first HEVs to reach production. Most modern AC traction motors work with voltages in the range 70–120 volts, the result of a compromise between motor bulk, efficiency and electrical safety. For the most part, current electric vehicles use a single-speed drive, exploiting the ability of electric traction motors to develop maximum torque at zero or at least at very low speed. With the aid of 'aggressive' engineering and positive cooling, electric motors can provide extremely high torque-to-weight ratios. A motor demonstrated by the British company Zytec produces 60Nm (44lb ft) for a weight of only 13kg (28.6lb), sufficiently light to make wheel-hub mounting a practical proposition.

Electronics provide the key to modern control of electric motors, and all modern motors are brushless. Most electric vehicles now have electronic motor control using the high frequency 'chopper' principle – in which the average power level is determined by the proportion of time (per standard system pulse) for which the supply is switched on. A possible and more advanced alternative is vector control, which has been demonstrated by Mitsubishi in a concept vehicle and which leads to even higher efficiency.

Electric vehicles can also save (regenerate) energy by 'reversing' their motors to reclaim some of the kinetic energy which would otherwise be lost (actually, turned into heat and radiated away) during braking. Regeneration may also take place, under computer control, on the overrun or on a downward gradient. Depending on the driving conditions, it can play a useful part in improving the energy economy of BEVs and HEVs.

# Hybrid power units

An obvious way of overcoming the limited range of the BEV is to add a small engine and generator to the vehicle to recharge the battery bank on the move. Coming from a slightly different direction, it can be argued that one way to create an economical vehicle with low emissions is to use an electric drive running on power supplied by an engine-driven generator. The size of this 'prime mover' engine can be chosen to deliver the *average* power requirement of the vehicle rather than the maximum needed for acceleration. The engine can then be run at its most fuel and emissions-efficient point all the time (or be shut down). Extra power for acceleration is drawn from an energy buffer.

In fact HEVs can be split into two classes, the **series** hybrid in which all the energy transfer is electric, and the **parallel** hybrid in which the prime mover is connected to the driven wheels by a mechanical transmission, and the flow of electric power runs in parallel – hence the name. The series type gives the vehicle designer the greatest flexibility, since all the connections (except the transmission from the traction motor to the wheels) are electrical and each unit can be housed wherever is most convenient. In the parallel type, on the other hand, the electric motor can be made much lighter and smaller. In a series hybrid, the motor must be able to deliver the entire driving force, while in a parallel hybrid it might need to provide as little as 30% of it.

For a long time, the general attitude towards the HEV was that the cost of fitting two drive systems,

internal combustion and electric, rather than one meant that the vehicle would be too expensive to compete with its rivals. More recently, detailed analysis has suggested that the HEV might be made competitive, with any extra cost offset by the better economy and lower emissions which result from the concept of 'energy management', using the flexibility of the system to conserve, recover and retain energy which would go to waste in a conventional IC-engined vehicle. This new attitude has already prompted Toyota and Honda to produce and sell HEVs, the Prius and the Insight.

The 4-door saloon Prius is powered by the Toyota Hybrid System (THS), an integrated driveline which combines a high-efficiency 1.5-litre IC engine and electric motor driving through an ingenious power splitter and CVT transmission (see Part 2), with a control system that ensures the best use is made of all available energy. The car is claimed to use only half as much fuel – and therefore to produce only half the $CO_2$ emissions – of a conventional car of similar size and performance. Other emissions (HC, CO, NOx) are said to be cut by 90%. Power output of the 1.5-litre Prius engine, which never exceeds 4,000rpm, is 58bhp, while its electric motor can add a further 40PS (and substantial torque) for 'sprint' acceleration. The engine output alone is enough to maintain a steady

*The hybrid vehicle, combining an internal combustion engine and electric power to achieve optimum use of available energy rather than wasting it through braking and use of*

*the engine at inefficient speeds and loads, may prove to be a halfway house to the eventual success of the fuel-cell vehicle. Nissan showed this drivetrain arrangement for a hybrid in 1999. (Nissan)*

■The system of the NEO HYBRID

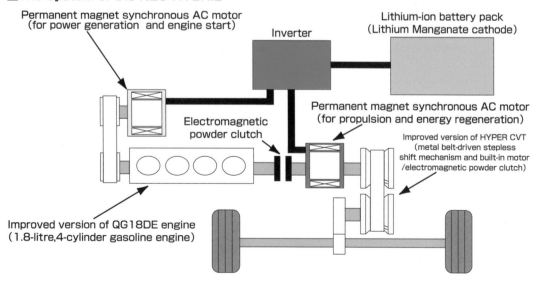

Permanent magnet synchronous AC motor
(for power generation and engine start)

Inverter

Lithium-ion battery pack
(Lithium Manganate cathode)

Electromagnetic
powder clutch

Permanent magnet synchronous AC motor
(for propulsion and energy regeneration)

Improved version of HYPER CVT
(metal belt-driven stepless
shift mechanism and built-in motor
/electromagnetic powder clutch)

Improved version of QG18DE engine
(1.8-litre,4-cylinder gasoline engine)

# THS-C Schematic

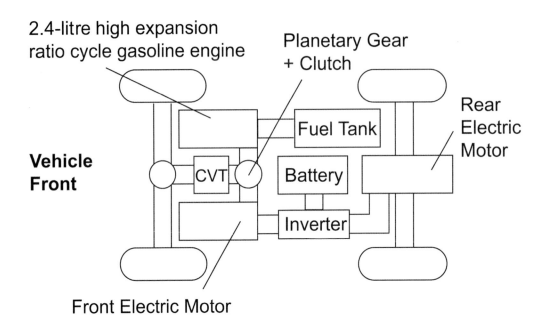

2.4-litre high expansion ratio cycle gasoline engine

Planetary Gear + Clutch

Rear Electric Motor

**Vehicle Front**

CVT

Fuel Tank

Battery

Inverter

Front Electric Motor

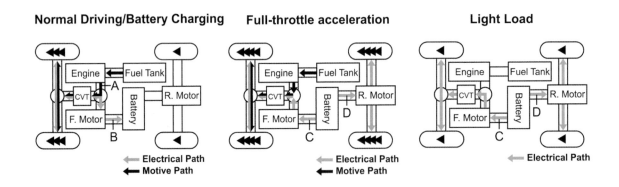

**Normal Driving/Battery Charging**

Engine | Fuel Tank
CVT — A
F. Motor | Battery | R. Motor
B

← Electrical Path
← Motive Path

**Full-throttle acceleration**

Engine | Fuel Tank
CVT
F. Motor | Battery | R. Motor
D
C

← Electrical Path
← Motive Path

**Light Load**

Engine | Fuel Tank
CVT
F. Motor | Battery | R. Motor
D
C

← Electrical Path

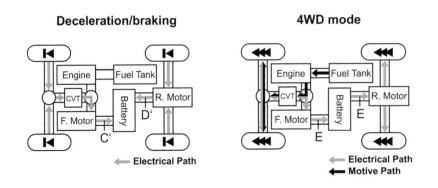

**Deceleration/braking**

Engine | Fuel Tank
CVT
F. Motor | Battery | R. Motor
D'
C'

← Electrical Path

**4WD mode**

Engine | Fuel Tank
CVT
F. Motor | Battery | R. Motor
E
E

← Electrical Path
← Motive Path

*Opposite: At the 1999 Tokyo Motor Show, Toyota showed its HV-M4 concept vehicle, in effect a second-generation hybrid following on from the Prius which was about to enter production. The HV-M4 used the same hybrid principle, but added a second electric motor driving the rear wheels when required. These diagrams show the way in which electrical and mechanical power flows are computer-controlled according to driving condition, always with the object of optimising the efficient use of energy. (Toyota)*

speed of 100km/h (62mph) on a level road with no drain on the battery bank.

The Honda Insight is a lightweight 2-seat coupé with a series hybrid layout. Its power unit, carefully integrated like that of the Prius, uses Honda's Integral Motor Assist (IMA) concept, and combines a 3-cylinder, 12-valve, 1-litre engine with a slender electric motor/generator sandwiched between the engine and the 5-speed manual transmission. The Insight engine itself has a power output of 68bhp, and maximum torque of 91Nm (67lb ft) at 4,800rpm. When the electric motor is providing full assistance, the power goes up modestly to 76bhp, but the maximum torque is increased to 113Nm (83lb ft) at only 1,500rpm, showing the effect of the way the electric motor develops high torque at very low speed. These figures also show however that the Insight is a good deal 'less hybrid' than the Prius, whose internal combustion and electric motor outputs are much more nearly balanced. From the hybrid point of view, the Insight is at the other end of the spectrum from the vehicles demonstrated in the late 1990s by Citroën and Fiat, both of which were basically BEVs with small internal-combustion engines and generators added in place of some of the batteries. With the batteries flat, and the engine operating in 'limp-home' mode, these pure series-HEVs could manage no more than around 30mph (50km/h). In such cases the engine is intended only as a 'range extender' to help out the batteries and increase the possible radius of operation from the recharging depot.

# Fuel **cells**

The fuel cell is the technology most of the experts think will provide the long-term answer to the problems of exhaust emissions and oil shortages. The basic principle of the fuel cell is that it reverses the school laboratory experiment of electrolysis, in which an electric current passes through water and oxygen and hydrogen are formed. In the fuel cell, oxygen (from the air) and hydrogen are fed to opposite sides of a reactive layer in which, encouraged by a catalyst, they combine to form water and in the process produce electric power. Several types of fuel cell have been developed though only one, the proton exchange membrane (PEM) type, works at fairly low temperature (around 80°C), making it by far the most suitable for use in vehicles. As late as 1990, however, even the PEM fuel cell was seen at best as expensive, bulky, and of doubtful energy-conversion efficiency. The failure to turn the BEV into a practical proposition led to massive fuel-cell research programmes, though, because the fuel cell was really the only alternative technology which looked like delivering the same environmental advantages. Sure enough, progress was rapid and by 1999 several car manufacturers including DaimlerChrysler, Ford, General Motors, Honda and Toyota had demonstrated prototype FCEVs with satisfactory performance and behaviour – though still at high cost.

Some indication of the progress made is seen in the DaimlerChrysler NECAR series of demonstrators. The company points out that in 1994, its van-based NECAR I had space only for the driver alongside its experimental power unit. Two years later, the power unit of the NECAR II, based on the V-class MPV, could be housed beneath the rear floor, leaving space for six seats inside the vehicle. By 1999 the NECAR 4, adapted from the small A-class car, had its entire fuel-cell system beneath its floor, leaving space for four seats and a load of luggage. Most of the larger car manufacturers now say they expect to be selling a trickle of cars to selected customers by 2004, and will be making them in commercial quantities (though still in far smaller numbers than IC-engined cars) by 2010.

In theory, the fuel cell produces nothing but electric power and water. In practice, the picture is unlikely to be so simple, though most of the potential problems are associated with the process of 'reforming' liquid fuels, either petrol or methanol, to produce the hydrogen needed by the cell. The alternative is to carry a pressurized or liquid hydrogen supply, but this makes refuelling much less convenient. Through 1999 and 2000 there has been a heated debate about the fuel options, with petrol, methanol and hydrogen enthusiasts all pushing their points of view. The petrol option is easiest, even though the petrol would have to be rather different from today's unleaded, with fewer additives and any impurities (especially sulphur) almost completely removed. Petrol still faces the problem that it will run out – or become unbearably expensive – when the crude oil runs out. Also, using petrol does little to help reduce 'greenhouse' $CO_2$ emissions. Methanol tanks can be filled in the same way as petrol tanks, but obviously a whole new network of refineries, distribution depots and special pumps at filling stations would be needed. Methanol can be made from natural gas (methane) and should face no supply problem this side of 2100. Hydrogen would make the fuel-cell system in the car much simpler but would need a huge shift in the way fuel is

*Interior view of the DaimlerChrysler NECAR 4 shows how the entire power unit has been packaged beneath the floor of this compact (but tall) 4-seater, based on the A-class. In the* *first vehicle of the NECAR series, only a few years ago, the same components took up most of the interior of a medium-sized van, leaving only two seats.* (DaimlerChrysler)

stored, distributed and dispensed, with some serious safety issues to be resolved. Hydrogen is theoretically available in unlimited quantity, but isolating it needs a lot of electric power. What everyone wants to avoid is a situation where there have to be two massive changes of supply system, from petrol to methanol and eventually to hydrogen. It will be some time before this question is resolved.

Fuel cells are potentially very efficient. The internal-combustion engine works through a cycle of compression and expansion, and the French scientist Carnot proved in 1824 that no such engine can ever be more than around 50% efficient in converting heat (produced by the chemical energy of burning fuel) into mechanical work. The fuel cell has no moving parts (at least, not within the cell itself) and is not subject to the Carnot limitations. It can certainly be more than 50% efficient, and gains especially at low load where the IC engine tends to be least efficient. Thus FCEVs are likely to be (and have already proved to be) more economical than conventional cars in real-life driving conditions.

The fuel-cell economy advantage may be greater

still in FCEVs which use the cell as part of a 'hybrid' system with an energy buffer, which allows overall energy management, including regeneration, to yield further improved efficiency. There is much debate among the fuel-cell experts about which approach is the best: to have a 'steady-state' fuel cell with an energy buffer and management system to smooth the peaks and troughs of demand, or to make the cell 'throttleable', able to change its power output very quickly on demand in the same way as an IC engine, by varying the flow of hydrogen and altering the pressure in the cell. The power output of a fuel cell can be expressed as kW per litre of cell volume. The latest cells to be shown by Ballard and General Motors reach up to 2kW/litre, which means that the 75kW Ballard cell has a volume of nearly 40 litres, about the same size as the petrol tank in a small car.

The fuel cell is not, in itself, an 'engine'. All it does is supply electric power. In order to drive the vehicle, that power must be turned into mechanical work, via an electric motor. So we have to think of the fuel cell plus the motor as the 'substitute engine'. Nor is the fuel cell a simple device. The cell itself may have no moving parts, but it needs to be supplied with hydrogen and air, and this calls for pumps and other ancillaries. It is easy to overlook the fact that if it is to supply as much power as an internal-combustion engine, the fuel cell needs to be supplied with roughly the same amount of air – in other words, quite a lot (as with the internal-combustion engine, the 80% of air which consists of nitrogen will pass through unchanged). So the fuel cell

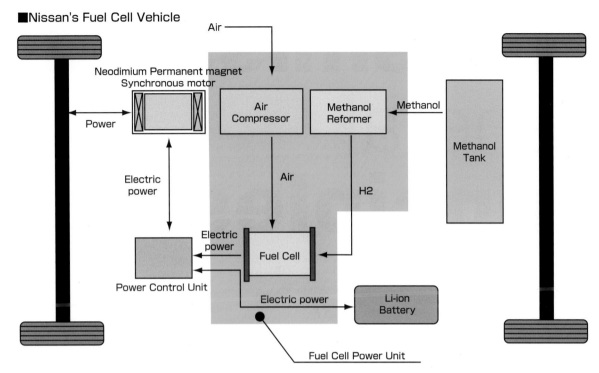

**■Nissan's Fuel Cell Vehicle**

At the 1999 Tokyo Motor Show, Nissan exhibited a fuel-cell-powered vehicle with the powertrain arrangement shown here in diagram form. Among other things, it makes the point that the fuel cell stack itself may be the heart of a complete fuel-cell power unit, but it is only a small part. The need to pass air through a fuel cell almost as fast as through a conventional internal combustion engine is often overlooked. (Nissan)

needs a large and efficient air pump, probably a compressor-expander unit in which the exhaust helps to drive the compressor, so as not to waste energy.

On the hydrogen supply side, everything depends on the choice of fuel. Pure hydrogen can simply be supplied direct, under pressure. If methanol or petrol is used, the fuel must be 'reformed' in a special unit which separates out the hydrogen and disposes of the rest as $CO_2$ and water. Reforming petrol is more difficult and involves higher temperatures – about 800°C compared with 250°C inside a methanol reformer. Almost certainly, the reforming process will be less than perfect and the 'exhaust' will need some kind of catalytic converter if near-zero emissions are to be achieved.

There are enough FCEV prototypes and demonstrators now running in various parts of the world to prove that the concept really works. The remaining challenges are technical and industrial. The technical challenge is to achieve further improvements in power output, and longer service life, while drastically reducing cost. The real price of an automotive fuel cell has come down by a factor of ten since 1990, but needs to be no more than one-tenth of the 2001 price before it becomes competitive as a power unit for production vehicles. The industrial challenge is, of course, to gear up to producing millions of fuel-cell power units a year – and to decide what is to be done with all the factories now making internal-combustion engines.

# Other 'green' alternatives

Aside from the battery and the fuel cell, there are several other strange, and not so strange ideas for doing away with the engine. Several research teams have studied designs for flywheels capable of storing large amounts of energy. The most promising approach seems to be one of very strong rotors (the strength needed to avoid bursting under centrifugal stress) turning extremely fast in a vacuum chamber, with energy added and retrieved electrically rather than mechanically. One very simple solution is to use compressed air released through a rudimentary 'engine', a solution which might give a lightweight vehicle performance approaching that of a BEV at a fraction of the cost. Any possible solution is worth examination, but with two golden rules always in mind. Given the need to store a certain amount of energy to achieve acceptable performance, what will it weigh? And how much is it likely to cost?

# 9 Transmission general principles

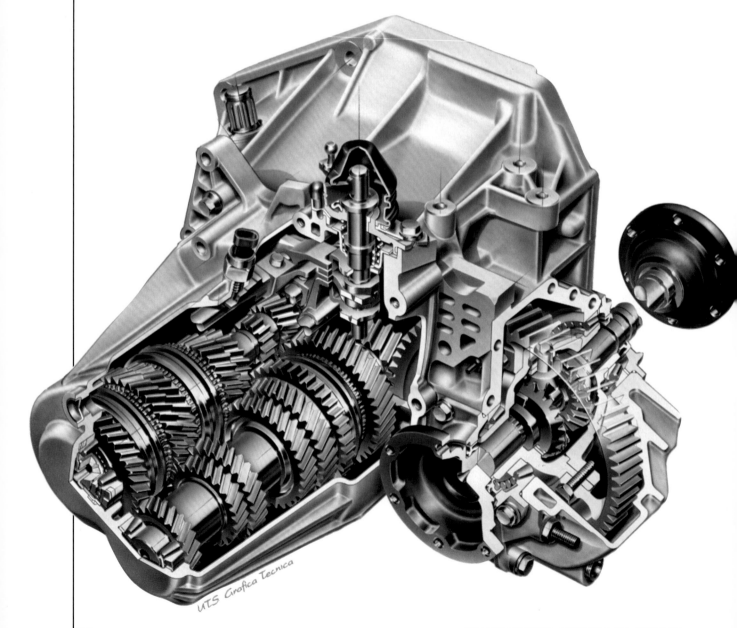

UTS Grafica Tecnica

The job of the transmission is to take the power (more strictly, the torque) from the engine to the driven wheels. Put like that, it's simple – yet the engineering challenges are many and varied, and have become more so since most cars adopted front-wheel-drive, rear-wheel-drive cars adopted independent rear suspension, and 4-wheel-drive became a major interest.

For the casual onlooker, the transmission in any conventional car with an internal-combustion engine consists of the gearbox and 'everything else'. The 'everything else' is far too often taken for granted, but first of all let's consider why we need a box full of different gear ratios at all. The problem is that the internal-combustion engine delivers such poor torque, especially at low speeds. Any car needs a certain amount of torque if it is to be driven away from rest, especially if it is pointing uphill with a caravan attached to the back, which is the yardstick most often applied when selecting the lowest gear ratio. This ratio allows the engine to run fast even when the car is moving very slowly: it steps-down the engine speed so that the output shaft from the gearbox is turning at (usually) around a quarter of the input speed. The transition from stationary to moving needs some means of feeding the engine output to the gearbox; this may be either a manual or an automatic clutch, or a fluid coupling – all to be discussed later. Whatever the chosen system, it enables the engine to remain running when the car is stationary, and by one means or another it can 'slip' to bridge that awkward gap between standstill and movement, and usually also has some means to damp out the shock and vibration of an over-sudden engagement of drive.

Once the clutch is fully engaged, the car is free to accelerate – but only until its engine reaches its maximum operating speed. In a typical family car, this usually arrives at around 30mph (50km/h) – and then what? You change up, of course, to a higher gear which will enable the car to reach a higher speed (but in which it would be more difficult to start from rest). This second gear may take you to around 60mph (100km/h); but even if you are happy to drive at this speed, you certainly don't want the engine running at its maximum speed all the time. So a third, higher gear is provided – and a higher fourth, and these days, almost always an even higher fifth, if not a sixth. Just as first gear is usually determined by the caravan-towing hill start, so the top gear – fourth, fifth or sixth – is generally chosen so that the car's maximum speed on a level road coincides with the engine's peak power speed.

This isn't essential, however. Some German manufacturers used to use slightly lower than 'ideal' top gears, so that if you were cruising flat-out (still theoretically possible on German autobahns) your engine would be slightly beyond its power peak. Then when you came to a slight uphill gradient, the first slight slowing of the car would bring the engine back to its peak power speed, which you could (hopefully) maintain without having to change down. At the other extreme, when we became more interested in fuel economy (and also in quieter cruising) the top gear could be set high enough to ensure the engine was turning quite slowly – somewhere between peak torque and peak power – even when the car was running at maximum speed. To achieve this, the top gear usually had to be an 'overdrive' – which literally means the gearbox output shaft is turning faster than the engine input, rather than slower. This certainly reduced fuel consumption and engine noise, but it also meant that even a slight uphill motorway gradient could see the car losing speed so quickly that it became necessary to change down early. In the 1980s especially, a good many cars with 5-speed manual gearboxes had a higher maximum speed in fourth gear than in fifth.

Today, with near universal speed limits outside Germany, it matters far less if the top gear is high in the interests of economy and quietness. What does matter is the actual number of gears and the way they are spread out (for the time being, we are still talking of any gearbox, manual or automatic). The more gears there are, the less the difference between any two 'adjacent' ratios. A large gap between two gears can make driving a misery. For example, if you are trying to overtake, starting in a lower gear, and feel the need to change up part-way through the manoeuvre – not that this is good, let alone recommended driving practice, but sometimes it happens – you may find acceleration is so much reduced in the higher gear that you have to rethink the whole situation. And if you feel the need to change down, perhaps when approaching a corner or a junction, a wide gap may leave you with a suddenly screaming engine and far more engine braking than you really wanted.

As drivers have become more demanding, and car performance has increased, the move to more gear ratios has become inexorable. During the 1940s, the average family car with a manual gearbox had three

*Opposite: It is difficult but not impossible to fit a transverse-engined, front-wheel-drive car with a two-shaft, 6-speed gearbox. This example is used in the Alfa Romeo 156 with the V6 engine option. Because the V6 is so compact, fitting the box is no great problem, although it cannot be done with the in-line 4-cylinder and 5-cylinder engines also used in the 156. The difference is that the V6, although of larger capacity, is only 'three and a half cylinders long' in terms of the width it occupies under the bonnet. Note, in this illustration, the way the output is taken to the final-drive unit and differential. (Alfa Romeo)*

forward gears. In the 1950s and 1960s there was a steady move towards 4-speed manual gearboxes (most automatics then were still 3-speed). By 1980 we were well into the transition to 5-speed manual and 4-speed automatic; and by 2000, 6-speed manual gearboxes and 5-speed automatic transmissions were becoming more common. The way has always been led by 'sporting' cars, partly because their drivers saw changing gear to maintain best performance as part of the fun of driving, and partly because they often had engines with high maximum-torque speeds which made more frequent down-changes more or less essential in many situations.

All through the history of motoring, there has been an anxiety to make driving as easy as possible. With a manual gearbox, which for a long time was all the engineer had, starting from rest was always a challenge, and changing gear was even worse for the driver with no natural 'feel' and no mechanical understanding of what was happening inside the gearbox. Eventually, as we shall see in Chapter 10, answers were found in both clutch and gearbox design – but in the meantime, others strove to produce a genuinely automatic transmission which called for no driver action other than to select 'D' before setting off. By the early 1940s, the definitive answer to this challenge had been found. At least, it remained definitive for half a century, but is now being called into question by newer and more ingenious systems.

There remains the 'everything else' of the transmission. For the first half of the 20th century, with a few maverick exceptions, the transmission downstream of the in-line, front-mounted gearbox consisted of a propeller shaft joining the gearbox to a final-drive unit which sat in the middle of a 'live' beam rear axle, with a driven wheel at each end. The propeller shaft was equipped with at least one universal joint and some means of altering slightly in length, so as to accommodate movement of the rear axle relative to the gearbox. The final drive had two purposes. First, it incorporated a further step-down ratio, usually of around 4:1 – without which the first gear in the gearbox would have needed to be around

*Portrait of a survivor: for very special reasons, the Porsche 911 is almost the only example of the once popular rear-engined layout to remain in volume production. Note, in this case, the 4WD driveline with an output shaft from the nose of the transaxle-type gearbox and final drive, to a second final-drive unit at the front. To overcome the handling problems inherent with an engine hung aft of the rear axle line, the modern 911 has a very sophisticated suspension layout with a complex multi-link arrangement at the rear, and MacPherson struts at the front (see how the axis of the coil spring is well offset from that of the damper strut). Note also the front-mounted radiators which are needed because the Porsche flat-6 engine is no longer air-cooled as in the original car. (Porsche)*

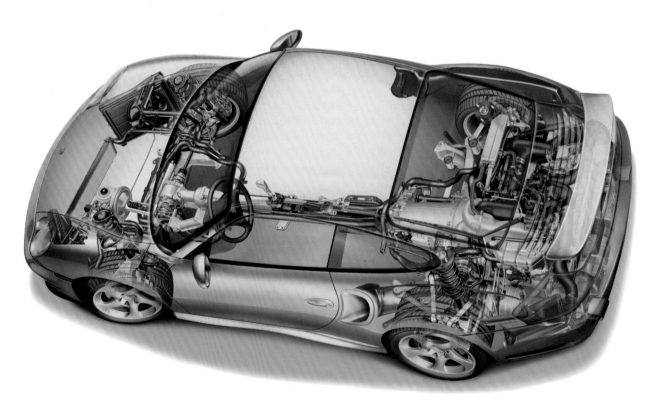

16:1. Second, it also contained a differential gear arrangement which meant the driven wheels could travel at different speeds, essential to enable the car to travel round corners without the inner and outer driven wheels 'fighting' each other. The stiff tube of the rear axle contained the fixed-length drive shafts which connected the differential outputs to the rear wheel hubs. This was an arrangement which Monsieur Panhard, who devised it in the 1890s, would have recognised in the vast majority of cars 60 years later. Today, he would have a lot more trouble.

# Big impact: the switch to front-wheel-drive

By far the most significant change, pioneered by Citroën and others in the 1930s but suddenly made immensely popular by the success of the Mini from 1958 onwards, was the change from rear-wheel-drive to front-wheel-drive. With front-wheel-drive, the engine might be installed lengthwise, or transversely, with a 'transaxle' combining the gearbox and final drive. In the Mini, the gearbox was housed in the sump of the transverse engine with a spur gear output to the final drive behind the engine, but almost every other transverse-engined car has kept its gearbox in-line with the crankshaft, which makes design simpler in many respects but means that the complete engine-and-gearbox package is significantly wider, which can pose installation problems. The in-line engine and transaxle solution was less challenging, not least because transaxles had already been engineered for a whole generation of post-war rear-engined cars including the VW Beetle, the Renault 4CV/Dauphine and others. On the other hand this layout had none of the 'packaging' advantages of the transverse engine, and offered designers a hard choice between mounting the engine ahead of the front axle line –

making the car potentially nose-heavy and ruining the aerodynamics of the nose – or behind the axle line with the gearbox in front, in which case the engine was forced almost to live in the front seat, as seen in all the big Citroëns up to the DS.

Whatever the chosen layout, front-wheel-drive (like the rear-engine layout) meant there was no propeller shaft. This meant some other way had to be found of allowing the wheels to move vertically relative to the engine and gearbox. In fact it more or less demanded the use of independent suspension rather than a beam axle, with the drive shafts, running directly from the differential to the front wheels, jointed and in some way splined to allow small changes in length and so accommodate 'plunge'. In the small rear-engined cars of the 1950s, independent rear suspension had been fairly easy to arrange with variations on the swing axle (see Part 3). But the failings of the swing axle could scarcely be tolerated when the wheels needed to be steered – and in any case, the need to steer meant that the joints in the drive shafts could no longer be simple universal joints, but something much more advanced – the constant velocity joint (CVJ – see Chapter 12).

What we have now, in summary, is two virtually standard transmission layouts – front-wheel-drive with transverse engine, and rear-wheel-drive with in-line engine, plus the specialised case of 4WD (Chapter 13). What this has done, over the last 20 years or so, is to allow chassis designers first, to concentrate on perfecting these arrangements without worrying too much about alternatives, but second, to indulge in some really advanced thinking about how the transmission could be used not only to drive the car, but also to help control it (Chapter 14). This, one imagines, will be the last great step forward in the transmission area before electric traction arrives to re-write the rules and make everything much simpler.

# 10 Manual transmissions

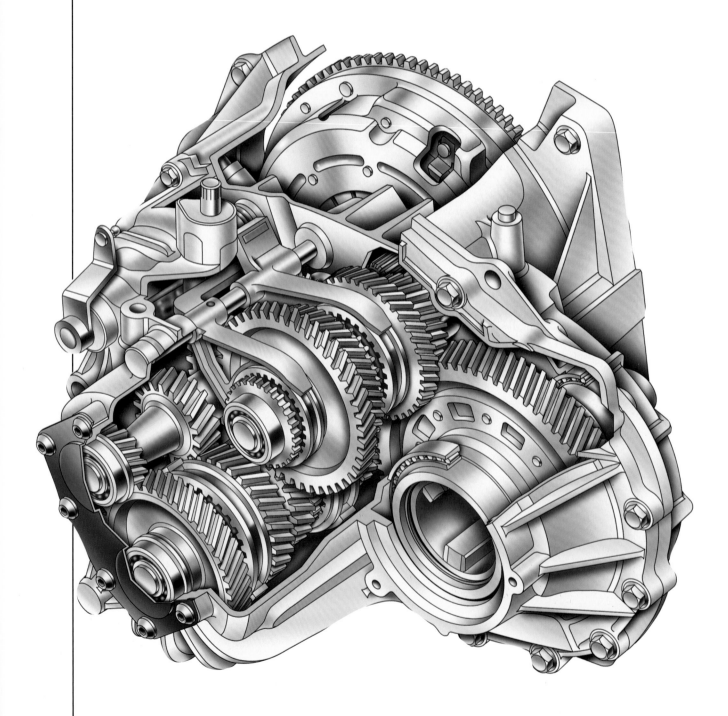

**T**here are two main technical aspects to any manual transmission: the clutch and the gearbox. What any engineer strives for in both cases – apart from low cost, low weight and bulk – is ease of operation. Customers understandably like their manual clutches and gearboxes to feel light and as near foolproof as possible. Anyone who doubts the advances which have been achieved should try driving a typical 1930s car and then a modern one. The casual student of car design might assume that the arrival of synchromesh made all the difference, but as so often, the truth is that a whole series of developments in clutch and gearbox design, and in the materials used, have had their effect.

# The clutch

The sole purpose of the clutch is to disconnect the engine from the rest of the transmission when necessary. The basic principle of the modern passenger car clutch is fairly simple: a clutch plate (the 'driven' plate) faced on both sides with high-friction material is sandwiched between the rear face of the engine flywheel and a pressure plate. The pressure plate in turn is pressed into place by a powerful spring. Its pressure can be released by the driver pressing on the clutch pedal, which operates a linkage to unload the spring. At some point in the linkage, account has to be taken of the fact that the clutch assembly is whirling at high speed, and the clutch pedal isn't. At that point, an operating fork has to bear against a thrust face, creating the final crucial component, the clutch release bearing. That is the principle; the practice is more complicated, and it took around 90 years of development to arrive at the kind of clutch we normally use today.

The main engineering requirement of the clutch – apart from disengaging and re-engaging when necessary – is to transmit all the torque produced by the engine, without slipping. Bear in mind that we are looking at two disc-faces connected only by friction and held together by spring pressure; if the load on the clutch plate is heavy enough and the torque applied to the flywheel is high enough, the clutch will slip. The torque capacity of the clutch – the torque it will transmit cleanly before it begins to slip – depends on the coefficient of friction of the lining material, the size of clutch plate (in other words its diameter) and the spring loading which holds the clutch plate against the flywheel. Facing the driven plate with friction material on both sides doubles the effective area of the clutch; the flywheel and pressure plate faces are plain metal, because contact between two faces of friction material would cause near instant lockup and very fast wear.

There isn't much which can be done to improve the friction of the material beyond a certain value if it is to take up smoothly, be strong enough to resist the various forces and temperatures involved, and last a long time (this is engineering compromise again; you can have much better friction, and thus a smaller and lighter clutch, if you don't mind replacing the clutch plate every few hundred miles). There is a sensible limit to the size of the clutch plate, depending on the size of the engine. The plate in a typical 2-litre family car normally has a diameter of 8 to 9 inches. If you want to transmit more torque, therefore, you have to use a stronger spring clamping force. This used to be a real problem in the days when the clutch plate was clamped by a pressure plate that passed on the shove of several small but stiff coil springs between the pressure plate and the clutch casing. It could take a real heave on the pedal to disengage the clutch of a powerful car in the 1950s, as the mechanism compressed those coil springs. The only way the clutch could be made lighter was to increase the pedal travel, a technique which has its obvious limits. Then the diaphragm spring was developed, and made life much easier for the designers of light-duty clutches. The diaphragm spring had so many advantages over the coil-spring type that the latter soon disappeared from use, except in large commercial vehicles.

In principle, the diaphragm spring operates like the dished end of a tin can: you can push its centre without any great effort to make it dish in the opposite direction, but when you let it go, it springs back to its original shape. In practice, the spring-disc is much more carefully designed, with radial slots to help it retain its proper shape without buckling, and to modify its spring characteristics, but the principle remains the same: in its 'natural' shape the spring provides strong pressure to hold the clutch engaged, but its pressure can be released by operating the clutch pedal, via its linkage (mechanical or hydraulic) and the release bearing. The spring is located on a 'fulcrum ring', with the release bearing at its centre and the load applied to the pressure plate at the periphery. The most modern form of clutch is the DSP (diaphragm-spring pull) type, in which the release bearing is pulled rather than pushed in order to declutch. In this case the fulcrum ring is around the periphery of the pressure plate – which makes for a stronger mounting – and the load is applied to the pressure plate within

*Opposite: The PK6 6-speed manual gearbox used in the highest-powered versions of the Laguna II, and in the luxury Avantime coupé, is an evolution of an earlier 5-speed unit. To keep the gearbox short enough for transverse installation, it uses a three-shaft layout to reduce the length of each shaft, a technique also used by Volvo in the transmissions for its front-wheel-drive 70- and 80-series cars. (Renault)*

the ring, which means the lever effect can be greater and the clutch even lighter. The release bearing itself is now more often a ball-bearing than a plain self-lubricated thrust bearing.

The design of the driven plate is anything but simple in a modern clutch. The friction facings are usually mounted on stiff springs which compress to give a gentler take-up of the drive, and the plate is most often attached to the central hub, on the splined forward end of the gearbox input shaft, by coil springs which compress as the drive is taken up. All these features make modern clutches far more 'forgiving' – a fact appreciated by test drivers who may 'drop' the clutch in a standing-start acceleration test with the engine doing perhaps 4,000rpm. This is certainly not recommended procedure, but is probably less harmful in the long run than using the clutch pedal as a support for the left foot. Although modern friction materials, from which all asbestos has long since been removed, resists wear and temperature quite well, 'riding' the clutch is still a recipe for trouble: the one example of driver malpractice for which a complete answer has never been found.

The single-plate clutch is the world standard for manual transmission passenger car use. A handful of cars with extremely high power, torque and performance, and many commercial vehicles, use multi-plate clutches to achieve high torque capacity without increasing the clutch diameter unreasonably.

In multi-plate clutches the driven plates and pressure plates, all splined to the gearbox input shaft, are pressed together in a multi-layered sandwich by a master pressure plate at the gearbox end. Multi-plate clutches are not only expensive, but need very careful design if they are to disengage and engage as cleanly as a single-plate clutch.

Over the years, several types of automatic clutch have been offered with the idea of allowing 'two-pedal' driving with a manual gearbox. In theory, any arrangement which completely disconnects the engine from the gearbox below around 800rpm, and engages progressively to a 'solid' drive at around 1,200rpm, should do the trick – were it not for the fact that changes between the higher gears, with the aid of synchromesh, are rarely carried out without the engine speed dropping as low as 1,200rpm, let alone 800rpm. Therefore any truly automatic clutch needs to declutch not only at a standstill, but whenever the driver is changing gear.

This requirement rules out the simple centrifugal clutch, in which friction shoes, resembling those of a drum brake, are mounted on an engine-driven shaft and thrust outward by increasing engine speed, overcoming the tension of springs which pull them into the disengaged position. Centrifugal clutches are very widely used in low-powered vehicles such as lawn mowers and snowmobiles where simplicity of operation is at a premium. They have also been fitted to a number of low-powered cars, including the early Citroën 2CV and the original DAF Daffodil. However, the difficulty of engineering a unit which provides suitably smooth take-up of the drive, increases rapidly with maximum drive torque. A further problem is that the clutch does not disengage until the engine speed has fallen sufficiently, requiring some additional means, such as a free-wheel, to allow immediate gear selection on the move.

A better alternative is the electromagnetic clutch, in which the drive is engaged by passing an electric current through a coil; the current can be interrupted when the gear lever is moved, allowing normal gearchanges to take place at any speed. During the 1960s and 1970s a number of cars, including the NSU Ro80, used an automatic servo clutch to allow clutchless changing at normal speeds, plus a torque converter (see Chapter 11) for stopping and starting

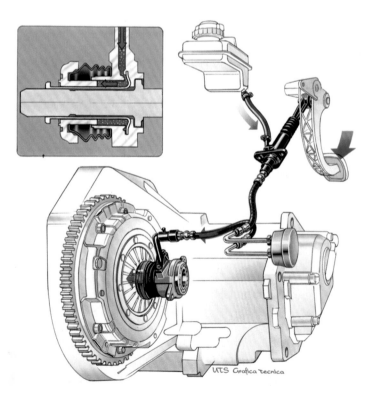

*Although most modern cars with manual transmissions use cable-operated clutches, some engineers still believe hydraulic operation gives a better feel at the pedal and more progressive operation. The Alfa Romeo 156 is one car which retains a hydraulic clutch system, its layout seen here complete with inset drawing of how hydraulic pressure pushes the sleeve which releases the diaphragm spring. (Alfa Romeo)*

from rest – an extremely clumsy arrangement which mercifully never caught on. Such cars were normally billed as 'semi-automatic' even though the driver had to make all the gear selections. Modern automatic clutches use a hydraulic servo, a number of sensors and an electronic control unit for their operation. The flexibility of electronic control means that the clutch (itself a more or less standard unit, the only difference being that the servo cylinder rather than the driver works the linkage) can be disengaged not only during gearshifting but whenever the operating condition demands it. Thus the clutch disengages smoothly as the vehicle comes to rest, or (with a suitable driver warning) if an attempt is made to drive in too high a gear for the conditions; no separate start-off device is needed, and the modern systems suffer none of the microswitch sensitivity which led to sudden, unanticipated declutching in early systems.

Among the modern servo-clutch systems, Renault offers its Easy unit, developed with AP, in a number of its smaller models, while Valeo supplies its generally similar system to Fiat for use in the Seicento, and also to the Korean manufacturers Daewoo and Hyundai. In all these cars, the driver remains responsible for selecting the gear in use. With this modern technology, a market of sorts seems to have emerged for small cars with two-pedal operation but also without the high cost of a fully automatic transmission. However, Saab's attempt – with its Sensonic system – to sell the idea to the better-off drivers of higher-performance cars on the basis that it was a good thing for the driver to be directly in charge of gear selection, was withdrawn from the market after a short time. Enthusiastic drivers, it seems, actually enjoy the feeling of perfect clutch and gear co-ordination.

# **Manual** gearboxes

To operate the finger-light gearchange of any modern small car is to have not the slightest idea of how difficult the process used to be – or rather, of how much skill, patience and mechanical sympathy used to be involved. The basic task of changing gear is to slide one pair of gears out of engagement and another pair in. At least, that is the obvious assumption and it was the one on which early gearboxes were based.

The basic layout of the gearbox was also established by the 1890s and so far as rear-wheel-drive cars with in-line engines are concerned, has not changed. The drive from the engine and clutch enters via a mainshaft, which carries a set of gears. Parallel to the mainshaft is a layshaft, carrying a second set of gears. At the output end of the gearbox, the mainshaft can be connected directly to an output

shaft to provide a direct drive which becomes one of the gear ratios, with the input and output speeds equal. In addition, one gear on the layshaft is also in permanent mesh with another gear on the output shaft. All that remains – apart from the need to provide a reverse gear, which involves introducing a third gear into the train so that the direction in which the output shaft turns is reversed – is to manoeuvre the gears on the mainshaft and the layshaft so that they mesh with each other as desired.

In early gearboxes, that was exactly what happened. Gear clusters were slid along the splined length of the mainshaft so that one pair of gears would engage, drive would be transferred from the mainshaft to the layshaft and then to the output shaft, via the permanently-engaged gears. For direct drive, all the gears would be disengaged and the mainshaft and output shafts would be connected via a dog-clutch; in this case the layshaft would still be driven via the permanently-engaged gears.

This was fine in theory but suffered from two practical problems. The first was how to engage two gears rotating at different speeds, whether changing up or down; given that the previously engaged gear speeds on the mainshaft and layshaft were perfectly matched, the speeds of the new pair of gears obviously couldn't be. A skilled driver could use the engine to adjust the speed of the mainshaft with the gearbox momentarily in neutral, and then slip the new gear into mesh: the process revered as double declutching. Minor differences in speed could be smoothed over by careful shaping of the gears where they began to mesh, with curves rather than sharp corners. Unskilled drivers might attempt to double declutch and make matters worse rather than better. With a combination of luck and brute force, a gear could eventually be engaged. Brave drivers who wonder how it felt might care to experiment with changing gear in a modern car without using the clutch at all – it can be done, and it gets easier with practice – simply pulling the gearbox into neutral on the overrun and trying to judge when the engine and vehicle speeds are just right to engage the next higher or lower gear (the most difficult thing is to get back into the gear you came out of; and on a practical note, if you ever suffer complete failure of the clutch operating linkage, it is possible to start from rest by starting the engine with first gear already engaged).

Aside from these extreme circumstances, however, it was always clear that the answer would be some kind of friction-clutching device which would match the speeds of the engaging gears before their teeth began to mesh – and which would also avoid the possibility of total baulking if at that moment their teeth were 'nose to nose' and unable to mesh. Eventually, although not until the 1920s, such

synchromesh mechanisms were devised – but they had to await an answer to the second gearbox problem before they became fully effective.

The second problem was that gears weigh quite a lot. Changing the speed of a mainshaft complete with its gear clusters took time and energy. Also, leaving space for complete gear clusters to slide back and forth meant that gearboxes had to be bulky. Eventually the answer emerged in the form of the constant-mesh gearbox principle, which quickly supplanted the original sliding-mesh gearbox for all practical purposes, at least in passenger cars. In the constant-mesh gearbox, as the name implies, all the pairs of gears are in mesh all the time. The gears on the mainshaft are connected to it as required by small selectors which slide on the mainshaft splines and key into the hubs of the gears. Moving these selectors needs much less space and effort than moving whole gear clusters, so the entire gearbox can be made more compact. Because they are much lighter, their speed can be synchronised with that of the gear far more quickly. And in the last thirty years or so, enormous effort has been devoted to refining the synchromesh mechanisms which are built into them, and which are now so effective.

It took time for synchromesh to spread. In the 3-speed gearboxes common in the 1940s, it was usually confined to changes between second and top gear, and a downshift to first on the move still called for double declutching. Today, we would scarcely contemplate a car which didn't have synchromesh on all gears, no matter how many – five, six, or even more. If anything, the centre of interest is now the way in which the selectors themselves are moved – the mechanism which connects the gear lever with the gearbox. There has been a steady move towards cable-operated shifts, partly to achieve easier installation, partly to overcome the problems created by the engine torque-rocking movement in transverse installations, but also to prevent the transmission of vibration along linkages consisting of rigid links. The problems of early cable-operated shifts appear to have been completely overcome. Future interest now appears to be shifting to the hydrostatic shift, which promises to be even lighter and more positive than the best existing linkages.

New gearbox layouts became necessary when rear-engined, and then front-wheel-drive cars became popular. With no in-line drive to the rear wheels, the need was for a gearbox which 'turned round' the drive to emerge from the clutch end. The output could then be fed straight into a final drive unit integrated with the gearbox (forming a transaxle, for rear-wheel-drive cars and front-wheel-drive cars with in-line engines), or sideways via a spur gear to a final drive unit behind the engine and gearbox, as in virtually all

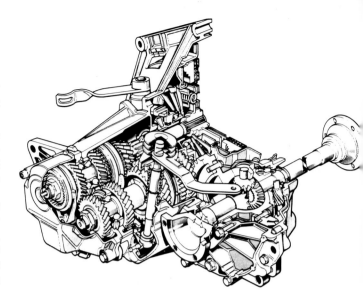

*The apparent complexity of any multi-speed manual gearbox becomes worse when it is installed transversely and shown complete with its integral final drive, as seen in this illustration of the Fiat Tipo transmission of 1988. This particularly clear* *drawing shows the two gearbox shafts, the clutch, the gearshift linkage and selectors and the final drive with its differential – and even the worm drive to the speedometer cable, something which has now given way to electronics.* (Fiat)

transverse front-wheel-drive designs. In such gearboxes, the option of a straight-through direct drive no longer exists. All the drive ratios must be created by gear-pairs, and the gearbox is often called 'all indirect' or 'two-shaft' – rather than a mainshaft, layshaft and output shaft, they consist simply of an input and an output shaft.

The move to more gear ratios, and thus more gear pairs, came as especially bad news to the designers of two-shaft gearboxes for transverse front-engined cars. An in-line gearbox can fairly easily be extended lengthwise to make space for the extra gears – many early 5-speed in-line boxes literally added a small extra casing to an existing 4-speed unit – but the transverse engine and gearbox is always restricted in the amount of width between the front wheel arches. Considerable ingenuity went into overcoming this problem (and, it has to be said, tightness of turning circle was sacrificed in some models) in two-shaft gearboxes; but an alternative was available in the form of the three-shaft layout, which with the help of a more complicated gear selector layout enabled the gearbox length to be reduced by reducing the number of gears on each shaft. The first production car to use this type of layout seems to have been the Volvo 850 with its transverse 5-cylinder engine. Volvo developed an extremely compact 5-speed gearbox, the Type M56, with three shafts and two pinion gears. Two of the shafts are secondary shafts, one carrying the idler gears for the first and second ratios, and the other the idlers for fifth and reverse; the idlers for third and

fourth gears are carried on the primary shaft. The engagement of reverse calls for the meshing of gears on the two secondary shafts. Both secondary shafts are in turn geared to the output shaft, avoiding the need for a separate idler gear. The three-shaft layout of the M56 gearbox makes it only 353mm (14in) long overall, enabling it to be fitted in-line with the 5-cylinder engine and still leave clearance for a typically tight Volvo turning circle.

The Ford B5S 5-speed gearbox fitted to the current Fiesta is more typical of modern two-shaft 5-speed gearboxes for small cars, and includes several features aimed at better refinement and ease of operation. External stiffening ribs have been added to the gearbox casing and the clutch housing to reduce vibration; it has been known for some time that bending of the clutch bell-housing joint under changing load is the cause of many noise and vibration problems, often solved by the addition of stiffening webs between the engine and the gearbox. The Fiesta gearbox also employs double-cone synchronising mechanisms on first, second and third gears, and large single-cone synchronisers on fourth and fifth gears, to improve gearchange quality. Easier gearchanging when cold has been achieved by moving to a new 75W90 synthetic gear oil.

Where 6-speed gearboxes are concerned, some interest lies in the very fact that they are being developed despite the fact that most luxury-class cars are now delivered with automatic transmission. In other words the 6-speed gearbox is finding its way into 'affordable' medium-sized cars, especially in their sporting versions – as models from companies like Fiat, Peugeot and Toyota have shown.

Renault's first production 6-speed gearbox, the PK6, was announced in 2000 as the standard transmission for the futuristic Avantime luxury coupé. Yet again, the PK6 is not all-new, but rather a reworking of the 5-speed PK1 gearbox used in the Laguna, Safrane and Espace, with an added pair of gears to provide the extra ratio. Renault claims the addition of a sixth speed reduces fuel consumption in most driving conditions and also reduces noise levels by 3dB. Renault stresses however that using a sixth speed to provide very high overall gearing is only realistic where the engine has enough torque to

ensure adequate performance without too much changing down – ideal, it suggests, for turbodiesel engines with their very high torque in relation to their more limited power. Audi obviously agrees, since it has for some time equipped the turbodiesel versions of its larger models with 6-speed boxes.

Among the detail changes adopted in converting the Renault PK1 into the 6-speed PK6, the company mentions that the selector forks are now mounted on Teflon coated rails or on needle bearings, for higher efficiency. The redesigned gear cluster is stronger, while also reducing internal friction losses by 20%, and a new synchromesh arrangement on the lowest two gears brings smoother gearchanges. A new lubricant contributes to achieving a uniform gearchange feel at low temperatures and when warm. The gate, with shorter movements made necessary by the 6th gear, gains in precision and in smoothness, with selection efforts reduced by 30%, despite a 40% narrower lever movement between the 1/2 and 5/6 planes (in a 6-speed gearbox, you need four distinct fore-and-aft planes of lever movement, three for the forward gears plus reverse). Fore and aft lever movements are reduced by 10%. It says something for the improvements which can still be squeezed out by clever design and new manufacturing methods that the PK6 gearbox is a fraction (2kg/4.4lb) lighter than its 5-speed predecessor.

At the other end of the size scale, Renault has also shown its latest thinking on an extremely light and compact 5-speed gearbox with a torque capacity of 140Nm (103lb ft), for future small cars. Still a prototype, this EM1 gearbox shows the way in which transmission engineers are thinking about the future. Its designers concentrated on making the gearbox as compact and light as possible – the EM1 weighs only 22kg (48lb) – and on reducing frictional losses in the bearings. Some of the savings depend on new manufacturing methods such as friction welding, avoiding not only the need for some machining but for making space in the design for the machining tools actually to reach in. At present the EM1 is a 2-shaft, 5-speed manual gearbox, but Renault says it can be extended to 6-speed and has been designed for easy 'robotisation' – but that is something for Chapter 11.

# 11 Automatic transmissions

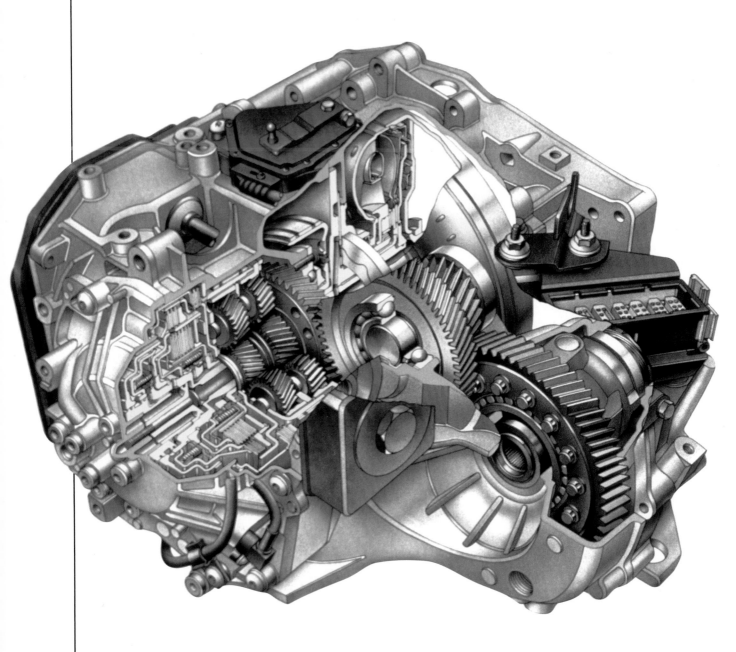

In the early days of motoring, changing gear was sufficiently tricky that many drivers – and inventors – were drawn to the idea of a gearbox that changed gear all by itself. Today, manual gearchanging is easy but traffic in many places is so congested that many drivers prefer automatic transmission to avoid the chore of having to operate the clutch and gearchange hundreds of times in the course of any trip through the centre of a large city.

The challenge of designing a truly automatic transmission comes in two parts. First, you need a gearbox which shifts up or down automatically at the right time. Second, you need some form of automatic clutch so that the car can stop and restart without the driver needing to operate anything more than the brake and accelerator. Early inventive thoughts tended to concentrate on ingenious mechanisms which would duplicate the gearchanging actions of a skilled driver. They didn't work, mainly because in the 1930s suitable technology for detecting and measuring the various factors involved – the engine speed and load, and the accelerator position – simply didn't exist. In the 21st century, thanks to electronics, those means do exist, which is why the 'automated manual gearbox' has attracted renewed attention. In the meantime, however, other forms of automatic transmission have become well established.

# The conventional automatic

The multi-speed automatic transmission with which we are most familiar depends on two main technologies: the torque converter and the epicyclic gearbox. The torque converter evolved from the earlier concept of the fluid flywheel, in which the normal flywheel is replaced by a 'doughnut' sliced into two, one half (the impeller) driven by the engine and the other (the turbine) connected to the gearbox input shaft. By part-filling the doughnut with fluid – with suitable sealing arrangements – and equipping each half of the doughnut with a large number of carefully shaped guide vanes, the engine's drive is transmitted to the gearbox input through the spiral circulation of the fluid within the 'doughnut', which transfers energy from the impeller to the turbine. When there is little or no drive force, the car can easily be held on the brake against any small amount of energy that is still transferred.

The simple fluid flywheel passes on the input torque unchanged, except for a small loss caused by churning of the fluid. However, if a set of stationary guide vanes – a 'stator' – is introduced between the two moving halves, the input torque can be multiplied. This is the

principle of the modern torque converter. Depending on the shape of the stator vanes, multiplications of up to around 2.4:1 can be achieved at low speed (the higher the multiplication, the less efficient the transmission tends to be at normal speeds). The value of the multiplication effect is that it gives much quicker, crisper movement away from rest and enables first gear to be higher, in turn possibly allowing the number of gear ratios to be reduced – although as we shall see, too much advantage can be taken of this option. As the engine speed rises, the multiplication is reduced and at normal driving speeds, there is no multiplication at all – unless, as has been tried in some experimental transmissions, the angle of incidence of the stator guide vanes is varied to align them with the fluid flow and maintain the effect. This is by no means an impractical idea: remember that many modern turbochargers have variable-incidence guide vanes, and most modern jet aero engines control the incidence of the stators which are set between each row of their axial-flow compressor blades. Maintaining torque multiplication at all speeds would enable the number of ratios in the automatic gearbox to be reduced, but on balance engineers have judged it easier to add more ratios than to tackle the complexity of building a variable-geometry torque converter.

The modern torque converter is now a well-tried and extremely reliable component, normally about the same diameter as the flywheel for a manual transmission. The ring of its 'doughnut' is often now flattened into an oval rather than a perfect circle, which saves space (especially in transverse engine, front-wheel-drive installations) without sacrificing any significant efficiency. Most modern converters are also now equipped with a lock-up device to prevent any slip at all when the higher gears are engaged, to improve overall efficiency.

*Opposite: Renault's DP0 automatic transmission is fairly typical of modern units engineered for installation in transverse-engined, front-wheel-drive cars. Renault calls it the 'Pro-active' transmission because of the care which has gone into programming its control unit to make it respond, as far as possible, in the same way as a skilled driver in a car with a manual gearbox. (Renault)*

The other vital component of the conventional automatic transmission, the epicyclic gearbox, depends on principles which have been known for a long time, yet still cause some confusion. The simple epicyclic gear train takes a central 'sun' gear and an outer ring-gear with its teeth on the inside, and connects the two with a series of (usually three) 'planet' gears mounted on a carrier frame. In theory, any one of the three parts can be driven while a second is held stationary by some kind of brake, and the output can be taken by the third. Several more

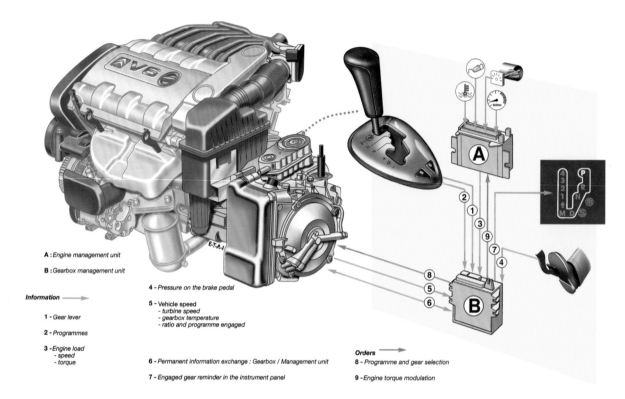

**A** : Engine management unit

**B** : Gearbox management unit

**Information** →

**1** - Gear lever

**2** - Programmes

**3** - Engine load
   - speed
   - torque

**4** - Pressure on the brake pedal

**5** - Vehicle speed
   - turbine speed
   - gearbox temperature
   - ratio and programme engaged

**6** - Permanent information exchange : Gearbox / Management unit

**7** - Engaged gear reminder in the instrument panel

**Orders** →

**8** - Programme and gear selection

**9** - Engine torque modulation

*The modern trend to make automatic transmissions capable of sequential shifting (one gear at a time up or down with each forward or aft movement of the selector lever) has involved extra complexity in the electronic control systems and the way in which signals are processed. Note the separate engine and transmission control units, in constant dialogue. (Citroën)*

complicated variations on this basic theme exist, some of them 'inside out' and others with doubled-up planet wheels, but the important aspect of all of them is that with a suitable layout of interlinked epicyclic gear trains, and of brake bands or automatic clutches to hold and release their various parts, different gear ratios can be selected without needing to disconnect the drive from the engine. The brake bands are wrapped around the outside of epicyclic gearsets to hold or release the outer ring gear, while the automatic clutches are multi-plate 'wet' units (that is, filled with transmission fluid) which can be made both compact, powerful and progressive in operation. Once the basic gearbox has been designed, all that remains is to design a control system which ensures the gearchanges take place at suitable times.

In fact, this is such a challenge that the first serious applications of fluid flywheel and epicyclic gearbox technology, on European luxury cars of the 1930s, of which Daimler was the best known (and also on a whole generation of London buses), left actual gear selection to the driver. The Wilson pre-selector

gearbox was operated by moving a small selector lever – in later cars, an electric switch – into position to select the next gear needed, up or down. The actual change was then effected by pressing once on a pedal – where a normal clutch pedal would be – which provided the hydro-mechanical impulse to release a brake band on the ring gear of one epicyclic train, and simultaneously (or near enough) apply another band to a different train. The fluid flywheel meant no action was needed when coming to rest and setting off (other than to engage first gear), and drivers who became used to the Wilson transmission actually enjoyed the way they could select the correct gear in advance, for instance when approaching a corner, and then engage it instantly with a single foot movement at exactly the right moment. The transmission also lent itself to what is now known as 'sequential' selection, with a simple fore-and-aft lever pushed one way to pre-select the next gear up, and the other way for the next gear down. Some post-war British luxury cars, such as the big Armstrong-Siddeleys, used the Wilson pre-selector transmission well into the 1950s.

Eventually, however, American engineers found satisfactory methods of making gear selection completely automatic, and from the 1940s onwards such transmissions became increasingly popular in the USA. European drivers largely resisted them on the grounds that they were heavy and expensive, that they reduced car performance and increased fuel consumption, and above all perhaps that the early automatics by no means changed gear when the driver would have chosen to. Certainly some of the early automatics offered in medium-sized European cars were poorly suited for their task. Probably the worst suited of all was the 2-speed Powerglide transmission offered as an option on the Vauxhall Victor during the 1960s; what was a passable transmission when coupled to a 'lazy' 5-litre V8 in a land of freeways became almost frightening when teamed with a 1.6-litre engine and confronted with the need to overtake on a busy two-way road. Eventually the automatic transmission specialists acknowledged that even with a torque converter to help with the standing start, the average medium-sized European car needed at least a 4-speed gearbox.

Meanwhile, the problem of better response and a feeling of more willing automatic gearchanging was tackled in two stages. First, the amazingly complicated hydro-mechanical control systems developed by the Americans were replaced by electronic control – Renault claims to have been the first manufacturer in the world to put an electronically controlled automatic into production, in the mid-1970s. Second, in a move led by the Japanese, the ability of modern computer systems to react in an 'adaptive' way, using so-called 'fuzzy logic', enabled automatic transmissions finally to be persuaded to change gear very much as a skilled and sympathetic driver might – not merely at certain combinations of engine speed and load, but according to driving conditions and even the driver's style and attitude. These control systems can not only distinguish between a smooth, gentle driver and an aggressive one, but any shade of attitude between the two extremes. As such, they are a step beyond the selector switches provided in some up-market transmissions, with which the driver can select 'comfort', 'normal' or 'sport' for him or herself. Such transmissions are always now programmed to avoid unwanted upshifts if the driver lifts off the accelerator, especially when travelling downhill; automatic downshifts during firm braking are another feature which would have seemed strange (but welcome) to the automatic transmission user of twenty years ago. The one thing which is still usually left to the driver in these 'fuzzy logic' transmissions is to select the 'winter' setting, which prevents the engagement of first gear to avoid the danger of wheelspin on snow or icy surfaces.

*The Mercedes 5-speed automatic transmission in the S-class demonstrates just how complex such units can be. Note the preference for multi-plate clutches rather than the brake bands so often used in early transmissions. Multi-plate clutch units can be 'tuned' for much smoother operation, to the point where shifting becomes almost imperceptible, except by engine note as the speed changes.* (Mercedes)

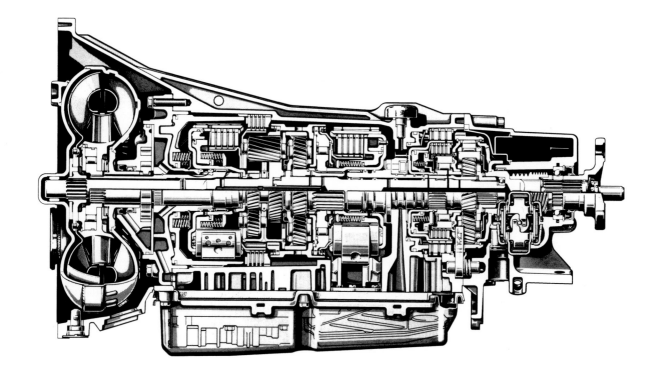

# The spread of the automatic

This change to flexible and capable electronic control should have removed one of the main objections to automatic transmission – the feeling that a skilled driver would do better selecting the shift points through sheer judgement. In Europe at least, many drivers have still to discover how good the new generation of automatics really is, and in southern Europe there remains a feeling that automatic transmission is in some way a denial of the driver's right and duty to be in charge. Elsewhere in the world things are different. Once they became sufficiently affluent, Japanese motorists mainly followed the American lead, although their manufacturers were careful to adapt their automatics to local needs. In 2000, the automatic share of the American market was around 90%, of the Japanese market nearly 80%, and of the European market only around 15%, with a higher proportion in the UK, Germany and Scandinavia, but a near insignificant share in Italy and Spain.

A few conventional 3-speed automatics remain in production in the USA but the vast majority in all markets now are at least 4-speed, with a growing number of 5-speed units and one or two offered with six forward speeds. There are two current trends in the European (and Japanese) development of 4-speed transmissions. The first is to improve their suitability for medium-sized and small transverse-engined, front-wheel-drive cars, in which demand for automatic transmission is slowly increasing. To meet this need, transmissions need to be not only compact, light and relatively cheap, but also efficient, since the owners of smaller cars are more likely to be aware of and sensitive to fuel economy.

One recently introduced 4-speed unit for small and medium-sized cars which reflects these needs was developed in a joint venture set up by PSA Peugeot-Citroën specifically for this purpose. Before the new transmission was developed, PSA bought almost exclusively from ZF, while Renault built some transmissions for itself, but had also created a joint venture with Volkswagen to build 4-speed transmissions for transverse-engined front-wheel-drive cars. The new transmission will serve most of the needs of both PSA and Renault except for their larger and more powerful models. Because the unit was from the start intended for cars as small as the Peugeot 206 and Renault Clio, it had to be small enough to fit – which meant it had to be 4-speed rather than 5-speed (and keeping down cost was also a consideration). Renault, which was first to introduce the new unit, says that developing a new automatic transmission costs roughly twice as much as developing a new manual gearbox. This makes the idea of sharing the cost with another manufacturer very attractive.

To keep the cost as low as possible, the transmission was designed above all to be cheap to make, and embodies several ingenious ideas for reducing the number of separate parts to a minimum. Unlike many earlier transmissions which needed their fluid changing at specified intervals, the PSA/Renault unit is effectively 'lubricated for life' with a specially developed lubricant intended to survive for at least 150,000km (93,000 miles). The lubricant depends for its long life on efficient temperature control, and for this purpose Valeo developed a new high-efficiency oil/coolant heat exchanger which forms an integral part of the transmission.

In its search for high efficiency, and hence good fuel economy, the PSA/Renault team chose to use several high-technology features, including torque converter lock-up in all forward gears, and an electronic control system (from Siemens) exploiting 'fuzzy logic'. The control strategy is not, in fact, completely 'fuzzy' in its decision-making, but instead uses 'fuzzy switching' between a number of characteristic curves stored in the control unit's memory, each suited to a particular circumstance.

'Adaptive' control strategies have been adopted for most of the 5-speed automatic transmissions now being produced in Europe and Japan. These are mainly used in large, luxury-class cars although Mercedes, which makes its own transmissions, has adopted 5-speed transmissions across its entire range, including the small A-class. ZF supplies its 5-speed transmissions to Audi, BMW, Jaguar and Volkswagen. Ford and GM (Vauxhall/Opel), both of whom make their own automatic transmissions in Europe, have been slower to move up from 4-speed to 5-speed automatics; the new Mondeo for example still uses a 4-speed unit. However, GM announced in 1997 that it had completed the engineering of a 5-speed unit for in-line transmissions, the 5L40-E, and would build it – together with the outwardly similar 4-speed 4L40-E – at its Strasbourg transmission plant. GM has also announced an agreement to supply Volvo with automatic transmissions (until now, the Swedish company has imported Japanese-built units from Aisin-Warner). The new front-wheel-drive Volvo S80 has thus become the first European application for the 4-speed 4T65-E transmission, designed for transverse front-wheel-drive installation, and supplied from GM transmission plants in the USA. This unit is used in the 6-cylinder versions of the S80, the less powerful 5-cylinder versions being equipped with a 5-speed automatic from Aisin of Japan.

The latest 5-speed transmission developed for

luxury-class Mercedes models shows just how sophisticated the most advanced multi-speed automatics have become. This completely new design achieves its five forward ratios (and two reverse ratios) with only three epicyclic gearsets and six selector brake units – all of which are multi-plate clutches – compared with the four gearsets and seven selector units of the previous Mercedes 5-speed unit. This has resulted in a significantly smaller and lighter transmission, especially bearing in mind that it has sufficient torque capacity to cope with the output of Mercedes's V12 engine. The complete unit is 600mm (23.6in) long and weighs 80kg (176lb), and the number of separate components has been reduced from 1,160 to 630. Much of the weight reduction is due to the use of pressed sheet metal parts instead of forgings and castings, an approach also seen in the PSA/Renault transmission.

Although the torque converter fitted to the new Mercedes transmission is generally conventional, with lock-up on third, fourth and fifth gears, it deliberately allows a small and controlled amount of slip, from 20 to 80rpm relative speed between input and output, at all times. Mercedes says this trick prevents the transmission from behaving like a solidly locked member which might suffer more severe noise and vibration problems. While a slipping torque converter is an excellent isolator of vibration, the company argues, a solidly locked converter is not. By allowing a small degree of slip, the need for other vibration-control measures such as torsional vibration dampers and balancing inertias, which add both weight and cost, is avoided.

It remains to be seen whether 5-speed automatic transmissions will spread downwards from the top end of the market, or whether the 4-speed unit will remain the standard for most small and medium-sized cars (other than the Mercedes A-class). In the longer term, if the quest for extreme fuel economy encourages a move towards smaller engines with high specific power output in relatively narrow speed ranges, it may become essential to use transmissions with more speeds and a wider spread of ratios. At that point, however, the growing challenge of the continuously variable transmission (CVT – see later in this chapter), with its ability to offer a very wide spread of ratios while also being able to allow the engine to run at whatever speed delivers the highest efficiency for the driver's demanded torque output, may become overwhelming.

Apart from its reluctance to embrace automatic transmission as readily as the other developed markets, Europe also presents engineers with a unique challenge because its market contains so many drivers who insist on retaining ultimate control over the choice of gear ratio, even with an automatic. This has led to the development of a number of systems which lack a common sense of purpose. On the one hand, automatic clutch arrangements such as Renault's Easy system, discussed in Chapter 10, are aimed mainly at removing the effort of manual clutch operation without going to the expense of a full automatic. At the other extreme are transmissions like BMW's Selectronic and Porsche's Tiptronic, in which automatic shifting can be inhibited and the driver shifts up or down, one gear at a time, by moving a lever backwards and forwards or by pressing buttons or 'paddles' built into the steering wheel, in the fashion of a Formula 1 racing car. Such an arrangement is easily added to the control electronics of a modern automatic transmission, with hardly any extra hardware apart from the selector switches. The well-off enthusiasts at whom these systems are aimed should note, perhaps, that modern F1 cars are steered with less than half a turn of the wheel (actually, more of a yoke) in each direction, so the racing driver never moves his hands away from the gear selector paddles. This can't be said of any road car – at least, not yet.

# The **belt-drive CVT**

The history of the CVT (continuously variable transmission) in passenger cars can be traced back through several decades and several forms of transmission. However, it was the DAF Variomatic transmission of the 1950s which provided the technical origin of the CVT as it is now generally understood. The Variomatic used continuous rubber drive belts running between conical pulley sheaves, the distance between the sheaves being varied so as to alter the operating radius of the 'master' pulley and therefore in turn of the spring-loaded 'slave' pulley, the whole arrangement being known as the 'variator'. The Variomatic was succeeded by the Van Doorne Transmatic, in which the rubber belt was replaced by a belt consisting of carefully shaped steel blocks strung on a flexible steel band. Although the Transmatic differed fundamentally from the Variomatic in that the transmission of drive from one pulley to another was now via belt-block compression rather than belt tension, the twin-pulley arrangement remained visually much the same. The advantage of the new arrangement was that for a transmission of given size, the Transmatic was capable of handling considerably higher torque, although it was some time before the system was asked to accept more than about 150Nm (111lb ft).

While providing any desired gear ratio between the upper and lower limits set by the shape and size of the pulleys, the belt-driven CVT has no neutral position and therefore needs some form of clutching

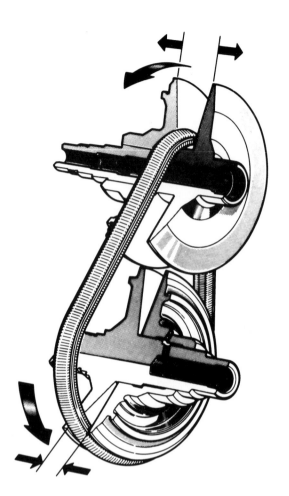
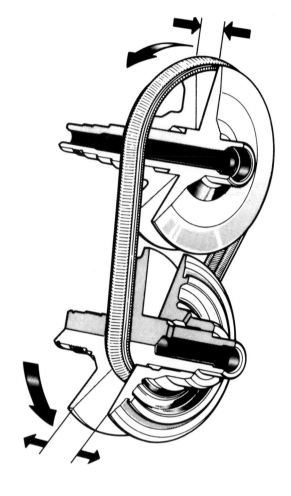

*The basic principle of the belt-drive CVT is shown in this diagram. In this case the belt is of the steel-block type developed by van Doorne for its Transmatic transmission, licensed to Fiat and Ford. (Fiat)*

arrangement as well as a means of reversing the drive. Without some form of automatic clutch, the belt-and-pulley CVT – and, indeed, other forms of CVT discussed later – cannot function as a fully automatic transmission. The easiest way to provide reverse is to fit a single epicyclic gear train and brake to reverse the output from the variator. Such an arrangement means the car can theoretically go as fast backwards as it can forwards (and the early DAF models would do just that) – but travelling very fast in reverse can be dangerous, and modern CVT systems generally provide some means of limiting speed in reverse, for instance by preventing the variator from moving out of its lowest ratio.

The Variomatic and early Transmatic systems used a centrifugal clutch to overcome the problem of stopping and starting from rest without undue cost penalty, but despite several stages of refinement, this

system never provided a completely happy solution with smooth starting from rest and stopping – there was always some jerkiness, even with 'two-stage' engagement as speed increased. Subaru, the first Japanese car manufacturer to adopt the CVT in its Justy supermini, achieved better results with an electromagnetic iron-powder clutch, with computer control of the clutching current. This solution was also adopted by Nissan when applying the CVT to the Micra.

Although it adds to the cost, one very good solution is a conventional torque converter. This provides much smoother starting from rest, and its torque multiplication effect can be used either to achieve quicker 'step-off' or to raise the lowest CVT gear ratio, which enables the pulley system to be made more compact. Such an approach was suggested by the German automatic transmission specialist ZF, which first showed its Ecotronic belt-and-pulley CVT in 1995. By 1998 the company had evolved the Ecotronic into a family of three units of varying size and torque capacity, the CFT13 (130Nm/96lb ft), CFT18 (180Nm/133lb ft), and

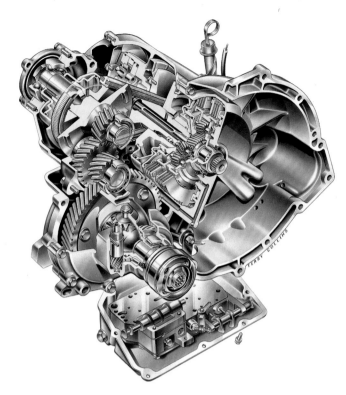

CFT25 (250Nm/185lb ft). On the basis that naturally aspirated modern engines deliver around 90Nm (66lb ft) per litre of capacity (Ford's 2.5-litre 24-valve Duratec V6, for example, produces 220Nm/162 ft lb of torque), the CFT25 is well matched to the needs of medium-large European cars – the Mondeo, Vectra and Passat class. The CFT13 and CFT18 use a 24mm (0.9in) wide belt; the CFT25 belt is 30mm (1.2in) wide. The variator pulleys are of larger outer diameter in the higher-capacity units, but the difference is smaller than might be expected; the CFT25 pulleys are 19% bigger than those of the CFT13.

The ZF Ecotronic's torque converter has mechanical lock-up, as in a conventional modern automatic. A single epicyclic geartrain between the converter and the input to the drive pulley provides reverse gear, engaged and disengaged through the operation of multi-plate clutch and brake units. Although the CVT is ideally suited to transverse-engine, front-wheel-drive packages, ZF has engineered layouts to suit both rear-wheel-drive vehicles, and front-wheel-drive vehicles with in-line rather than transverse engines (in this case, very clearly with existing customer BMW in mind). The design approach to creating these different layouts was 'modular', making the greatest possible use of components from the basic transverse-engine front-wheel-drive package.

The Ecotronic uses an advanced electronic control system, borrowing in some respects from ZF's huge experience of adaptive control for its current production 4-speed and 5-speed units. Fuzzy logic is used to specify the operating point at any moment, taking information from a number of sources, naturally including the driver's input and stored knowledge of the engine characteristics. In principle, says ZF, the operating point is that which yields optimum specific fuel consumption, but is modified by an 'adaptation factor' which is infinitely variable between the two extremes of optimum fuel economy and maximum power. Engine speed increases whenever the driver demands higher output, or when road conditions dictate that more engine power is needed, such as when climbing a hill.

Honda, which developed its own CVT technology using the steel-belt-and-pulley principle, went a stage further by adopting a computer-controlled multi-plate 'wet' clutch for starting from rest. It fitted this transmission to the medium-sized Civic, powered by a 1.6-litre engine developing a maximum 140Nm (103ft lb) torque output. Among other significant developments adopted by Honda was computer-controlled (from the engine and transmission management system) pressure on the moving sheaves of both pulleys, ensuring that the pressure was always sufficient for reliable transmission without being excessive. Too tight a 'squeeze' on either pulley reduces mechanical efficiency as well as increasing the risk of belt wear and of noise problems. The programming of the Civic CVT was specifically aimed at achieving a good match with the engine's best specific fuel consumption, and it was claimed that the CVT's fuel economy in the urban cycle was 15% better than achieved with a conventional 4-speed automatic.

These claims appear to have been borne out by results achieved by the Civic in service, but it is worth noting that in the latest Civic, launched in 2000, Honda has chosen to offer a 4-speed automatic option rather than the CVT. This is partly because many drivers have a problem – in effect, a psychological problem – because in a car with a CVT, the engine noise is not directly related to what the car is doing. With manual gearboxes or multi-speed automatics, the driver hears a rising engine note all the time the car is accelerating, punctuated by sudden drops with each shift to a higher gear. But with a CVT, the car can be accelerating hard but with a constant engine note, because the CVT is holding the engine at the best rpm for acceleration. The performance is actually good, but because it doesn't *sound* good in the conventional sense, the driver has the impression that the car is sluggish and unwilling. This has led some manufacturers to adapt their CVT control systems to provide a number of fixed gear ratios, thus overcoming the psychological problem. In theory, any number of ratios could be provided but six or seven seem to be the most frequent choices. It is then easy to provide the driver with a 'flick-shift' facility for manually selecting one ratio up or down at a time; and true fully-variable CVT operation can still be retained as a separate mode if desired.

## ■Gear ratio of EXTROID CVT

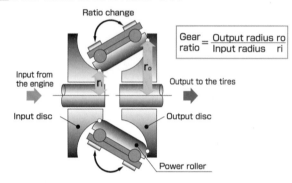

*Nissan has become one of the main exponents of the belt-drive, variable-pulley CVT,* *and brought a new level of refinement and efficiency to the concept.* (Nissan)

Nissan seems to have been the first manufacturer to adopt this approach with its Hyper CVT-M6, announced in 1997 with a control system that included six predetermined ratios – the lowest and highest possible, and four evenly spaced between them. The Hyper CVT-M6 allowed the car either to operate in its most economical auto-CVT mode, or in any of the six predetermined ratios – subject to protection against engine overspeeding, for example. Nissan's example has since been followed by some other CVT users. Nissan had developed the Hyper CVT, which uses a torque converter for starting from rest, for installation in cars with engines up to 2-litre capacity. The transmission was claimed to improve fuel economy by 20% in the Japanese 10–15 mode emissions cycle, when compared with a conventional 4-speed automatic, without any sacrifice in performance. By 1999 the Hyper CVT was offered in a wide range of Nissan models in the Japanese market, and it appeared in Europe (in the Primera and the Tino mini-MPV) in 2000. Nissan has also now developed a smaller version, still working on the same principles, for Micra-class models with engines up to 1.3-litre capacity. The company has also exploited the characteristics of the CVT by teaming it with its own new direct-injection gasoline engine, whose engine management unit works on the basis of interpreting

the accelerator pedal position as a torque output demand. The control unit transmits 'drive-by-wire' outputs both to the engine itself and to the CVT, using the latter to 'position' the output so that the torque is as required by the driver. At the same time, as far as possible, the engine's operating regime remains within the limits of the stratified-charge, 'lean-burn' envelope, for improved fuel economy.

Audi's new Multitronic CVT uses a slightly different approach, allowing the engine speed to increase with road speed at a rate fast enough to satisfy the driver that the car is accelerating strongly. This sacrifices some of the theoretical performance and economy advantages of 'pure' CVT operation, but not nearly as much as shifting between a fixed set of ratios. Like the Honda system, the Multitronic uses a wet multi-plate clutch to take up the drive from rest. Audi's drive belt works under tension and transmits torque through the friction of pins running through the links of the belt and bearing against the pulley faces. Audi claims that in the A6 2.8 V6, the Multitronic achieves strong economy and performance gains over a conventional 5-speed automatic transmission, and marginal gains even when compared with a manual transmission.

In the future, the appeal of the CVT may become stronger because of the ease with which it can be adapted to different powertrains, especially hybrids. The Toyota Prius hybrid car uses a CVT as standard; and indeed virtually every Japanese manufacturer has shown a concept vehicle or a technology-demonstrator drivetrain with a CVT. In most cases the units used torque converters to connect the transmission to the engine. Mitsubishi's HSR-VI concept car, for example, was powered by the company's GDI (gasoline direct injection) engine driving through a CVT. Mitsubishi makes the interesting point that it has adapted its INVECS-II 'fuzzy logic' programming – the first to be applied to a conventional 4-speed automatic transmission – to its CVT, indicating the inherent flexibility of this programming approach.

# Toroidal drives

Another CVT concept uses a tilting roller running between two bowls, one driven by the engine, the other with an output to the driven wheels. The two face-to-face bowls form something like a doughnut or toroid, hence the name often applied to this kind of transmission. According to the angle of the roller, the output roller may be driven at the same speed as the input – when the roller is horizontal – or faster, or slower. Again, a separate clutching provision needs to be made for starting from rest, and for providing a reverse gear. Although such transmissions were actually offered during the 1930s as the Perbury-Hayes system, durability and torque capacity suffered through lack of the right materials and technology. The key problem is that the transmission of torque depends entirely on the friction contact between the rollers and the bowls, and the higher the torque, the higher the friction needs to be in the very small area available. Thus pressures need to be higher, and the danger of damage to bowl and roller

*At the 1999 Tokyo Motor Show Mazda displayed this ingenious transmission which combines two half-toroidal CVT units (lower section) and a two-speed epicyclic geartrain, plus two automatic clutches. For starting, the epicyclic train gears down the overall ratio for greater torque output; at high speed, the drive is taken directly from the output of the toroidal unit. The final-drive unit is at top left; the whole unit is clearly engineered for a transverse engine and front-wheel-drive. (Mazda)*

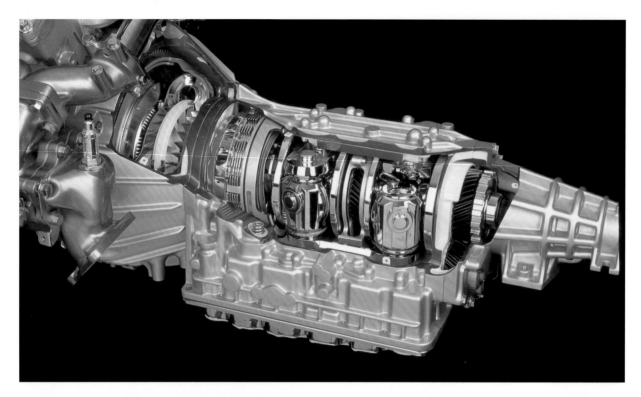

*Nissan's Extroid transmission uses twin toroidal CVT units with the drive split between them to keep the overall unit slim. This transmission has been engineered for in-line installation in a powerful rear-wheel-drive car and is now in limited-volume production, but only for the Japanese home market.* (Nissan)

becomes greater. This happens despite the fact that the contact is not metal-to-metal, but (as in engine main bearings) actually takes place through a very thin layer of fluid lubricant. The trouble is that this lubricant must protect the two surfaces, yet at the same time transmit the torque: to achieve both these aims it cannot be too 'slippery'.

For many years, pioneering development work on the toroidal drive was carried out by a British company, Torotrak, which achieved a number of vital advances in detail design and control, and demonstrated a number of successful prototypes. Torotrak's work continues, but in the meantime Nissan took an interest in the concept and now uses it in small-scale production.

Nissan calls its design the Extroid CVT, and has engineered it as an in-line unit for use in rear-wheel-drive cars. In 1997 the company showed a demonstration unit in which the input torque was split between two toroidal variators operating in parallel, thus reducing the diameter of the unit as a whole. At that time Nissan pointed to the use of special steels, and to extensive research carried out

into the properties of the high-shear lubrication/transmission oils, as two of the factors which had enabled this type of transmission to be made both reliable and efficient. By 1999, Nissan had put the Extroid into low-volume production for the luxury-class Cedric and Gloria saloons for the Japanese market only. These two related models are powered by a 3-litre V6 engine, indicating the level of torque which the transmission is able to handle.

# Automated manual gearboxes

There has been some European interest in the idea of the 'automated manual gearbox', using electronic control and modern transducers to achieve a result which proved beyond so many inventors, using purely mechanical means, in the 1930s. BMW was the first manufacturer to offer such a unit, which it designates Sequential M Gearbox (SMG). This transmission, offered as an option on the high performance M3 version of the 3-series, has six forward speeds and two alternative servo-controlled operating modes. In the first, which BMW has elected to call 'Economy', gearbox operation is entirely automatic, as in any conventional automatic transmission. The unit defaults to this mode whenever the ignition is switched off. In the second, 'Sports' mode, the driver selects upward and downward shifts in 'Tiptronic' fashion. The driver switches between the two modes by rocking the selector lever sideways. Upshifts can be made without lifting off the accelerator. There is no 'safety' upshift, although the engine is protected from overspeeding by an ignition governor. A safety override is provided, however, to prevent engine damage resulting from downshifting at too high a speed. The gearbox also automatically downshifts to second gear if the speed falls below 15km/h (9mph), and to first gear if the car comes to rest. The electronic control settings of the SMG can easily be reprogrammed according to need, and BMW says its Economy-mode shift points were reset for the UK market, to avoid 'hunting' between the lower gears when negotiating roundabouts.

A similar concept was later announced by Valeo and Renault, though without the sporting overtones. The Boite de Vitesses Automatisée (BVA) uses the Valeo servo clutch unit (described previously) together with an adapted version of a Renault 5-speed manual gearbox with full servo operation of gear selection. The advantages claimed by Renault for the BVA include lower weight, lower cost and higher efficiency than a conventional automatic, with equivalent or better performance.

Although, when viewed in a world-wide perspective, these robotised-manual developments seem rather on the fringe of the technical mainstream, they have been backed by the respected research company Ricardo, which says that in some of its latest studies on economy optimisation in simulated conditions, its best figures have been achieved using its own automated layshaft transmission (ALT), whose operating principle resembles that of the SMG although not offering the 'flick-shift' sporting option. Ricardo points to the small but decisive advantage enjoyed by constant-mesh layshaft gearboxes in terms of mechanical efficiency; such units are usually around 97% efficient, while the best a conventional automatic may hope for, even with torque converter lockup and minimised oil pumping losses, is around 95%.

# 12 Propeller shafts, driveshafts and final drives

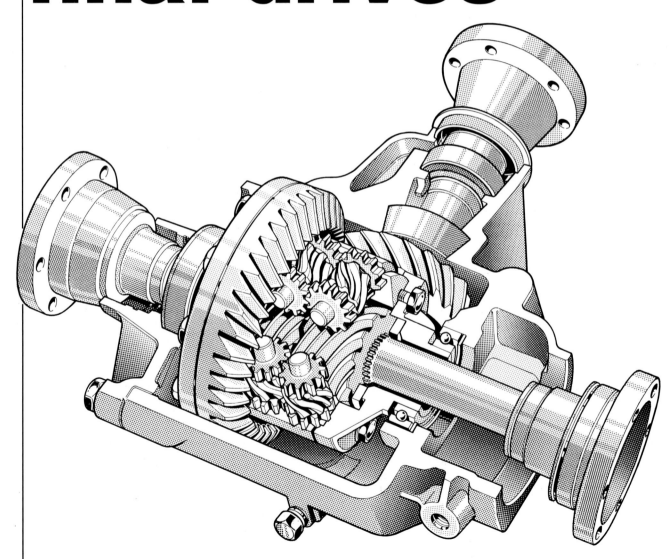

**T**he components which take the output from the gearbox and deliver it to the driven wheels tend to be the 'ugly ducklings' of the transmission business, but they are vital none the less. Some tricky engineering challenges must be overcome, because the wheels must be free to move up and down as they are driven, and in front-wheel-drive cars they need to be steered as well. Looming over the transmission engineers, like all their counterparts, is the need to do the job at minimum cost, weight and bulk, and with maximum reliability.

In a rear-wheel-drive car, of the kind which used to be regarded as conventional until the 1960s, the transmission downstream of the gearbox consisted basically of a propeller shaft taking the drive to a final-drive unit between the rear wheels, and drive shafts from the final drive to the wheels themselves. The rear wheels, the final drive and the axle connecting them might be free to rise and fall as a single unit, in which case the drive shafts were housed within the axle tube and the entire assembly was known as a 'live' axle. Alternatively the final drive might be attached to the body, and the drive shafts taking the torque from the final drive to the wheels would (in most cases) need to be equipped with joints and with some means of allowing for small changes in length as the wheels moved up and down independently – the arrangement known as independent rear suspension, to be discussed in more detail in Part 3. In a few cars, the gearbox was moved to the rear to form a single unit with the final drive; all such cars used independent rear suspension. Virtually all the rear-wheel-drive cars in production today also use independent rear suspension, although many commercial vehicles retain live rear axles.

In a front-wheel-drive car of the kind which now accounts for the vast majority of production worldwide, the final drive forms a single unit with the gearbox, and the 'downstream' transmission consists only of the two drive shafts, neatly underlining the great advantage of front-wheel-drive in doing away with the weight and cost of the propeller shaft and the space its tunnel takes up in passing through the body. The penalty is the need to use more complicated and expensive joints to carry the drive 'round the corner' when the front wheels are turned through a large steering angle.

# Final-drive units

So long as only two wheels of a vehicle are driven, the transmission needs to include only a single final-drive unit, to split the single input from the gearbox into twin outputs to the wheels. This final-drive unit normally combines two functions. It acts as a reduction gear to drop the speed of the gearbox output to the speed of the wheels, and it includes a differential assembly to split the input torque exactly 50:50 between the driven wheels, while also allowing them to turn at different speeds when the vehicle is cornering (since the inner wheel of the two turns more slowly than the outer). The needs of vehicles in which all four wheels are driven are discussed in Chapter 13.

The reduction gear ratio of a conventional final-drive unit is created by a small input drive pinion gear meshing with a much larger 'crownwheel'. The reduction ratio is normally between about 3:1 and 5:1. There are two reasons for using the final drive to gear down the speed. First, if the entire ratio of first gear – normally between 16:1 and 20:1 – had to be built into the gearbox, the box would become horribly large and heavy, because first gear would call for a pair of gears of which one was 16 times the diameter of the other. Dropping the speed in two stages makes everything lighter and more compact. This apart, in rear-wheel-drive cars, if the entire reduction was built into the gearbox, the propeller shaft would need to be strong enough to withstand the entire multiplied torque of first gear, rather than around a quarter of it, and would (again) become bigger and heavier. As things are, in any rear-wheel-drive car, the fully multiplied torque only emerges from the final-drive unit – and then it is split in two, so that each drive shaft need (normally) only be strong enough to withstand half of it. It is worth noting that if a car's transmission fails through gross overstressing – for example, by 'dropping the clutch' with a fast-revving engine in an attempt to start from rest up a steep hill – the failure normally takes place either in one of the small output gears from the differential, or at the wheel end of one drive shaft, usually through spline failure. Propeller shaft failures are rare; gearbox failures are usually due to other causes.

Because the final-drive ratio multiplies the main gearbox ratios, a higher (numerically lower) final drive ratio both raises the overall gearing, and spreads the gear ratios. It is therefore normal practice to adjust the overall gearing – for example, to allow for engines of different sizes and torque outputs in different versions of the same model – by the relatively cheap and easy process of changing the

*Opposite: The Torsen (TORque SENsing) differential transfers torque towards the side with the best grip in a purely mechanical way. Exactly how it does it, via the geared-together worm wheels which bridge the input gears to the two drive shafts, is something that takes a working model fully to understand! More seriously, the amount of precision machining and assembly involved means the Torsen is very expensive. (Lancia)*

final-drive ratio while retaining, as far as possible, a standard gearbox. Some manufacturers used to offer buyers a choice of final-drive ratios, but this practice has ceased with the need to certify cars as meeting exhaust emission standards with standard overall gearing. The final-drive ratio is normally changed by fitting an input drive pinion, and if necessary a crownwheel, with different numbers of gear teeth. Designers normally ensure that the number of teeth on the crownwheel is not a perfect multiple of the number of teeth on the pinion, so as to avoid any danger of the gears 'resonating in phase' with the risk of failure. Thus the majority of final-drive units use primary numbers of teeth, typically 37, 41, 43 or 47, on the crownwheel.

All modern final-drive units in rear-wheel-drive transmissions use 'hypoid' or spiral-bevel rather than straight-bevel gearing. This form of gearing enables the drive pinion gear, and therefore the aft end of the propeller shaft, to be set below the centre-line of the crownwheel, in turn enabling the propeller shaft tunnel to be made shallower and smaller. Hypoid gearing also means that more than one pair of gear teeth is in contact at any time, which spreads the driving stress and helps to alleviate noise problems. For the same reason, spur-gear drives to transverse front-engine final drives always use helical rather than straight-cut gears. The only technical drawback is that hypoid gearing means that contact between gear teeth involves sliding as well as rolling motion, calling for the use of special lubricants capable of resisting higher shear forces.

The conventional differential unit splits the input drive exactly 50:50 between its two outputs, whatever the circumstances. This is normally what is needed, since an uneven split would tend to make the car veer off course; for special applications, such as the centre differential of a four-wheel-drive vehicle (see Chapter 13) the differential can be designed to split the input torque in any desired ratio. The drawback of the perfect 50:50 split in all circumstances is that if one wheel of a driven pair is unable to transmit any significant torque – if it is sitting on an ultra-low friction surface, for example, or if it has lifted clear of the road surface on the inside of a sharp corner – then no significant torque can be delivered to the opposite wheel, and drive is lost. In the first of these cases, the vehicle is immobilised; in the second, there is some danger of loss of control, either immediately or when the inside wheel suddenly regains its grip at the exit from the corner. Accordingly, there has long been interest in devising means of limiting the differential action – hence 'limited-slip differential' – to enable the better-gripping wheel to transmit some torque. The simplest approach is to provide some means, usually a form of dog-clutch, to lock the differential completely, but such a lock can only be engaged at a standstill and is useful only in off-road vehicles. Other, more complex units employ a variety of means to limit the amount of slip progressively, and on the move. The principle is usually to sense a growing difference in speed between the two driven wheels (as the 'cage' of the differential unit spins faster and faster) and to apply what amounts to a braking torque to the faster-spinning wheel. The slower-turning wheel – the one with the better grip – can then transmit at least that much torque, plus any torque which the faster wheel can still accept.

The challenge is to limit the amount of slip without interfering with the very necessary action of the differential in allowing the driven wheels to turn at slightly different speeds in normal cornering – if the slip limitation engages too early, it can be a serious nuisance. Too much slip limitation when fully engaged is also a bad thing, not only because of the danger of upsetting the car's handling by transferring the entire drive torque to a single tyre which will probably not be able to handle it, but also because the drive shaft will need to be made stronger and heavier to avoid the risk of failure. Limited-slip arrangements for final drives are therefore normally designed to transfer no more than a proportion of the drive torque to the 'good' wheel. The older mechanical devices were often referred to as (for instance) '20% limited-slip', meaning that only one-fifth of the drive torque would be transferred if one wheel was spinning helplessly. Such a proportion is a reasonable compromise for a high-performance road-going car; racing cars may use much 'tighter' units.

The means by which drive torque can be transferred from one side of a differential to the other can include friction plate or cone clutches, or viscous couplings which bridge the two output sides of the differential. The viscous coupling resembles a multi-plate clutch in containing sets of closely spaced, interleaved plates attached to the shafts coupled to either side, in a housing filled with special viscous fluid. This leaves the shafts free to rotate slowly relative to each other, but as the speed difference increases, the viscous fluid acts more nearly like a solid, binding the plates together and preventing excessive slip. Units based on the viscous coupling have been adopted for limited-slip applications by several vehicle manufacturers, and specialist companies have engineered transmission units which incorporate these devices, for application in both rear-wheel-drive and front-wheel-drive transmissions.

Another type of limited-slip unit is the Torsen (TORque SENsing) differential, in which a complex worm-drive mechanism positively transfers torque towards the higher-capacity side whenever a speed

*GKN's Visco Lok differential uses an extremely compact viscous coupling to transfer torque from one output to the other whenever a speed difference occurs. It can be used as a centre differential, or as a limited-slip final drive differential with a crown wheel bolted to its outer flange. The amount of torque transfer and the speed of the limited slip effect depends on the spacing of the coupling plates and the properties of the viscous fluid. (GKN)*

difference arises. The unit has the appeal of virtually instant response and a wide and progressive range of torque split, the limited slip being determined by the geometry of the unit. Its main drawback is high cost, since the design calls for a large number of parts machined and assembled to close limits. Although the two devices are often discussed as alternatives, there are fundamental differences of principle between the Torsen differential and the viscous coupling. The Torsen is a true differential unit which, when provided with an input, will split its two outputs 50:50, but with the ability to vary that split if the output speeds vary. The viscous coupling, on the other hand, can either bridge the input and output of a conventional final-drive unit, so as to modify its torque split as a function of difference in output speed, or be used as a direct in-line replacement, in which case drive is provided to the output only when there is a significant difference between the input and output speeds.

The principle of limiting differential slip can be taken further. If the effect of the slip-limiting device is capable of being positively controlled, then the distribution of drive torque around the transmission can be altered at will, for the benefit of handling and stability. The result is 'active transmission', discussed in more detail in Chapter 14.

# Propeller shafts

Inevitably, the propeller shaft is a minority interest these days – but since most of the surviving shafts are in expensive, high-performance cars feeding lots of torque to the back wheels and whose owners place high value on smooth and quiet operation, the technical requirements for their design are considerable. Obviously the shafts must be strong enough to withstand the maximum torque output from the gearbox, but they must also be well balanced to avoid vibration, and as small and light as possible.

Early propeller shafts, taking the drive from the gearbox to a live rear axle which might move up and down by anything up to a foot, were one-piece components with plain universal (Hooke) joints at either end, plus a splined section to accommodate plunge – the fact that at full suspension travel, the propeller shaft must be slightly longer than it is at the mid-position. With independent rear suspension, the final-drive unit moves much less in relation to the gearbox, but still sufficiently (through body flexing and torque-reaction effects) to call for joints at both ends of the shaft to allow for less than perfect alignment – and also to simplify assembly.

In a shaft whirling at high speed, any out-of-balance will tend to bend it in the middle. If the out-of-balance is significant and the shaft not stiff enough, the problem can become 'divergent' in engineering terms – the bending makes the out-of-balance worse, which further increases the bending, which further increases the out-of-balance … until the whole thing ends in tears, or at least in severe vibration and high loads which reduce the life of the propeller shaft joints. The longer the shaft, the greater the danger of encountering this problem. The choice of engineering solutions is either to stiffen the shaft by making it out of larger-diameter tube, which increases bulk and cost, or to split the shaft into two shorter and less whip-prone sections with an intermediate steady-bearing – which adds the cost of the bearing itself and two extra joints, but allows the shafts themselves to be made smaller, lighter and cheaper. The centre-bearing solution is almost standard today, though care must be taken with the design and mounting of the centre steady bearing to avoid the feeding of noise, vibration and harshness (NVH) into the body. Problems of this kind are more noticeable because the centre bearing is inevitably mounted nearly enough in line with the backs of the front seats. Apart from the design of the centre bearing itself, this problem has also been addressed by using constant-velocity joints (CVJs – see next section) to attach the propeller shafts rather than plain Hooke joints.

Propeller shafts are normally made from a plain tube 'plugged' at each end with an attachment for a joint. Steel tube is still by far the most commonly used material, but aluminium alloy and reinforced composite materials have been used in cars where weight saving was more important than cost. New forging techniques have made possible tubular one-piece shafts which can be 'tuned' to avoid noise

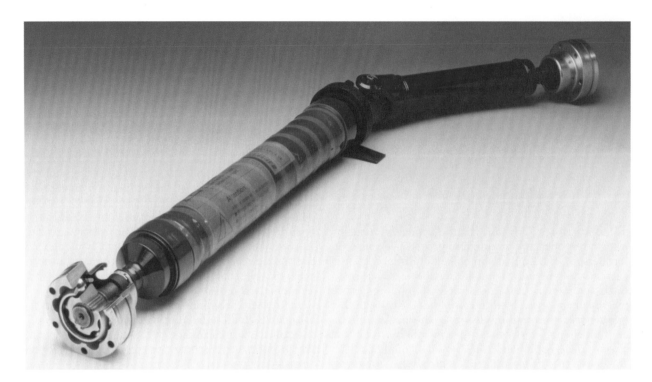

*Two-section propeller shaft from GKN shows combination of composite material (nearest camera) and metal. Composite shaft is stiffer and considerably lighter, but also much more expensive. Normally it would be used to make a single-section shaft where the metal equivalent would need to be in two sections. Note the constant-velocity joints (CVJs) at either end of the shaft, plus the centre steady bearing. (GKN)*

problems. These shafts are also lighter than those of conventional design. Joints, normally CVJs, can be attached to the shaft ends in a variety of ways: plugged and clipped, bolted, or friction welded.

# Drive shafts, joints and CVJs

Drive shafts, whether in front-wheel-drive cars or at the back of rear-wheel-drive cars with independent suspension, are essentially propeller shafts in miniature – with the important difference that because they are shorter and because their outboard ends move with the wheel they are driving, the angles through which they move are much larger. Weight is an important factor because, as explained in Part 3, the shafts form part of the 'unsprung weight' which affects ride comfort and roadholding. But the shafts must also be as slender as possible, because they have to be 'threaded through' the suspension while leaving room for all the other components – such as brakes

and brake lines – which form part of the wheel assembly. Thus drive shafts may be tubular, but are more often solid because this makes them slimmer and cheaper.

However, the design of the shaft itself is less important than the engineering of the joints at each end. The basic purpose of any drive joint is to enable two linked shafts to run at an angle to one another. To avoid vibration, the joint must maintain the shafts in a properly centred relationship. The design of the joint may be complicated by the need to produce a uniformly smooth output, to run at an extreme angle, to accommodate plunge movements, or to minimise frictional losses.

The most basic form of drive shaft joint is the universal or Hooke joint, which works extremely well for many purposes. Simple alternative designs substitute flexible material, either a rubber 'doughnut' or a disc of tough plastic, for the mechanical heart of the Hooke joint. But all these designs have one drawback: when the two shafts are running at an angle, with the input shaft at a constant speed, the speed of the output shaft varies during each revolution of the shaft, above and below the input speed. The larger the angle between the shafts, the greater the speed variation. This may not matter too much – or at all – in shafts which are turning slowly or where the angle is small, but clearly it cannot be accepted in the drive shaft to a front wheel which has been turned through a steering angle. The wheels need to turn at constant speed, and not with a faster-and-slower vibration several hundred times a minute. Thus practical drive-shaft joints need to make sure that the output shaft turns at the same constant speed as the input shaft – hence the term constant-velocity joint (CVJ).

There have been several successful CVJ designs since the 1930s, and refinements are still being introduced by transmission specialists like GKN. Citroën, the earliest mass-producer of front-wheel-drive passenger cars, used a carefully engineered 'back-to-back' double Hooke joint to overcome the problem, but most CVJs work by linking the input and output shafts via a 'cage' in which a series of ball bearings or rollers run in grooves in the ends of both shafts. Instead of a cyclic variation of output shaft speed, the joint produces a cyclic movement of, and variation in the stress on, the balls or rollers as they force the output shaft to rotate at the same uniform speed as the input. It is also possible to allow the balls or rollers to move axially within their housing, thus accommodating a degree of plunge. In drive shafts for front-wheel-drive cars, it is the inner joints, which do not need to flex through such large angles, that take care of the plunge while the fixed-length outer joints look after the steering angle.

The loads within CVJs increase with operating angle, and if large angles are maintained for any length of time they can threaten durability and refinement. However, the very large angles available to outboard front-wheel-drive joints, and the large internal loads which accompany them, are not maintained for any length of time, since they are only reached with the steering on full lock. CVJs have in general proved extremely durable as long as adequate lubrication is

*Component parts of the GKN UF-type constant-velocity joint (CVJ). The ball bearings in their cage are constrained to rotate between the inner 'gear' and the outer cage, so that input and output speeds are always the same. Any angular difference is accommodated by the balls running along their channels, creating cyclic forces which must be absorbed by the outer cage. Good lubrication is vital for the long life and quiet operation of any CVJ. (GKN)*

maintained; the flexible 'boots' which retain lubricant and protect against dirt and dust are vital components whose importance is sometimes not recognised. As already noted, CVJs are now widely used in rear-wheel-drive propeller shafts as well as drive shafts. Indeed, the modern transmission engineer's first thought when tackling an NVH problem is usually to replace any plain universal joints with CVJs.

# 13 **4-wheel** drive

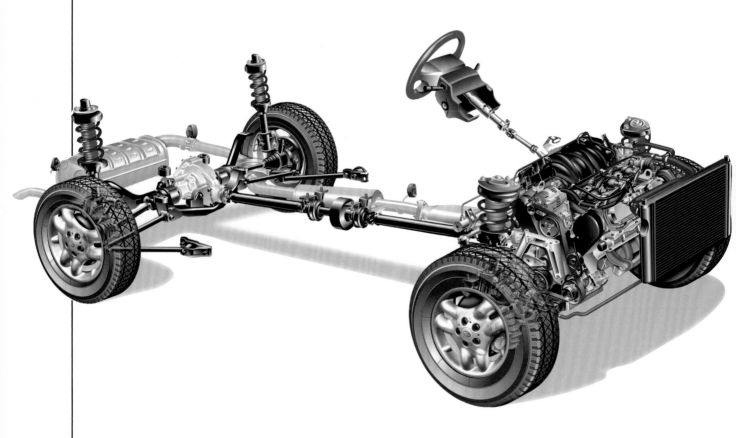

There are two possible reasons for driving all four wheels of a vehicle (4WD, or 4x4). One is to achieve maximum traction, in order to keep going in poor conditions. The other is to seek the best possible road-going performance in terms of handling and acceleration. The first reason has given birth to the now huge family of off-road and all-terrain vehicles, often referred to as RVs (recreational vehicles) or even more commonly as SUVs (sports utility vehicles). The road-going concept was really begun by the original Audi Quattro (though nobody should forget the Jensen FF, and the 4WD research programme pursued in Britain from the 1950s onwards by Harry Ferguson and L. T. C. Rolt). There are still plenty of 4WD road-going cars from which to choose, although not quite as many as there were in the early 1990s, when every major manufacturer seemed to feel obliged to offer 4WD adaptations of one or two of its volume-production models.

It is worth beginning any discussion of 4WD by underlining its disadvantages when compared with 2WD (front or rear). Driving all four wheels adds considerably to the cost and weight of the transmission, and increases the mechanical losses which occur whenever bearings roll or gears mesh in a bath of oil. The extra weight and the extra mechanical losses will reduce the performance in absolute terms, and also the fuel economy. If an engineer chooses 4WD, he (or she) does so acknowledging these penalties, and confident that for the purpose for which a particular vehicle is designed, they are outweighed by the advantages.

Where off-road vehicles are concerned, two more factors are important. When driving over rough ground, the true value of 4WD in many situations is that it enables the driver to creep slowly and carefully when with 2WD, there would be no alternative but to 'stand off and charge' with serious risk of damage or of getting stuck anyway. With 4WD, there is a much better chance of backing off before the going gets impossible (all too many newcomers to 4WD have learned the hard way that once a 4WD vehicle is stuck in soft ground, it 'digs in' twice as fast as a 2WD). In no way is 4WD a means of crossing rough country any faster than a soundly engineered 2WD vehicle – it simply makes getting to the other side more certain and less risky. This apart, other features besides the 4WD transmission itself are equally important. If you are going to creep forward carefully, very low gearing is essential, which is why all serious off-road vehicles are equipped with a transfer gearbox – an extra 2-speed gearbox which gives the driver a choice between the standard set of road-going gear ratios and an extra-low set. Maximum ground clearance is also crucial: there is no point in having a clever 4WD transmission if the middle of the vehicle gets stuck on a hump. All expert 4WD drivers also agree that tyre equipment is critical, and that different types of tyre are best suited to different types of going. And the advantages of 4WD can be completely cancelled unless the system is designed to prevent the loss of traction at one wheel bringing the whole vehicle to a stop. Especially in expert hands, a 2WD vehicle with low gearing, good ground clearance and suitable tyres will probably get further than a 4WD vehicle lacking the other essentials – especially since the 2WD vehicle will be lighter, and weight is one of the enemies of cross-country performance.

The case for 4WD on the road is different, and less clear. Obviously 4WD is an advantage in a powerful car on slippery surfaces, because it will be able to accelerate more quickly (though it won't be able to stop any faster). The effect of 4WD on handling and roadholding is more complicated, and probably better discussed in Part 3; but in essence, the evidence is that 4WD gives only a marginal advantage in roadholding in slippery conditions, but makes it much easier to control the car right up to the limit (and in particular, much easier to control than a rear-wheel-drive car). On dry, high-grip surfaces this advantage is more problematic.

*Opposite: Chassis and power-unit drawing of Land Rover Freelander shows how a drive to the rear wheels can be taken from what is basically a transverse-engine, front-wheel-drive package, using a two-piece propeller shaft with a centre steady bearing. Freelander is relatively unusual for a 4WD in using all-independent suspension; live axles give guaranteed constant ground clearance but at a cost in ride comfort, especially when driven on the road. (Land Rover)*

# 4WD transmission layouts

Regardless of how the engine is installed, any vehicle with 4WD needs two final-drive units, one front, one rear. It also needs some form of central unit to split the single output from the gearbox into two, to deliver to the front and rear final drives. Apart from splitting the drive torque between front and rear, this central or intermediate unit usually also includes a differential; it may include a two-speed transfer gearbox and some means of disconnecting the drive to one pair of wheels, usually the front wheels, so that the vehicle can function more quietly and economically in 2WD when the conditions don't demand 4WD – for example, when driving an off-road vehicle on the road.

There is a virtually standard basic transmission layout for all 'off road' 4WD vehicles in the RV/SUV

## LANCIA Y10 4WD

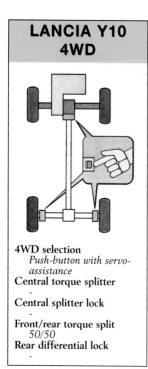

**4WD selection**
*Push-button with servo-assistance*
**Central torque splitter**
-
**Central splitter lock**
-
**Front/rear torque split**
*50/50*
**Rear differential lock**
-

## ALFA ROMEO 33 4X4

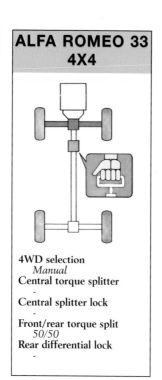

**4WD selection**
*Manual*
**Central torque splitter**
-
**Central splitter lock**
-
**Front/rear torque split**
*50/50*
**Rear differential lock**
-

## FIAT PANDA 4X4

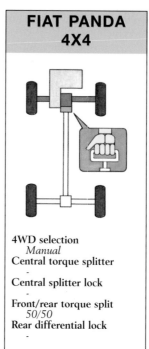

**4WD selection**
*Manual*
**Central torque splitter**
-
**Central splitter lock**
-
**Front/rear torque split**
*50/50*
**Rear differential lock**
-

## HONDA CIVIC SHUTTLE

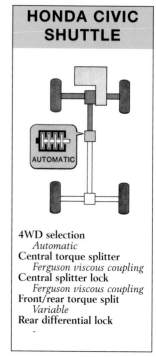

**4WD selection**
*Automatic*
**Central torque splitter**
*Ferguson viscous coupling*
**Central splitter lock**
*Ferguson viscous coupling*
**Front/rear torque split**
*Variable*
**Rear differential lock**
-

## NISSAN SUNNY 4WD

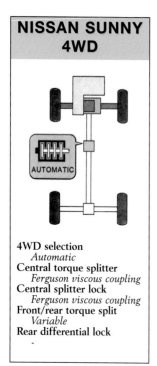

**4WD selection**
*Automatic*
**Central torque splitter**
*Ferguson viscous coupling*
**Central splitter lock**
*Ferguson viscous coupling*
**Front/rear torque split**
*Variable*
**Rear differential lock**
-

## SUBARU JUSTY REX COMBI

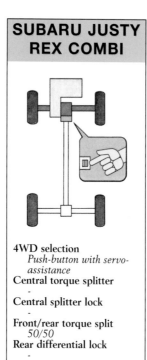

**4WD selection**
*Push-button with servo-assistance*
**Central torque splitter**
-
**Central splitter lock**
-
**Front/rear torque split**
*50/50*
**Rear differential lock**

## VW GOLF SYNCRO

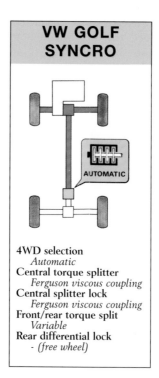

**4WD selection**
*Automatic*
**Central torque splitter**
*Ferguson viscous coupling*
**Central splitter lock**
*Ferguson viscous coupling*
**Front/rear torque split**
*Variable*
**Rear differential lock**
*- (free wheel)*

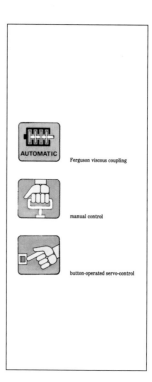

Ferguson viscous coupling

manual control

button-operated servo-control

Several years ago, when Lancia was producing three different models with four-wheel-drive (the Integrale, Dedra and Y10) the company issued this diagram detailing all the variations on selectable 4WD transmission layout then in production, showing which types of unit were involved in each case. (Lancia)

## LANCIA PRISMA INTEGRALE

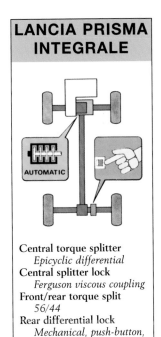

Central torque splitter
*Epicyclic differential*
Central splitter lock
*Ferguson viscous coupling*
Front/rear torque split
*56/44*
Rear differential lock
*Mechanical, push-button, servo control*

## LANCIA DELTA INTEGRALE

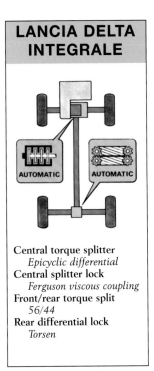

Central torque splitter
*Epicyclic differential*
Central splitter lock
*Ferguson viscous coupling*
Front/rear torque split
*56/44*
Rear differential lock
*Torsen*

## AUDI 80/90 QUATTRO

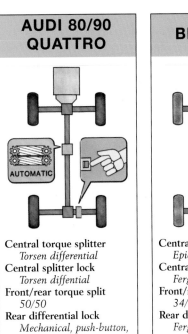

Central torque splitter
*Torsen differential*
Central splitter lock
*Torsen diffential*
Front/rear torque split
*50/50*
Rear differential lock
*Mechanical, push-button, servo control*

## BMW 325iX

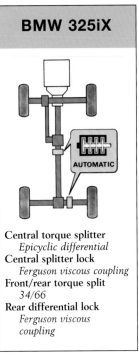

Central torque splitter
*Epicyclic differential*
Central splitter lock
*Ferguson viscous coupling*
Front/rear torque split
*34/66*
Rear differential lock
*Ferguson viscous coupling*

## FORD SIERRA/ SCORPIO 4X4

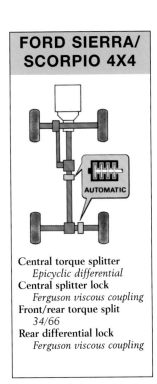

Central torque splitter
*Epicyclic differential*
Central splitter lock
*Ferguson viscous coupling*
Front/rear torque split
*34/66*
Rear differential lock
*Ferguson viscous coupling*

## MAZDA 323 4WD

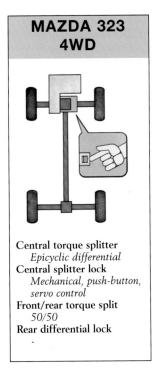

Central torque splitter
*Epicyclic differential*
Central splitter lock
*Mechanical, push-button, servo control*
Front/rear torque split
*50/50*
Rear differential lock
*-*

## TOYOTA CELICA 4WD

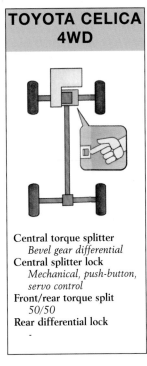

Central torque splitter
*Bevel gear differential*
Central splitter lock
*Mechanical, push-button, servo control*
Front/rear torque split
*50/50*
Rear differential lock
*-*

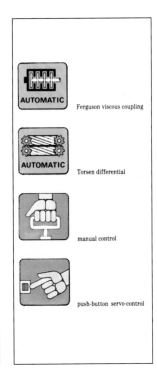

Ferguson viscous coupling

Torsen differential

manual control

push-button servo-control

*In parallel with the survey of selectable 4WD transmissions already shown, Lancia also surveyed all the variations on permanent 4WD then in production. There are some interesting variations, not only between cars which were originally front-wheel-drive and rear-wheel-drive, but also in the degree of automatic operation and torque splitting.*
(Lancia)

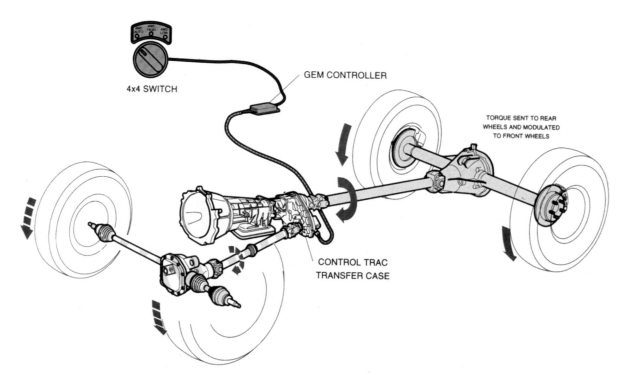

GEM CONTROLLER

4x4 SWITCH

TORQUE SENT TO REAR
WHEELS AND MODULATED
TO FRONT WHEELS

CONTROL TRAC
TRANSFER CASE

*Above: This diagram shows the layout of the Ford Explorer 4WD transmission, with live rear axle but articulated drive shafts to the independently suspended* front wheels. *In modern 4WD models, a lot of emphasis is placed on the ability to switch between low and high ratio, or 2WD and 4WD, on the move.* (Ford)

*Below: Complete Jaguar X-type driveline shows take-off of rear drive from transverse front gearbox and final drive, with two-piece propeller shaft to* rear final-drive unit. *Note the use of both conventional Hooke-type universal joints and constant-velocity joints.* (Jaguar)

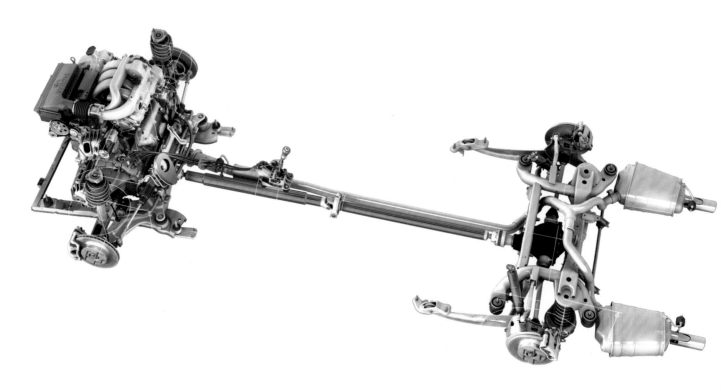

4-WHEEL DRIVE

*This diagram shows how each major component of the 4WD driveline in the Syncro version of the Volkswagen Caravelle is installed. Note that the viscous coupling is installed in such a way that drive to the rear only takes place if the front wheels begin to spin.* (Volkswagen)

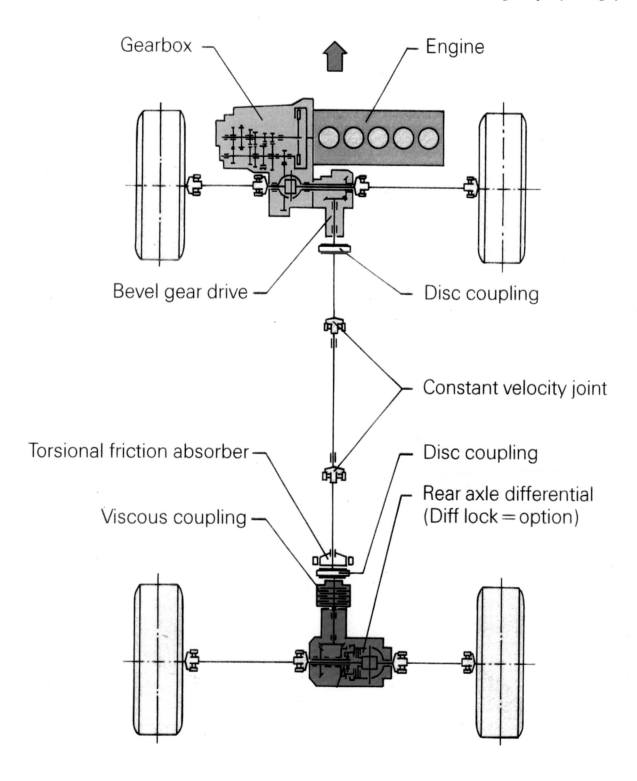

Gearbox

Engine

Bevel gear drive

Disc coupling

Constant velocity joint

Torsional friction absorber

Disc coupling

Viscous coupling

Rear axle differential
(Diff lock = option)

class, with an in-line front-mounted engine driving through its primary gearbox and then via a short propeller shaft to the centre transmission unit which may, as already described, include a transfer gearbox as well as a front/rear drive splitter and centre differential. In some SUVs with short wheelbases, the primary propeller shaft is eliminated and the centre transmission unit forms a direct extension of the primary gearbox. The centre differential is needed because when a vehicle corners, not only do the inner wheels turn more slowly than the outer ones, but the back wheels travel more slowly than the front ones. Without the centre differential, the front and rear wheels would 'fight' and tyre wear would increase. This can be tolerated in a vehicle which uses 4WD only on loose surfaces and which reverts to 2WD on the road, but all modern SUVs use a centre differential so that they can keep 4WD all the time.

From the centre transmission unit, two more short propeller shafts carry the 'split' drive to the front and rear final-drive units and thus to the four wheels. The output to the rear wheels may be in line with the input, and the output to the front wheels offset to one side, with drive transfer either by spur gear or, occasionally, by a multiple chain. Even when offset in

this way, the front final drive is close to or even beneath the engine sump. The offset is especially important when a live front axle is used, since it creates enough space for the final-drive casing to move up and down. In some models, the front and rear propeller shafts are in line with each other, and both final-drive units are offset – the layout is really a function of the way the transfer gearbox and torque splitter is designed. The advantage of a live axle in an off-road 4WD vehicle is that the clearance beneath the final drive casing is constant, while with independent suspension it could come much closer to the ground with the suspension fully compressed. The final-drive units need high torque capacity if the vehicle uses a two-speed transfer gearbox, since the low range gearing multiplies the engine output so much, and if the centre differential has a slip-limiting

*The current Land Rover Discovery, introduced in 1998, is typical of modern medium-sized SUVs in its layout. It has a live rear axle rather than independent rear suspension, and a central transfer gearbox to split the drive between front and rear while also providing two sets of gear ratios (high-range for the road and low-range for off-road) and a centre differential. (Land Rover)*

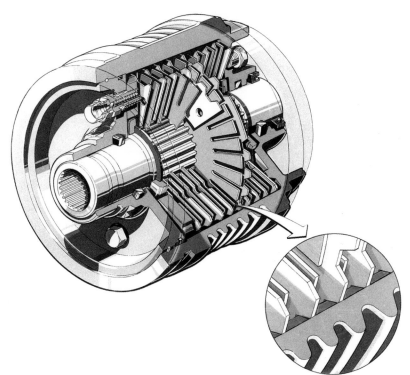

device, the final-drive torque capacity must be even greater. Consequently, the front and rear final-drive units in specialised off-road vehicles are usually larger and heavier than in normal road-going cars.

As briefly discussed in Chapter 12, the centre differential can be designed so that it splits the torque unequally. If the split is not 50:50, the higher proportion generally goes to the rear wheels, for three reasons. First, when the vehicle is climbing or accelerating, there is a rearward transfer of weight which means the rear wheels can handle more torque than the front. Second, it is easier to design the drive to the rear wheels with the strength to accept the greater share of torque – it doesn't have to find its way past the engine to the front final drive. Third, limiting the share of torque delivered to the front wheels makes the steering lighter and less likely to suffer from the effect of variations in drive torque.

Of the other units in the centre transmission unit, the 2-speed transfer gearbox may either provide a direct drive and a reduction gearing of about 2:1 for low-speed operation, or it may be a two-shaft gearbox in which both outputs are geared – normally one gear-down for low ratio, and the other an overdrive for high ratio. Low-ratio first gear is normally low enough to enable a vehicle with manual transmission to travel comfortably at a slow walking pace with the clutch fully engaged; this ultra-low gear is also useful for descending very steep slopes without touching the brakes, which can be dangerous. Early transfer

*This drawing shows how the components of a multi-plate viscous coupling is assembled. Half of the interleaved plates are keyed to the central shaft, and the others to the outer casing.*

*When the shaft rotates relative to the casing, the viscosity of the fluid between the plates begins to transfer drive from one side of the unit to the other.*
*(Volkswagen)*

gearboxes used dog-clutch engagement of gears and to shift from high to low ratio, it was necessary to come to a stop or very nearly so; modern 4WD transmissions allow the change to be made at moderate speed. If a clutch unit is fitted to allow the drive to two of the wheels to be engaged or disengaged, its operation is often automatic, with 4WD engaged when low-ratio drive is selected, and disengaged when high-ratio is in use. The provision of any such system classifies the transmission as 'selectable' rather then 'permanent' 4WD. A long established alternative approach, popular for example on early Land Rovers, is to provide the front wheel hubs with a free-wheeling mechanism, enabling the wheels to travel their extra cornering distance without having to 'fight' the rear wheels. Depending on just how serious are the off-road intentions of an SUV, the transfer gearbox may be omitted altogether to save cost, weight and space.

Having engineered this complex transmission, there remains the question of maintaining the drive if any one wheel loses its grip, bearing in mind that the use of three differentials means that if this happens,

*Mercedes's first application of 4WD to a road-going car was 4Matic, whose main components are illustrated here. It was a complex system which worked well but was heavy and extremely expensive. Mercedes appeared later to decide that many of the same advantages could be achieved with rear-wheel-drive and electronic aids to traction and stability. (Mercedes)*

# Road-going 4WD

When 4WD is applied to a road car, it is generally the case that the car has started life with 2WD, either front-wheel-drive or rear-wheel-drive. A few cars, including the Jaguar X-type introduced in 2001, were designed from the start to use 4WD.

When the original car was front-wheel-drive, the adaptation is fairly straightforward. With an in-line front engine and transaxle, as in most Audis or the Subaru Impreza range for example, the added-on 4WD can be extremely neat, taking a second output from the rear of the standard gearbox, into a propeller shaft to the new rear final-drive unit. The centre differential is normally built into the extended gearbox casing. Adapting a rear-engined car (such as the Porsche Carrera) to 4WD is the mirror-image of this procedure, with the second output connected to a propeller shaft running forward to meet the newly installed front final drive. Mid-engined cars pose more potential problems but in practice there have been hardly any 4WD mid-engined models. One such car was the apparently stillborn Bugatti EB110, which used a mid-engined in-line layout with a 4WD transmission. A similar layout was proposed for the Jaguar XJ220 and actually fitted to the original concept car, but the limited-production version reverted to rear-wheel-drive. In the Bugatti, the front-to-rear torque split was nominally 27:73, although the centre differential (and that at the rear) had limited slip. The front final-drive unit was therefore relatively small, which at

no torque can be transmitted to any of the other three wheels. The first move is to provide the centre differential with a lock, so that if a wheel spins at one end of the vehicle, torque can still be transmitted to the wheels at the other end. With a positive lock, all the available torque is transmitted in the one direction, which means that the output propeller and drive shafts have to be made twice as strong to avoid the risk of overstressing and failure. Many modern 4WD transmissions replace the centre lock with a viscous coupling which automatically transfers an increasing proportion of the torque as it senses a speed difference which implies wheelspin at either end of the vehicle. The most 'serious' RVs are also provided with a positive lock for the rear differential, so that if a single rear wheel is spinning in a mudhole or similar obstruction, drive to the other three wheels can be maintained. Differential locks on the front axle are not really to be contemplated, because of the effect on steering in the event of malfunction. In any event, it is far more often a rear wheel which gets stuck in off-road conditions – and when all else fails, serious RVs are also provided with an engine-driven winch and cable.

least eased the otherwise considerable problems of installing the front driveline. Mid-engined cars with transverse engines, like the MGF and Toyota MR2, would be very difficult indeed to adapt to 4WD.

Front-wheel-drive cars with transverse engines may seem awkward to adapt, but in practice it is easy to redesign the final-drive casing behind the engine to provide a second output to the propeller shaft and thus to the rear final drive, a layout adopted by Lancia in its outstandingly successful Integrale series, by Mitsubishi, by Volkswagen in the Golf Syncro, and most recently by Jaguar in the X-type, whose 4WD transmission is standard – there is no front-wheel-drive version. The real engineering challenge when adapting a front-wheel-drive car is to design the new back-end layout, starting with undriven wheels and a relatively simple rear suspension system, and finding space for the propeller shaft, rear final drive, drive shafts, and a new, heavier and more complex rear suspension arrangement.

Where the original car is front-engined and rear-wheel-drive, the end result of a 4WD conversion usually resembles an SUV transmission, with the torque splitter and central differential housed in a rearward extension of the in-line gearbox. In such cars, a rear-biased torque split is always used, often around 35:65 front-to-rear. Unlike off-road vehicles, 4WD cars intended for normal road-going use are equipped with independent suspension, so the final-drive units at both ends of the car are attached to the body, simplifying the design of the propeller shafts – and making it easier to install the front propeller shaft alongside the engine sump – but calling for more complicated drive shafts to all four wheels. However, the main interest in many 4WD road cars is their use of limited-slip mechanisms in the centre and rear differentials. Recent models have used viscous couplings and Torsen units, sometimes mixing the two – viscous coupling on the centre differential, Torsen at the rear. An even more advanced technique is to use what amounts to a 'controllable' viscous coupling whose effect can be adjusted by squeezing the plates closer together. Such a device can be used to alter the front-to-rear torque split under electronic control, according to a program which takes various factors such as vehicle speed, individual wheel speeds and cornering force into account. The designers of modern 4WD road cars prefer these subtle means of maintaining traction and controlling behaviour to the fitting of simple differential locks.

# **14** **Electronic control** and the **future**

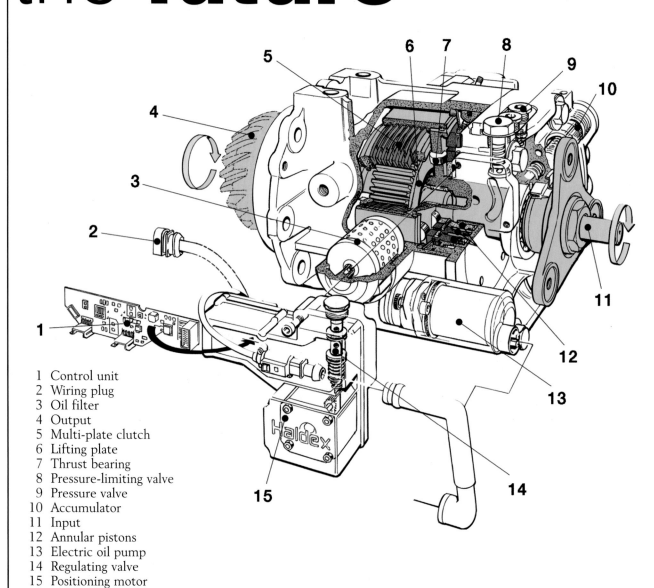

1 Control unit
2 Wiring plug
3 Oil filter
4 Output
5 Multi-plate clutch
6 Lifting plate
7 Thrust bearing
8 Pressure-limiting valve
9 Pressure valve
10 Accumulator
11 Input
12 Annular pistons
13 Electric oil pump
14 Regulating valve
15 Positioning motor

The designers of the most advanced cars are no longer content to allow the differential – and the driver's judgement – to determine the way in which the transmission operates. As we have already seen, the differential can be a fairly 'dumb' device in any situation where the driven wheels don't enjoy identical grip (the so-called 'split-mu' situation, typically with one wheel on the dry centre of the road and the other close to the slippery verge). Sadly, the driver can be even dumber, often applying power through the transmission in a way which is guaranteed to cause trouble. Possibly the most common fault is to apply too much power when cornering a rear-wheel-drive car on a slippery surface, to cause wild oversteer and even a spin. While some drivers enjoy the challenge of seeking to maintain control 'on the limit', and the most skilled drivers actually succeed, electronic control systems today provide the means of detecting problems in their early stages and countering them before they become serious.

# Traction control systems (TCS)

One of the commonest driving problems in slippery conditions is the ease with which the driven wheels spin when the car moves away from rest. Too much acceleration quickly induces wheelspin, but if the driver feeds in torque slowly and carefully to avoid it, there is always the feeling that progress could have been quicker. Maintaining as much acceleration as the tyres will accept without spinning, without overdoing it, used to be a matter of fine judgement. Today, many cars automatically prevent wheelspin no matter how hard the driver hits the accelerator pedal, thanks to traction control systems.

The principle of TCS in a car with 2WD is to sense when a driven wheel is beginning to spin (by checking its speed and assuming it is about to spin if that speed begins to increase when compared with the speed of an undriven wheel) because it is being asked to transmit too much torque, and then to reduce the torque so that wheelspin is prevented. As soon as the wheelspin ceases, the torque is allowed to increase, until wheelspin is again detected. Depending on the response time of the system, a driven wheel can be maintained very close to maximum traction. In a 4WD car, there is less point in having TCS to begin with, but if it is fitted, a more subtle approach is needed for the detection of wheelspin, since there is no undriven wheel to provide a reference speed.

Most TCS systems operate in two ways. The most obvious is to reduce the engine torque as soon as wheelspin is detected. This is much more easily achieved in cars with 'drive-by-wire' accelerator linkages (see Part 1). Where the linkage is mechanical, some means must be provided for the TCS to intervene in the linkage. In a few early cases, a complete second throttle body was installed, with the valve operated by the TCS.

However, cutting back the engine output may not provide a fast enough reaction, especially at low speed. Most TCS systems therefore also automatically apply a 'dab' of brake to a wheel which is beginning to spin. This is done via the anti-lock brake system (ABS) which is described in more detail in Part 3. Indeed, in many ways TCS and ABS are such closely complementary systems that they might be considered as one. ABS automatically releases the brake for a fraction of a second when a wheel slows down and threatens to slide: TCS automatically applies the brake for a fraction of a second when a wheel speeds up and threatens to spin. Both systems depend on the accurate measurement of wheel speed through hub-mounted sensors, so it makes sense for them to share a single set of wheel sensors – and quite a lot of the control electronics.

TCS is more complicated, however, because of its need to combine control through braking and control of engine output. At low speed, control is mainly through individual wheel braking: at high speed, entirely through control of engine power. A typical system depends on braking up to around 9mph (15km/h) and then gradually changes over to engine-based control by around 31mph (50km/h). The braking operation has much the same effect as a limited-slip differential, in that the the 'good' wheel of the driven pair can transmit as much torque as the brake is applying to the wheel which lacks grip. In a crude way, the same principle is used by skilled drivers who use the handbrake as a 'poor man's limited slip device' when starting off on snow and ice surfaces – so long as the handbrake operates on the driven wheels, which means the technique can't be used on most front-wheel-drive cars – many Citroëns and Saabs being among the exceptions. In any event, braking is an acceptable technique at low speeds where the main effect of wheelspin is to reduce traction. At higher speeds, it is more likely to affect vehicle stability and control, and the safer option is

*Opposite: While the viscous coupling and the Torsen differential are 'passive' devices, positive control can be exerted over the way in which torque is split front to rear or side to side, although the devices needed to do this are complicated and expensive. This is the Haldex coupling used by Volkswagen in some advanced 4WD systems. Control is achieved via a multi-plate 'wet' clutch – requiring a complete hydraulic system pressurised by an electric pump, with a pressure accumulator and an electronic control unit. (Volkswagen)*

then to control the spin by directly controlling the engine's output.

Modern TCS systems have proved so effective that they have probably discouraged the development of 4WD road cars, simply because it provides assured traction (though not as much of it as with 4WD) at a fraction of the weight, cost and complication. They have also provided the basis for new 'stability enhancement' systems with a greater range of abilities, discussed in Part 3, Chapter 20. These systems use basically the same hardware, but take information from an additional series of sensors which enable them to deduce exactly how the car is behaving.

# Towards 'active' transmission

During the late 1990s, the concept of active transmission grew out of the limited-slip differential, with the addition of some means of positively and continuously varying the degree of slip. This makes it possible, while retaining the improved limited-slip traction, to modify a vehicle's stability and handling by controlling the side-to-side torque split, and in a 4WD vehicle, the fore-and-aft split also. As briefly mentioned in Chapter 13, control of the torque split can be achieved with a 'wet' multi-plate servo-controlled clutch, internally resembling a viscous coupling, operated according to decisions taken by an electronic control unit on the basis of information gathered from a variety of sensors. The torque split varies according to the degree of slip permitted within the clutch; control is exercised by hydraulic pressure, pressing the clutch plates more or less tightly together, either to increase or decrease the amount of torque transferred from one side of the torque-splitter to the other. When used between a pair of wheels on the same axle, these devices always bridge a conventional differential and therefore act as a limited-slip differential with full control of the amount of split which is allowed to take place. When used in a 4WD vehicle, the device may work in exactly the same way, or it may simply be inserted into the centre of the propeller shaft, transmitting anything from 0% upwards of the available torque to the wheels – usually the rear wheels – at the far end of the shaft.

The first challenge for the transmission engineer when using these devices is to decide exactly how control needs to be applied. In other words the first vital step is to answer the question: these devices can split the torque any way you wish, so how do you wish? The usual answer is that the torque split should be matched to the vehicle's dynamic weight distribution, so that when the side-to-side split is controlled, a higher proportion of the available torque is fed to the driven wheel on the outer, and thus more heavily laden, side when cornering. In a 4WD vehicle, given control of the split across all three differentials, the torque can be divided so that it exactly matches the load on each individual wheel (the greater the load carried by a wheel, the more traction it can exert without spinning). This basic approach however ensures only that the best possible use is made of the available grip. The torque split can be further altered to affect the way the vehicle actually behaves, and in particular to correct any failure to follow the driver's intended path.

Clearly, this kind of control demands knowledge of what the driver is trying to achieve, which is normally measured by sensing steering wheel position and rate of movement, and of how the vehicle is actually behaving, which calls for at least two 'advanced' sensors – one to measure the sideways acceleration or cornering force, and the other to measure the yaw rate (the rate at which the vehicle is changing the direction in which it is pointing). The same result can be achieved with two accelerometers, one at either end of the car. A great deal of care needs to go into the design of the software for such a system: for example, the system needs to concentrate on the driver's basic intention and not follow every movement of a steering wheel which is being alternately 'sawn' in each direction, as sometimes happens if the driver fights for control near the limit of grip.

With the right information from the sensors and good interpretation of the driver's wishes, there are several ways in which the vehicle's path can be corrected when it begins either to understeer (to run wide of the intended cornering line) or to oversteer (to 'hang out the tail' and tighten inside the intended cornering line). Corrections can be applied through differential action of the brakes, and eventually perhaps directly through the steering – techniques we shall discuss in Part 3, Chapter 18. But they can also be applied through 'active' operation of torque distribution, both side-to-side and, in a 4WD car, between front and rear. It is worth noting, in passing, that the software can interpret running in a straight line as turning a corner of infinite radius, enabling the system to apply an automatic correction if, for example, the car begins to yaw because of an uneven road surface when the driver hasn't moved the steering wheel.

Where such a system wants to tighten the cornering line of an understeering 2WD car, it transfers extra torque to the outer wheel, possibly in combination with a cutting back of the engine's output, which will itself tend to tighten the line and will also slow the car, reducing the risk of running out of room before the adjustment of line can take effect. Much of the interest in such active systems has been in Japan. In 1996, Honda introduced its ATTS (Automatic Torque Transfer System) for front-wheel-drive cars and installed it on some of its most powerful medium-sized models in the Japanese domestic market. The ATTS was notable for deducing all its information about car behaviour from a single yaw sensor mounted aft of the car's centre of gravity. Honda has also adapted the ATTS principle for use in the rear final-drive unit of a 4WD vehicle, which has the advantage that there are no worries about interfering with the steering (in a front-wheel-drive car, altering the torque split may well have a direct effect on the steering feel).

With 4WD, a more subtle option is to change the front-to-rear torque split. Sending a greater share of torque to the front wheels will reduce any existing oversteer, and vice versa. In a system with active control of all three differentials, a bias to one side – to maintain the best cornering traction – can be maintained while still adjusting the front-to-rear torque split to modify the vehicle's handling. It remains to be argued whether this level of complexity is really needed, except by rally drivers. The real object of the exercise for most purposes is to maintain good vehicle behaviour and safe handling in situations where the driver has made a misjudgement and lacks the skill to rescue the ensuing situation without assistance.

Volkswagen-Audi showed an early interest in such controllable torque-split units, installing one in the centre differential of the Audi V8 in 1988. Another application was in the 4WD Passat G60 Syncro of 1989, in which a unit was installed across the front differential, controlled by a program which took wheel-speed signals from the ABS computer. In Japan, both Mitsubishi and Subaru have shown systems in which the transmission could be controlled to modify the car's yawing behaviour. Towards the end of 2000 the British specialist Prodrive announced its own system, which it calls Active Torque Dynamics (ATD). This system has been developed for 4WD vehicles, and can be applied with different degrees of sophistication depending on need. At its simplest level, ATD locks the rear differential only to prevent an oversteering spin from developing; the locking action applies more torque to the inner wheel and tends to straighten the car. At higher levels of control, ATD 'tailors' the torque delivered to each individual wheel. Prodrive says the active transmission approach works more quickly than individual wheel braking, and also feels more natural to the driver. The company expects ATD-type technology to become 'a common feature' of high-performance 4WD road cars and SUVs.

# Other kinds of **transmission?**

Over the years, many inventors have sought ways of replacing the apparent complication of transmitting torque mechanically from the engine to the driven wheels. There are two promising-seeming alternatives: hydrostatic and electric transmission.

In the hydrostatic system, pipes carrying hydraulic pressure take the place of rotating mechanical shafts, with the engine driving a hydraulic pump and each wheel provided with a hydraulic motor (in effect, a back-to-front pump). The system has the advantage of doing away with the conventional gearbox, because the overall 'gear ratio' can be altered by changing the characteristics of the hydraulic motors relative to the pump. This system has two drawbacks. One is the weight of the hydraulic motor which must be built into each driven wheel, adding to the unsprung weight – to be discussed in Part 3 – and creating problems for ride comfort and roadholding. The other is that hydrostatic systems, which have been used with success in earthmoving and other construction machines, are inherently noisy in operation. No answer to this problem – a serious one for any passenger vehicle transmission – has so far been found.

In a purely electric transmission, the mechanical shafts are replaced by flexible conductors carrying electric power from an engine-driven generator to wheel-mounted electric motors. The advantages and problems of such a system are in some ways remarkably similar to those of the hydrostatic approach, except that electric drive can be made extremely quiet. One large advantage is that a gearbox is not needed because most electric motors deliver high torque from zero speed (this is an advantage even where a mechanical drive is taken from a 'central' electric motor to each wheel). The disadvantage of the motor-in-wheel concept is again that the weight of the motor adds considerably to the unsprung weight of the wheel assembly. Some question marks also arise over the safety of high-voltage power supply cables which are subject to constant flexing with suspension movement, and to the water and dirt thrown up beneath the car.

On balance, therefore, it seems likely that even when cars begin to switch from internal-combustion engines to electric motors for their propulsion, the transmission of the driving force to the wheels will still be mechanical.

# 15 Chassis general principles

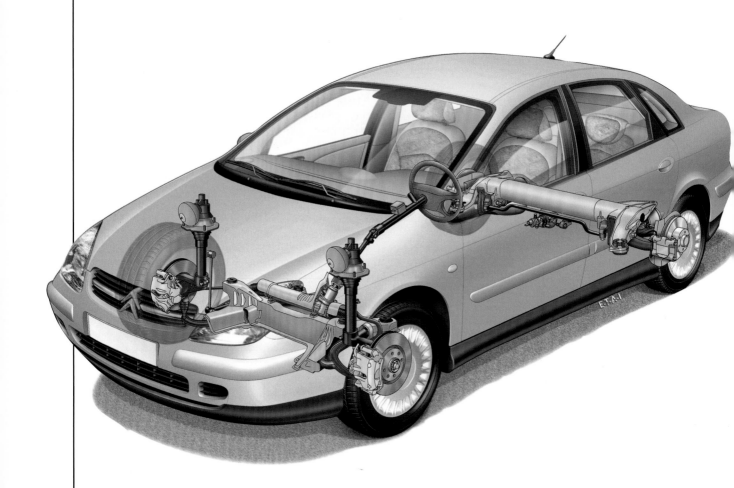

In the early days of motoring, the chassis was often taken to be the frame – two lengthwise members joined by various cross-beams – on which the body was mounted. Even then, in the wider sense, the chassis was actually this frame plus all the mechanical components of the car – including the engine and transmission. The body, however beautifully made and impressive to see, was essentially to house the seats and their occupants, and to keep the rain off; hence such descriptions as 'a Mulliner body on a Rolls-Royce chassis'. Edwardian owners bought their chassis and then sent them to the coachbuilder of their choice.

Modern passenger cars – and even some modern 4x4 off-road vehicles – no longer have a chassis frame as such. Indeed, such frames began to vanish (see Part 4) in the 1920s with the arrival of unitary body construction. Now, chassis engineering has come to mean anything to do with the parts and systems which connect the vehicle body to the road, and which therefore contribute to passenger comfort and to enabling the driver to maintain control. Thus the suspension, wheels and tyres, steering and braking systems have all become aspects of chassis design.

The two basic targets of chassis design are comfort and control. The car's occupants and their luggage (and the engine, and a lot else besides) sit in what amounts to a large box, and prefer to ride with the minimum of disturbance. Beneath them, the wheels pass over whatever the road surface has to offer – from billiard-table smoothness to ruts, bumps and potholes, or even (in RVs and SUVs) a completely unprepared surface. Linking the wheels to the cabin is a set of linkages, springs and dampers – the suspension (see Chapter 16). From the comfort point of view, the suspension must allow the wheels as much freedom as possible to ride over the humps and dips of the road surface, while passing on as little as possible of this movement to the cabin above. It is worth bearing in mind that body movements have to be controlled in three senses – in heave (up-and-down), pitch (fore-and-aft) and roll (side-to-side).

Although the *basic* targets of chassis design are comfort and control, in the real world there are two other factors which the designer must take into account. The first of these is space efficiency. The chassis components, and most of all the suspension linkages, must as far as possible 'fit around' the cabin and luggage space and the main mechanical components. It is not normally acceptable, except in specialised sports cars, to have suspension linkages taking up a substantial amount of the space available inside the body. The second consideration is structural efficiency. If the suspension mountings feed loads into the body at convenient and preferably well-separated points, the body itself can be made lighter. Having to carry most of the loads away from mounting points which are too low and too close together – which can happen in some otherwise admirable double-wishbone suspension systems, for example – can impose a considerable weight penalty.

# Steering, handling and roadholding

This is probably the best place to establish the important differences between three often confused qualities: steering, handling and roadholding, all of which are determined by the chassis design. Steering – not to be confused with handling – is the simplest one, since it refers only to the ease with which the driver can 'tell' the car which way to go. Steering is all about the driver input, and about the feedback of some vital information to the driver through the steering system, which is why it has a chapter to itself. Roadholding – again, not to be confused with handling – is also relatively simple, since it refers only to the grip between the tyres and the road, principally when cornering. Handling is more difficult to define exactly, but it can be thought of as the way a car behaves when subject to cornering forces. The steering provides the initial signal: what happens after that is handling. The car may turn into the corner quickly or slowly, it may settle into a comfortable 'steady cornering state' or it may not, and it may exit the corner and return to travelling in a straight line more or less easily. It is handling, far more than steering, which determines whether a car feels easy to control. It depends on many factors, not only the design of the suspension linkages and anti-roll bars, but also the car's weight distribution and the tyre pressures, plus the characteristics of the tyres themselves. Perhaps the best way to make the point that steering, handling and roadholding are different is to observe that there have been cars with great roadholding but dismal handling (the Citroën 2CV is probably the best example of all time), and cars with great handling but limited roadholding (the Ford Lotus Cortina Mk1 on its original cross-ply tyres set a standard which may remain unsurpassed). Equally, there may well be cars with great handling but poor steering – but how would you ever find out?

This is also the best place to discuss the main terms

*Opposite: Citroën C5 suspension, with front MacPherson struts and rear trailing arms, looks amazingly simple compared with some modern layouts, but great care has gone into the detail, especially of the way the suspension is mounted to the body, to improve stability and the filtration of noise and vibration. (Citroën)*

associated with handling, to avoid having to state them in Chapter 16 and again in Chapter 17. Most car enthusiasts know there are two contrasting conditions, understeer and oversteer. Understeer is technically defined as a cornering state in which the slip angle of the front tyres (the slip angle being the angle between the direction in which the tyre is travelling, and the direction in which it is *pointing*) is greater than that of the rear tyres; an understeering car tends to run wide of the chosen steering (cornering) line. In oversteer, by contrast, the rear tyre slip angle is the greater, and the car tends to tighten inside the originally chosen cornering line. The safest handling for most drivers is achieved by maintaining a moderate amount of understeer, as consistently as possible in all circumstances. It is possible, in some conditions, to achieve true 'neutral steer' with the same slip angle front and rear, but it can't be consistently maintained, and when it gives way to oversteer, the driver may have problems controlling the car.

Many enthusiast drivers feel they might prefer a naturally oversteering car, but most of them are mistaken. The grip of the rear tyres in a powerful rear-wheel-drive car can be reduced by applying excessive power, and the tail will 'hang out' in an exciting way for a second or so, but the taming of consistent oversteer demands great skill and fast reflexes. The most beautiful examples of true oversteer can be seen in the four-wheel-drift cornering of Grand Prix cars before the days of cotton-reel shaped tyres; what is rarely commented on is that the most delicate part of the process was straightening up at the exit from the corner without being flicked out of control by the back tyres as they suddenly gained more grip. Another safer way to experience oversteer is on a really slippery skidpan, where a back-to-back comparison between a front-wheel-drive and a rear-wheel-drive car will reveal that the latter may be more fun, but the former needs less skill and concentration to maintain control at the same speed, because excessive understeer can be checked simply by lifting off the accelerator, while oversteer control and correction needs combined use of accelerator and steering.

In the final analysis, handling depends on the way the weight of a cornering car is distributed between the four wheels. The harder you lean on a tyre, assuming nothing else changes, the more cornering force the tyre will develop. Thus altering the weight distribution between the tyres also changes the cornering force developed by each one, and it is these changes (together with the effect of camber change and other factors) which determine the handling. Without going into all the details of why it should be so – which would need a book in

itself – more side-to-side weight transfer at the front increases understeer, while at the back it increases oversteer (more realistically, in most cases it reduces understeer).

Most modern cars carry more weight on the front wheels than the rear, and therefore naturally tend to understeer, although some rear-wheel-drive designs still advertise the appeal of a 'perfect' 50/50 distribution. When a car is cornering, however, the cornering force acts on the car body, leaning it outwards, compressing the springs on the outside of the corner and unloading the ones on the inside. This, in fact, is how most of the weight is transferred from one side to the other. The situation becomes even more complicated if the driver accelerates or brakes while cornering. Exactly how much weight is transferred from inside to outside during cornering depends on the layout (the 'geometry') of the front and rear suspension, and the way the geometry changes as the car body rolls or pitches.

The simple way of looking at weight transfer is that the mass of the entire vehicle is represented by its centre of gravity (CG) at a certain height above the road, and for any given cornering force there is an overturning moment acting through the CG, as well as the weight of the vehicle acting downwards. If the resultant of these two forces moves outside the outer tyre line, you are in trouble: at maybe 2g cornering force for a low-slung sports car, 1.3g for a typical family hatchback, or 0.7g for a high-built SUV. Below this 'toppling limit', the overturning moment simply transfers load from the inner tyres to the outer ones.

Sadly, this neat little exercise in basic maths is far too simple to provide any clue to vehicle handling. The starting point for a realistic approach to handling is to think of the car's mass not as a single point at the CG, but rather as a 'dumb-bell' with two unequal masses (according to the front/rear weight distribution) in line with the front and rear wheels. But remember, the body is not directly connected to the ground; it rests on its springs. So when cornering forces acting on these two masses pull the body sideways, where is the point around which the body tilts? The answer is at the roll centre – in fact two roll centres, one at each end of the car, which define the roll axis.

# Roll centres and **roll axis**

Again in simple terms, each roll centre is determined by the layout of the suspension linkage at that end of the car, and the amount of side-to-side weight transfer during cornering at that end depends on the height of the 'dumb-bell weight' above the roll centre. The lower the centre, the more the body will try to tilt and the more weight will be transferred. So if you have a nose-heavy car and you don't want it to understeer like a pig, you arrange that the rear roll centre is lower than the one at the front, so there is more cornering weight transfer at the rear, which reduces the natural understeer caused by the basic weight distribution. It follows that if the roll axis slopes up towards the front, the result will be less understeer; if it slopes down, there will be more understeer. Thus logically, a front-engined, front-wheel-drive car should have a roll axis that slopes upward towards the front, and a rear-engined car like the old VW Beetle and the Porsche 911 should have one that slopes down – and it is largely so in practice.

The picture can be complicated by other factors, such as anti-roll bars. These reduce body roll angles during cornering, but in effect they 'buy' this benefit by increasing the side-to-side weight transfer. This is why a front anti-roll bar increases understeer while a rear one reduces it – often a handy way of 'tweaking' a car's handling, perhaps for its most sporting version, without the expense of a major re-engineering of the suspension. There are other and less desirable ways of doing this, such as fitting different size tyres front and rear, or even changing the tyre pressures (smaller front tyres or lower front tyre pressures increase

understeer). The need to check natural oversteer was one reason why the rear-engined Hillman Imp had tyre pressures of 30psi at the rear, but only 18psi at the front.

Nor should we forget that if a driver asks any driven wheel to develop more traction, its tyre will respond by delivering less cornering force. That is why adding more power in a front-wheel-drive car increases understeer (and the rate of tyre wear) while opening the throttle in a cornering rear-wheel-drive car reduces understeer – or even induces oversteer. This, however, is rather beside the point. The important thing is that each chassis designer selects his suspension layout, and develops it in detail, according to the car's handling needs. Comfort is much more a question of spring and damper choice, which is a slightly separate issue. The only other point which needs to be made, if only to show how

*Audi TT roadster is a modern application of well-tried 'quattro' principles to achieve well balanced handling with superb traction. In the case of this dedicated two-seater there is more room to install both the rear driveline and a complex suspension – yet Audi has kept the multi-link rear suspension very compact (note the short, variable-rate coil spring) and so created a lot of luggage space in such a compact car. Wrapping the front suspension around the engine and drive shafts calls for greater care. (Audi)*

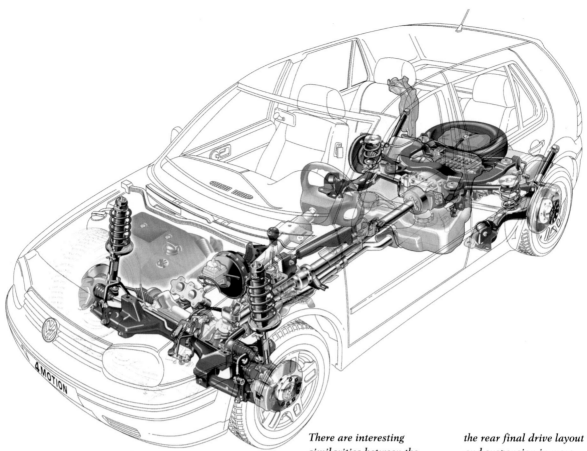

complicated the whole task can become, is that the roll centre rarely stays in the same place once the body has assumed a roll angle and the suspension linkage has 'deformed'. It can in fact move quite a long way, both vertically and sideways, and this can have important implications, especially from the point of view of 'transient' handling – the car's behaviour when turning into a corner or straightening up at the exit.

# Fighting noise and **vibration**

Another aspect of comfort, now seen as increasingly important yet often overlooked, is the need to filter out road noise and vibration before it reaches the cabin and its occupants. This is becoming more of a challenge as the engine, the exhaust system and the transmission become quieter. Road noise and vibration begin with the tyres. The tyre tread creates a more or less constant roar as it rolls along the road surface, and every obstruction in the surface – every ridge and pothole – catches the tyre and tries to force it backwards, each one creating a 'thump' which tends to make the entire car structure vibrate. To reduce this effect as far as possible, the suspension mountings in modern cars are designed to allow the wheel to 'give' in the fore-and-aft direction so that less of the shock is passed to the main body structure.

*There are interesting similarities between the layout of the Audi TT on the previous page and this VW Golf 4Motion, a 4WD adaptation of the standard front-wheel-drive Golf. Since both companies are part of the same group, the general resemblance is not surprising. The Golf shows the rear final drive layout and suspension in more detail, including the forward-inclined dampers which avoid intruding too much into luggage space (note also the 'space saver' spare wheel). But these are not identical layouts - look at the design of the rear trailing arm in each car. (Volkswagen).*

So the wheels must be as free as possible to move up and down, and – in moderation – also fore-and-aft. Yet at the same time, and however much the wheels move in these two directions, the direction in which each wheel is *pointing* must be closely controlled. If the wheels are free to point in any direction very far from straight ahead (except for the front wheels when they are being steered), the car's stability will be poor and – perhaps even worse – unpredictable. Good stability is the first requirement for proper control, and there is no point in having a suspension which is wonderfully absorbent if it fails in this vital respect. This gives rise to the basic challenge of suspension design: to allow the wheels sufficient freedom in two senses while exerting close and accurate control in the third. It is equally worth remembering that both ride comfort and stability have to be preserved, as far as possible, whatever the load in the car. Invite a couple of hefty passengers into the back seat of a front-wheel-drive supermini and the load on the back wheels may double.

# Sprung and unsprung weight

There is one principle which governs almost everything to do with suspension design, and that is the distinction between 'sprung' and 'unsprung' weight. Logically enough, the 'sprung' weight of a vehicle is the weight of everything which has springs between itself and the ground. Equally logically, the 'unsprung' weight is everything that doesn't – principally the wheels, tyres, wheel hubs and brake drums or discs. When a wheel passes over a bump, it will not only move upwards but will also try to push the body upwards, working through its spring. Just how much it succeeds will depend on how heavy the body is relative to the wheel and everything attached to it – in other words, the ratio of sprung to unsprung weight. This is why so much of suspension design in recent years has concentrated on reducing the unsprung weight, mainly by moving from live axles (Part 2) in which the entire axle including the final drive forms part of the unsprung weight, to independent suspension in which the only truly unsprung weight is the wheel itself and everything that moves with it.

It is not always realised that a high ratio of sprung to unsprung weight also benefits roadholding. The heavier the body relative to the wheel, the more quickly the wheel will be forced back into permanent contact with the road after it has passed over a bump – and as Colin Chapman knew very well and showed in his early Lotus designs, a wheel not in contact with the ground contributes nothing to the grip. It sounds simple enough, yet the principle was not understood in the early days of motoring. Some early competition drivers strapped extra weight to their axles in search of better roadholding, and succeeded only in destroying it, together with what little ride comfort they enjoyed to begin with. Equally, some designers and car owners today seem determined to fit larger and wider wheels and tyres in search (so they say) of better grip, when the wheels they fit are much heavier, and on anything but the smoothest of surfaces have the opposite effect – to say nothing of the harm they can do to decent steering.

The wheels and tyres themselves are of course a vital part of chassis design as a whole, yet some aspects of their importance are not properly understood, which is why a whole chapter (Chapter 17) of this part of the book is devoted to them. Among other things, most suspension designs are developed with a particular size and type (or even make) of tyre in mind, and changing the wheel and tyre specification can have unpredictable effects.

Aside from stability, proper control also involves steering and braking (Chapters 18 and 19 respectively). The development of good steering has been a long and painful process; the designers of the earliest cars made just about every mistake possible, beginning by copying the steering principles of horse-drawn carriages, and evolution was slow. Today we take decent steering very much for granted, and power-assisted steering at that. Yet this is one area of car design in which there is probably still a lot more to come. As for braking, we have come a long way indeed from the days when it was thought undesirable, perhaps even dangerous, to fit brakes to the front wheels. The technical challenges of steering and braking the same wheel seemed formidable to the early designers, who preferred to let the front wheels do the steering and the back wheels do the braking – possibly with an additional brake on the propeller shaft.

The idea that you might control the brake to prevent it locking, that you might apportion the effort applied to each brake individually to achieve the best braking performance, let alone that you might do away with any kind of mechanical connection between the brake pedal and the brakes themselves, would have seemed very strange to any vehicle engineer up to the end of the 1940s at least.

These are the elements of chassis engineering as understood by modern vehicle engineers. Compared with the engine or even the transmission, the chassis has something of an unglamorous aspect, perhaps because so much of it is out of sight beneath the car. Yet many of the virtues of the modern car, which many of us take so much for granted, owe more to recent developments in chassis engineering than anything else. s briefly explained in Chapter 15, the suspension system – consisting of mechanical linkages, springs and dampers – is responsible for ride comfort, the filtration of noise and vibration, and vehicle stability and handling (handling as distinct from steering). Any modern suspension system consists of five distinct though closely associated parts: the mechanical linkages which determine the way in which each wheel moves; the anti-roll bars (now fitted to the majority of cars, though often only at the front) which reduce the amount the car rolls while cornering and also influence the handling; the springs, which absorb the energy created when a wheel is displaced by a bump, and which feed the energy back again afterwards; the dampers – so often referred to as the shock absorbers, which they aren't; and finally, the attachments which locate the linkage members, the springs and the dampers to the car body.

# 16 Suspension

**A**s briefly explained in Chapter 15, the suspension system – consisting of mechanical linkages, springs and dampers – is responsible for ride comfort, the filtration of noise and vibration, and vehicle stability and handling (handling as distinct from steering). Any modern suspension system consists of five distinct though closely associated parts: the mechanical linkages which determine the way in which each wheel moves; the anti-roll bars (now fitted to the majority of cars, though often only at the front) which reduce the amount the car rolls while cornering and also influence the handling; the springs, which absorb the energy created when a wheel is displaced by a bump, and which feed the energy back again afterwards; the dampers – so often referred to as the shock absorbers, which they aren't; and finally, the attachments which locate the linkage members, the springs and the dampers to the car body.

## Suspension linkages

In specific engineering terms, the most basic requirement of the suspension system is simply to attach the wheels to the vehicle. Beyond that, suspension engineering has three aims:

- To keep the wheels as nearly upright as possible regardless of body movement in roll or heave.
- To allow the wheels to move vertically relative to the vehicle body, so as to cushion the ride over an uneven road surface.
- To control the movement of the wheels relative to the body in such a way as to achieve acceptable vehicle stability and handling.

The original suspension linkage, inherited by the motor industry from the horse-drawn carriage, attached wheels to opposite ends of a rigid axle which in turn was attached to the body (to a chassis member) by means of a pair of multi-leaf springs. When the disadvantages of this system became evident with increasing vehicle performance, there was a rapid move to 'independent' suspension systems, first for the front wheels and later for all four. An 'independent' suspension linkage consists of articulated members between the body and a single wheel hub.

The wheels need to be kept as nearly upright (zero camber angle) as possible because when wheels and tyres are allowed to lean at an angle to the vertical, the grip of the tyre is reduced. Also, the resulting asymmetric shape of the tyre contact patch creates a sideways force, which tends to destabilise the vehicle.

It is not difficult to design an independent suspension linkage so that its wheel and tyre move vertically over bumps in the road surface without any change in the camber angle when a car is running in a straight line. It is very difficult indeed to do so while also maintaining the wheel vertical when the body to which it is attached assumes a roll angle during cornering. Any real-world suspension linkage is a compromise between the two, maintaining the wheel as nearly vertical as possible in all circumstances. Suspension designers now have the confidence to turn any remaining camber change to good advantage, improving the roadholding and the handling beyond what can be achieved with completely upright wheels.

# Suspension configurations

A mechanical engineer would say that the design of a suspension linkage involves removing four of a wheel's six degrees of freedom while allowing it to retain the other two – rotation around its spindle, and vertical movement. This theoretical ideal cannot be achieved in a practical system without serious engineering disadvantages: in particular, it is very difficult simultaneously to remove all freedom in rotation about the fore/aft axis (camber change) and in sideways movement (track change). In practice, as the designers of independent suspensions quickly realised, it is in any case better to allow camber change but to try to make it equal and opposite to any body roll, since this keeps the wheel upright during cornering.

Of all the types of suspension linkage used in a century of car design, only five are now of major importance. These are the double wishbone, the MacPherson strut, the trailing arm, the torsion beam, and the multi-link. Of these, the trailing arm and the torsion beam are used only for the rear suspensions of front-wheel-drive cars; the other three may be used at either end, for any wheel. Unlike the other four, the torsion beam concept is not a fully independent arrangement, although as we shall see, it has compensating advantages of its own.

Of the suspension arrangements now rarely encountered – except in 'classic' and historic vehicles – the oldest is of course the axle beam with a wheel at each end, the axle being 'live' if the wheels are driven and 'dead' if they are not. As explained in Part 2, the 'live' axle remains an option in off-road vehicles (and in purpose-designed rear-wheel-drive light

*Opposite: Front suspension of the current Ford Mondeo uses MacPherson struts, like all European Fords for many years. The layout has been steadily refined however, not only in the design of the struts themselves, but even more in that of the lower wishbones with their wide-spaced attachments to the subframe and the careful design of the mounting bushes to provide thump-damping 'compliance'. Note also the way the anti-roll bars are attached to the dampers through long, articulated links. (Ford)*

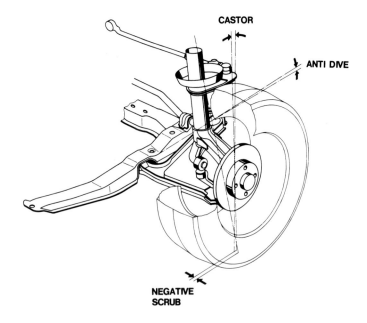

CASTOR

ANTI DIVE

NEGATIVE
SCRUB

*Not a very modern car – actually the last Vauxhall Cavalier, introduced in 1988 – but this diagram shows the subtle 'tweaks' applied to any front suspension (in this case, a MacPherson strut with the coil spring omitted for clarity). The angles involved are small (although some cars use a much larger caster angle) but they have a significant effect on the way the car behaves.* (Vauxhall)

axle, which created serious handling problems in some situations, and the de Dion axle which offered all the virtues of a 'dead' axle yet allowed the wheels to be driven, but which became a victim of its own complication.

As noted in Part 2, any combination of independent suspension and driven wheels, at front or rear, normally calls for drive shafts of variable length. However, some layouts – including the original rear suspension designed for the Jaguar E-type – have used a fixed-length drive shaft as a suspension link (in effect, as an upper wishbone), thus overcoming this need, though at the risk of other problems.

# Double wishbones

The double wishbone is the 'classic' independent suspension system, consisting in its pure form of two wishbone-shaped arms, one above the other, the forked ends attached to the body and the single ends swivel-jointed to the top and bottom of the wheel-hub carrier. A front wheel-hub carrier can then be allowed to swivel around its two joints for steering. In practice, only one of the wishbones needs to be of actual wishbone shape: the other can take the form of a single link.

commercial vehicles), because of the constant ground clearance beneath its centre. The 'dead' axle is an efficient rear suspension layout for front-wheel-drive cars, so long as it is properly located, and was used by Saab in particular until recently. It does, however, suffer from packaging difficulties, getting in the way of the exhaust run and stealing space from the fuel tank (the whole axle must be free to move up and down, remember).

Early independent front suspension systems included the sliding pillar (Lancia and Morgan), the single leading arm (Citroën 2CV) and double trailing arm (early Volkswagen Beetle), but these are now of historical interest only. Of the early independent rear suspensions, the one which survived until most recently, notably in most BMWs until the early 1990s, was the semi-trailing arm, a relatively simple system for rear-wheel-drive cars but one which led to poor handling in extreme conditions. Earlier casualties of engineering pragmatism were the swing

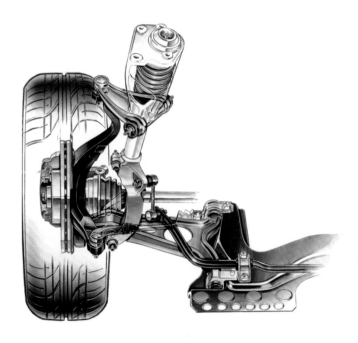

*Double-wishbone front suspension of Alfa Romeo 156. Features to note: the need to arrange components to make room for the drive shaft, lower wishbone with widely separated mounting points, much smaller upper wishbone with its axis making a large angle with the car's centre-line, 'swan-neck' upward extension to hub carrier to enable upper wishbone to be mounted really high, compact coil spring wrapped around the upper section of the damper, anti-roll bar with articulated link to pick up on the base of the damper, ventilated front disc brake. A typical modern double-wishbone layout in many respects, although some designers use other lower wishbone mounting arrangements to improve compliance (insulation against shock-loads caused by road surface bumps). (Alfa Romeo)*

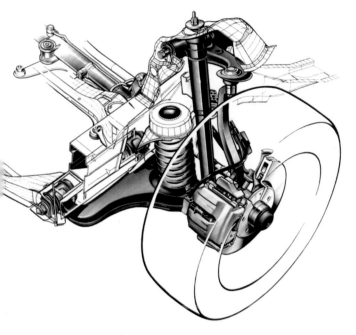

*Front suspension of the Mercedes E-class uses widely separated double wishbones with an upwards-extended wheel hub carrier and, unusually, the coil spring completely separate from the telescopic damper rather than being wound around it. This enables the spring and damper characteristics to be independently calibrated.* (Mercedes)

Two wishbones of equal length create no camber change during vertical wheel movement (although a track change does occur). When the body rolls during cornering, however, the camber angle is the same as the roll angle, and roadholding can suffer alarmingly. Normally, therefore, the wishbones are of unequal length, the upper one being shorter. This causes small camber changes during vertical wheel movement, but the camber change due to body roll during cornering can be virtually eliminated, at least so far as the heavily loaded wheel on the outside of the corner is concerned.

The geometry of a double-wishbone layout – normally, as viewed from the front – can be varied not only by altering the length of the wishbones, but also their angle to the horizontal in the static position. The axes formed by the body mountings, around which the wishbones rotate, can be (and these days, usually are) subtly angled away from the horizontal – and sometimes also the fore-and-aft – in order to create vertical forces (anti-dive or anti-squat) on the body under braking and acceleration, or to 'tweak' the geometry to achieve an advantageous camber change in a critical manoeuvre. Understanding exactly how to apply these subtle variations – in other words, the precise effect they have on camber, track and alignment as the wheel moves vertically through full suspension travel – calls for an ability to think in three dimensions. A computer and a computer-aided design (CAD) programme help.

One advantage of the double-wishbone layout – and the reason why it is the favoured layout for racing cars – is that its geometry can be altered to provide (within reason) any desired roll-centre height. Better

still, by comparison with some systems, the roll centre moves relatively little with body movement.

One evolution of the double-wishbone layout, apparently first used by Honda but now more widely seen, is to extend the wheel-hub carrier upwards by more than the radius of the wheel. At the cost of some penalty in unsprung weight, this enables the upper wishbone to be positioned very high, and well away from the area where it would come into conflict with the space requirements of the transverse engine and gearbox. It also makes it easier to achieve a fairly high roll-centre if needed.

Modern wishbones, in this layout and at the bottom end of MacPherson strut systems, are often now L-shaped in plan, with the long leg of the L forming the mounting axis and the wheel attached to the end of the shorter leg. This arrangement makes it much easier to build 'compliance' or thump-absorbing flexibility into the mountings without affecting the accuracy of wheel location. This is done by installing the rubber bush of the front mounting horizontally, and the rear one vertically, which is becoming almost a standard technique in modern suspension design.

# MacPherson strut

The MacPherson strut is a more space and structurally-efficient alternative to the double-wishbone layout. The strut is created by clamping the wheel-hub carrier to the lower end of a telescopic strut (which houses the hydraulic damper unit). The bottom end of the strut is located transversely and lengthwise by a lower wishbone link or a pair of single links. The MacPherson strut gives a high roll-centre – usually desirable – and as long as the strut is of reasonable length, wheel camber changes during vertical wheel movement or body roll are small. However, the system suffers two drawbacks. First, the roll centre can travel ('migrate') a long way from its static position during cornering, and this can lead to handling problems. Also, steering the attached wheel involves swivelling the entire strut, which can make the steering heavier and calls for careful low-friction design of the upper swivel-joint.

The MacPherson system feeds the suspension loads into the body shell via three conveniently separated points (the upper 'turret' attachment of the

*Left: In effect, the rear suspension of the Alfa Romeo 156 is a MacPherson strut with a careful multi-link location of its lower end. While the strut itself keeps the wheel upright, the large trailing arm provides fore-and-aft location, and the two transverse links not only locate the wheel sideways, but also control toe-in and toe-out. Allowing a very small amount of toe-in or toe-out movement in cornering by careful choice of stiffness of the mounting bushes can enhance handling and stability. Note also the articulated attachment of the anti-roll bar, and the plain disc brake. (Alfa Romeo)*

*Below: Saab 9-5 front suspension: an extremely sturdy subframe for this tough car, but essentially a standard MacPherson strut layout with broad-based lower wishbones, and the steering rack in the usual position, tucked well out of harm's way behind the transverse engine. Note the equal-length drive shafts to the front wheels, and the massive brake calipers. (Saab)*

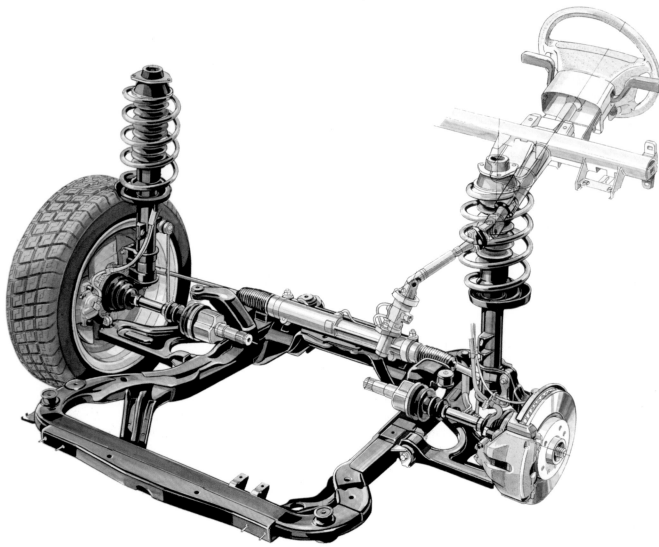

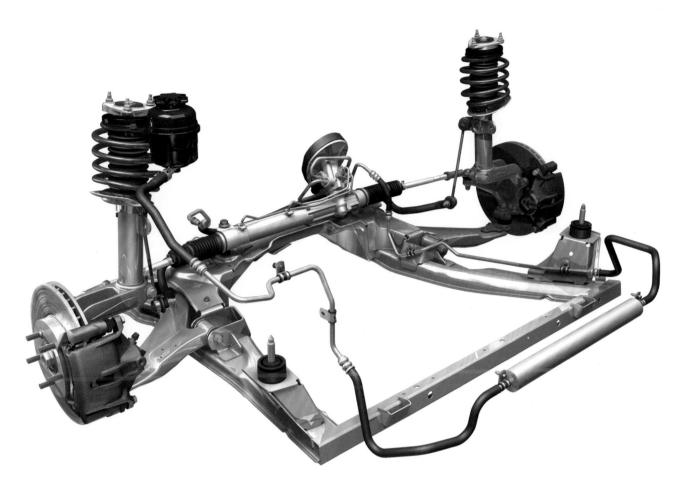

strut itself, and the attachments of the two lower links). It leaves the engine bay with no serious intrusions beyond the 'turrets'. These advantages are sufficient to give it a place in modern vehicle engineering, whatever its drawbacks. For example, Jaguar recently adopted MacPherson strut front suspension for its new X-type, the first time the company has ever used the system.

Normally, MacPherson struts use coil springs wound around the damper strut itself, but this is not the only option. In the past, for example, Fiat used MacPherson struts for the rear suspension of the 128, with springing and lower-end location provided by a single wide transverse leaf spring – a system which worked perfectly well. It has also been found that installing the spring so that it is not perfectly concentric with damper strut reduces the problem of 'stiction' when the vertical forces applied to the wheel are small. Stiction – the tendency of the strut not to move until a threshold force is reached, and then to move suddenly – can lead to an unexpectedly harsh-feeling ride on smooth surfaces.

# Multi-link

In a sense, the multi-link suspension is like a double-wishbone suspension each of whose wishbones has been split into two separate links – sometimes with the addition of a fifth link. Each link then becomes

*Jaguar X-type front suspension is a completely new departure for the company, using MacPherson struts instead of double wishbones, so as to fit around the transverse engine package. Also clearly evident, although the drive shafts themselves are omitted in this view, is the provision which has been made to 'thread' them through to the front wheels. Note also the subframe which provides mountings for the engine as well as the suspension.*
(Jaguar)

responsible for controlling one particular aspect of wheel behaviour – its camber change for example, or its transverse location. The links can be designed so that they work together yet without interfering with each other, and also shaped to avoid taking up space which the designer needs for the body interior or other features. The three-dimensional design process is so complicated that it can only be properly performed with a computer and a suitable CAD program. As with double wishbones, the roll centre can be precisely positioned almost as desired, within sensible limits, and roll-centre migration can be well controlled.

Now that all design offices have the necessary computer equipment, multi-link suspension is becoming more popular, especially for the rear suspension of up-market models. A typical application comes on the new Jaguar X-type; Jaguar calls its arrangement a 'torsion control link'

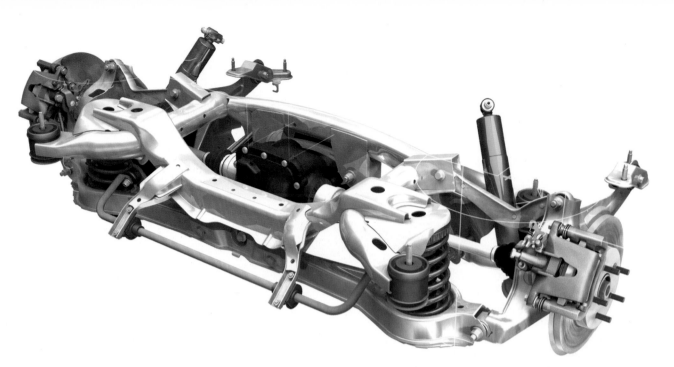

Above: Jaguar X-type rear suspension assembly, mounted on a substantial subframe, is a typical modern multi-link layout. Not easily seen in this view are the thin 'blade' trailing links which locate fore and aft without interfering with the links responsible for transverse location. Note the very wide separation of the coil springs and the dampers. (Jaguar)

Below: The rear suspension of the Ford Mondeo uses what the company calls its Quadralink arrangement. This uses twin transverse links for sideways location with built-in 'passive steer' to improve cornering stability, plus a trailing link for fore-and-aft location, plus vertical coil spring and damper struts. All but the trailing links are mounted to a rear subframe to provide double insulation against road noise and vibration. (Ford)

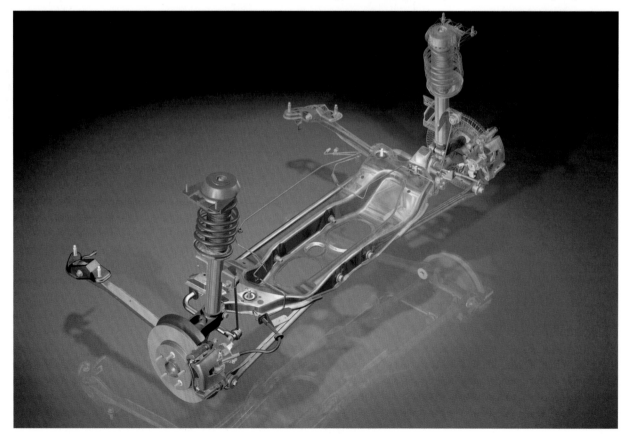

suspension. BMW, Mercedes and several of the Japanese manufacturers use broadly similar arrangements. Oddly enough, however, one of the first true multi-link suspensions to appear was at the front of the Audi A4 when it was introduced in 1995. This suspension used forged-aluminium links, with the upper two pivoted to the body via rubber bushings, and to an upward extension of the hub carrier by means of ball joints. The lower arms are rubber-bushed to the front subframe, and connected to the lower end of the hub carrier via a single ball-joint. In appearance, the arrangement is not unlike a wishbone system with widely separated upper and lower members, but the use of individually ball-jointed arms serves to modify the suspension characteristics.

# Trailing arms

One very simple form of independent suspension is to attach each wheel at the end of trailing arm, the arm itself being hinged to a beam running across the body. This beam often takes the form of a transverse tube which acts as a subframe and as a distributor of sideways forces. The trailing arm layout maintains the wheels parallel to the centre-line at all times – neglecting any bending of the arm or deflection of the mounting bushes – but the wheels are forced to adopt a camber angle identical to the body roll angle when cornering. Some chassis engineers actually welcome the resulting reduction of grip from the rear tyres in order to help balance what might otherwise be excessive understeer, although it means that overall cornering grip is reduced. The original Mini used trailing-arm rear suspension, and the system has been

*Rear suspension of the Saab 9-5 is conventional in principle, with vertical damper/coil spring struts, transverse and trailing links, but the links themselves are exceptionally strong, and the design of the subframe is rather unusual, a departure from the rectangular shape seen far more often. Saab was one of the last exponents of the 'dead' rear axle, which it used in well-located form in the 9-5's predecessor the 9000. (Saab)*

used in many of the smaller cars built by the French manufacturers. In many of these designs, from the Renault 5 onwards, useful space was saved by using transverse torsion-bar springs, and compact damper units compressed by bell-cranks, enabling the rear suspension to be housed almost entirely beneath the floor of the luggage compartment.

# The **torsion beam** system

This layout, now probably the one most widely used for the rear suspensions of small and medium-sized front-wheel-drive cars, first appeared in the original Volkswagen Golf and Scirocco of the mid-1970s. It consists of two trailing arms, joined by a cross-beam part-way along their length, forming an assembly in the shape of a shallow H, with two hinged joints to the body at the top, and the wheels attached at the bottom. The cross-beam itself is an open channel section, and so can twist quite easily, allowing the trailing arms to move up and down independently, while remaining stiff enough to keep the arms a constant distance apart. The torsion beam is good from the point of view of structural and packaging efficiency, and provides most of the advantages of truly independent suspension while overcoming some of its disadvantages. It is also relatively cheap to make and easy to assemble to the rest of the car on the production line.

The virtues of the torsion beam were borne out early in 1998 by the appearance of the Renault Clio II, equipped with torsion-beam rear suspension rather than the trailing arm system which the company had carefully developed and used in so many of its earlier models. In 2001, Renault gave the torsion beam a further vote of confidence by using it in the larger, more powerful and more luxurious Laguna II.

# Spring **media**

As observed in Chapter 15, any spring is really a device which temporarily stores mechanical energy when it is compressed, only to release the energy again as it expands. One of the objects of any spring design is to store as much energy as possible within a light and compact device. Any spring has a stiffness or 'rate' expressed as the load which will compress it by a certain distance (for example, pounds per inch or kilograms per centimetre). Equally, any spring has a 'natural frequency' at which it 'bounces' up and down if stretched and then released. This frequency is a function of the spring rate and the load on the spring – in the case of a car suspension spring, the weight of that corner of the car body that it supports. This

rightly implies that the natural frequency, especially of the rear suspension, increases as the car becomes more heavily laden.

The chassis engineer can choose from many different types of spring when designing the suspension. Whatever the choice, compromises are involved. One crucial factor is the chosen spring rate. A very soft rate allows a wheel to pass more easily over single bumps, but it also creates a low natural frequency which, on undulating roads, may cause a floating sensation which upsets some passengers. A soft spring rate also calls for a greater wheel travel, without which large bumps may 'run the suspension out of travel', bringing into play the bump-stops fitted to prevent damaging metal-to-metal contact within the linkage (by the same token, 'rebound straps' are needed to limit downward wheel movement if the body bounces upwards, perhaps causing the wheels to leave the ground). Soft, long-travel suspension calls for large wheel arches and reduces the space inside the cabin. On the other hand, an over-stiff spring rate results in sharp, jarring reactions to an uneven road surface. The natural frequency is much higher, and may again cause discomfort (various parts of the human body have their own natural frequencies which may resonate in sympathy with the movement of suspension springs). Thus the choice of spring rate is always a compromise; but there are some techniques which help. One approach, for example, is to engineer springs in which the rate is not constant, but increases as the springs are compressed.

Two factors also worth noting are first, that tyres are also (extremely stiff) springs and any complete analysis of vehicle behaviour has to take this into account; and second, perhaps surprisingly to the casual observer, the presence of a damper has little effect on the basic spring rate. Even a very stiff damper will cause the rate to change by less than 10%.

For many years from the early days of motoring, all cars used multi-leaf springs. Today, the vast majority of cars use coil springs, although torsion bars are still quite popular, and several more complicated alternative spring systems exist.

# **Leaf** springs

Leaf springs have two advantages. They can provide adequate (as opposed to good) location for one end of an axle without needing any additional linkage – and a transverse spring can act as a link in an independent suspension, as mentioned earlier in the case of the Fiat 128. Also, the inter-leaf friction which occurs during the flexing of multi-leaf springs provides a useful if inconsistent damping effect which enabled most early motor vehicles to do without separate dampers. Eventually, the design of leaf springs become more subtle and complex. By the 1970s, the last such springs to be used in road-going cars (such as the Ford Capri) consisted of single long leaves of carefully tapered section, to which the axle was attached some way from the centre of the leaf, this having been found to provide greater resistance to axle-tramp.

# Coil springs

The most familiar form of spring is the linear or constant-rate coil, whose rate remains constant when it is compressed or extended by a load. Any uniform coil spring has a definite minimum length, set by the point at which its coils come into contact, turning it in effect into a solid cylinder. To prevent this happening (with severe discomfort and some risk of loss of control) coil springs are always supplemented by elastomeric (these days, normally polyurethane) bump-stops to limit suspension movement in compression. These bump-stops are often deep enough to give a progressive-rate effect as the spring is compressed beyond a certain point.

Compared with the leaf spring, the coil spring is light and compact in relation to the amount of energy it can store, and this together with its ease of manufacture accounts for its huge popularity today. Its shape brings the further advantage that the spring can be installed co-axially with a telescopic damper, to produce a single compact, easily installed and exchanged unit. This is a particular advantage in the case of the MacPherson strut suspension. Some car manufacturers, however, prefer to feed the vertical loads of the spring and damper into the body at separate points, especially at the rear, claiming to achieve better refinement by giving each mounting its own vibration-absorbing characteristics.

Another valuable feature of the coil spring to chassis engineers is the ease with which its rate can be adjusted or even made non-linear, becoming stiffer towards its extremes of travel. A 'sports' suspension, for example, may be created simply by removing part of one coil from each of a vehicle's springs, which both lowers the ride height and stiffens the remaining spring, both of which are probably desirable for that particular purpose.

A variable-rate coil spring can be made by designing it with coils whose spacing decreases towards the ends, so that compression then collapses the coils into direct contact one by one from each end towards the centre of the spring, the remaining length of 'free' spring therefore becoming stiffer. Alternatively, the coil spacing can be kept constant but the spring made from a bar which tapers towards each end. As already mentioned, an easy alternative is to extend the bump-stops to form elastomer-in-compression progressive-rate springs.

Coil springs can also be wound in a conical or 'beehive' shape rather than as a cylinder. This creates a spring with variable rate, but with the significant advantage that it saves space by collapsing to a much smaller volume when fully compressed. Such springs have been used in the rear suspensions of several small, front-wheel-drive European cars.

# Torsion-bar springs

In effect, a torsion bar is a coil spring which has been unwound and located at one end, the load being applied to the other end by means of a lever arm (in other words, a suspension member). Several cars designed in the 1930s and 1940s, including the Morris Minor, used longitudinal torsion-bars for their front suspension, the rear end anchored to a substantial body member beneath the floorpan and the load applied to the front end of the bar by the lower suspension wishbone. This arrangement is still used in some 4WD vehicles with independent front suspension. Transverse torsion-bars are still used in rear suspensions, notably by Renault. In small front-wheel-drive cars, rear torsion-bars have the advantage of running beneath the load platform without creating any significant intrusion.

# Alternative spring systems

In practice, with a very few exceptions, vehicle springs have always depended on the elastic deformation of metal as their energy storage mechanism. A few other types of spring have been applied to vehicle suspensions with apparent success, yet without gaining widespread acceptance. Three obvious examples are the rubber-in-torsion springs of the BMC Mini, the more advanced Hydrolastic system fitted to the Austin/Morris 1100, Allegro and 1800, and the high-pressure gas springs used in the larger Citroën models.

The Citroën 'hydropneumatic' system uses hydraulic fluid to transmit forces from the suspension to spherical gas-spring units. It also maintains constant vehicle attitude and ride height by adding to or subtracting from the amount of fluid in the system. One of the drawbacks of the system, apart from the expense of making the vital and complicated control valves, is that the system needs a pressure pump to keep it 'topped up', absorbing engine power and adding to fuel consumption. On the other hand, damping can be provided simply by inserting restrictors at appropriate places in the fluid pipes.

Another alternative is the air spring, in which an upper chamber in the suspension struts is pressurised to maintain a constant ride height; the greater the load, the higher the pressure. Such systems have been used in up-market cars (such as the Lincoln Continental and the Toyota Lexus, and most recently the Mercedes S-class) for several years. Compared with the Citroën hydropneumatic approach they have the advantage of not using high-pressure liquid, and of needing no separate fluid reservoir. On the other hand they need to handle greater gas volumes, because all the air in the system is compressible, and they do not readily lend themselves to integral damping, but use conventional dampers built into the suspension struts. As with hydropneumatic systems, the air-spring charging system calls for either an engine or an electrically driven pump, plus a pressure storage accumulator and a control valving system.

# Anti-roll bars

The anti-roll bar is a specialised type of spring, in effect a torsion bar linking the suspension members of the wheels at one end of the car. The bars modify the natural 'roll-stiffness' of a vehicle, which depends on the stiffness of its springs and their distance apart. Minimum roll angles while cornering are of course desirable, but the spring rates needed to achieve high roll-stiffness can make the ride uncomfortable. The anti-roll bar provides an answer.

Most modern passenger cars are equipped at least with a front anti-roll bar. As already mentioned, the bars increase the sideways weight transfer effect and so can be used to 'trim' vehicle handling. A front anti-roll bar increases understeer, while a rear bar reduces it. Some chassis designers now work on the basis of selecting main front and rear spring rates for ride comfort, adding front and rear anti-roll bars to reduce roll angles as far as possible, and then adjusting the ratio of front to rear roll-bar stiffness to optimise the vehicle's handling.

*Citroën's Hydractive suspension is arguably the most advanced system in production anywhere. With the aid of the centre spheres and damping orifices, both the spring and damper rates can be varied according to need. The latest version of Hydractive, fitted to the C5, uses lighter and smaller control units and has more sophisticated reactions to car movement and driver input. (Citroën)*

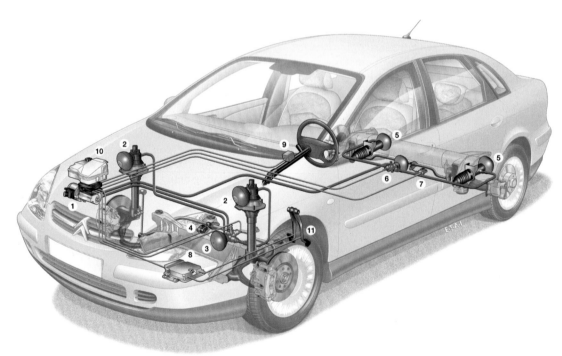

| | | |
|---|---|---|
| 1 *Integrated hydrotronic unit* | 5 *Rear hydropneumatique cylinders* | 9 *Steering wheel sensor* |
| 2 *Front suspension Struts* | 6 *Rear Stiffness regulator* | 10 *Hydraulic fluid reservoir* |
| 3 *Front Stiffness regulator* | 7 *Rear electronic position sensor* | 11 *Accelerator-pedal and brake-pedal* |
| 4 *Front electronic position sensor* | 8 *Built-in Systems Interface* | |

——— *Electronic*
▬▬▬ *Hydraulic*

Inevitably, anti-roll bars create problems of their own: very few engineering features deliver something for nothing. The sideways weight transfer effect of a stiff anti-roll bar can lead to the lifting of the inner wheel in some extreme situations, and thus to loss of traction if the wheel is driven. Also, when a wheel attached to an anti-roll bar runs over a single large bump, the bar reacts to the wheel movement by trying to roll the body. On poor surfaces this can be felt as a sideways 'jiggling', most noticeable at head level.

# Dampers

As we have seen, when a car wheel passes over a bump, the suspension spring stores the energy created by the wheel's upward movement, and its compression brings the wheel's movement to rest. After the bump, the wheel is free to move down again and the spring releases its energy. The problem is that left to itself, the spring will then carry on bouncing up and down at its natural frequency, until eventually – after maybe eight or ten hops of the wheel, in the case of a coil spring – air resistance, heating of the spring metal and scuffing of the tyre finally bring it to a stop. This is clearly unsatisfactory. What we need is a device which will bring the wheel as nearly as possible to a 'smooth landing' without bouncing. That device is the damper, which applies a force proportional to the speed at which the wheel is moving vertically. When there is no movement, there is no damping force, and hence the damper has no effect on the actual spring rate or on its natural frequency.

In the English language, dampers are often and completely wrongly called 'shock absorbers'. In fact it is the spring which absorbs the shock of the wheel being forced upwards by the bump. The damper is there to stop it misbehaving afterwards.

Almost all the dampers used in modern cars are telescopic hydraulic devices. In the earliest days of motoring, as already mentioned, cars managed without separate dampers: friction between the leaves of the multi-leaf springs happened to provide some damping effect. As car performance increased, the need for extra damping was realised. The earliest devices to provide it were multiple friction discs with an adjustable clamping force. However, the hydraulic damper provided a better solution from the late 1920s onwards.

The basic principle of all hydraulic dampers is that the suspension movement drives a piston through a cylinder of hydraulic fluid. The fluid is forced through an orifice, and in so doing sets up a force which opposes the movement of the piston and therefore of the suspension. Several forms of hydraulic damper have been developed, differing most notably in the way they transmit the motion of the suspension to the damper piston. Today, light-duty vehicle dampers are overwhelmingly of the direct-acting, telescopic hydraulic type. Different sized orifices, closed by reed valves, are used to achieve different damper rates during bump and rebound movement.

The design of telescopic damper units has become more complex as engineers have sought to provide more progressive characteristics and to overcome problems such as hydraulic fluid leakage, minimum breakout friction – dampers never 'start' smoothly from a static position – and damper fade brought about by overheating (by its action, the damper turns the kinetic energy of vertical wheel motion into heat, which must be dissipated) and by frothing of the hydraulic fluid. Many dampers, particularly those for higher performance cars, are filled with pressurised gas to improve fade resistance. Modern dampers may be of the monotube or twin-tube type, the latter consisting of concentric tubes in which the intermediate space forms a separately valved fluid reservoir.

# Adaptive damper systems

As long ago as the 1950s, some luxury cars were equipped with systems like the Armstrong Selectaride, which allowed the driver manually to select from a range of predetermined damper settings, from soft to stiff. Modern systems operate automatically (though often with a driver-selected override), using computer control to select the most suitable setting for any speed, road surface and driving condition. Most of the systems used on luxury-class cars up to 2001 work through one or two solenoid-operated bypass valves which are opened or closed to provide two or three different damper characteristics. In a three-level system, the stiffest characteristic, achieved with both valves closed, is often designated 'sport', with one valve opening to achieve a 'normal' setting. Opening both valves results in the softest, 'comfort' setting. Mercedes has developed a more sophisticated system (the Adaptive Damping System or ADS) which uses bypass valves of different sizes, allowing four different damper settings in all. Mercedes estimates that the system setting is fully soft more than half the time even when the car is being driven as quickly as possible.

A completely different approach has been adopted by the systems supplier Delphi, with its Magneride concept. This exploits the fact that some viscous fluids can be made sensitive to electric fields, their

upsetting the headlamp aim and quite likely interfering with the handling. A level ride can be restored by fitting a device – most commonly an air spring – to 'pump up' the rear suspension height to its centre position. Levelling systems are fitted to several luxury-class saloon cars, for the sake of optimum ride comfort, and to some large estate cars and SUVs, to enable them to carry heavy loads without the rear end sagging.

Self-levelling systems are of two kinds. They may be slow in operation, essentially to trim the vehicle's static attitude according to load, or they may operate fast enough to react to transient pitching movements. The simplest slow-acting types are driver operated and use an air supply from a small electric pump, via a control valve to inflate (or vent) an auxiliary air-spring reservoir. More expensive units are completely automatic in operation, using a ride-height sensor, a means of adjusting the height, and some form of power supply to operate the adjustment. Boge offers a self-contained unit whose reservoir is maintained at constant pressure by suspension movement.

The system offered by Mercedes in the original S-class used two hydraulically adjustable spring struts, with gas-filled pressure reservoirs, operating in parallel with the standard springs. The struts thus acted as auxiliary springs, while the main springs always carried their design load. A rear ride-height sensor linked to a control valve admitted pressure to, or vented it from the struts as necessary – the pressure supply coming from an accumulator fed by an engine driven pump. As already noted, the current Mercedes S-class has switched to an air-spring suspension, in which self-levelling is integral.

# Mounting the suspension

The suspension mountings are the 'Cinderellas' of chassis design, yet vitally important. There is no point in designing a superbly precise suspension system only to throw away the precision through sloppy mounting. On the other hand, few customers (other than racing drivers) would thank you for offering them that same precise system at the expense of feeding most of the tyre noise and the thump of every

viscosity increasing with the strength of the field as the molecules 'line up' in a more resistive way. Delphi has shown cars equipped with dampers in which the conventional orifices are replaced by shallow passages in which the fluid passes between electric field-coils. Magneride has the great advantage that the fluid viscosity and therefore the damping rate is completely variable, depending on the computer-controlled strength of the applied field. Dampers using this technology are expected to appear in production before long.

It is worth bearing in mind that rate-adjustable dampers are just that and no more. Adjusting the damper rate has little effect on the spring rate, and for a true 'magic carpet' ride, the spring rate needs also to be adjustable. That is a far more difficult thing to achieve, but some of the ways it might be done are discussed in Chapter 20.

# Suspension levelling systems

In a conventional vehicle with static springs, placing a heavy load in the back weighs down the tail, ruining the ride comfort because the rear springs are operating around a compressed static position,

bump in the road into the cabin interior. In the last 20 years especially, the science of designing elastomer mounting bushes for suspension members (and of blending the elastomer materials from which they are made) has advanced enormously. So has the way in which they are used. The 'L-arm principle' used in so many modern double-wishbone, MacPherson strut and multi-link suspensions has already been mentioned. Another widely used technique is to double-insulate – to mount the suspension to a stiff subframe which in turn is flexibly mounted to the body. Today, almost all luxury-class cars use this approach in some degree.

Further refinement is possible using mounting bushes which are profiled so that they are stiffer in one direction than another, and which contain closed 'capsules' of viscous fluid. Depending on its volume, the fluid helps to damp out critical vibration frequencies, while the selective stiffness enables the chassis designer deliberately to allow the suspension to deform very slightly in a carefully planned way. This is the basis of 'passive rear steering' in which the side force acting on the suspension during cornering makes the tyres run at a slight 'into-corner' slip angle which improves stability and handling. Renault has used such mountings in the latest Laguna II, and gives them much of the credit for the car's widely admired combination of refinement and good behaviour.

A growing consumer demand for low levels of noise and vibration inside the cabin has led to more extensive and more careful isolation mounting of suspension members to the body, to shut off road noise paths into the structure. There is a trend towards more complex and efficient mountings, and even to electronically controlled 'active' mountings at the top end of the market.

# Manufacturing
## requirements

Suspension components may be manufactured 'in house' or bought-in from suppliers. Suspension members have generally been fabricated from steel tubes and pressed sheet, though there is a trend towards cast or forged light-alloy members among up-market car models. Suspensions are also increasingly mounted to subframes rather than directly to the body: apart from affording 'two-level' isolation of road noise (suspension-to-frame and frame-to-body) this approach makes it easier to prepare complete mechanical sub-assemblies for subsequent attachment to the body on the final assembly line. The use of subframes for mounting the suspension to the platform is likely to become a more standardised approach in future.

# 17 **Wheels** and **tyres**

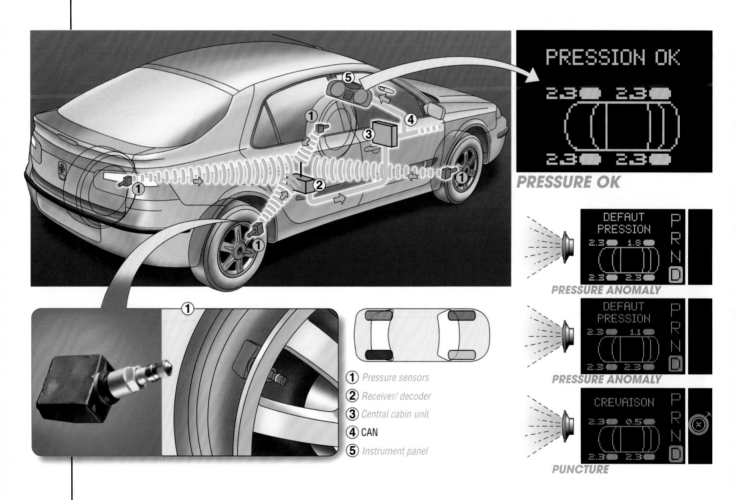

① Pressure sensors
② Receiver/ decoder
③ Central cabin unit
④ CAN
⑤ Instrument panel

PRESSION OK
**PRESSURE OK**

DEFAUT PRESSION
**PRESSURE ANOMALY**

DEFAUT PRESSION
**PRESSURE ANOMALY**

CREVAISON
**PUNCTURE**

**U**ltimately, a car's stability and handling depend on what happens within four patches of rubber-based compound in rolling contact with the road surface. These are the tyre contact patches. Within these patches are generated all the forces which make the car accelerate, brake, or go round corners.

The scientific detail of what actually goes on in the contact patches is unbelievably complicated. Tyre engineers and technologists have only begun to crack the principles since they had access to supercomputers. The most complex situation of all arises when the car is cornering and the tyres are running at a slip angle. In that case, the tyre tread 'wriggles' through the contact patch to create two important forces: the sideways force which keeps the car following a curved path, and a 'self-aligning torque' which tries to pull the tyre straight and restore normal (straight-ahead) running. The self-aligning torque generated by the front wheels provides an important part of the steering 'feel' which tells a skilled driver how hard the tyres are working and how close the car may be to breakaway – a total loss of tyre grip at one or both ends.

Although the 'classic' driving school advice is never to brake in a corner, and to be very careful about accelerating through one, drivers do – and with modern tyres, there is really no reason not to so long as you are aware of the danger that too extreme a combination of braking and cornering may cause a spin because the forward weight transfer will unload the rear tyres to the point where they lose their grip. Skilled racing drivers talk about 'trail braking', the technique of driving deep into a corner with the brakes applied before quickly, but very smoothly, transferring to the accelerator. Accelerating out of a corner is easier, but can still present dangers on a slippery surface. But what is happening in each contact patch when the driver is simultaneously cornering and either braking or accelerating? The tyre works within a so-called 'circle of force' or 'friction circle' – it can create its maximum total force in any direction. The geometry of the circle means that a tyre can simultaneously deliver up to about 70% of the maximum 'pure' tractive or braking force, plus 70% of the maximum 'pure' cornering force, which is usually enough to give the average driver a large margin of safety, at least on a dry road.

Remember, though, that when a car is cornering, and especially when it is cornering with braking or acceleration, the loads on each tyre will be different. In extreme circumstances, a single tyre, usually the outside front, may be supporting half the weight of the vehicle. It will be working very hard indeed – and even though the amount of braking and cornering force a tyre can transmit increases with vertical load,

there are limits. Meanwhile, the other three wheels will be carrying less of the load and will be less able to contribute to braking and cornering. The shape and size of each of the four contact patches will be different, and so will what is happening within each patch. This, in the end, is what determines a car's handling characteristics.

# Wheels

Before we look at tyre behaviour, however, we ought briefly to look at the wheel. A lot of drivers set great store by their wheels and spend a lot of money on them. But the job of any wheel is a simple one. It is to form the link between the tyre and the wheel hub, and to transmit all those vital forces from the contact patch, after they have travelled through the tyre walls and beads, into the hub and thus the rest of the car. So long as a wheel does this, it should logically be as light, simple, cheap and easy to make as possible. The fact that so many people treat wheels as car fashion accessories has nothing to do with technology. All else apart, a lot of the beautiful aluminium alloy wheels bought by enthusiasts weigh just as much as (sometimes more than) the steel wheels they replace, so there is a technical penalty in fitting them. And that is without even thinking about vulnerability to 'kerbing' damage and attraction for thieves. Take a look at the undoubtedly efficient – light and strong – alloy wheels (almost always magnesium) used by the leading rally teams: for the most part, they look extremely simple and not particularly attractive.

*Opposite: The Renault Laguna II was one of the first European volume-manufactured cars to be equipped with a tyre pressure monitoring system to warn the driver of dangerously low pressures. Such systems are useful in any vehicle but become absolutely vital with 'run-flat' tyres, with which the driver might otherwise carry on driving at high speed on a punctured tyre. (Renault)*

So far as materials are concerned, the fact remains that pressed and welded steel disc wheels are structurally efficient, and capable of transmitting very large loads. Their appearance is nowadays generally improved with the addition of light, snap-on trims, mainly made from moulded nylon. Of the light-alloy wheels, the forged type has superior grain structure and ultimate strength, but cast wheels are cheaper. Alloy wheels of any type are relatively expensive, not only because of their material costs but also their need for finish-machining. Wheels have been made (and are used in competition) from reinforced composite materials, which offer weight savings when compared even with the best light-alloy designs. As long ago as 1971, Citroën offered carbon-fibre-reinforced wheels as a production option on its SM sports saloon. These wheels weighed slightly more than 4kg (8.8lb) each, compared with 9.5kg (21lb) each for the standard pressed-steel wheels. Unfortunately, they were also extremely expensive, and enjoyed very limited sales despite their technical advantages. On balance, it seems unlikely that non-metallic wheels will ever be widely accepted, unless and until extremely light wheels are needed to improve the economy and the ride comfort of ultra-light cars in the '3-litre' economy class.

Wheel sizes and rim widths have increased in the last decade, following a period in which many chassis designers used the smallest possible wheels for the sake of low unsprung weight and minimum wheel arch intrusion into the front footwells and the back seat and luggage space. In the 1970s, 10-inch diameter rims were in use and many medium-sized family ('D-segment') cars had 13-inch wheels. Today, 13-inch wheels are the smallest in normal use, the most common size for D-segment cars is 15-inch, and many luxury and specialised high-performance cars have 17-inch or 18-inch diameter wheels. In the same way, rim widths have also increased, to cater for the fashion for wider-section tyres.

One less obvious, and less appreciated aspect of a wheel is its offset. Any wheel must 'wrap around' the hub to which it is mounted, so that the centre of the tyre contact patch is offset from the vertical axis through the centre of the hub, by a small amount carefully chosen by the suspension and steering system engineers. The offset is critical for the front wheels, since the positioning of the contact patch relative to the 'king pin axis' (king pins themselves went out with vintage cars – these days we mean 'steering axis inclination', the axis around which steering movement takes place, which is the angle, when viewed from the front or rear of the car, between the vertical and an imaginary line drawn between the upper and lower wheel-hub pivots) plays a vital role in determining the vehicle's steering characteristics. This is often sadly not apparent to those who fit wider, aftermarket-supplied wheels with the wrong offset. The effects of increased stresses in the wheel hub, also resulting from increased offset, take longer to appear but can be extremely serious.

However radically different some of them may look, almost all wheels conform to a common standard, so that on any vehicle, wheels and tyres can be interchanged. Thus with a few exceptions, all wheels have a nominal diameter in an exact number of inches – and they all use a related 'family' of standard rim shapes designed to accept any normal tyre of near enough the right section width (the rim shape also allows easier tyre fitting – the first tyre bead drops into the well in the rim while the second bead is eased over the flange – plus some form of

subtle hump or slope which retains the bead and discourage it from rolling over and off the rim should the tyre suffer a puncture).

The means of attaching wheels to hubs are not so standard. Whatever the means, accurate centring on the hub is essential. Even a small amount of eccentricity can mean an uncomfortable ride, with rapid and uneven tyre wear. The two basic approaches are either to locate the wheel on a central spigot and attach it by bolts (or, in some vintage and classic cars with the now obsolete wire-spoked wheels, by a single large 'knock-on' retaining nut), or to slide it over four or five accurately positioned studs protruding from the hub, to which the wheel is secured by specially shaped nuts which, as they are tightened down on the studs, pull it into an exactly centred position. Similar accuracy is needed in the roundness of the rim, and (of course) the mechanical balance of the wheel and tyre assembly.

From time to time, the major tyre manufacturers have tried to introduce new and radically different standard rims with claims of better handling and roadholding, more comfortable ride, and (especially) behaviour following a puncture. None of these initiatives has succeeded, although in 1998 Michelin announced a new attempt to break the existing pattern with the rim for its PAX run-flat tyre, discussed later in this chapter. One problem with any such move is that it must be made physically impossible to fit a conventional tyre to the new rim, since this could be highly dangerous. In the case of the PAX, not only are the rims made in metric rather than inch diameters, but the diameters of the two tyre beads are different, giving the tyre an asymmetric section.

# Tyres

The engineering tasks of any tyre are first, to support the weight of the vehicle, and second, to generate and transmit all the loads concerned with accelerating, braking and steering. As already briefly explained, all the main (non-aerodynamic) forces acting on the vehicle are generated within its tyre contact patches, which change shape as the force changes – symmetrically for acceleration and braking, and asymmetrically for cornering. This asymmetric deformation gives rise to the self-aligning torque – created by the contact patch trying to regain symmetry – which is felt by the driver as self-centring of the steering. The main purpose of the tyre tread pattern – at least, in normal road driving – is to clear any water within the contact patch to achieve sufficient grip on a wet surface; if you could guarantee never to encounter a wet road, a 'slick' tyre would be much quieter and would last longer. Rolling resistance is created by the absorption of energy (then converted into heat) due to the compression and extension of tread pattern blocks as they pass through the contact patch. Vibrations generated within the patch pass around the tyre tread and generate tyre noise. Looking at all these different effects taking place within a few constantly-changing square inches of rubber, it is perhaps not surprising that many experts regard the mathematical physics of contact-patch behaviour as among the most complex in any field of engineering.

The steel-braced radial-ply tyre has long been the industry standard for all light-duty road vehicles. Recent technical developments have concentrated on the reduction of rolling resistance for the sake of fuel economy; on the improvement of grip, especially in wet conditions, and on reducing noise. Tyre-generated noise is often the major contributor towards external 'drive-by' noise levels, which are now tightly regulated for new vehicles, and there have been many improvements in this area.

As regards the actual shape of the tyre, there has been a trend towards reducing the height of the tyre section in relation to its width (the aspect ratio, expressed as a percentage). Lowering the aspect ratio by reducing the height of the sidewalls allows the wheel to be made bigger without increasing the overall diameter of the tyre. This creates extra space for the installation of larger and more effective brake discs, for example. It also leads to a tyre which responds more quickly to steering inputs. The reduction of sidewall flexing also reduces heat build-up and allows safe operation to higher speeds. On the debit side, ride quality normally suffers, and the shape of the road surface contact patch becomes shorter and wider, usually reducing self-aligning torque and steering 'feel' unless the steering geometry is adjusted to compensate. These drawbacks have discouraged the adoption of low aspect ratios in mass-produced cars, most of which use tyres of 60, 65 or 70% aspect ratio. Specialised high-performance road car tyres may have aspect ratios as low as 30%.

The 1990s saw a tendency for tyres also to become wider, especially in sporting and up-market cars. In many cases this trend reflected fashion rather than engineering needs, and today many cars are fitted with tyres which are wider than chassis engineers would consider the optimum. There is a widespread assumption that a wider tyre 'puts more rubber on the road' and therefore improves grip. Actually, the amount of rubber on the road – the combined area of the four contact patches – depends only on the weight of the car and the tyre pressure; a car weighing 2,000lb with tyre pressures of 25psi will stand on a contact patch area of 80in² (the tyre sidewalls don't

support any weight worth thinking about). If wider tyres are fitted but the tyre pressures remain the same, the shape of the contact patch changes, becoming shorter and wider. This is not necessarily what the chassis engineer wants in his search for good steering feel and progressive handling towards the limit of grip. The only way to put more rubber on the road is to reduce the tyre pressure, which is why – in practice – the recommended pressures for wider tyres tend to be lower in any particular vehicle application. But the penalty generally has to be paid in terms of higher rolling resistance and extra noise, not to mention the sad fact that the car may be less pleasant to drive.

Despite the near universal speed limits, the safe speed ratings of tyres have steadily risen. Tyres are speed-rated according to a letter code: vehicle manufacturers always fit OE tyres rated higher than a vehicle's actual maximum speed. Most tyres for medium-sized cars are now at least T-rated (maximum 190km/h, 118mph). The highest speed rating, Z, indicates a tyre designed to exceed 240km/h (149mph) with no stated maximum. Tyres with very high speed ratings have taken an increasing (though still small) share of the European market since 1990.

The major tyre companies have worked hard to reduce rolling resistance to help improve fuel economy. Even at 100km/h (62mph), rolling resistance accounts for some 20% of a car's resistance to motion. The proportion is greater at lower speeds, when the aerodynamic drag falls sharply by comparison. All the tyre companies have moved in a similar technical direction, seeking tread compound materials which absorb less energy in compression and expansion through the contact patch, while retaining the strong surface grip. This research involves aspects such as the molecular structure of elastomers, carried out with the aid of supercomputers. Compounds containing a proportion of silicon (replacing the more usual carbon black) have been found to offer improved characteristics, enabling rolling resistance to be reduced while at the same time maintaining or even improving grip, especially in the wet. Michelin, for example, claims that its 'green' tyre range reduces rolling resistance by up to 35%, according to circumstance, without loss of grip and with little change in tyre pressures. The saving in fuel consumption in normal driving is calculated at between 3 and 5%.

There is a growing market for specialised tyres, especially for off-road vehicles. Skilled off-road drivers know that the choice of tyre can be crucial – and also that different tread patterns are needed for different surfaces such as soft sand, deep mud and wet grass. Many of the aggressive, 'knobbly' tread patterns seen on SUVs are at best a compromise between these distinct needs. They also suffer badly from high rolling resistance and noise levels when used on normal roads.

Another specialist area, though of little importance in Britain, is the 'winter' tyre. Although these often have 'off-road' type tread patterns to cut through and clear away snow, the main feature of true winter tyres is that they are made from a different tread compound which grips the surface much better at temperatures below freezing. Improvements to winter tyres in recent years have made studded tyres much less popular even where they are still permitted (and in many countries and areas they are banned for fear of road surface damage). The drawback of winter tyres is that they wear out much more quickly when the temperature rises much above freezing. Motorists in the Scandinavian and Alpine countries often keep two complete sets of wheels, with summer and winter tyres, changing over twice a year.

Conventionally, all cars have carried a spare wheel and the means of fitting it in the event of a puncture. The consumer fear of tyre puncturing remains strong, even though statistics show that the average interval between punctures on any well-maintained vehicle not subject to overloading is now of the order of 90,000km (56,000 miles) and rising. However, the trend to larger and wider wheels and tyres has resulted in problems creating a neat stowage for the spare, especially in sports cars. This has led to the development of 'space saver' spare wheels of standard radius, but with a much narrower tyre capable of supporting the standard load (subject to fairly severe speed and cornering force limits) by virtue of running at substantially higher than standard pressure. Attempts to sell this idea to a wider motoring market have varied considerably from country to country. British consumers in particular have not taken to the concept, and some cars in the UK market are equipped with full-size spare wheels and tyres protruding from wells which were clearly intended for a space-saver. In the longer term, the answer to this problem may lie with the 'run-flat' tyre.

# Run-flat tyres

The 'puncture-proof' tyre has been one of the ultimate goals of the motor industry for the best part of a century. The technical approaches have included self-sealing tyres, tyres capable of running even when punctured, and systems to warn the vehicle driver of any significant loss of tyre pressure (any 'run-flat' tyre system needs to let the driver know when a puncture has occurred). Interest in the concept remains strong, and recent research and development effort has been concentrated on enabling tyres to run-flat – to remain

safely in place on the wheel rim and provide sufficient (though reduced) grip and control to allow driving to continue for a limited range at a limited speed, enabling the user at least to reach the nearest workshop. The teams developing tyres of this kind now tend to refer to them as 'extended mobility' concepts rather than 'run-flat'.

The run-flat concept might have remained confined to high-cost products for a few specialised markets, such as security vehicles, had not a potential mass market arisen in the USA, where people in some parts of the country began to feel concern that stopping to change a wheel would make them ready targets for criminals. Michelin quickly produced a modified version of a standard tyre, the MXV4 ZP (zero pressure) with heavily reinforced sidewalls which could carry the weight of one corner of the car for 50 miles (80km) at 55mph (90km/h) – still the most widespread US speed limit – following deflation, without damage or loss of vehicle control. Goodyear has since introduced a tyre, the EMT, working on the same principles but claiming to offer greater 'run-flat' range with better behaviour, thanks to the tyre having been designed from the outset with this requirement in mind. In effect, both the ZP and the EMT become twin narrow, solid rubber tyres when punctured. They cannot in normal circumstances be pulled off the rim, and so their zero-pressure characteristics depend on the detail design of the sidewall. Inevitably, there is a small weight penalty due to the thicker, heavier walls.

In 1997, Michelin announced a radical new tyre, now known as the PAX but originally the PAV (*pneu accrochée verticale*, or vertically anchored tyre). The PAX is designed to work with an internal reinforcing ring which extends the deflated driving range well beyond 100 miles/160km (though still with a 55mph/88km/h speed restriction). Several other advantages are claimed for the PAX in normal, as opposed to deflated, running including improved wet grip, steering response and ride comfort. The big drawback of the PAX is that it is designed around a completely new wheel rim design and is not, therefore, interchangeable with standard tyres. As a result it faces a hard task gaining acceptance: as with so many developments in chassis engineering, it is not a question of the product being better, but of needing to be much better in order to overcome any drawbacks. Four years after the concept was announced, the PAX only recently found its first production car application.

The puncture-proof, as distinct from the run-flat tyre seems as much of a technical mirage as ever, and understandably so: engineering a tyre to deliver satisfactory performance in normal use yet also to be proof against severe misuse (kerbing, running under-inflated and overloaded, and worse) strikes most specialists as an unreasonable and well-nigh impossible challenge.

One of the often-claimed virtues of the run-flat tyre is that it enables the spare wheel to be deleted, to the benefit of weight and interior space. Consumer surveys, however, have indicated that car owners are disinclined to do without the psychological reassurance of a spare wheel, even when assured of continued mobility following a puncture. Consumers seem less impressed by run-flat concepts when it is suggested to them that they should accept four wheels and tyres to replace their existing five.

Michelin and Goodyear stress that the PAX and the EMT will only be fitted in combination with a deflation warning system, to avoid the possibility of an extremely unaware driver continuing without realising that any deflation has occurred. Even without the special tyres, such a system has considerable value, since many punctures (especially the dangerous violent blowouts) are caused by continuing to run with tyres that are well below recommended pressure. The pressure in a standard tyre can be halved without it looking disastrously flat and without any serious effect on steering and handling 'feel', at least so far as the average driver is concerned. Yet at half pressure, a tyre driven at motorway speeds will quickly overheat and the danger of a blowout is serious, especially if the tyre has at any time suffered sidewall damage through 'kerbing' – and a great many tyres have, even though no damage is visible from outside. A reliable pressure warning system would greatly reduce this risk, and would probably extend the average distance between punctures to well over 100,000km (62,000 miles). Renault has begun offering such systems in its latest models, starting with the Laguna II introduced at the end of 2000, using a sensor and transmitter unit developed in collaboration with Michelin.

# 18 Steering

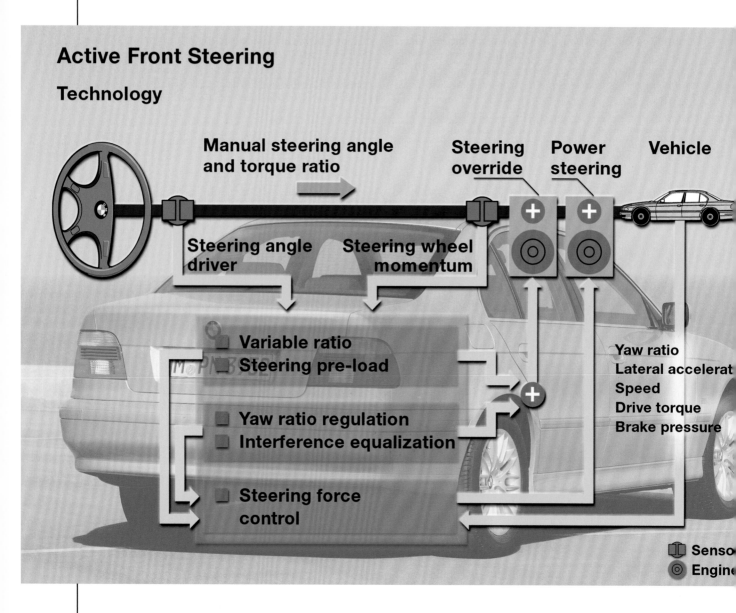

## Active Front Steering

**Technology**

**Manual steering angle and torque ratio**

**Steering override**

**Power steering**

**Vehicle**

**Steering angle driver**

**Steering wheel momentum**

- Variable ratio
- Steering pre-load

- Yaw ratio regulation
- Interference equalization

- Steering force control

Yaw ratio
Lateral accelerat
Speed
Drive torque
Brake pressure

Senso
Engine

On the face of it, there should be no problem designing a linkage to join the wheel in front of the driver to the ones at the front of the car, so that when the driver turns his wheel, the front wheels steer the car. However, there are three problems which between them make the task much less simple. First, the steering needs to be light enough for the driver to manage the car without undue effort. This implies at least some kind of gearing, and possibly power assistance. Second, while good steering 'feel' is desirable if not absolutely essential, the steering still needs to be protected against the sometimes harsh shocks felt by the front wheels at the road surface. In other words, feedback needs to be selective. Make the steering 'irreversible' (in practice, far from easy) and you end up with no feeling at all, and therefore no natural self-centring, which is an inherent part of good steering feel. Elementary safety demands that if the driver lets go of the steering wheel, it should return to the straight-ahead position and not wind itself onto full lock. So do you then try to add self-centring feel in some kind of artificial way? A few years ago that would have been thought ridiculous, but no more. The third problem is that the front wheels can move up and down by anything up to a foot, as the suspension travels from full bump to full rebound. The steering system has to be designed so that these movements result neither in unwanted feedback to the driver through the steering wheel, nor unwanted steering of the car.

Through the early years of the car, chassis designers made just about every possible mistake when it came to steering systems. They were, after all, starting from a background in the horse-and-carriage business in which the front axle was usually simply pivoted at its centre, and swivelled when the horse changed direction. It was quickly realised that the front wheels of a car had to be made to swivel separately, otherwise loss of control became almost inevitable. Even then, early drivers were expected to cope with 'tiller' steering and other arrangements which might almost have been designed to make the task as difficult as possible. Eventually it was realised that there were two vital aspects of steering: the 'geometry' of the front wheels, and the design of the steering linkage. Later, there also came the challenge of power assistance, now so widely used.

Incidentally, it requires only a short demonstration to show why it is the front wheels that are steered. Although rear-steered vehicles exist for special purposes (fork-lift trucks, for example) they are inherently unstable, require special driver skills and can be operated only at low speeds. Certain advantages (which we shall look at) can derive from steering all four wheels, with most of the contribution coming from the front wheels, but conventional front-wheel steering is sufficient for all normal road-going purposes.

# Steering **geometry**

When a front wheel – or rather, a front wheel hub – is connected to the front suspension, the 'geometry' is determined by the relationship between two axes. One of them joins the swivel joints and is the axis around which steering movement takes place (the 'steering axis'); the other is the vertical axis through the centre of the tyre contact patch. You might think that the ideal solution would be to align the two exactly, but it isn't so. For one thing, everything has to be packed into the centre of the wheel. There is no room for decent brakes, scarcely even for strong swivel joints, while the wheel hub itself is pushed well outboard. What is more, you get almost no steering feel or self-centring.

In that case, why not move the steering axis – still called the 'king-pin axis' although the king-pin itself doesn't exist in modern designs – inboard of the wheel axis? This was the first thought of the early car designers, as any visit to a good museum will confirm. But if that is all you do, you still end up with no self-centring to speak of, and you end up suffering badly from the wrong kind of steering feel – every bump of the tyre is felt sharply through the steering wheel. The clever thing, the first real breakthrough towards decent steering, came with the

*Opposite: This diagram shows the way in which information is gathered and decisions taken in operating BMW's Active Front Steering system, in which an electric steering motor acting through an epicyclic gear adds to the driver's own input to create a faster steering response in suitable operating conditions (mainly at slow speeds and when parking). The system is designed so that any failure of the electric input still leaves the driver with conventional steering. (BMW)*

thought that you could keep the swivel joints inboard of the wheel axis, but cant the swivel axis outwards at an angle – the 'king-pin inclination' – so that it met the wheel axis at the centre of the tyre contact patch. Now you have your space, you avoid the bump-feedback problem, and you gain some self-centring effect (beyond what the tyres provide in self-aligning torque) because as the wheel turns around the swivel axis, it has to lift the front of the car very slightly – in some cars with extreme kin-pin inclinations, like the Hillman Imp, you can actually see it happen.

So far we have only looked at the steering geometry from the front, but it needs viewing from the side as well. A much more positive, and usually desirable self-centring effect can be achieved by also tilting the king-pin axis forward at the bottom, and running it slightly forward of the centre of the wheel, to provide a castoring effect. All that remains then is to exercise some fine-tuning. The wheel itself can be given a camber angle (positive with its top leaning outwards, negative with it leaning inwards) and a small amount of toe-in or toe-out (front-wheel-drive cars often have a small amount of static toe-out, so that they are pulled straight-ahead when they are actually driving). Finally, the point where the steering axis meets the ground can be 'tweaked' relative to the centre of the tyre contact patch. The amount by which it is forward of the centre – which in practice it always is – is the 'castor trail'. When it falls inside the line through the centre, there is 'offset'. When it falls outside the line, there is 'negative offset', which is sometimes claimed to create a self-stabilising effect when braking with the front wheels on surfaces with different grip: the difference in braking pulls the car one way, but the steering is gently tugged in the other. Moderate offset makes the steering lighter, because when the steering is turned, more of the tyre can roll around the steering axis rather than scrubbing round it – obviously a consideration mainly at low speed.

What we end up with, therefore, is no less than six measurements – four angles and two distances – which completely define the steering geometry of any car. The angles are the king pin inclination, the castor angle, the camber angle and the toe-in; the distances are the castor trail and the offset, positive or negative. It is open to the chassis designer to adjust any of these to achieve exactly the desired result, which is not to say the task is easy. Here as everywhere else in the chassis, compromise is at work. Powerful self-centring gives strong natural stability but also creates heavy steering, for example, and may also mask the more subtle messages being fed back by the self-aligning torque, which is what provides the driver's hands with information about how the tyres themselves are behaving.

Even six measurements may not be the end of the story. One steering problem which has emerged in powerful front-wheel-drive cars is that of 'torque steer', which tends to wrench the steering towards full lock if the driver floors the accelerator while cornering. There are various theories about what causes torque steer, but Volkswagen has suggested that one of the keys to its control is to reduce the 'spindle offset' – the distance between the steering axis and the wheel-hub centre. This principle was applied to the Golf series 3 front suspension, in which the spindle offset was reduced from 52mm (2.0in) to 40mm (1.6in).

# The steering linkage

Ask the average driver what he wants in the way of steering, and he (or, especially, she) will ask for it to be light enough to call for no real effort. At the same time, most drivers feel uncomfortable with steering which is so light as to give no 'feel'. Pressed beyond this, drivers often ask for steering which is responsive without being 'abrupt' – an area in which subjective opinions can vary widely. Most drivers tend to value and admire cars with tight turning circles, even though the ability to turn the front wheels through extreme angles can cause severe engineering problems, especially in front-wheel-drive cars.

To reduce driver effort, all steering systems employ some form of gearing. Modern cars typically have steering ratios of up to 20:1, in other words it takes about four turns of the steering wheel to turn the front wheels about one-fifth of a full turn (36 degrees in either direction) from full lock in one direction to full lock in the other. This is sufficient to enable the front wheels of a small car to be steered without undue effort. Larger and heavier cars need either lower-geared steering, or alternatively some form of power assistance.

A number of gearing systems have seen popularity over the years. Until the 1960s, the recirculating-ball evolution of the worm-and-nut type proved the most satisfactory for most light-duty purposes. Eventually, however, the rack-and-pinion system, earlier rejected because of its susceptibility to fight-back and to backlash, became the favoured type as ways were found to overcome its faults. Today it is almost the only type used in passenger cars and light commercial vehicles. Ways have since been found to design the teeth of the moving rack to deliver variable gearing, with a gentle response to pinion movements around the straight-ahead position to allow for delicate adjustments when cruising on a near-straight road, and a much faster response once the steering wheel has been moved through more than around a quarter-turn in either direction.

As already pointed out, smooth and accurate control is extremely difficult if the wheels do not tend to return to the straight-ahead position. The self-centring effect should not be too strong, however: apart from increasing the steering effort, there is a danger that if the driver simply releases the wheel when exiting a corner, the steering will overshoot the straight-ahead position and set up a potentially dangerous oscillation. To guard against this, and to provide additional protection against the transmission of road shocks, some steering systems are equipped with dampers which resist movements of higher frequency than the driver would normally be capable of applying.

Attention to detail can usefully reduce steering effort, and also – through the removal of friction – improve feel. In the 1995 Ford Fiesta, for example, effort was reduced and feel improved through a 50% reduction in the lower steering ball-joint friction, a reduction of the steering column universal joint angle from 39 to 28°, and a general tightening of tolerances compared with the preceding model.

# Power-assisted
## steering

Almost certainly, more new production passenger cars are now fitted with power-assisted steering (PAS) than with manual steering. Two factors have contributed to this. One is the tendency of chassis engineers to take advantage of PAS to do things that would otherwise make the steering heavy or low-geared. The other is the ability (and readiness) of the consumer to pay for systems which take the effort out of driving.

In theory, the factor which decides the changeover point from manual to power steering is the effort needed, especially at low speed and towards full lock, without the need for lots of turning of the wheel. Modern drivers are simply not tolerant of steering which needs more than four turns of the steering wheel from lock to lock. Yet at the same time, they want the steering to be as light as possible and the turning circle to be as tight as possible. PAS provides the only possible answer, especially with the almost universal move towards front-wheel-drive cars which place a high proportion of their weight on the front wheels.

Apart from reducing steering effort, one of the advantages of PAS is that it enables steering characteristics to be adapted more readily to suit different consumer requirements. In particular, the gearing of the system can be varied almost at will. Modern PAS-equipped cars are generally geared at around three turns of the steering wheel between extremes of steering lock; cars have been offered with gearing as high as two turns of the wheel between locks but these were generally disliked, although it is increasingly argued that much 'faster' steering would be acceptable, given proper shaping of the steering response curve to overcome the problem of a twitchy 'go-kart' reaction to small movements around the straight-ahead position.

PAS can also be made to offer varying degrees of assistance, from a great deal, to a more moderate amount which retains a greater impression of 'feel' for enthusiastic drivers. This technique now extends to speed-sensitive assistance, in which the degree of assistance is high at low speed – for parking and general manoeuvring – but becomes less as speed increases, to decrease the risk of driver over-control.

For many years, the standard method of providing PAS has been to use an engine-driven hydraulic pump whose pressure can be applied to either side of a steering jack, through valves operated by movement of the steering wheel. As time has gone on, such systems have become more highly developed, to provide such features as the speed-sensitive assistance just described, and to provide a higher standard of feedback to prevent the driver's feeling of being 'disconnected' from the front wheels, a fault of many of the earliest PAS installations, especially in American cars.

PAS systems normally work, through the design of their control valve arrangements, to provide assistance to reduce steering effort, rather than operating the steering directly via a servo-valve system, which would require higher pressures. Citroën is the only manufacturer to have used a fully-powered system in large-scale production, tapping pressure from its hydropneumatic suspension system in the DS, SM, CX and XM. In the vast majority of hydraulic PAS systems, pressure from the engine-driven pump is 'spilled' when not needed. This wastes energy; it has been estimated that a conventional PAS pump can absorb up to 2kW even when no steering assistance is being provided.

Full power operation as used by Citroën offers a number of advantages, including the interesting ability of the steering to centre itself when the vehicle is stationary, as long as the engine is running to provide power. For the sake of safety, provision must be made for reversion to manual steering in the event of hydraulic circuit or other failure.

Although specialist suppliers like ZF have continued to seek ways of making hydraulic PAS lighter, cheaper and less wasteful of energy, especially when fitted to smaller cars, there is now far more interest in PAS which works through electric or electro-hydraulic operation. In the second case, the system retains hydraulic assistance but pressure is provided via an electric pump rather than an engine-driven pump. The alternative is to do away with hydraulics altogether and adopt a system in which the power assistance (or even fully powered operation) is provided by an electric motor. In either case, the system is generally known as EPAS – electric power-assisted steering.

Both approaches consume power only when steering assistance is needed, and their installation is easier because there is no need to align a mechanically driven pump with a belt drive from the crankshaft. The pure electric system consists essentially of an electric motor geared to the steering linkage, a control module and suitable sensors, the most important being a steering torque sensor. The electro-hydraulic approach still requires a reservoir, the electrically driven pump, an hydraulic output jack or motor and associated piping, although given flexibility of installation, these can be engineered into an extremely compact module.

The pure electric EPAS has the additional advantage that it is extremely easy to incorporate speed sensitivity by modulating the control signal to the motor. A minor advantage is that steering assistance is available, drawing on battery capacity, even when the engine is not running. The greatest disadvantage of any EPAS, other than the existing body of experience and investment in production facilities for hydraulic systems, is the extra load placed on electric power-generation systems which in many cases are already being run close to their limits. Things will become much easier when cars begin to be fitted with higher-voltage electrical systems (see Part 4, Chapter 25).

Among the earliest cars to use EPAS were the mid-engined Honda NS-X, MGF and Toyota MR2 sports cars, in which conventional hydraulic PAS would involve long high-pressure pipe runs through the cabin from an engine-driven pump to the steering rack. Beyond these special cases, the first production EPAS applications in small front-wheel-drive cars have already appeared, for example in the Renault Twingo and Fiat Punto, and other 'B-segment' models are set to follow. In these small cars, sufficient power for steering can be supplied from a compact 12V electric motor. Applying EPAS to larger and heavier vehicles will probably have to await the arrival of 36V electrical systems.

Delphi, which supplies its E-steer EPAS for the Fiat Punto, says that switching from hydraulic to electric operation helps performance and economy. The company's tests on a B-segment car fitted with E-steer instead of a standard hydraulic system have suggested savings of up to 0.3 litres/100km (approximately 0.1 gallons/ 100miles) in overall fuel

*One gentle step towards 'steer-by-wire' is Delphi's Quadrasteer system for applying a steering input to the rear wheels of large US-market SUVs and light trucks. The steering signal is transmitted to the rear electrically and is therefore 'by wire' but with the advantage that the wheels can be centred in the event of any failure. This assumption cannot be made for the front wheels, of course. (Delphi)*

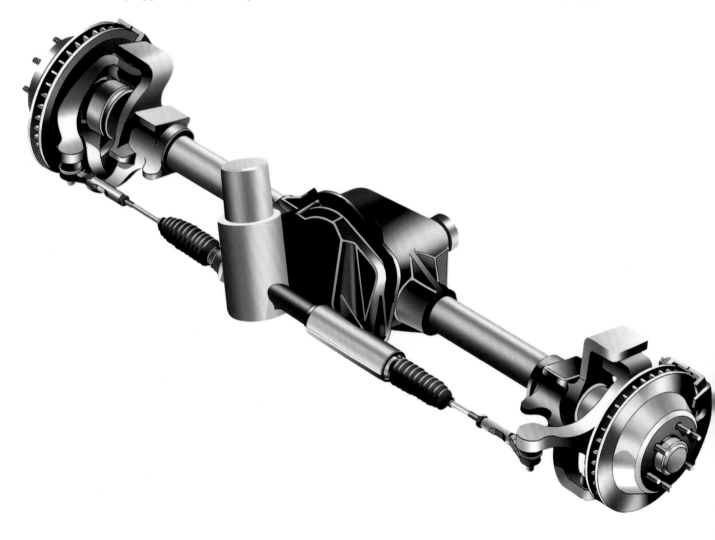

consumption, of 0.5sec in the time taken to accelerate from rest to 100km/h (62mph), and of 3sec in the time taken to cover 400m (a quarter-mile) from rest. As a bonus, Delphi suggests that incidents with hydraulic pump and hoses (which E-steer doesn't have) account for 53% of steering system warranty claims throughout the industry. Delphi also points to the ease with which EPAS characteristics can be changed to suit different needs. The Fiat Punto has a driver-selected switch which halves the steering effort at low speed for city driving and parking.

# Rear-wheel and four-wheel steering

Four-wheel steer (4WS) systems have been offered on a handful of Japanese models for more than a decade, but have made little headway in other markets. In Japan, the much tighter turning circle which can be achieved by steering the rear wheels in the opposite direction to the front wheels has a strong appeal for drivers who must frequently manoeuvre in extremely confined spaces. Elsewhere, the cost, weight, complication and possible safety implications of 4WS have proved too much of a discouragement. Clearly, the only practical way to make 4WS 'fail-safe' is for the rear wheels to automatically return to the straight-ahead position in the event of any problem.

The main technical question with 4WS is whether – or rather, when – the rear wheels should steer in the same sense as the front wheels, and when in the opposite sense. As already pointed out, opposite-sense steering allows much tighter turning circles for manoeuvring in crowded car parks. On the other hand, similar-sense steering provides better behaviour at high speeds, especially in lane-change manoeuvres where it enables the car to 'move sideways' without having to change direction so much; it is the change of direction which can lead to control problems in extreme situations. It is now generally accepted that to fulfil its potential, 4WS needs the ability to steer in either sense according to speed, with opposite-sense rear steering at parking speeds, same-sense steering at high speeds, and a 'cross-over' between the two at around 20mph (32km/h). However, some advanced studies have suggested maximum benefit would be provided if, even at high speed, the rear wheels were steered momentarily in the opposite sense before assuming a same-sense steering angle. Mitsubishi, which actually demonstrated such a system in its HSR-III concept car, claimed better 'turn-in' resulted, but clearly any such system depends on extremely rapid signal processing and

transducer response. Any advanced 4WS system would probably take into account not only steering wheel position but also the speed of steering wheel movement, and try to deduce whether the driver was changing lane or steering through a continuous corner.

Despite its apparent technical promise, 4WS has recently fallen from favour even among the Japanese manufacturers. European chassis engineers generally took the principle and achieved some of the same benefits by 'passive' means, discussed in earlier chapters, controlling the deformation of rear suspension mounting bushes under cornering loads to achieve a calculated rear-steer effect to enhance stability. The rapid development of electronically controlled stability augmentation systems, which mainly use existing hardware and can more convincingly be programmed to 'fail-safe', may well have written the end to the use of 4WS in production passenger cars.

*Any rear-wheel steering system which adds an input to the front steering needs to be carefully tuned. At very low speed, the wheels should turn 'pro-steer' to tighten the turning circle; at moderate to high speed they should 'counter-steer' to improve stability and reduce yaw angles during lane changes. The tuning curve for the Delphi Quadrasteer system is shown here. (Delphi)*

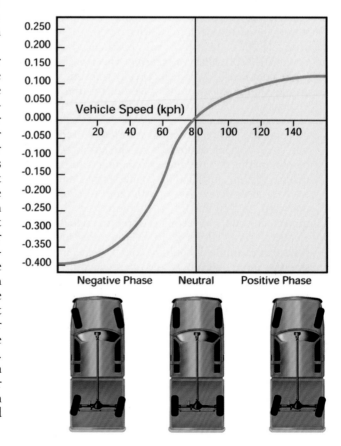

Despite this feeling, from 1999 onwards Delphi began developing its Quadrasteer system, applying the same 4WS principles of operation, but aiming at the very large American market for luxury-equipped light trucks and very big off-road vehicles. Even in American car parks, the biggest of these vehicles can be awkward to manoeuvre and would be helped by opposite-sense rear steering. At the same time, their stability in lane-changes, especially when towing a heavy trailer, would be improved by same-sense rear steer. Delphi accordingly developed Quadrasteer for the rear axles of such vehicles, and expects to have a production application in the near future. An interesting aspect of Quadrasteer is that steering signals to the electric motor which operates the rear wheel steering are themselves transmitted electrically – making this one of the first true examples of 'steer-by-wire'.

# The future:
## steer-by-wire?

As described in Part 1, 'drive-by-wire', in which the cable linkage from the accelerator pedal to the throttle valve (or diesel injection pump) is replaced by an electrical linkage from a pedal sensor to the engine control unit, is becoming commonplace. Chassis engineers are now looking at applying the same general approach to steering, to create 'steer-by-wire' (SBW). In SBW, the mechanical steering column is replaced by a steering wheel position and movement sensor which electrically transmits data to an electronic control unit. The control unit in turn instructs an EPAS system to position the front wheels at a certain angle.

There are two big potential advantages to SBW, and one large, nagging doubt. Taking the advantages first, by eliminating the mechanical steering column, SBW makes system installation much easier and saves weight, also doing away with any worries about rearward movement of the column in a frontal impact. Second, converting the steering signal into an electrical form allows it to be processed in useful ways. For example, it could be told to disregard driver steering inputs which would cause loss of control (while allowing the maximum available cornering force to be maintained without loss of control), or it might accept inputs from advanced forward-looking sensors which could trigger automatic avoiding action.

The big doubt is what happens in the event of a system failure (including electric power failure). There is no natural 'fail-safe' for primary steering: returning the wheels to the straight-ahead position as a reaction to a computer failure could, in the wrong circumstances, send you over the edge of a cliff.

There is no easy answer to this fear – or rather, there are two answers. The first is that SBW must be engineered as nearly as possible to eliminate the risk of complete failure, using duplicated electric signal paths with channel self-checking and cross-checking. A back-up battery would guard against simple power failure. The second answer is more philosophical. Every year, a handful of people drive over cliffs anyway, because they lose control of their vehicles on mountain roads. If the considerable abilities of SBW enabled some of those people to retain control, the balance would be in its favour. Beside such considerations, the problem of providing the SBW system with artificial 'feel' seems almost trivial.

Despite these misgivings – and the fact that under existing law, SBW is actually illegal in the European Community in any vehicle capable of more than 40km/h (25mph) – the advantages of SBW are such that systems are likely to appear in production cars within five years. Prototype systems have already been demonstrated, and some remarkable layouts have been proposed. One startling idea comes from Delphi, which as long ago as 1998 showed a system which eliminated all mechanical connection not only between the steering wheel and the front wheels, but also between the front wheels, instead using a separate steering actuator for each wheel with electronic movement synchronisation. This arrangement has the incidental advantage that the steering relationship between the two wheels need not be constant. Instead, each wheel can be steered to take account of the slight difference in steering angle (the so-called Ackermann angle) between the inner and outer wheels when cornering: the inner wheel, following the tighter radius, ideally needs to turn through a greater angle. With correct electronic control, the Delphi system could eliminate 'scrub' in low-speed manoeuvring without paying any high-speed penalty in stability or handling.

'Halfway-house' systems are possible, as BMW showed in a demonstration in 2000. The company produced two experimental 3-series cars, one with a full SBW system and the other with an ingenious hybrid 'active front steering' (AFS) system. BMW's AFS works by using an epicyclic gearbox built into the steering column to enable an SBW signal to add (or in principle to subtract, but in practice usually to add) to the driver's own input. Thus at low speed, AFS can turn the steering more quickly, in effect raising the gearing of the steering system as perceived by the driver. One obvious advantage of this concept is that in the event of a fault, the system can be disabled, leaving the driver with a conventional manual input. The 'full-house' SBW system had the ability directly to vary the steering ratio according to speed (and to achieve a smooth non-linear relationship with the driver's input, increasing the gearing towards full lock at low speed). For the sake of safety, signal paths in this system were triplicated, with a 'majority voting' system to identify and isolate a faulty channel. Both systems were engineered so that turning the steering wheel through 160° in either direction gave full lock.

Another route towards SBW has been seen in some of the 'automatic lane keeping' systems which have been demonstrated by several manufacturers including Jaguar. These systems are more fully discussed in Part 4, but in principle the lane markings are tracked by a camera whose signals are analysed by a computer which then issues steering instructions to keep the car in the centre of the lane. The actual steering is done by a small steering motor 'strapped on' to the steering column, with a friction contact so that the driver can easily override it if he wishes; but the automatic steering corrections are undoubtedly SBW.

Eventually, SBW opens up the possibility of steering by 'joystick' rather than a conventional wheel, with the system applying lock in response to a combination of movement and pressure. Mercedes and Saab have already run experimental cars equipped with joystick steering, and the conclusion of tests seems to be that most drivers find it much easier to steer than they expected before setting out. There are obvious advantages with this concept: if the joystick was mounted on the centre console (and especially if it also moved forward to accelerate the car and backwards to apply the brakes, using other 'X-by-wire' electronic linkages) then either front seat occupant could drive the car, and there would be no need to build separate left-hand and right-hand-drive versions, while identical front airbags could be installed on both sides. It all sounds very attractive – but even the optimists think it may be 10 years before we see production cars using the idea.

# 19 **Brakes**

The motoring pioneers had enough trouble keeping going, without worrying too much about stopping. As car performance increased, however, stopping quickly became a major problem, and it has been so ever since. Keeping up with the rise in car performance, and in the number of stopping situations created by increasing traffic density, has called for advances not only in the design of braking systems as such, but in the materials – especially the friction materials – used to make them. Nor should we forget that in the final analysis, brake performance can only be as good as the grip of the tyres on the road, which may be plentiful on a good, dry surface but distinctly lacking in wet or icy conditions. This is why the development of anti-lock braking systems, now universally referred to as ABS (although strictly speaking, ABS is a Bosch trademark), was so important. It still doesn't deliver dry-road braking performance, but it allows any driver to make the most of what grip there is.

Fundamentally, braking involves removing some of the energy of motion (kinetic energy) of the vehicle and turning it into another form of energy. In conventional brakes, this other form is always heat, generated by the friction of the brake linings (shoes or pads) rubbing against metal (drums or discs). Cars of the future, using electric traction, have the alternative of re-creating electrical energy and feeding it back to the batteries, a process known as regenerative braking. But the sheer rate of energy conversion involved in maximum-rate stopping means that even these advanced cars will still need efficient friction brakes too. One graphic illustration of the amount of energy involved was given by an Aston Martin engineer who had calculated that the energy dissipated in stopping a DB7 quickly from 100mph (161km/h) would heat a pensioner's flat for two weeks in winter.

Early chassis engineers had some strange ideas about braking, as they had about suspension design and steering. A popular device in the pioneer days was the transmission brake: you installed your brake on the propeller shaft rather than at the wheels. This does actually have the advantage of reducing the unsprung weight – not that this was much appreciated at the time – but it has the big disadvantage of forcing a large part of the transmission, between the brake and the tyre contact patch, to withstand the braking torque. In fact, all those early engineers were trying to do was avoid the complication of installing a brake unit actually in the wheel, with due allowance for the way the wheel was moving around (this became much easier with the invention of hydraulic brakes, but that came later). Even when wheel braking was adopted, most cars up to the mid-1920s had brakes only on the back wheels, which did nothing for their stability if the brakes were applied when cornering or if the brakes were locked in an emergency stop: if the front brakes lock, the car slides straight ahead but if the rears lock, you must fight to retain directional control.

Eventually the modern braking system emerged from chaos. Brakes were fitted to all four wheels, cable operation replaced pushrods and then hydraulics replaced cables, vacuum servo units were invented to reduce braking effort, drum brakes were replaced with discs, ABS was perfected and asbestos was eliminated from friction materials. Yet there are still more advances to come …

# Braking systems

The typical modern brake system consists of disc brakes on all four wheels, the front discs being ventilated, operation of the brake calipers being hydraulic with a vacuum servo to multiply the driver's pedal effort, plus ABS.

The master cylinder (acted upon by the brake pedal) has tandem pistons and the brake hydraulic circuits are 'split' according to one of a number of standard patterns, to ensure that no single failure completely disables the braking system. A mechanically operated parking brake, serving also as the ultimate emergency back-up, completes the system. Many braking systems also have a rear brake pressure-limiting valve which as far as possible restricts the pressure in the rear brake lines to make sure the back wheels will not lock, rendering the car unstable, in any circumstances. Modern brake discs are invariably integral with the wheel hub, even though this adds to the unsprung mass. From time to time over the years, designers have tried 'inboard' brakes connected to the wheels via what amounts to a small propeller shaft (or have simply mounted them at the inboard end of the drive shaft, where the wheel is driven) but the benefits have never managed to outweigh the additional cost and complication.

The basic modern system sounds fairly simple, yet a lot of work has gone into achieving the present high levels of braking performance. Effective braking depends on the generation of heat: the faster we can safely and effectively generate heat, the faster we can slow the car. Exactly how fast we can generate that

*Opposite: The majority of modern cars are now equipped with ventilated front disc brakes; this unit is from the current Ford Mondeo. For this car, the disc is 300mm in diameter and 24mm thick. For high-performance and competition cars, the face of the brake disc is often perforated for even better ventilation, and grooved to help disperse the dust created by brake pad wear. (Ford)*

heat depends on two things only: the way in which the friction surfaces work together, and the rate at which we can conduct heat away from the friction surfaces after it has been generated, before the surfaces melt, catch fire or explode.

This way of looking at it simplifies the situation so that only two things really matter: the materials from which the friction surfaces are made, and the design of the discs, pads and calipers to withstand very high temperatures and at the same time to transmit heat away from those surfaces as quickly as possible.

Up to around 1960, braking involved jamming high-friction shoes against the inside of metal drums. Almost all the heat was conducted away by the metal and, hopefully, radiated to the surrounding air. Sufficient radiation was achieved only when the drums were hot enough – and by that time, being metal, they had generally expanded enough to move away from the shoes so that the brake pedal gradually slumped to the floor before finding any bite, the classic problem of 'brake fade'. So the drums for high-performance cars were made mainly of light alloy (a better heat conductor) and equipped with surface fins (to increase surface area and therefore radiation); and the wheels were made as open as possible, by using wire spokes, to allow as much air as possible into contact with the drums. Even then, for passable performance, the drums had to be absolutely huge, adding enough unsprung weight to have a serious effect on ride comfort, roadholding and steering effort.

The brake fade problem was largely overcome by the switch to disc brakes, because the disc couldn't expand away from the pads, making the system (in theory) 'fade-proof'. However, when they are worked hard, disc brakes become very hot. Night-time pictures of racing cars often show the brake discs at a bright red heat. It is essential to conduct this heat away from the friction surfaces, which requires huge rates of transfer. Failure to achieve this means the friction surfaces and calipers may overheat. If too much heat lingers in the caliper assembly, the brake fluid can boil, causing symptoms uncannily like drum-brake fade, but even more suddenly encountered. So if disc brakes have done anything, they have concentrated engineers' minds even more on the basic questions of friction material and of effective heat dissipation.

Where the material is concerned, modern brake pads are a cunning (asbestos-free) blend of metallic filaments and tough resins: the resin generates the friction, and the metal keeps the shape stable while conducting some share of the heat away from the surface (most of the heat, of course, is carried away by the continually rotating disc). Any friction material has a 'temperature characteristic': its friction rises to a peak at a certain temperature and then falls away again as it gets hotter still. A 'gentle' material which works well at low temperatures, as used in the average car, will lose quite a lot of its friction if it is forced to a really high temperature, perhaps by driving fast down a mountain road with repeated heavy braking. This loss of friction can again feel like classic brake fade. So-called 'racing' brake pads have much higher peak-friction temperatures – at the cost of very little friction at low temperatures, which is why such pads have little bite until they are properly warmed through. This correctly suggests that any friction material is a compromise, both in its friction characteristics and in its wear rate. The more friction a pad generates in a given situation, the faster it will wear away (the disc hardly wears at all, or at least, it shouldn't).

*The possible shape of brakes to come: Siemens have developed an electromechanical unit with no hydraulics at all – the brake pads are pushed into contact with the disc by a highly-geared electric motor drive, which has to be reversible to pull them out of contact when the brake pedal is released.* (Siemens)

BRAKES

However, accepting that great advances have been made over the years by improving friction materials and optimising caliper design, we should still look at the other half of the system – the disc. The greatest step forward was to realise that a thicker disc could be cast with integral air channels, sucking air in at the centre and throwing it out, through centrifugal force, around the periphery. This creates a huge increase in radiation transfer rate and therefore in the rate at which energy can be shed. Especially in racing cars, great care is taken to duct cool air from a high-pressure intake to the hub of each ventilated disc. Most road cars have ventilated discs at the front only, because the front brakes inevitably carry the greater part of the braking effort. The average road car is nose-heavy anyway: the forward transfer of load under hard braking can see the front brakes doing 80% of the work, which is why the front brakes (like the front tyres) generally wear out faster than the rears.

The disc can also be made from advanced composite materials rather than cast metal, though only at great expense. For years, the fastest aeroplanes have used discs made mainly of carbon fibre, because for a given performance they can be made far more compact and lighter – cost, of course, being almost no object. Eventually, the technique was taken up by the top levels of motor racing, where the cost meant just as little. This in turn set the manufacturers of the highest-performance road cars thinking, and even though pure carbon discs remained out of the question, some advanced alternatives were available. This is how the current interest in 'ceramic' discs, now used in top-performance models by Porsche and Mercedes-Benz, arose. They are not pure ceramic, but a composite of carbon and ceramic, capable of withstanding very high temperatures and mechanical loads.

# Anti-lock brakes

As already pointed out, the term 'ABS' has become universal shorthand for an anti-lock brake system, although strictly it belongs to Bosch, the acronym deriving from that company's Anti-Blockier System or anti-wheel lock system. The basic principle of ABS is that wheel speed sensors feed information to a central processing unit which deduces when a wheel is about to lock, and the processor then acts through a servo valve system momentarily to release the brake on that wheel. In order that the brake can then be re-applied, the system needs its own source of hydraulic pressure; otherwise the driver's brake pedal would descend towards the floor every time an ABS pulse was delivered. The essential components of an ABS system are therefore the wheel speed sensors, the electronic processor, the servo valves, an electrically driven hydraulic pump, and a pressure accumulator. Non-electronic (pure hydro-mechanical) ABS systems were devised and offered during the 1980s, but eventually were 'seen off' by electronic systems which were not only more capable, but which quickly became cheaper.

Some early ABS systems were 'three channel', controlling the front brakes individually but releasing all rear wheel braking if either rear wheel began to lock. This saved a certain amount of cost and complication, but gave slightly inferior performance to a full four-channel system in which each brake is controlled individually.

A potential problem in ABS design is how to deal with 4WD transmission systems which embody limited-slip or differential locking devices. The mechanical linking, via the transmission, of wheels which the ABS system is seeking to control can produce the wrong messages. Some transmission systems have provision to disconnect drive to the rear wheels when ABS braking takes place. An alternative approach is to fit extra sensors to make system operation more flexible.

ABS has much in common with the traction control system (TCS), whose operation might be considered as 'ABS in reverse', since it depends on the detection of a (driven) wheel beginning to rotate faster, indicating incipient spin, rather than slower, indicating incipient locking. The wheel speed sensors can be shared, and because it has been found that the most effective way to prevent wheelspin at low speeds is to apply a momentary (and if necessary, repeated) brake operation, braking pulses can be drawn from the ABS valve block. In effect, once ABS is present, all that is required to provide a TCS is some extra software and an additional control output to reduce engine torque if necessary, either by reducing the amount of fuel being injected, or by direct intervention in a drive-by-wire accelerator control system.

A relatively recent concept related both to servo operation and to ABS is that of 'emergency brake assist' (EBA), first introduced by Mercedes and since adopted, in more or less similar form, by an increasing number of manufacturers. The principle of EBA is to ensure that the maximum possible braking effort is maintained throughout an emergency stop, since research has shown that many drivers fail to do so of their own accord, adding several metres to their minimum possible stopping distance. The research showed that even when an ABS system had been invoked and was cycling, stopping distances could be reduced by increasing the pedal pressure and thus the ABS cycling rate. Accordingly, EBA seeks to detect any pattern of brake pedal movement which indicates beyond question that the driver has initiated an emergency stop. A positive detection results in the maximum servo braking force being 'locked on', until either the car has come to a complete stop or the driver has completely released the brake pedal. Logically, EBA can only be employed when ABS is fitted.

At a technical seminar in mid-1998, BMW presented its plans for developing a fully integrated electronic brake management (EBM) system using its existing DSC stability-enhancement system (which includes the ABS and TCS functions) as the core. The development goal, according to BMW, is to define a system architecture which embraces all existing brake components and software (control systems) and which will allow the immediate integration of new functions as they become available. The first two functions to take advantage of this approach will be dynamic braking control (DBC), and active cruise control (ACC). The DBC system is essentially a refined interpretation of EBA; ACC calls for an interface between forward looking sensors and the braking system to achieve automatic slowing of the vehicle when the measured headway is less than the minimum permitted for the existing speed.

# The future: dynamic braking **and** brake-by-wire

Ever since the introduction of ABS, the way has potentially been opening towards what chassis engineers call either electronic brake management (EBM) or dynamic brake control (DBC). As a system, ABS works well but is limited in its application: it doesn't begin working until one of the wheels begins to lock up under braking. Yet as we have already seen, in many situations a car's weight is not evenly distributed on its four wheels or even from side to side, and in these circumstances some wheels will be

*BMW has demonstrated this electromechanical braking system, with no hydraulics at all: very high-geared electric motors wind the pads into contact with the discs and lift them clear again. The system needs 36V electrics to provide sufficient power for rapid brake operation. Brake pedal feel has to be synthetic, and the effort to each wheel can be adjusted individually. (BMW)*

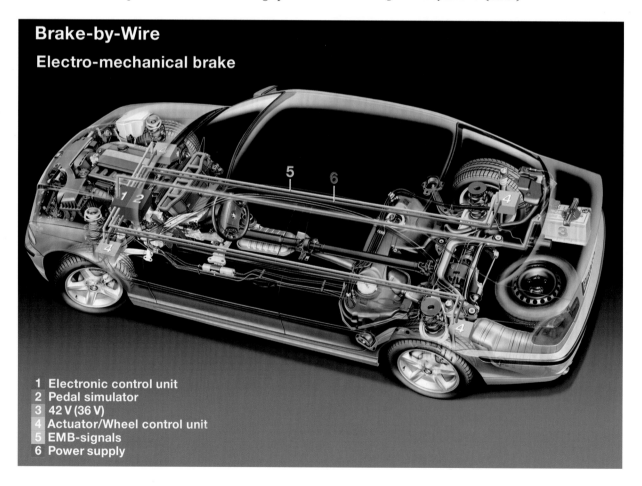

**Brake-by-Wire**

**Electro-mechanical brake**

1 Electronic control unit
2 Pedal simulator
3 42 V (36 V)
4 Actuator/Wheel control unit
5 EMB-signals
6 Power supply

able to accept more braking effort than others. What is more, distributing the braking according to wheel load might benefit vehicle stability – and the way would also be open to use differential side-to-side braking to achieve positive control of stability (discussed in more detail in Chapter 20). Before these ideals can be achieved, two things are needed. One is the ability to work out the loads on the individual wheels. The second is the ability to control at all times (not just when the ABS is working) the braking effort to each wheel. The first requirement needs the right sensors and a computer. The second will come when we have the other great braking advance – brake-by-wire (BBW). As in the case of steer-by-wire (SBW – Chapter 18), the brakes can be applied through the use of electrical rather than mechanical signalling between brake pedal and whatever device actually applies the brake. In exactly the same way as SBW, the advantages of BBW include the ability to modulate the driver's output signal at will in the interests of easy and consistent operation, and of safety. In the case of DBC, the computer would take the driver's signal – pressure on the brake pedal and speed of application – and divide it into four separate signals, one for each wheel, to apply the right amount of braking effort in the best possible way. BBW would also open up the possibility of an easy interface with, for example, an 'intelligent cruise control' system, permitting automatic braking of the car to maintain safety distance – down to a standstill if necessary. Physically, BBW brings other advantages: for example, there is no need for any linkage passing through the bulkhead to a master cylinder on the other side, which is better for passive safety and the transmission of noise and vibration. But the brake pedal needs some kind of 'artificial feel' for the driver to push against.

At the wheel end of the system, BBW can be purely electric or electro-hydraulic. In the first case,

the brake pad would be forced into place (and positively released) by an electric screw-jack arrangement. At a technical demonstration in 2000, BMW showed a car with pure electric BBW, using the recirculating-ball principle for its screwjack actuators to minimise friction and achieve rapid response. As with so many of these new-generation developments, the system worked from a 36V rather than a 12V electrical supply. It was notable for its totally smooth action deep into the ABS regime, rather than having the usual thumping feedback from the pedal. The smoothness was the result of control being genuinely analogue, unlike existing ABS in which control is 'digital', applying brake pressure at one threshold value and releasing it at another. Control was, of course, wheel-by-wheel; and BMW made the point that any braking function one cared to think of could be catered for within the software.

In electro-hydraulic BBW, a motor driving a pump pressurises the brake fluid accumulator. A set of solenoid valves controls the flow of pressurised fluid to each caliper. Valve operation is controlled by a brake system controller which accepts, and processes, signals from brake pedal force and travel sensors. In many respects, in fact, this option resembles an ABS package plus electric signalling and electronic processing. This approach has the advantage of being able to use existing caliper units and may therefore be the first type to come into use, by 2005 at the latest, although BMW – and maybe some of the other car manufacturers – may be keener to move quickly to the all-electric solution. Whatever type comes first, there are likely to be savings in weight and in ease of installation and servicing. Confining the hydraulics to a small closed circuit at each corner of the car – or doing away with them altogether – will make a big difference. But the real difference will come when the brakes no longer merely stop the car, but contribute to its stability and safe handling.

# ⑳The future for chassis design

## TRW Integrated Vehicle Control Systems

### *Sensor & Communication Technologies:*

❶ Contact Tyre Patch Sensors (CTPS)

❷ Safety Critical Data Bus Structure

❸ Plug and Play Software

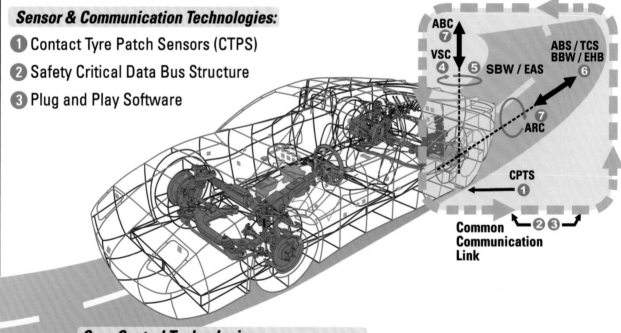

### *Core Control Technologies:*

❹ Enhanced Vehicle Stability Control (VSC)

❺ **Steering** – Steer by Wire (SBW) or Electrically Assisted Steering (EAS)

❻ **Braking** – Brake By Wire (BBW) or Electro Hydraulic Braking (EHB)

❼ **Suspension** – Active Roll Control (ARC) & Active Body Control (ABC)

A t various places in Part 3 we have looked at future prospects for various aspects of chassis design, especially those offered by steer-by-wire and brake-by-wire. But there is one area we have only briefly mentioned, and another where the various strings need pulling together, so to speak. The first area is that of truly 'active' ride control – the prospects for a magic-carpet ride in the cabin whatever the state of the road surface, using electronic control of the suspension. The second is what the chassis engineers call 'stability enhancement', which essentially means that as far as possible, using all the means available to it, the car will be made faithfully to execute what the driver intends without the risk of losing control.

Active ride is an area where only two manufacturers, Citroën and Mercedes, have made even limited steps towards the ideal. Experimental prototypes which approach it more nearly have been demonstrated, but it seems more than ever likely that fully active ride may never reach production, and we need to understand why. Stability enhancement on the other hand is already fitted to an increasing number of cars, and the question is mainly one of how much more capable it can become.

# Active ride

Although Citroën exploited the benefits of its hydropneumatic suspension system for years to give benefits like a constantly level body attitude and adjustable ride height, it was only during the 1990s that the company moved in the direction of truly active ride control – and even then, it didn't move very far in relation to the often expressed ideal. In a truly active ride, springs and dampers give way to a system which actually drives the wheels up and down in relation to the body, so that (in theory) the wheels follow every contour of the road surface and the body doesn't move at all. The trouble with this theory is that because any such system needs a response time – it cannot respond instantaneously – the only way to achieve perfection is to measure the profile of the road surface before you cross it. Some work has actually been carried out on ultrasonic sensors scanning the surface ahead of the front wheels, but most experimental active ride systems work on the basis of constant load. The system knows how much load each wheel should be supporting: if the load on one wheel starts to increase, it must be because that wheel is climbing over a bump, and the system lifts the wheel to keep the load constant, lowering it again as the load reduces on the far side.

The problem with any such system is the amount of energy needed to 'drive' all four wheels vertically all the time. A power consumption of 10kW has been suggested for operating four high-pressure, high-speed hydraulic jacks in a heavy car on a normal road surface. Even in a big luxury car, this imposes a significant penalty in terms of performance and fuel consumption, even before thinking about the extremely high cost of any jack which would do the job. System failure also needs thinking about – if the hydraulic pump fails, the car will sink quickly onto its emergency bump-stops, with limited ground clearance. Thus, although various experimental cars, notably from Lotus, produced impressive results not only in terms of ride comfort but also such features as automatic adjustment of handling characteristics by altering the ratio of front to rear roll stiffness, the full concept never came anywhere near a production application. There were alternative suggestions for systems in which the movement of a suspension unit would itself 'pump up' a hydraulic accumulator whose pressure could then be used to improve the ride quality without draining power from the engine, but little has been heard of that approach since the mid-1990s.

Citroën, which had the best starting point in the form of its existing high-pressure hydropneumatic suspension system, adopted an indirect approach. It did not try to achieve the surface-tracking ability of fully active ride, but instead modified its suspension to switch between two different settings – the important point being that the settings involved different spring rates as well as different (matched) damper rates. The Citroën Hydractive system, which first appeared in the XM, switches between two spring-and-damper settings, achieved by providing an extra gas-spring sphere at each end of the car, to which the adjacent wheel units can be connected by opening a pair of valves. The connecting passages contain damper orifices, enabling the damper rate to be matched to the reduced spring rate. The valves open and close under computer control, shutting the valves to switch to the stiffer setting when, for instance, the electronic system senses that the driver is turning the steering wheel to enter a corner.

Hydractive achieved worthwhile benefits, at some extra cost but without adding very much to the power drain of the basic hydropneumatic system. Citroën followed its technical success with the Activa anti-roll system, which first appeared on the Xantia.

*Opposite: One of the giant American 'tier-one' suppliers to the motor industry has a development programme which it foresees leading to the close integration of all the main vehicle control systems for optimum safety and efficiency. The broad outline of the TRW concept is seen in this diagram, which comes from the 2000 SAE Congress. TRW clearly sees 'by-wire' operation of systems as the desirable goal, but feels that it may be reached in two stages. (TRW)*

The Activa system requires two extra hydraulic jacks between the body and the suspension, at diagonally opposite corners of the car. The high-pressure system operates these jacks to limit body roll to half a degree, which from a driver's point of view means no perceptible roll at all. The half-degree allowance is sufficient to prevent the system from 'hunting' every time the driver makes a small course correction, while ensuring that the body stays almost perfectly upright when cornering. This ensures that the wheels and the tyres also remain upright, leading to much improved cornering behaviour and grip.

Other companies have looked at the benefits of artificially limiting cornering roll angle, and Delphi supplies Land Rover with a system to reduce roll angles in the Discovery – not completely, but enough to make driving more comfortable, and safer, when travelling quickly on normal roads.

In 1999, Mercedes came to fully active ride when it announced its Active Body Control (ABC) system. Mercedes's key move was to throw away the idea of a completely magic-carpet ride and settle for a system with 'limited authority'. In ABC, the hydraulic system only takes care of suspension movements at rates of up to 5 Hertz (5 cycles per second), the significance of this being that most of the suspension movements which our bodies interpret as 'ride comfort' rather than 'vibration' are less than 5Hz, and are thus taken care of by ABC. Higher-rate movements are soaked up in the normal way by a conventional coil spring and damper suspension. By accepting the 5Hz limit, the Mercedes engineers were able to reduce the power consumption to a reasonable 3kW in the 'worst case' of a driver pressing on down a twisty lane with a poor surface (and some of that power drain is regained because the tyres, maintained more nearly upright, have lower rolling resistance when cornering). It also proved possible to achieve a big reduction in component cost – although in normal car terms, it remains high (the system comprises one hydraulic pump, two pressure accumulators, 13 different sensors, two computer units, four very complicated and expensive spring/damper struts and a number of smaller items, and ties them all together with an advanced databus electronic system; it can never be cheap). Other benefits of active ride, such as being able to do away with anti-roll bars and anti-dive geometry, and being able to adjust handling by altering the ratio of front to rear roll stiffness, remained. And because the ABC actuators work in parallel with conventional coil springs and dampers, any failure of ABC leaves the car perfectly driveable, if less comfortable.

While Mercedes's ABC works well, giving a combination of luxury-car ride with sports-car handling, it is too expensive ever to be applied to ordinary family cars. Mercedes thinks the lower limit of ABC application may eventually be the top-range versions of its E-class; and even this is a system which fails to deliver the full benefits of 'ideal' active ride. Future solutions are going to have to depend on lateral thinking, like Citroën's (in what circumstances do we really need to control the ride characteristics more flexibly?) or on simpler concepts like Delphi's Magneride, discussed in Chapter 16. Chassis engineers don't need to ask what is theoretically possible – the answer is almost anything. They need to ask what they can do at moderate cost and with minimum, if any, additional power consumption.

# Artificial stability

It has been sadly evident since the beginning of motoring that some drivers are more skilled than others. This is especially obvious during certain tricky manoeuvres. One of these is the high-speed 'chicane' or double lane-change (change lanes to avoid an obstacle, then regain your own side of the road as quickly as possible). For a number of complex engineering reasons there is a danger of losing control on the exit from this manoeuvre; instead of straightening up, the vehicle oscillates in a series of wild swoops until it either spins to a stop or rolls over. During 1997, this exercise and its risks suddenly became celebrated as the 'Moose Test', after a Scandinavian motoring magazine which used it as a standard test procedure rolled the then-new Mercedes A-class in the process.

Among the several measures Mercedes then took to improve the behaviour of the A-class was to fit the car with what it called the ESP (Electronic Stability Programme) system. As it happened, ESP was immediately available because Mercedes had already developed the system and since 1995, had been offering it in its powerful rear-wheel-drive cars – as had its competitor BMW, which called its system (different in detail but not in principle) DSC, or Dynamic Slip Control.

Stability enhancement systems like ESP and DSC take as their starting point the well established principles (already discussed) of anti-lock braking (ABS) and traction control systems (TCS). Remember that in most TCS installations, at moderate speeds, a driven wheel is prevented from spinning by automatic momentary application of its brake, an action which also allows the opposite wheel to transmit extra torque. When operating in this sense, the system not only uses the ABS wheel speed sensor to detect when the wheel is starting to spin, but also takes the brake pulse from the ABS pressure accumulator and valve block. In fact, as previously pointed out, basic traction control can be added to almost any ABS system simply by writing some extra software for the control computer; although further complications arise because real-life TCS usually also generates a signal to control engine torque output, and this involves the addition of extra hardware and electrical connections.

Stability enhancement systems like ESC take the principle a stage further by using the same momentary application of an individual brake to modify the yaw rate (the rate of change of direction) of a manoeuvring car. If, for example, the driver of a powerful rear-wheel-drive car on an icy road uses too much power in cornering, the rear wheels begin to slide outwards, and control may quickly be lost. But if, as soon as the rear wheels begin to slide, an ESC system applies brake to the rear wheel on the outside of the corner, then the effect will tend to yaw the car in the opposite sense – nose out of the corner rather than into it. At the same time, the car will be slowed down. Again, if the driver enters a corner too abruptly and the front wheels begin to run wide, application of the nearside front brake will pull the car back towards its proper cornering line. Thus the working principle of ESC is that if the car begins to depart from the driver's intended line, small, rapid 'dabs' of brake, normally on a single wheel at one corner of the car, will restore the condition the driver is trying to achieve. In fundamental terms, ESC uses individual wheel braking to modify a car's handling.

The key to the concept is to determine the driver's intentions, to compare these with the car's actual behaviour, and to reduce the difference to zero. This requires careful sensing of the driver's control movements, and especially of steering wheel operation, together with sensing of the car's movement. This latter calls at the very least for a lateral accelerometer, and preferably for a direct-reading yaw-rate sensor. All the signals have then to be processed through the stability system control unit. The final output takes the simple form of a series of brake pulses to one wheel, possibly accompanied by an automatic reduction in engine power, until the car has returned to the driver's intended path.

Stability enhancement is by no means foolproof. It cannot allow cars to be driven into low-friction corners at absurdly high speeds. But it has proved effective at providing powerful rear-wheel-drive cars on low-friction surfaces with the stability and ease of control normally to be expected of front-wheel-drive cars. Part of the appeal of such systems is that they require only three significant pieces of hardware – the steering-angle/rate sensor, the yaw-rate sensor (both of which can be useful for other purposes) and an electronic processing unit – plus an investment in software over and above a conventional four-channel ABS/TCS installation.

Ever since it provided part of the answer to the particular handling problem encountered in the Mercedes A-class, stability enhancement has been fitted to an increasing variety of cars, some of which should logically have little use for it. To some extent this is a commentary on the fact that most of the hardware is already now fitted to most moderately expensive cars, and it is relatively easy to 'wire them up' to deliver this extra feature, which can then be sold as a valuable addition to the specification. The wiring-up process should become easier still if brake-by-wire becomes accepted, and if sensor information is distributed around the car by means of a 'databus bar'.

Stability enhancement may become even more powerful if advantage is taken of the potential – discussed in Part 2, Chapter 14 – of 'active' transmissions, able to vary the side-to-side split of drive torque to influence vehicle behaviour. Paradoxically enough, the one input which is less likely to play a part is steering itself, even if steer-by-wire eventually becomes a reality. If steering created the handling problem to begin with, the car needs an alternative way of sorting it out. Consciously or otherwise, skilled drivers have always used the accelerator to 'trim' their car's handling – and really skilled ones, especially Scandinavian rally drivers, have used the brakes too. Stability enhancement, by whatever means, delivers some measure of that skill to any driver who has overdone a manoeuvre.

Among other things, ESC has proved to be a further nail in the coffin of four-wheel-drive for road use. Just as traction control overcame the basic problem of wheelspin on slippery surfaces in a car with two driven wheels, so ESC has achieved with less weight and cost the other main advantage of 4WD, ease of control up to the natural limit of roadholding. Such systems are likely to see an increasing number of applications, especially towards the top end of the market. ESC may well be accompanied, where handling qualities are at a premium, by 'active transmission'.

# 21 Body design general principles

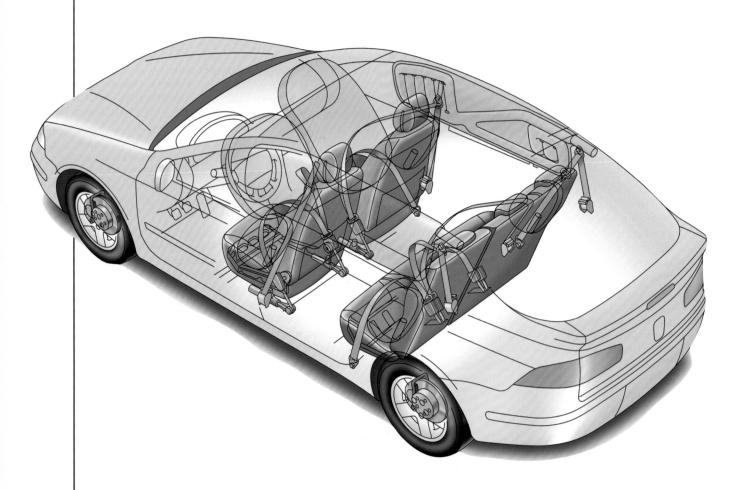

Ever since the 1930s, most car bodies have in effect been three-dimensional jigsaw puzzles of pressed-steel panels, spot-welded together in a carefully determined sequence to form a self-supporting 'unitary' structure to which the engine, transmission, chassis components, seats and all other equipment are attached. This part of the book deals with that body and with the systems that go into it – other than the major components covered in the first three parts.

So far as the body itself is concerned, the interest divides neatly into three. There are the efforts which have been, and are being devoted to making the conventional body structure as efficient as possible – in other words, as light and cheap as possible in relation to the amount of space inside. Then there is the research which is being devoted to doing things another way, using different materials and getting away from the unitary concept. Finally, there is the work devoted to making the body more efficient and more comfortable – covering everything from improved aerodynamics for better fuel consumption, to more effective noise insulation for a quieter ride.

Where the body systems are concerned, they have spent a hundred years growing from seats and upholstery, a few crude instruments and perhaps some acetylene lamps, into the amazing complexity we face today – a complexity which is still growing fast. It is difficult, now, to accept how crude the earliest cars were when it came to equipment. Heaters, for example, only became widespread during the 1940s, yet now we are beginning to take air conditioning for granted. But the biggest growth has been in electrical systems of all kinds. A century ago, you could buy a car which literally had no electrics at all, except a magneto to operate the ignition. Today, the demand of the average car for electric power is beginning to outstrip the ability of a 12-volt system to supply it. Another area of intense interest which would have astonished our great-grandfathers is that of safety systems. Today, we take safety belts and airbags for granted in new cars – but the engineers are still looking to the future. We shall look at various aspects of systems engineering in Chapters 23 to 26, with electrical systems and safety engineering each deserving a chapter to themselves.

# Catering for the particular

This is a book about technology, not about styling or 'pure' design. The closest we shall come to it is in observing that the body engineer, while always trying to make the body as light and cheap to make as possible, has to work from various starting points depending on the type of car. A sports 2-seater, a family hatchback, a 7-seat 'people carrier' and an SUV represent a wide range of products to engineer using the same basic principles, yet this is largely what happens. By the time the body engineer starts work, the product planner and the designer have already laid down the basic requirement – the size and outline shape of the car, the kind of features and equipment it must carry. After that, the basic rules apply: as light and cheap to make as possible, assuming of course that a number of other needs are also satisfied. 'As possible' implies that the body will offer sufficient durability – in other words, that nothing will break, fall off, creak, squeak or rattle for a specified distance of average driving (these days, at least 100,000 miles/161,000km). It also means that the body must be stiff enough not to writhe around when the car is driven on poor surfaces. Stiffness and durability usually go together, but stiffness is also important for stability and handling – and for quietness, another factor that car consumers value more and more. Noise is not just about rattles, squeaks, or even whether engine and road noise filter through the mountings: it is also about whether and how body panels vibrate. Stiffness helps.

Body stiffness, therefore, is a big factor. To complicate things, there are two separate stiffnesses which are important in any car body – stiffness in torsion (twisting), and stiffness in bending, thinking of the car as a beam slung between the front and rear axles. The forces that impose twisting and bending come mainly from the road surface, but also to some extent from the engine, because the body reacts to the engine's torque output (there are some powerful sports cars which you can actually feel twisting as you blip the accelerator). In general, the road surface reactions are more important, which means the wheelbase is crucial to stiffness. The shorter the wheelbase, the stiffer the car will be, all other things being equal. Probably, though, they will not be equal, because shorter cars tend also to be taller – look at the design trend in the modern supermini class, with cars like the Fiat Punto, Renault Clio and VW Polo – and this helps to add even more stiffness. The long, low-slung car can be a structural nightmare for the body engineer. The preference of modern drivers for sitting higher, so that they can see more of what is happening – one of the reasons why SUVs are so popular – has also

*Opposite: The extent of modern occupant restraint systems is seen in this diagram of the current Renault Laguna II. Inertia-reel safety belts for five occupants include pre-tensioners (a two-stage unit for the driver) and load limiters, while there are three different airbag systems: frontal, installed in the dashboard, side, installed in the backs of the front seats, and 'curtain', installed in the roof cantrails. The firing of airbags and pre-tensioners has to be carefully co-ordinated. (Renault)*

*Ghosted view of Porsche Boxster shows the layout of this most carefully engineered of mid-engined sports cars. Unlike 'big brother' 911 in which the flat-6 engine is cantilevered aft of the rear axle line, the Boxster installs its smaller engine between the cabin and the rear axle. This gives the best balance and the lowest polar moment of inertia (making the car quicker to respond) but creates problems of access to the engine for servicing, of noise for the occupants, and of limited stowage space in and around the cabin.* (Porsche)

helped the body engineer, as well as the cause of safety in general.

Note, by the way, that there is no such thing as a rigid car body (or a rigid bridge, building, ship or aeroplane). Some structures are stiffer than others. Any engineer can make a structure (within reason) as stiff as he likes. All it takes is more metal and more money. The trick is to make it sufficiently stiff for the least metal and the least money. And how stiff is sufficiently? That is where the judgement of the gifted engineer comes into play. Exactly how he proceeds is something we look at in Chapter 22.

# Aerodynamics

During most of the 1980s, car manufacturers were keen to quote the aerodynamic drag coefficient (Cd) of their cars. Until then, nobody cared very much. It was only when the world suffered its first great politically-created fuel crisis that attention turned to the amount of fuel which was wasted pushing badly designed bodies through the air. In very crude terms, the Cd figure indicates how 'streamlined' a body shape is. Armed with the Cd and the frontal area of the car, you can work out how much power is needed to overcome air resistance at any speed (remember, though, that the rolling resistance of the tyres, and the less than perfect mechanical efficiency of other components from the gearbox to the wheel bearings, all take their own share of the power). Aerodynamic drag usually becomes the biggest single factor at something between 30 and 50mph (48 and 80km/h), depending on a number of factors. For economy in motorway cruising, it is obviously desirable to keep the Cd as low as possible.

During the 1950s it was quite common to find cars with a Cd of 0.5; it was also common to find cars in which nobody ever bothered to measure it. The car which did more than any other to set the low-Cd fashion was the Audi 100 of 1982, which achieved a Cd of 0.28 and set a standard for later designs. Sadly, it also created a fashion in which the Cd figure was quoted in advertising and press releases without sufficient appreciation of what it really meant and what the possible pitfalls might be.

After all, there are six ways in which airflow forces act on a car, of which four (drag, lift, sideforce, and the yawing moment, which tries to deflect the car and can affect its stability) are important. Specialists in vehicle aerodynamics point out that when the wind is coming from anywhere but dead ahead, some cars with admirably low Cd figures can suffer from noticeable lift at one or both ends, and poor stability in sidewinds. These specialists argue that other coefficients besides Cd need to be carefully considered and should be regarded as equally important. Other observers pointed out that where a car existed in a range of versions, the one with the best (and therefore advertised) Cd figure was usually

*The Ford Explorer is typical of the type of 4WD vehicle seen as medium-sized in the USA but large in Europe. (Ford)*

the 'entry level' version with the narrowest tyres, the smallest radiator, the shallowest front bumper, and so on. One might buy the luxury version of a car with an advertised Cd of 0.28 and end up with something that actually achieved 0.32.

What caused interest in the Cd figure to wane, however, was the way it stubbornly refused to come much lower through the late 1980s and all of the 1990s. The lowest Cd claimed for any volume production car in all that time appears to have been 0.26 for the Opel/Vauxhall Calibra. Today, Honda claims 0.25 for its Insight hybrid, but that is something of a special case. Prototypes and concept studies have been shown with much lower Cd figures down to well below 0.2, but they seem only to have proved the arguments of those who feel that beyond a certain point, lower-drag shapes suffer a penalty of decreased comfort and convenience: inferior driver vision, more difficult entry and exit, greater danger of body damage in 'real life' parking and manoeuvring situations, and problems with things like wheel changing. Also, body engineers have found it difficult to achieve very low-drag shapes without driving up weight or manufacturing cost, or both.

In short, it has become accepted that there is a point at which the quest for lower aerodynamic drag becomes counter-productive in other respects. It seems likely therefore that while those aerodynamic features which have become widely established (sealed front ends and smoothed undertrays, semi-flush glass, faired door mirrors, careful control of internal cooling and ventilation flows) will continue, the future thrust of aerodynamic development will concentrate more on improving stability and to achieve minimum lift without increasing drag.

The question of 'add-on' aerodynamic devices, of front spoilers and rear 'wings' is slightly different. It was often claimed in the 1980s that such devices reduced the drag coefficient. If they did, either the basic body design was fairly poor or the add-on designer had been lucky, or both. There were arguments that massive front 'beard' spoilers 'reduced drag because they forced air to go over the car rather than under it'. In practice, either the air got in at the sides anyway, or if side-skirts were fitted as well, the lower air pressure beneath the car created (modest) downforce and added to the rolling resistance, so what you gained aerodynamically you lost in the tyres – to say nothing of the added frontal area of the car. A better reason for fitting such devices (and the original reason, in cars like the earliest Porsche 911 Turbo) was to reduce lift at one end or other of the car, to keep the wheels more firmly in contact with the ground. The late 1980s saw some designers adopt moving aerodynamic surfaces, extended automatically at high speed, for a few high-performance models, but the trend has not continued. Future cars are, if anything, more likely to benefit from the ability of advanced suspension systems to maintain constant body attitude and to control ride height according to speed.

# **22** **The body**
# structure

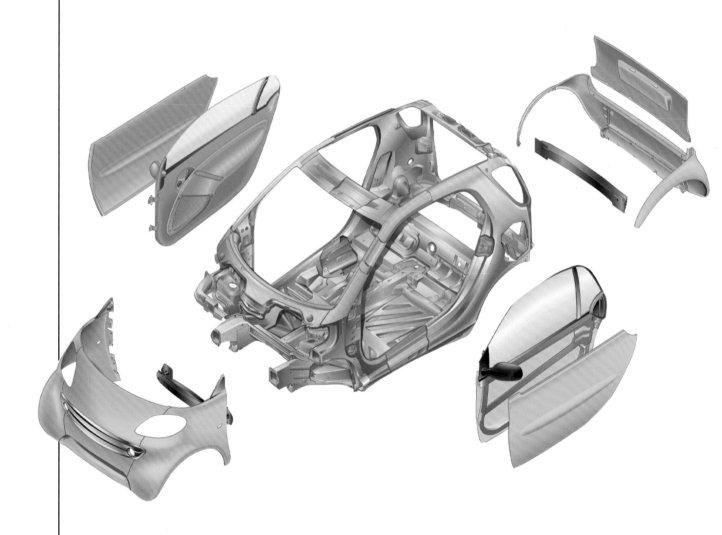

The first cars were built using techniques familiar to the builders of horse-drawn carriages. The loads were taken through a chassis, essentially two long beams joined by a series of crossbeams, and everything was mounted on this chassis, including the body which was no more than a 'little house' enclosing the seats. In some early cars, it wasn't even that: just a floor, the seats themselves, a folding hood and some kind of protective front bulkhead.

A big change came in the 1920s, when a few pioneers realised the potential strength of the body was being wasted, because if you were looking for stiffness, especially torsional stiffness, it is much easier to achieve in a three-dimensional box than in an essentially two-dimensional ladder-frame. This was why we quite quickly arrived at unitary construction, which is still used for most car bodies today.

Some people still talk of 'monocoque' construction, but modern bodies are actually far from monocoque – a term which implies a complete shell whose stiffness arises because each element supports those adjacent to it. Something like a true monocoque is found in aircraft fuselages, but very rarely in cars except for a few competition machines. Car bodies are not continuous shells. They need openings for doors, windows, bonnet, boot lid or rear hatch, and very often also a sunroof. By the time the structural designer has run frames around each of these openings to divert the loads which cannot be carried across them, the modern car body is much more like a steel skeleton-frame to which a few diaphragm panels – the bulkheads, the body sides, the floor and the roof – have been attached. The frame members are often closed hollow beams, created by welding together two or more concave pressings, because such 'box sections' are much stronger than open sections. But the construction is still unitary – it is made up almost entirely of sheet-metal pressings spot-welded together to form a complex three-dimensional structure.

The only features of a modern car body which an engineer from the 1930s would not recognise are those parts which have been added in the interests of passive safety. Those parts can be of two kinds. Some are added to keep the cabin space as intact as possible, to maintain the 'survival space' inside. Others are deliberately positioned so that in a particular kind of impact they crumple and, in so doing, absorb a lot of the energy where it does least harm. Design for passive safety has made modern car bodies even more complex, and even less 'monocoque' in any true sense.

Today, there are three main avenues of research in car body engineering. The first takes the existing unitary structure and seeks to make it even more efficient – in other words, lighter yet safer and more durable for a body of a given size. The second looks at the way we do things at the moment, in terms both of body structure and the way we manufacture bodies, and seeks to come up with a better alternative. The third looks at the material we use – sheet steel – and studies alternative materials which may do a better job.

# Better **structural efficiency**

Although we have been using the same basic approach to car body design and manufacture for so long, we are still improving. Computer-aided design (CAD) has allowed us to study ways of distributing loads through the structure in the most efficient way, making sure each part carries its fair share but that no part is actually overloaded. Standard practice is now to break down a body into a large number of 'finite elements' each of which can be represented by a single equation in a computer programme, and then linked to all its adjacent elements to form a 'network'. The tighter the mesh of the network, the more lifelike the model becomes – and the longer it takes to perform the calculations on any given computer. Finite-element modelling (FEM) is now used for basic strength calculations, to study the behaviour of the structure during an impact, and to examine the way it vibrates in sympathy with inputs from the engine, transmission, suspension, or airflow. When it was first introduced around 1980, CAD enabled designers to save substantial body weight, but this is an area where the main lessons have now been learned. The benefits now are mainly in the areas of safety and refinement (low levels of noise and vibration).

At the same time, without moving away from the unitary construction principle, materials and processes have improved. The sheet steel itself has been developed, especially during the 1990s, to meet the demands of body engineers in terms of weight reduction and passive safety performance. The main trend has been to develop steels which, although much stronger, retain the 'ductility' needed to enable them to be deep-drawn in the huge hydraulic presses which are normally used to shape individual body

*Opposite: Small cars lend themselves best to the use of composite body panels, because the panels themselves are not too large to be produced on existing machinery. Here, the tiny 'Smart' car shows its strong metallic basic structure and the way in which its plastic outer panels, which make up the majority of the visible surface of the car, are attached.*
*(DaimlerChrysler)*

*Modern volume-production cars are mostly made from pressed-steel panels which are then jigged and welded together. Here, a complete body side panel for a Citroën C5 is seen being extracted from between the upper and lower parts of the die tool immediately after pressing. Panels like this usually pass through several stages before they are fully shaped and ready for welding.* (Citroën)

panels. High tensile strength steels had been made for many years, but until the 1980s such steels could be shaped only by simple rolling or folding, not by the deep-drawn pressing. Modern high-strength steels are used for the body panels which carry the highest loads, whether in providing torsional or bending stiffness, or in distributing or absorbing impact energy. Because the steel is stronger, the panel can be thinner, with a consequent weight-saving. In some recently designed car bodies, up to 50% of the sheet steel is 'high strength' according to conventional definitions. Most of the passenger car bodies engineered during the mid-1990s use a significant proportion of high-strength steel. European examples include the Volkswagen Golf (10%), the Saab 9-5 (25%), the Mercedes A-class (45%) and the BMW 3-series (50%). The key areas for high-strength steel are around the 'corners' of the passenger compartment safety cage, and in door and windscreen frames including, crucially, the centre pillar (B-post) and its junctions with the sill section and the roof side rail (the 'cantrail'). Strength here is essential if the body is to resist side impact intrusion.

One limitation of using sheet steel (or any sheet metal) for making car bodies in this way is that the sheet comes in huge rolls of uniform thickness, which are cut to length and then 'blanked', with spare metal cut away, before being pressed into shape. A new technique to overcome the single-thickness limitation, and to reduce the amount of metal wasted in offcuts, is that of tailored blanks, in which two or more individual blanks can be edge-welded together,

using laser welding, before pressing. This allows single large pressed panels to be made from steels of different thickness or strength according to need, with consequent savings in body weight, or material cost, or both. Tailored blanks have quickly become popular despite needing special workshops and equipment to carry out the laser welding. The New Mini, for instance, has very large one-piece side panels (over 3 metres long and 1 metre high) pressed from tailored blanks using three different thicknesses of steel for the nose, mid and tail sections. Other manufacturers use tailored blanks for parts which are crucial to cabin stiffness and safety.

The standard technique for steel body panel shaping remains the heavy-duty hydraulic press, now very highly developed into fully automated and enclosed multi-station machines which work much faster than traditional press lines. In order to make the best possible use of these very expensive machines without allowing large 'buffer stocks' of finished panels to build up between the press shop and the body assembly line, it has become a standard technique to lay out shop floors, and design the machines, in such a way that the interchangeable die-sets which give the panels their shape can be switched in a matter of minutes, rather than the hours it might have taken twenty years ago.

The largest single pressings are normally those used in the floor – the 'platform' – of the car, and its body sides. It is possible to make the entire side of a small or medium-sized car – that is, from the front door pillar (the A-pillar) aft – as a single pressing; to include the front wings would be impractical from several points of view. Large one-piece body sides have a number of advantages but also some compensating disadvantages. The advantages include a high level of manufacturing accuracy and a smaller number of spot-welds required; the body structure will be at least slightly lighter and stiffer. The disadvantages include the size and cost of the press needed to produce such a large single panel (typically, a 2,000-tonne machine is needed), the amount of offcut waste which results, the styling inflexibility which can result, and the implications for the repair of minor body damage.

Although hydraulic press-forming remains by far the most popular way of shaping steel body panels, an alternative technique which is steadily gaining ground is hydroforming, in which a tube is expanded against a mould by a pulse of high internal hydraulic pressure. It is therefore an attractive alternative way of making the closed box-sections which form such an important part of unitary body structures, and could for example be used to shape door pillars, roof rails, sill members, or parts of the nose structure which

*Above: The Land Rover Freelander body is much closer to a conventional passenger car in its construction, rather than a previous-generation off-road vehicle which would have had a separate chassis frame to which the body would have added little in the way of* strength. The Freelander saves considerable weight with this approach, to the benefit both of economy and off-road performance where lightness is always an advantage. This is the Freelander V6, a recent addition to the range. (Land Rover)*

*Left: Most of the welding on a modern body line is applied by robots which can manoeuvre around the shell in a way that is computer-calculated to apply the most spot-welds in the shortest time without any robot interfering with another one, as here on the Citroën C5 body line at Rennes in France. Robot welding is better than human: each spot in the right place every time, and none missed out. (Citroën)*

need to absorb, or to help distribute, impact energy. Some of the first large hydroformed parts have indeed been used in nose structures.

## Platform considerations

In practical terms, a modern unitary passenger car body can be thought of as an upper body section carried on a 'platform'. The platform essentially comprises three sections: the nose sub-assembly, the centre floor and the rear sub-assembly. The latter two are often combined into a single sub-assembly, especially in front-wheel-drive cars in which the rear structure is relatively simple.

The key features forming part of the nose sub-assembly are the engine and front suspension mountings, the front bulkhead, the inner wheel arches and those structural members concerned with the distribution and absorption of frontal impact energy. The rear sub-assembly similarly includes the rear suspension mountings, the rear wheel arches, and

those members involved in absorbing rear impact energy. While these two sections are designed to collapse progressively during an impact, the centre section must be as stiff as possible, to help maintain the cabin space intact. Stiffness is normally achieved with the help of box-section sill members and additional box-section longerons beneath the floor panels. Cross-members, again of box-section, carry loads between the longerons and sill members while also stiffening the floor against deformation during side impact.

Apart from providing the attachments for the powertrain and suspension, the platform normally also houses the exhaust system run, the fuel tank, and the greater part of the braking and fuel systems. These features, together with the crucial importance of its structural design for passive safety, make the platform difficult and expensive to modify in any major respect. Consequently the platform usually remains little changed no matter how many different versions of a particular car model are built on the foundation it provides. The platform of a unitary body shell is normally too weak in bending to be self-supporting, and requires the addition of the upper body before it is able to pass along a production line unsupported.

Today, a single platform may also be shared between several apparently different car models, in

*Knowing more about what lies beneath the surface of the Jaguar X-type makes it easier to appreciate the skill involved in fitting a stylish body around the entire assembly without conflict.*

*This 'ghosted' view makes it clearer why the transverse engine is such an advantage in terms of creating extra cabin space in a relatively compact car.* (Jaguar)

the interests of keeping design, development and production costs as low as possible. Although in the past the platform has been a single 'frozen' design, and all the vehicles sharing it have shared a common wheelbase, modern platforms are themselves becoming a little more flexible, so that they can be adapted to the widest possible range of models. This may be done by altering the length of the centre floor section, and therefore the wheelbase; or the centre and rear sections may be designed so that while retaining the same pressings, they can be overlapped to a greater or lesser extent while being jigged for body assembly. The nose sub-assembly, which is the most complex part of the platform, is normally left unchanged. A typical variation of wheelbase for a medium-sized passenger car is 10cm (4ins), the longer wheelbase serving saloon and estate car versions while the shorter one is more suitable for the hatchback and the sports coupé derivatives.

From the rear, the main interest of the 'ghosted' Jaguar X-type is the compactness of the rear suspension, from which only the dampers rise to any significant height. However, since they are separate from the coil springs, their housing within the body can be kept slender and unobtrusive. The conventional saloon body shape makes structural design of the back end easier, for torsional stiffness and to resist rear impact. (Jaguar)

# The convenience of subframes

The increasing use of common platforms may save cost, but it creates a number of practical problems of which the most obvious is the need to cater for a range of different engines. This can be done through the suitable adaptation of engine mounts direct to the body, or alternatively by mounting the engines on a range of subframes, each adapted to one engine but all designed to pick up on the same body mountings. The subframe solution has two further advantages, first that the subframe can also provide convenient (and similarly adaptable) lower suspension mountings, and second that the layout provides a double filtering action for engine and suspension noise and vibration, at the mounting of the unit to the subframe and again

at the attachment of the subframe to the main body. Similarly, a rear subframe can provide suitable mounting points, and improved insulation, for the rear suspension, while also carrying the rear final drive in the case of rear-engined or 4WD vehicles.

Subframes can play a valuable part at the final assembly stage, allowing the main mechanical units to be prepared as a major sub-assembly before 'marriage' to the body shell. This advantage becomes extremely marked in the case of powerful rear-wheel-drive or 4WD vehicles, in which front and rear subframes have become the norm.

Front subframes, especially for transverse-engined, front-wheel-drive cars, are normally roughly rectangular in plan, forming a cradle beneath the engine, with the lower suspension mounts picking up on its sides. The frame is usually made up of pressings which are welded, upper and lower, to form box sections. This is a manufacturing area in which hydroforming looks a promising alternative to hydraulic press-forming.

The front subframe is generally too stiff to act as an energy-absorbing member in a frontal impact, and has to be treated as an essentially rigid mass in the same way as the engine itself and the front wheels. As such, account must be taken of its behaviour during impact, and if necessary, measures must be taken to deflect it rather than allowing it to penetrate the cabin space. For example, Renault, in the Clio II, has located the rear of the subframe with swinging links attached to the body, ensuring that the frame (and the engine it carries) moves downwards after impact rather than directly rearwards.

## Corrosion protection and painting

For the body engineer, steel has one overwhelming advantage: by comparison with any other possible material, it is cheap. It also has one big drawback: unless carefully protected, it rusts. Bad experiences with some car models in the past have led consumers to expect a high degree of protection, backed up by several years' warranty against 'body rot' – corrosion which completely pierces the thickness of a body panel.

The approach to corrosion protection and painting has become far more standardised during the last 20 years. Basic protection is now largely sought through the zinc-dipping or galvanising of the sheet steel prior to pressing, the coating being applied on one or both sides. This protection is usually selective, and used for those parts of the body which are most exposed to corrosion-inducing conditions: the underside, wings, door panels, wheel arch interiors and structurally important box-sections. Some manufacturers, however, protect the entire body structure through the use of 100% galvanised steel. The increasing effectiveness of basic corrosion protection has reduced the need for additional underbody protection. Additional materials now applied to the body mainly take the form of mastic sealants applied, manually or by robot, as beads to crucial seams.

To an increasing extent, body painting is now carried out in 'clean room' conditions, the entire shop being slightly pressurised to exclude dust, and provided with an atmosphere in which temperature and humidity can be closely controlled. As new paint shops have been commissioned at passenger car factories, there has been a steady move towards the use of water-based colour coats, in order to reduce the emission of solvents which threaten the environment. Most colour coats are now applied by robots, using 'rotating bell' sprays or powder dispersal with electrostatic adhesion.

Topcoat technology is becoming more complex in response to consumer tastes. Metallic finishes now account for a substantial proportion of all car sales, especially towards the top of the market. More manufacturers are now offering other 'exotic' finishes such as pearlescent types in which the visual effect is achieved with mica 'scales' within the paint layer, and paint suppliers have also developed finishes which change colour according to viewing angle.

## New structural and manufacturing approaches

One problem created by the conventional pressed-steel unitary approach to body design and manufacture is that it is uneconomic for the production of vehicles in small numbers. A full set of steel press dies for a vehicle body may, depending on the complexity of the design, cost $15–20 million. Such dies will, with proper maintenance and refurbishment, yield 500,000 panel-sets before needing replacement. Dies can be made much cheaper, using techniques such as metal spraying over an epoxy core, but have a life of perhaps 100 panel-sets before deteriorating to an unacceptable degree. Such dies are extremely useful for prototyping and especially for pilot build. No satisfactory 'middle way' has been devised between the high-cost, long-life die for volume production and the low-cost, short-life type.

This limitation has led smaller manufacturers in particular to study other ways of building cars. Mostly this has involved moving to other materials, because steel has several important limitations. As we have already seen, it is cheap, but it rusts. More important from the manufacturing point of view, there are only two ways of making steel structures. One is the unitary method already discussed; the other is to cut, fit, and bolt or seam-weld – fine for bridges and ships, and also the method used for making old-fashioned chassis, but hopelessly uneconomic for making complete cars which have also to be reasonably light and very safe. Two techniques in particular which are very difficult, if not impossible to apply to steel are precision casting (the right kind of iron can be cast, but steel is much more difficult and expensive to handle) and extrusion – the process of squeezing soft metal through a die to form a beam which can be of complex (and hollow) section. As it happens, aluminium can be cast and extruded, and this is one reason, apart from its lightness, why it has attracted the attention of engineers looking for alternatives to steel construction. But aluminium too has its rivals.

It is possible to create a skeleton-frame quickly and easily (not necessarily cheaply) by slotting together extruded beams with precision-cast 'nodes' at the junctions. This approach has formed the basis for many recent body-building studies and a few car models which have entered limited production. Interesting among these is the Fiat Multipla, which uses a skeleton-frame approach but with the skeleton made up of carefully formed and joined steel pressings rather than using an alternative material.

*BMW's Z22 concept car has the wheelbase of a 7-series, the cabin space of a 5-series, and better economy than a 3-series, mainly thanks to lightweight construction. It is unlikely, however, that BMW would put a car that looked like this into production, or that it would adopt its rear-mounted 'on its side' 4-cylinder engine. (BMW)*

# Alternative **materials**

## *Aluminium*

The main appeal of aluminium-based alloys for the vehicle body engineer is lightness. An aluminium-alloy body can be made approximately half the weight of an equivalent steel body with similar stiffness and passive safety performance. Also, aluminium does not rust; in fact it is protected by surface oxidation (which is not to say it does not corrode, especially in the presence of salt – although sea-water-resistant alloys are available).

The main drawback of aluminium is cost, which is substantially higher than that of high-quality steel. Aluminium is also more difficult to spot-weld than sheet steel, though by no means impossible; success demands extremely accurate control of welding current and timing. Some recent experience suggests that with experience and careful tuning of equipment, aluminium and steel bodies can be spot-welded on the same lines using the same machines. Honda's Tochigi factory does this in the manufacture of the Insight hybrid car and large parts of the S2000 sports car. Other research teams have developed alternative approaches to body structural design, generally seeking to carry the principal loads through a jointed framework of extruded aluminium tubes of complex section. Morgan, in developing its new Aero 8 sports car, evolved a system in which the main chassis and body members could be assembled from accurately cut aluminium sheet and assembled with a combination of welding and riveting, with a minimum of jigging.

The aluminium industry has suggested that eventually, most of the raw material needs of the motor industry could be met by recycling, since in contrast to the expense and difficulty of its extraction as a raw material, aluminium is easily and efficiently recycled. The problem remains of how to inject sufficient aluminium into the manufacturing cycle in the first instance.

It is worth noting that the weight savings quoted for aluminium construction can be misleading. A conventional steel body accounts for approximately 30% of the total weight of a passenger car, so a switch to all-aluminium construction would result in an overall saving of no more than 15% in the vehicle's kerb weight. Such a saving is still well worth having, but the 'aluminium car' will not halve fuel consumption in one bound. This is one reason why vehicle body designers remain reluctant to abandon a material which they have known and trusted for so long, and which their factories are equipped to handle in huge volume. It is worth noting, by contrast, the way cast aluminium has been generally accepted as a material for engines, transmissions and most recently, suspension parts.

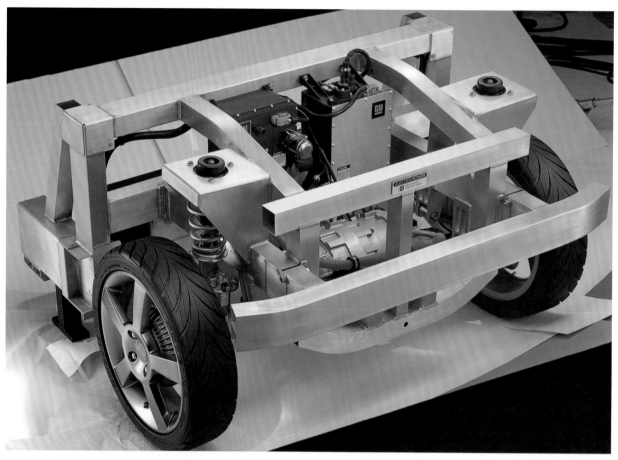

Above: At the 1999 Tokyo Motor Show Suzuki showed this 'nose module' for an electric car, with an all-aluminium structure welded from square-section extrusions. The structure in any volume production car would be a great deal more sophisticated, but the point about light weight is made none the less. Note the almost invisible electric traction motor nestling in the lower part of the bay, and the boxes of motor control gear carrying General Motors badges – Suzuki having a close relationship with the US giant. (Suzuki)

Where the vehicle body is concerned, there are signs that the vehicle manufacturers are beginning to seek a middle way through the use of aluminium for the hinged members (doors, bonnet and boot lid or rear hatch). This results in a useful weight saving while confining the aluminium to units which can be separately assembled and then attached to the main stress-bearing body shell by purely mechanical means, avoiding many of the engineering problems associated

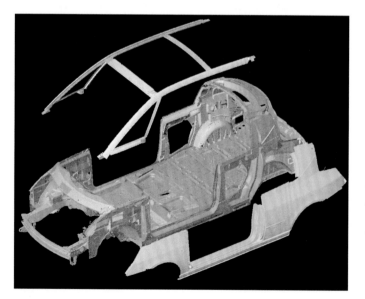

Left: Renault's futuristic new Avantime coupé has a main platform (related to that of the Espace) manufactured from dip-galvanised steel, with an upper structure of extruded and jointed aluminium and external body sides of plastic composite. The layout was chosen partly because of features the designers wanted to include, such as extremely large side doors (1.4 metres long and weighing 55kg, with a special double-hinged mounting) and an extremely large glass sunroof. (Renault)

THE BODY STRUCTURE

with the material. Early in 1998, Renault announced that high-performance versions of its new Clio model would be equipped with aluminium alloy bonnets, and Citroën has followed suit in its recently introduced C5.

## Plastics

Plastics are still, potentially, an alternative to aluminium as lightweight body materials. However, their challenge has been blunted throughout the last decade by anxieties about recycling. The term 'plastics' embraces a variety of materials offering a wide range of physical properties. Despite this, most of them tend to look and feel much the same. Most plastics are petrochemical derivatives. All of them are 'corrosion-free' in a conventional sense although they may be subject to attack by specific chemicals (including motor fuels). Degradation by ultra-violet light is another problem in some plastics.

Freedom from corrosion is an engineering bonus in one respect but a drawback in another, in that plastics are seen as difficult and expensive to recycle. Even the 'thermoplastics' cannot simply be melted down, purified and reformed in the manner of most metals (and especially aluminium). Recycling worries have done more to hold back the progress of plastics in

*The 2-litre mid-engined Renault Sport Spider, shown as a concept in 1995 and later built in small numbers mainly for competition, used an aluminium chassis frame and lessons learned in the company's MOSAIC weight-reduction programme. If anything, its kerb weight of 930kg showed that saving body weight went only part-way to achieving a truly lightweight car. (Renault)*

vehicle bodies during the last decade than have engineering drawbacks such as questionable dimensional stability at high temperatures, the need for special paint processes (not in all cases) and the need to develop mechanical attachment systems to replace the spot-welding technology used for steel.

Before recycling became a major issue, vehicle manufacturers used a wide range of plastics, singly or in combination as 'polymer alloys'. Today the same manufacturers seek to restrict themselves to a few 'pure' plastics – among which the most commonly used are polyamide (Nylon), polycarbonate, polyethylene, polypropylene and polyurethane. Plastics containing the halide gases – polyvinyl chloride (PVC) and polytetra-fluoroethylene (PTFE) being the most prominent – have fallen from favour due to the 'ozone layer factor'. It is now almost universal practice to provide plastic parts of any size with identifying marks as an aid to sorting prior to correct recycling.

Plastics have survived as a major material because for some purposes, their advantages are overwhelming, in moulded bumpers for example. As noted in Part 1, precision-moulded engine intake manifolds are now commonplace. However, apart from the bumper application, in which resistance to minor impact damage is extremely valuable and a surface finish different from the rest of the body can be tolerated), plastic body panels are still not used on a large scale. The tendency of large, horizontal plastic panels to 'sag' in very high temperatures means that the most promising applications are vertical panels like the front and rear wings and the door panels. Of these, the front wings are the most likely candidates since they are most frequently subject to minor accident damage, and are therefore already usually designed to be mechanically attached (bolted in place) for ease of replacement. Renault already installs moulded plastic front wings (in GE Noryl polycarbonate) on its Mégane Scénic and Clio models.

## Composite materials

The so-called 'plastic' car bodies which have been made in small volume for many years are actually almost always made from plastic composites. The original 'composite' material in vehicle body use was glass-reinforced plastic (GRP) in which a polyester or epoxy resin matrix is injected into a mould containing a pre-positioned core of bundled or woven glass fibre. Essentially, in the finished (cured) component, the glass fibre provides the bulk of the mechanical strength while the resin matrix holds it in position and provides

*In 2000, BMW showed its Z22 lightweight concept car which used several advanced technologies to create a car the size of the 5-series which weighed less than the 3-series. One feature was this one-piece body side in carbon-fibre composite, moulded around 'lost' foam cores (which vaporise during manufacture). The complete side moulding is very stiff and comes complete with moulded-in-place attachments for door hinges, etc, yet weighs only a few kilograms. (BMW)*

THE BODY STRUCTURE

the surface finish. An alternative approach is seen in sheet moulding compound (SMC), in which pliable 'sheets' of reinforced resin are prepared and then shaped in a curing press. This allows the process to be semi-automated and avoids the need for precise pre-positioning of the reinforcement in the mould. Smaller but thicker components can be similarly formed from dough moulding compound (DMC). A more advanced alternative can be employed with polyurethane. If chopped or pulverised glass fibre is added during the moulding process known as reaction injection moulding, the moulded component is significantly stiffened. The process is then known as reinforced reaction injection moulding (RRIM). The same type of reinforcement can be added to polyamide (Nylon) during moulding, with similar results.

By far the most commonly used reinforcement in all such materials is glass fibre, which is cheap, manufactured in consistent quality and has a very high ratio of stiffness to weight. Higher cost alternatives for special applications include the even stiffer carbon fibre and the much stronger Kevlar, which are often used in woven combination in the manufacture of racing car 'tubs' and other components in which cost is not a serious issue when set against superior mechanical performance. The weaving of reinforcement mats for such purposes has become a science in itself, and knitted mats have also been studied.

A different type of composite material which is now gaining acceptance is the 'sandwich' of a plastic layer between two thin layers of steel. Panels made from this type of material can act as effective noise and vibration dampers with only a small weight penalty.

# 23 **Design** for safety

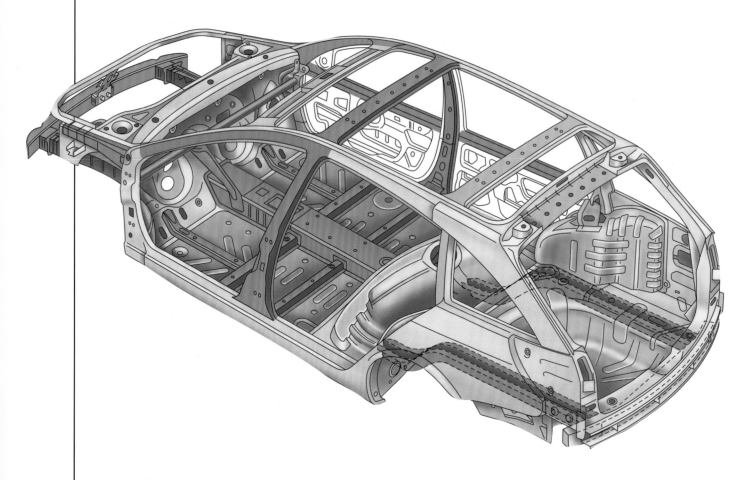

E ngineers usually begin by pointing out that there are two types of safety. There is active safety, which means designing the car to help avoid having an accident, through safe and predictable handling, good brakes, a good view for the driver, and so on. Then there is passive safety, which covers all aspects of designing a car to help its occupants survive an accident. This chapter is about passive safety; active safety aspects were covered mainly in Part 3.

Passive safety itself divides neatly into two parts. First, there is the importance of the car body in cushioning the shock of an impact, especially a frontal impact. It can make a big difference for occupant protection if the energy of an impact can be absorbed at a steady rate over a reasonable distance, even though that distance is measured in centimetres rather than metres.

Second, there is the need to restrain the occupants. At best, a car which collides with one coming the other way at around 60km/h (37mph) is going to stop in perhaps 50cm (1.6 ft). This is an average deceleration rate of 30g, and the peak will certainly be higher. You don't brace yourself against that kind of deceleration; you hurtle forward and collide with the dashboard, or the steering wheel, or the windscreen, with fatal force – unless you are restrained. That is why safety belts were invented, to be followed by airbags. It is worth saying straight away that airbags are not a substitute for safety belts. It is very foolish indeed to say 'my car is fitted with airbags, therefore I don't need to wear a safety belt'. The world's best safety engineers all agree that the best protection of all is a carefully blended combination of the two, working together.

In the majority of developed countries, the law now requires car occupants (at least in the front seats) to wear safety belts. In the USA, however, such legislation is enacted state-by-state and is not yet universal. Thus airbags for the US market have to act as 'primary' restraint systems, capable of preventing occupant injury in a stipulated frontal impact situation. 'American' airbags therefore tend to be bigger and to expand faster – something which has proved to bring dangers of its own. In other markets, safety engineers regard airbags as Supplementary Restraint Systems (SRS) and not as a substitute for three-point safety belts. There has been less concern of late to develop 'passive' safety belts which automatically wrap themselves around occupants when they enter cars. Such belts were fitted to a number of US-market cars, but opinion seems now to be that the interests of vehicle occupants who elect not to wear safety belts is better served by optimised airbag systems.

# Safety structures

Modern cars are designed with structures that afford reasonable safety against impacts from any direction. However, statistics from every developed country show that the majority of car occupants who are killed in accidents die in frontal impacts, and that remains the most important case. Around 35 years ago, the first official crash safety regulations were written around frontal impact requirements. Today, tests are also called for to check protection against rear-end and side impacts. Most car manufacturers also run their own tests for roll-over safety.

Over the years, the general approach has been to evolve structures in which the cabin space remained intact, surrounded by the stiffest possible 'cage', while the nose and tail structures were able to deform progressively while absorbing impact energy.

Collapsing nose and tail structures absorb impact energy through plastic (that is, permanent) deformation of the metal. Engineers have developed increasingly clever techniques not only to absorb as much energy as possible, but to do so in the most progressive possible manner in order to minimise peak deceleration. One of the principal methods is to make sure the box-section members collapse lengthwise in 'concertina' fashion. Care is taken, through the positioning of structural notches, that the collapse of struts, always begins in the correct place, thus ensuring as far as possible that the collapse takes place exactly as calculated during the design stage. The overall pattern of collapse, especially at the nose, is now calculated to take account of the sudden extra inertia and stiffness as the engine and the front wheels are contacted.

An early frontal-impact concern for safety designers was to ensure not only that the steering column would not be forced rearwards, but also that it would collapse progressively to absorb energy when struck by the driver's chest. Today the main concern is to ensure that the steering wheel provides a well-located platform from which the airbag, contained in its hub, can inflate to support the driver as intended.

Frontal impact testing now seeks more accurately to reproduce the contact pattern which actually occurs in head-on accidents. These are rarely 'nose to nose' but rather offset, driver side to driver side. Early offset testing involved impacting the car into a barrier

*Opposite: No matter how good the occupant restraint systems, good protection also calls for a cabin that remains essentially intact, and crumple zones which absorb energy, especially in a frontal impact, over a distance of up to a metre and as progressively as possible. This diagram shows some of the safety-critical structural members of the Renault Laguna II and the way they form a 'cage' around the cabin. (Renault)*

*Right: Among the many crash cases which have to be taken into account in car design and testing is the rollover. Here, a perfectly good Mercedes C-class is about to become a*

*write-off in the interests of passive safety research, having been launched from a 'sledge' brought to a sudden halt while the car continues on its way.* (Mercedes)

set at an angle, usually 30° from the orthogonal. Now the preferred approach is to make the test impact literally offset, the car striking the edge of the barrier. This has the disadvantage that a sideways error of a centimetre or so could make quite a difference to the final result, so great care is needed in positioning the test car and analysing the results. Offset impact resistance calls for a structure which can transfer loads from the impact side of the car, as far as possible across the entire width of the front bulkhead.

Various degrees of offset have been suggested, but a standard in which 40% of the car strikes the barrier has been widely accepted. The barrier is provided with a collapsible metal honeycomb face to represent the crushability of the vehicle coming in the opposite direction. The choice of test speed remains a matter of debate. The higher the speed for which the body is designed to perform acceptably, the better protected the occupants will be; on the other hand, the vehicle will not only be heavier and bulkier, but also more 'aggressive' in

*Below: Good passive safety performance in a frontal impact depends on the impact loads being distributed as widely as possible throughout the body structure, so that the only parts which are overloaded are those which are*

*deliberately designed to crumple in order to absorb energy. This diagram shows the way in which loads are distributed through the highly efficient structure of the latest Mercedes C-class, introduced in 2000.* (Mercedes)

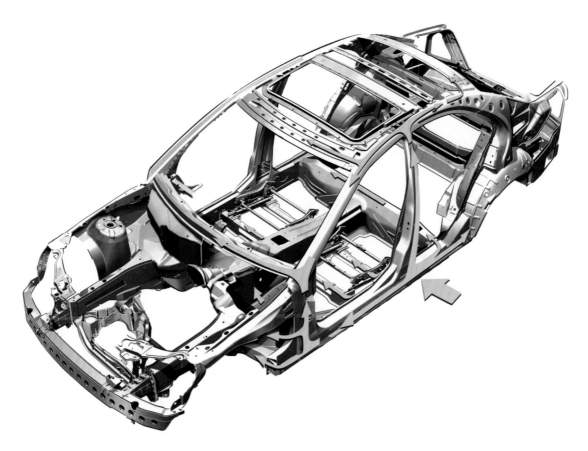

other types of impact, such as when striking another vehicle in the side, or hitting a pedestrian. The Euro-NCAP standard (Euro-NCAP is not a legislated standard, but is 'quasi-official', backed by a number of government and other organisations), calls for a 40mph (64km/h) impact. Most of the major car manufacturers carry out 'in-house' tests at higher speeds. It should be remembered, though, that the impact energy increases as the square of the speed, so that in a 50mph (80km/h) impact, the structure needs to absorb 56% more energy than in the 40mph (64km/h) case.

In practical terms, even at Euro-NCAP impact speed, car bodies designed since around 1990 generally perform well. One remaining area of real concern is the driver side footwell, which is frequently distorted or penetrated, and within which the pedals can themselves move through long distances and impose large loads. The latest designs further strengthen this area, while 'breakaway' pedal clusters and lower-leg restraint devices are also being studied.

Another frontal impact issue now being examined is that of 'compatibility' between colliding cars. Renault has pointed out that, all other things being equal, when a lighter car collides with a heavier one coming the other way, the lighter car will absorb the larger share of the impact energy, because conservation of momentum means it will end up moving backwards. The only way to overcome this is

*In side as in front impact, it is vital that the loads should be distributed as widely as possible through the car's structure, to ensure that no part is overloaded to the point where it would collapse and allow serious intrusion into the cabin. This diagram shows the structure of the Mercedes C-class of 2000, and makes it clear that the strength and the design of the junction between sill and centre pillar is crucial.* (Mercedes)

to design cars so that their front-end 'softness' is proportional to their mass, in other words to give smaller cars stiffer nose structures. The problem here, until recently, was that such stiffness resulted in the small car's occupants being subjected to intolerably high deceleration. The latest developments in occupant restraint systems mean there is now a much better chance of protection against injury in a small, 'compatible' car.

# Side impact **protection**

For many years, it was assumed that side impact protection could never be made as effective as protection against frontal impact, because cars could never be made wide enough to provide any significant impact-absorbing crush depth. Eventually it was realised that considerable protection could however be provided by concentrating on three areas.

First, care must be taken to distribute the impact load through as much of the structure as possible, using a strong sill structure, centre pillar and floor-level crossmembers. Next, intrusion must be minimised by strengthening the internal door structure and the door latching arrangements, while making sure the doors can still be opened following a frontal impact. Finally, the risk of occupant injury can be reduced by spreading loads across the body with the aid of side airbags and internal foam padding. The most recently designed cars have applied these principles to good effect, and side impact casualties have been reduced. Engineers admit, however, that success depends on what is responsible for the impact. With a soft-nosed vehicle, the chances are good, but in the 'nightmare scenario' of skidding sideways impact into a tree or rigid pole, protection is much more difficult.

# **Restraining** the occupants

## *Safety belts*

While airbags have been the subject of most publicity about vehicle safety in the last few years, the three-point safety belt remains the primary and most effective means of restraining occupants. There have been significant recent developments in three areas of safety-belt design: improving their ergonomics, providing some means of pre-tensioning belts in the event of an impact, and limiting the load imposed on the chest by the diagonal belt.

Ergonomic developments have concentrated on ensuring that the belts are more comfortable to wear, and that the belt is correctly positioned to provide maximum protection. The provision of height adjustment for the upper (shoulder) belt runner is important, while the inboard buckles are now usually attached to the seat rather than the tunnel structure, ensuring correct lap belt position and angle whatever the size of the wearer. Pre-tensioner devices may be mechanical or pyrotechnic; in either case the objective is to remove any slack in the harness, ensuring that the wearer remains in much closer contact with the seat. To gain maximum benefit, the pre-tensioner is often complemented by a 'grabber' clamp which prevents slack packing around the belt reel from being paid out following an impact. 'Grabbers' may also be fitted alone, with reduced but worthwhile benefits. Some safety systems now include two-stage pre-tensioners, to pull the belt fairly tight in a moderate impact, and much tighter if the impact is severe. Pre-tensioners may be triggered internally, or by a signal from the same 'crash event sensor' that fires the airbags.

Belt load limiters work on the basis that it is preferable to allow the wearer some small extra amount of forward movement in order to avoid exceeding a chest load which might present a threat of serious injury. The belt system works normally until the maximum permitted load is reached, after which a mechanical device within one of the belt attachments allows the wearer to move forward while maintaining the load at a nearly constant level. Renault was the first manufacturer to introduce such a system in a production car, but the technique has since been widely adopted.

Considerable strides have been made in recent years in the area of child car occupant safety, including rearward-facing carriers for very small infants and 'booster' seats for older children (who are now legally required to sit in the back in most of the major car markets). Most car manufacturers now develop their own child-safety equipment in partnership with a reputable specialist, or test available equipment and recommend a range of approved items. A recent development has been the ISOFIX standard for the easy and correct installation of child safety devices to standard anchorage points, which are now to be found in more and more cars in the European market.

## Airbags

Airbags are now produced in very large numbers to satisfy industry demand, and reliability of operation, both of the bag itself and of the impact sensor and control mechanism, appears to be extremely high. Apparently undemanded inflations occur in small numbers; most appear to result from spurious signals picked up by the sensors, and in general their results are less serious than was once feared.

However, as pointed out earlier, airbags meeting the primary restraint requirement need to be of larger volume and to inflate faster than airbags acting as an SRS. In the USA, this led to serious problems relating mainly to small occupants of the front passenger seat, especially children, sitting so far forward that following a frontal impact, they are struck by the bag while it is still rapidly inflating. The safety concept is that the occupant should contact the airbag rather than the other way around. The problem was made worse for small people and children because the expanding airbag could strike the head rather than the chest, forcing it backwards. This led to some fatalities. The problem is far less likely to occur with the smaller European-standard airbags, although most European manufacturers now offer devices – from driver-selected switches to automatic sensors – which will prevent airbag inflation if a suitably equipped child seat is installed opposite the airbag housing.

Systems have now been developed to overcome the American problem. They depend on two main technical features: airbags capable of being inflated at more than one rate, and sensors which can detect the size and position of a seat occupant. The typical dual-rate airbag inflator uses a simple mechanism which either directs the full gas charge into the bag, or allows half of it to vent. The sensors may take several forms, including measurement of seat position and occupant weight, or direct sensing of occupant position via roof-mounted units. Information regarding the occupant may be combined with sensing of the impact severity to command, by way of the airbag inflation controller, either a full inflation, part-inflation, or no inflation at all, depending on which choice is calculated to give the seat occupant the best chance of survival.

It is now accepted that airbags provide worthwhile extra protection for the head and upper torso in a single frontal impact. Clearly, though, they are 'one-shot' devices which cannot protect if, for example, a heavy but glancing collision with another vehicle is followed by an impact with a tree. Statistics gathered in the USA in the early 1990s showed that while airbags were effective overall in reducing injury severity, the incidence of major injuries was almost four times as high where the occupants were not also wearing safety belts.

Renault, working with Autoliv, has worked on the careful matching of the airbag with the characteristics of an advanced type of safety belt. The airbag is provided with a positively controlled vent allowing a degree of deflation to take place once the seat occupant has contacted the airbag. This 'programmed-restraint' belt-airbag system has been shown to reduce chest loads from the 900kg (1980lb) typically encountered with a conventional safety belt, to only 400kg (880lb). Other European manufacturers have begun adopting the same approach, with minor differences of technology and emphasis.

Following the success of the frontal airbag, which is now virtually standard on the driver side of all new cars and often fitted for the front seat passenger as well, side airbag protection, guarding the pelvis and chest (and to some degree also the head) against side impact is now offered on an increasing number of cars. The effectiveness of the side airbag, which is generally of much smaller volume than the front airbag, depends on extremely rapid inflation, since there is very little crush depth between the impacting object and the victim. These side airbags are now being joined by 'curtain' airbags which inflate downwards from the cantrail to give better head

*The latest addition to the range of airbags for production cars is the 'curtain' airbag which descends from the roof side rail (the cantrail) to protect the occupants' heads in the event of a side impact. This is what the interior of the Volvo V70 looks like when the curtain airbags are inflated. Both front and rear passengers are protected. (Volvo)*

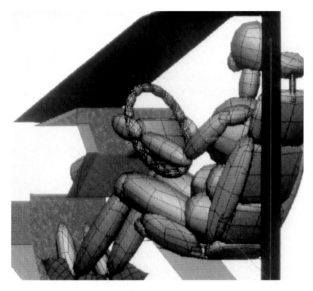

protection. Airbags have also been suggested, and shown at least in prototype form, for installation in the backs of the front seats or built into the rear safety belts, for the benefit of back seat occupants, and inflating within the footwells to reduce the risk of foot and lower leg injury.

# Safety in the future

It would be unwise to venture that safety system design has gone about as far as it can sensibly go. At various times in the last decade it has seemed so, and still the safety system experts have come up with, for example, the safety belt load limiter, the optimised

*Above: Ever more effective safety belts and head/chest airbags mean a greater number of crash survivors are suffering leg injuries.*

*Hence the growth of interest in small airbags installed in the footwell as seen here, to protected the shins, ankles and feet.* (Siemens)

*Below: One European initiative which is beginning to take wide effect is the establishment of the ISOFIX standard for attaching child safety seats. These diagrams show how the ISOFIX principle is applied in the Volvo V70. The broad*

*intention is that seats complying with the standard should be easy to install in any ISOFIX equipped car without risk of error, and in a way which ensures proper retention of the seat and child in the event of an impact.* (Volvo)

## ISOFIX Child/Baby Seat Fittings

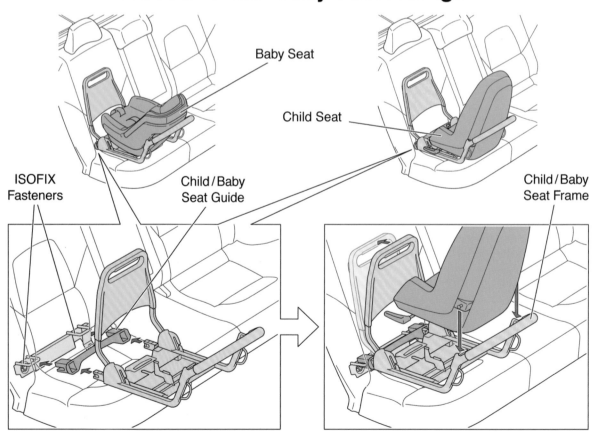

Baby Seat

Child Seat

ISOFIX Fasteners

Child/Baby Seat Guide

Child/Baby Seat Frame

avoidance zone

Normal Driving State · Warning State · Collision Avoidable State · Collision Unavoidable State · Post Event State

mitigation zone

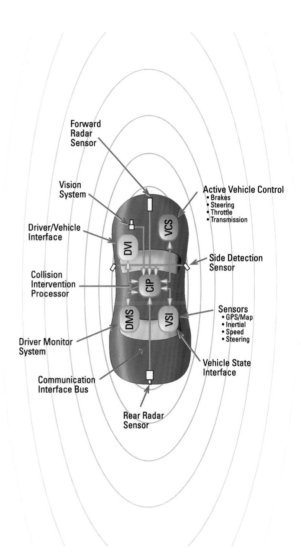

Forward Radar Sensor

Vision System

Driver/Vehicle Interface

Collision Intervention Processor

Driver Monitor System

Communication Interface Bus

Rear Radar Sensor

Active Vehicle Control
· Brakes
· Steering
· Throttle
· Transmission

Side Detection Sensor

Sensors
· GPS/Map
· Inertial
· Speed
· Steering

Vehicle State Interface

VCS · DVI · CIP · DMS · VSI

*In 2000 the American components and systems giant Delphi announced its concept for an 'integrated safety system' in which the conventional distinction between active (collision avoidance) and passive (collision survival) safety was blurred by advanced thinking and the use of some devices to serve both purposes. This is how Delphi explained the overlap between the passive and active areas. (Delphi)*

combination of belts and airbags, the 'programmed' airbag, the side curtain airbag and the ISOFIX child seat attachment system.

It does seem, however, that the next stage in safety design may be to extend the 'cushion' around the car by electronic means. We already have sensors which can detect nearby but invisible objects to help the driver park safely; there is no reason why similar sensors, together with ingenious electronic signal processing, should not detect moving objects and decide whether they represent a threat – in fact, whether they are going to impact. Take the case of side impact: the biggest engineering problem here is that the protective side airbag has to inflate near-instantly, because there is so little time to take action once the impact has begun. If a sideways-looking sensor could give even a fraction of a second earlier warning of an impact, better protection could be provided. Even in a frontal impact, engineers argue, early warning could mean for example that belt pretensioning could be applied before contact, and that the airbag system could be pre-informed about the likely severity of the impact, so that it could set itself up to operate accordingly. Early warning of a rear impact might allow head restraints to be positioned automatically to provide the best possible head protection.

This is why many advanced safety systems engineers now talk of creating a 'cocoon' of electronically protected space around the car, using sensors looking in various directions. Such systems would need to be extremely 'smart' even by modern

*These are some of the main sensors which Delphi feels it needs to create a completely integrated safety system. High-speed communication between the sensors and computers is absolutely vital, because some decisions about whether or not an impact is inevitable have to be made quite literally in a split second. The 'collision intervention processor' is the core of the entire system. (Delphi)*

standards. You would not want your side airbag to be set off simply because you had parked very close to another vehicle, or your garage wall. The system would have to be certain that the threat was not only close, but coming closer at a speed which made impact certain (and even then, you would not want the airbag to inflate if you merely misjudged and slightly grazed the garage wall). In short, many problems remain to be solved, but this is probably the most important direction in which safety systems design is now evolving.

# 24 Helping the driver

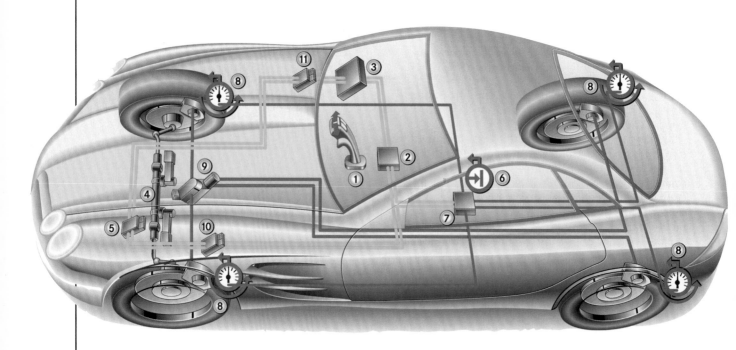

1 Joystick with applied force and angle sensors
  for steering, brakes and acceleration
2 Joystick control unit
3 Vehicle dynamics controller
4 Steering actuator
5 Steering control unit

6 Vehicle attitude sensors
7 Sensor electronics
8 Wheel rotation sensors
9 Electronic hydraulic pressure regulator
10 Sensortronic brake system control unit
11 Engine management system control unit

In the early days of flying, inventors were so concerned with getting their machines to fly that the means by which they were to be controlled seemed of secondary importance. So it was also with early motor cars. The means by which the driver exercised control, and via which he was informed what was going on, were engineering afterthoughts. To this day one finds cars, especially small-volume, high-performance cars, where the same attitude seems to prevail. The early aviators very quickly discovered that decent control and information were just as important as the basic feat of becoming airborne. Unfortunately a car driver can usually muddle through even when the quality of controls and instruments is diabolical. The car driver enjoys the luxury of being able to stop at any time and sort things out. It should not be an excuse for anything less than excellence.

Almost since the beginning of motoring, the driver has exercised control through a steering wheel and three pedals – accelerator, brake, and clutch – plus the gear selector. With automatic transmission, the clutch pedal vanishes and the selector takes a different form. Most of this has been discussed in detail in Parts 1, 2 and 3. Here, it suffices to say that the most important trend of the last few years, and one which will continue, is to do away with mechanical linkages and replace them with electrical ones, the so-called 'X-by-wire' principle.

As explained in Part 3, it may be that one day cars have a radically different control layout, possibly a single stick-control with sideways movement for steering, forward for acceleration and aft for braking. With X-by-wire, it would certainly be possible, and experimental cars with such arrangements have already been demonstrated. But the world's drivers are used to a steering wheel and pedals, and if 'joystick' arrangements are ever going to take their place, it will probably happen by slow expansion, starting with a few specialised cars built in relatively small numbers.

Meanwhile, engineers everywhere are facing the challenge of helping the driver to stay safe and perform efficiently in an increasingly complicated and demanding environment. Sometimes we fail to appreciate how much motoring conditions have changed. For example, for more than half a century cars have been equipped with headlamps with a far-seeing 'main beam' and a sharply cut-off 'dipped beam'. Yet today, plenty of drivers undertake night-time journeys on roads where the traffic flow is so constant that they never use main beam – which ought to suggest that we re-think lighting systems, as is beginning to happen. Again, the driver has three means of signalling intention: indicators, horn and headlamps. Yet many drivers hardly ever use the horn, there is

great argument about how and whether to use the headlamps for signalling, and the best you can do with the indicators is switch them on and hope other drivers notice. It is now technically possible for vehicles to communicate automatically, so that a car can tell any other car nearby that it is going to turn right, regardless of whether the driver remembers to check for other traffic and switch on the indicator – and sooner or later, it will happen, to the benefit of safety.

Beyond this re-thinking of existing functions, new ones are emerging. We are already becoming used to systems which help us navigate, and radios which automatically broadcast local traffic information. The first cars have already appeared with 'intelligent cruise control' which enables them to follow another vehicle at a safe distance – for the time being, only on a motorway or main road – even though the other vehicle's speed may keep changing. Eventually, we shall have cars which automatically stay in the centre of a motorway lane, opening up the possibility of a driving 'autopilot', which raises some interesting questions of its own. All these functions, and others, are aspects of a technology which has become known as telematics, whose application may eventually bring benefits we can barely guess at.

*Opposite: Mercedes took steer-by-wire to its logical conclusion by fitting one demonstrator car with a 'joystick' to operate all the driver inputs. Steering (duplicated) and braking systems are seen here. (DaimlerChrysler)*

At the heart of all this, however, is one basic question: how exactly does the driver communicate with the car? It may be all very well to have a car with 'autopilot' ability, but the driver still has to tell the autopilot what is supposed to happen. The question of the car-driver 'interface' remains one of the more vexed questions in the design of the modern car.

# Driver controls

As we have already stated, the layout of the major controls in any car has been made almost standard throughout the world. The greatest difference between modern cars so far as major controls are concerned is the number of American-market models fitted with a pedal-operated parking brake with a hand release, while virtually all European and Japanese cars, except for some luxury models, are fitted with a central handbrake. The adoption of brake-by-wire will make possible a switch-operated or pushbutton parking brake, which would free some valuable cabin space for other purposes, but this is the most radical change in prospect so far as the main driver controls are concerned.

The standard method of making a steering wheel is now to use a foam-covered steel 'skeleton' with

*The joystick control of Mercedes's demonstrator in use. Obvious advantages include perfect vision of all the instruments, and a full-size airbag for the driver. In addition, the central stick could be used from either side of the car, and would have obvious benefits for disabled drivers. (DaimlerChrysler)*

deeply padded boss, for the sake of driver safety in a frontal impact. The central boss, now occupying much of the area within the rim, provides the housing for the driver airbag, whose fitting is now virtually standard. Steering columns are still designed to collapse and absorb the energy of the driver colliding with the hub, but as mentioned in Chapter 23, there is now more of a concern to ensure that the wheel provides a 'stable platform' from which to deploy the airbag. Most steering wheels can now be adjusted for height, and some also for reach, to help drivers of widely different sizes find a safe and comfortable position. More and more minor controls, such as those for the audio system and for cruise control where fitted, are being housed in the steering wheel hub, or on 'stalks' within fingertip reach of the wheel. Suggestions have been made for steering wheels whose hub remains stationary, with only the wheel rim actually rotating.

Where pedal controls are concerned, specialist engineers continue to worry about the balance between pedal travel (a relatively long travel being seen as contributing towards progressive rather than 'sudden' operation) and the need to save footwell space, to limit pedal movement during frontal impact to help protect the driver from foot and lower leg injury, and to avoid the problem of having to lift the foot from the accelerator to the brake pedal in an emergency-stop situation.

Trends in the design of gear levers, especially to cope with 6-speed gearboxes, and of automatic-transmission selectors giving the driver the choice between fully automatic operation and 'flick-shift' manual override, were discussed in Part 2, Chapters 10 and 11.

# Minor control layouts – **now simpler?**

Most of today's cars have two stalk controls mounted on the steering column, one to control wipe/wash operation, the other for indicators and headlamp operation. Many cars however retain a dashboard-mounted rotary master selector switch for the

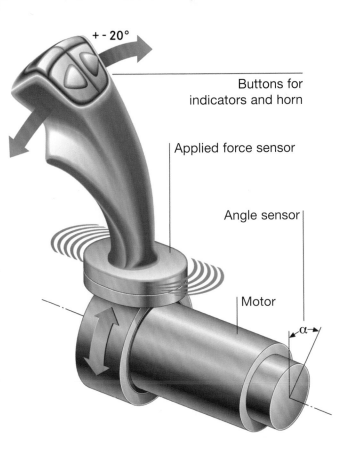

+ - 20°

Buttons for
indicators and horn

Applied force sensor

Angle sensor

Motor

α

*Technical 'close-up' of the
Mercedes joystick control,
showing the way in which the
various driver inputs are*

*sensed for onward
transmission to the 'X-by-
wire' control units.*
*(DaimlerChrysler)*

lighting system, often with other lighting functions
such as foglamp control built in. Most of the switches
for minor or less often used functions (heated rear
window, hazard warning flashers, etc) now take the
form either of push-push or slide switches to avoid
unnecessary projections and thus improve impact
safety. Modern lighting techniques (optical fibres,
etc) have greatly improved the identification of such
switches at night. The design trend is away from rows
of adjacent switches which, while looking neat, need
careful visual identification to ensure correct
operation by the driver.

There are three potential problem areas when it
comes to minor controls: heating and ventilation
controls, audio system controls, and manual overrides
for automatic systems. Most cars now use rotary
rather than slide controls for heating and ventilation,
and the actual number of controls has been reduced
with the arrival of 'intelligent' electronic systems.
These could eventually reduce the driver's need to
select heating distribution at screen, face or foot level.

Most audio system controls are much simpler than
they used to be. Several car manufacturers and their
audio system suppliers have developed 'satellite'
audio control modules to duplicate the main control
functions, such as frequency and volume change, and

waveband selection, in a switch cluster close to or
actually built into the steering wheel. Ergonomics in
this area will become an increasing concern as the
audio system becomes the 'front end' of a
communications and information-handling system.

Manual override switches are an area of potential
difficulty. In cars equipped with automated systems,
the need can also exist to provide the driver with the
means of overriding automatic selections, or to choose
between two or more automatic control patterns. We
already have switches to select, among other things,
'winter' and other modes of automatic transmission
operation, adaptive damper systems to a permanently
hard setting, to disable the rear electric window
switches (as a child safety measure), and sometimes to
switch off the ABS or traction control system. As X-
by-wire systems find wider use, the number of such
override switches could increase. A driver might be
offered, for example, a choice between 'quick' and
'relaxed' steering, or between 'fast' and 'progressive'
braking. In order to avoid undue complication, the
eventual answer is likely to take the form of adaptive
systems which continuously tailor themselves to
reflect driver behaviour – as is already happening in
the case of automatic transmissions.

There is growing interest in voice recognition
systems to control things like heating and ventilation,
the audio system, and perhaps even the windscreen
wipers, as well as any navigation system. With this
technology, already offered in some of the latest
luxury cars including the Jaguar S-type and X-type,
the driver simply 'talks' to the car in order to make
something happen. At the moment, the driver has to

*BMW has fitted its 'brake-by-
wire' demonstrator cars with
this type of steering wheel,
reminiscent of the old Austin
Allegro wheel. When there is*

*less than one turn of the
wheel between locks,
however, the shape is more
logical. Note the many built-
in controls. (BMW)*

learn a small repertoire of standard phrases in order to use such systems, but enthusiasts claim the advance of 'artificial intelligence' will make them far more flexible – and will allow the car to talk back. Sceptics point out that it takes less time (for instance) to switch on the windscreen wipers using a switch than it does to issue the same instruction by speaking clearly, but it seems certain that for some applications, voice recognition will prove a valuable as well as an interesting technology.

# Lighting systems

Headlamp design continues to be an issue in modern cars, because drivers want (and need) to see as much as possible without dazzling drivers in front of them, or coming the other way. Europe has usually led the way technically in this area because of its higher speed limits and often inferior driving conditions. Halogen headlamps have become standard, and discharge-type headlamps are now being fitted to more and more cars in the mid-range as well as luxury models. Reflector and lens technology has radically changed in the last few years.

In a discharge-type headlamp, the light is generated by an electrical discharge between two electrodes within a quartz bulb containing a high-pressure mixture of inert xenon gas and metal halides. The technical advantages of HID (high intensity discharge) lighting are lower power consumption, longer life and better light output, in terms of quality and quantity. A 35-watt HID lamp produces twice the light output of a 60-watt halogen

bulb, while its colour temperature is 'near daylight' in quality. Beam shaping is extremely precise, and bulb life is claimed potentially to match car life. Valeo, which together with Bosch and Hella has become one of the major suppliers of HID lamp assemblies, says its units achieve a 3,000-hour life, of which, in today's driving conditions, 2,500 hours are spent on dipped beam. Early HID headlamp units used HID for the dipped beam only, with a halogen main beam, but all-HID units are now gaining ground.

Valeo has quoted research to suggest that the volume of HID headlamps in the world market will grow to 7 million by 2005, a high proportion of them in Europe. The company also foresees the application of this technology to other areas of lighting, suggesting for instance that signal lamps could be made 25mm (1.0in) deep (i.e. reflector to lens) compared with 90mm (3.5in) at present, making them much easier to install. Such lamps would also enjoy a 5,000-hour life, making bulb failures virtually a thing of the past.

While HID looks the most likely headlamp technology for the future, alternatives have been suggested. Several suppliers have proposed systems in

*The modern trend in headlamp technology is towards xenon discharge units, as seen here in the unit for the Ford Mondeo, built into a complete front-corner cluster. In modern headlamp installations, beam control is a function of each individual unit, mainly through computer-aided design of 'complex' reflectors. The outer cover is just that – a protective moulding which plays no significant optical function. (Ford)*

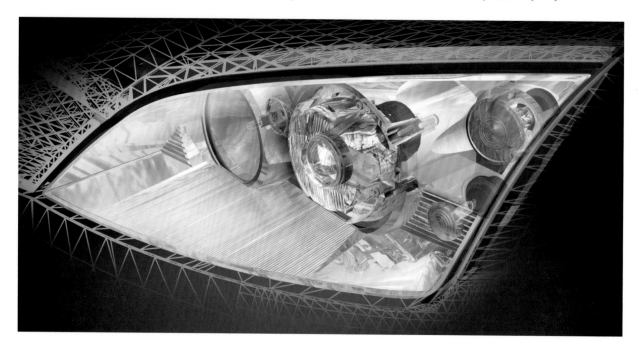

which extremely bright light would be generated from a single HID source inside a special enclosure within the car, to be transmitted to headlamp units by means of fibre-optic cables. Such a system would reduce the number of lamp units needed, would make it easier to accommodate the high-voltage system, and would protect the most expensive components from minor accident damage. Advantages would also accrue from the fact that at the visible lamp unit, the light would be 'cold', allowing the use of transparent plastic materials which are not compatible with the temperatures in conventional lamp units. The central source would obviously need to be duplicated to avoid the danger of a single failure leaving the driver with no light at all.

Apparently serious research has also been conducted into the use of ultra-violet headlamps to eliminate glare. The value of such lamps would be increased by using suitable reflective paint in road markings. Several practical problems remain to be solved before ultra-violet headlamps could be considered for production. Long-term studies are also being conducted into 'vision-enhancement' systems, mostly based around infra-red camera systems which are much better able to detect detail in the dark or in foggy conditions, especially when used in conjunction with infra-red projector 'headlamps'. Promising results have been shown in prototypes, but any practical application needs some form of head-up display panel on which the infra-red image can be projected, superimposed on the real, if dark or fog-bound, world.

Headlamp-cleaning systems are required by law in some countries. Small wiper units are still used by a few manufacturers, but high-pressure sprays of cleaning fluid are now the technology of choice. Headlamp levelling is another desirable feature, to prevent the glare caused by changes in vehicle attitude, whether under acceleration or because of a tail-heavy load. Levelling is an European Community legal requirement for cars equipped with HID headlamps. Systems are usually based on a rear suspension height sensor with hydromechanical or electrical signalling to a beam-height actuator.

# Wipe/wash systems

While, sadly, most engineers see little practical alternative to the apparently crude mechanical wiper arm for rain clearance, other approaches have been tried including treatment of the glass with a durable coating which almost eliminates surface tension, so that water on the windscreen forms a uniform transparent film.

Various techniques have already been used to improve the quality of mechanical screen wiping, to avoid smear without loading the wiper arm so heavily as to increase power consumption and the danger of judder. Some manufacturers have used complex wiper-arm linkages in an attempt to clear the 'blind spots' left by a conventional circular-arc pattern. Some of these systems have used a single wiper arm on a linkage which, during the sweep, pushes the blade towards the upper corners of the screen, clearing slightly more of the screen area than two conventional blades. Such an approach also overcomes the inconvenience of having to install 'handed' wiper patterns for left and right-hand drive.

An obvious step forward, suggested by both Bosch and Valeo, is to use twin synchronised motors, one for each wiper arm, instead of a single large motor with a complex and space-consuming linkage. Electronics can allow motors to be made reversible, yielding a useful mechanical simplification even when a single motor is used; and electronic control makes it easy to arrange for the wipers to be parked not only clear of the screen, but completely out of sight. Rain detectors, able to 'see' water drops on the screen and to switch on the wipers automatically, are now beginning to appear in production cars.

# Driver information systems

Many years ago, luxury and sports car manufacturers boasted of providing a 'full set' of analogue instruments which might display such information as oil pressure and temperature and electrical system voltage. Today the tendency is to 'display only what the driver really needs to see'. In theory, the only essential information is speed, since a speedometer is normally a legal requirement. Most product planners (and car drivers) would however add fuel quantity remaining, distance covered, and time as practical essentials. In practice, a very large number of cars today also add coolant temperature gauges and rev counters – although it is doubtful whether the majority of drivers make any good use of engine speed information.

While the majority of car instruments are still traditional round dials, many now make use of electronic display technology. The early enthusiasm for digital readings presented on an obviously 'electronic' panel has evaporated in the face of consumer resistance; instead, full use is made of the facilities created by modern display technology to create a representation of conventional analogue instruments, with the added advantages of clarity, accuracy, and flexibility of illumination. Surviving instruments with true electromechanical analogue mechanisms almost always now use electronic

signalling. It is much easier, and probably also more accurate, to take an electronic speed reading from the ABS computer than it is to run an old-fashioned speedometer cable from a special gear installed at the output end of the gearbox.

Supplier companies continue, from time to time, to demonstrate advanced display technologies, either of the head-up display (HUD) type, or of the virtual-image type. The HUD, based on technology which has been successfully used in aircraft, projects an image, focused so as to appear a considerable distance ahead of the car, onto the windscreen. The virtual display generates a 'head-down' image, but one which is again optically processed to appear some distance away. In both cases, the object is to reduce the need for refocusing between the display and the road.

A lot of information is now conveyed to drivers by warning lights. Some cars now carry a large 'central warning' light which draws the driver's attention to the need to examine the individual warnings. In some cases, warning lights have been integrated into a graphic 'check panel', often showing the vehicle in plan with indications of doors, etc, not properly secured. This approach is likely to extend if tyre pressure monitoring (see Part 3) becomes widespread. Audio warnings are also now found, with 'warning chimes' to remind drivers if, for example, the vehicle's lights are left on when the door is opened. Some manufacturers still retain warning systems using voice synthesisers to generate spoken messages, but for the most part drivers do not appreciate them once the novelty value has worn off. Spoken instructions from a navigation system (see later in this chapter) are a different matter.

Many more cars are now offered with some form of electronic parking aid, using ultrasonic proximity detectors. An example is provided by the BMW 7-series, which is offered with the option of park distance control (PDC), which uses ultrasonic sensors to 'guard' the four corners of the car and inform the driver, via an audio signal, how far away from the nearest obstacle the car is. The PDC system is switched on whenever reverse gear is selected, and disengaged whenever 30km/h (18.6mph) is exceeded or when the car has travelled more than 50 metres (164ft). Simpler systems 'guard' the rear bumper only, and warn the driver of closing distance by means of coloured lights in the corner of the rear window.

# Driver-assistance systems

Many systems are now on the market which provide the driver with navigation guidance: an indication of present position, and of how best to proceed to a selected destination. Many Japanese systems (though only for the Japanese market) provide drivers with other selected information and entertainment.

The principles of 'automatic' navigation are now well established, and rival systems differ only in the detail of the hardware and software. Geographic information is stored on CD-ROM (and more recently, on DVD), enabling it to be updated as necessary, and also allowing switching between different areas for long journeys. The vehicle's position is determined from Global Positioning System (GPS) satellite data, with a 'dead reckoning' backup to continue calculation should the GPS signals drop out (as happens in tunnels, and sometimes also in the radio 'shadows' of large buildings in dense urban areas).

Other facilities can be added to the basic navigation concept. Probably the most useful is the ability to accept real-time inputs from traffic information systems, either to warn the driver or even to allow the navigation system automatically to recalculate its 'shortest time' route if traffic congestion begins to affect the one it first set up. An almost limitless range of other information can be supplied and displayed on a navigation system, generally on a 'where is the nearest?' (vacant parking space, hotel, service station, hospital, golf course . . .) basis. Renault, which has worked with Philips in developing the Carminat series of navigation systems, plans to make available information from the celebrated *Guide Michelin*.

One problem with all existing systems, to a greater or lesser extent, is the difficulty of programming them – of inputting a new destination – quickly and easily. Today's systems mainly use the simplest possible input device, which may be no more than a

*Most of today's luxury cars are equipped with navigation systems that guide the driver on the best route to a chosen destination. With electronic adaptation and changes in the basic data stored in system memory, such systems can work well in any market, as seen in this unit shown by Mercedes at the 1999 Tokyo Motor Show! (Mercedes)*

pair of two-way rocker switches, but which force the user to scroll through and select from a series of menus. Other approaches, including touch-screen technology, trackball-and-cursor, or even the ability to plug a laptop computer into the navigation unit, have been suggested. This is one application where voice recognition may in the end prove the best solution.

Where guidance information is concerned, most experts now agree it is better to have the display – as large, bright and sharp as can be managed – high up on the dashboard so that the driver can see it without having to look down and away from the road. The latest displays are much improved, and use either TFT (thin film transistor) or advanced colour LCD technology, as in 'laptop' or notebook computers. Research continues into the best way to present visual information, as a map or a simplified diagram; an interesting variation is the 'Birdview' display developed by Nissan with its suppliers. Birdview shows the car, running through simplified scenery showing the calculated route, as seen from above and behind the vehicle.

Most current navigation systems offer some form of voice guidance, which many users find helpful. Careful development has enabled voice guidance to avoid some of the anticipated pitfalls of complex situations (especially in the older European cities) where junction layouts are complicated and the road layout is irregular. In systems intended for pan-European sale, the system 'voice' must obviously be multilingual. In practice this has not proved difficult.

# 'Intelligent-highway' systems

It is now technically possible to achieve substantial operating economies, improve safety and make better use of existing road space by using electronic-based systems to smooth traffic flow and prevent conflicts. Research programmes to encourage developments of this kind have been run in Europe (the PROMETHEUS programme), in Japan (the INVECS programme) and in the USA.

The success of all these projects depends on the ability of vehicles to communicate with the environment – more specifically, with transmitter-receivers forming part of an information gathering, processing and re-transmitting network – and with each other. Inter-vehicle communication could make possible systems to measure and control separation in traffic streams, with the main aim of maintaining an orderly, regularly spaced flow rather than of preventing nose-to-tail collisions. Communication between vehicle and environment covers a huge range of possibilities from receiving traffic-pattern data for navigation planning, through links with 'intelligent' road signals, to the automatic tracking of lane markings and the application of steering corrections for 'hands-off' driving. In some of these areas, manufacturers have continued hardware and software development to the point where advanced systems are now close to production. Intelligent cruise control is already being offered in some luxury models including the Jaguar S-type and the Mercedes S-class. Automatic lane tracking will probably appear in production by 2003. By that time, intelligent cruise control should have extended to automatic stop-go operation, permitting its use at low speeds and in dense traffic. The potential for an 'autopilot' will have been created, and the arguments will begin about the extent to which the driver remains not only fully responsible for the vehicle – which he must – but to what extent he should remain alert to take back control and resist the temptation to read the newspaper, send an e-mail or even doze off. Small wonder that another aspect of recent research has been into systems which detect when a driver's awareness begins to fail; scientists have studied various means of doing this, from analysing eye movements and blink rate to measuring the number of small steering corrections in a given time.

# **25** Electric
# power

The earliest cars functioned without any electric power at all: their engine ignition systems used magnetos (which need no external power source) and the lamps worked with acetylene gas (and probably created more noxious emissions than a modern engine). Starting was by handle, of course. Then came electric lamps and modern ignition systems, and once electric power was available designers began to use it for other things – not only electric starting but also windscreen wipers, and eventually all manner of systems.

In the early days, and for a long time afterwards, electrical systems were designed on the simplest possible basis. A supply lead was run from the battery to each component, interrupted at some point by a switch, usually driver-operated, which allowed the current to flow or not as required. Earthing was direct, via the metal body of the car. This is the way most vehicle electrical systems are still designed, but signs of change are emerging. In the new generation of electrical systems, there will be a distinction between power supply and control, which will eventually lead to systems which are physically lighter and easier to 'troubleshoot'.

This, however, is only one aspect of the new trend. It has been clear for some time that the car's demand for power has begun to exceed the ability of a powerful 14V alternator (supplying a 12V system, since the alternator always needs to work at a slightly higher voltage than the system it feeds) to supply, and the search has begun for alternatives. Most engineers now expect that within a few years, new cars will be equipped with alternators generating power at 42V instead of 14V, feeding a 36V system. Thus when looking at new-generation electrical systems, we need to consider two separate issues. First, what is the new power generation equipment going to look like? Second, what technology is going to be used in the new power-distribution and control systems?

# Generating more power

Where has the need for more power in the car come from? For a long time now, power has been needed for lighting, and for maintaining a high state of battery charge for engine starting. These demands were and are relatively modest, but as time went on they were joined by others: first windscreen wipers, heater fans and car radios, then electric cooling fans and heated rear windows, and most recently by heated windscreens, power-operated sunroofs, seats and mirrors. Engine management has itself become a

power consumer as it provides ignition, operates fuel injection, controls the movement of a number of auxiliaries (variable valve timing, variable inlet manifold geometry, EGR, and – with drive-by-wire – the throttle itself). Braking and chassis systems now need a power supply for ABS, traction control, and variable damping.

In a luxury car, these systems are already pushing the peak power requirement close to the 2kW which is all that can be squeezed out of a 14V alternator before hitting some fundamental limitations. If you need more power, you need a second alternator, or you need an alternator working at a higher voltage. The problem is, there are many new power-consuming features waiting in the wings. Entertainment systems are greedy for power, and cars are starting to offer features like refrigerated compartments and plug-in power points, but this is are only the beginning. Systems engineers are keen to replace many of the mechanical drives, now taken directly from the engine crankshaft via pulley and belt drive, with electrical drives. Such drives would be more efficient, because they would always absorb as much power as was needed and no more, while mechanical drives have to be designed to provide adequate output at near-idling speed, so most of their output is wasted when the engine is running fast. In addition, electrically driven accessories can be installed anywhere convenient, without having to worry about aligning pulleys and arranging belt drives.

So far, these solutions have been discouraged by the lack of electric power, but this will soon change. Even without them, luxury-class cars already need more power, which in effect means they need electrical systems running at a higher voltage – the only way is to raise the output of a single alternator to 5kW or more, which is what the system engineers say is a realistic requirement for the future. What is now certain to happen is that by 2005, most new-car alternators will work at 42V instead of 14V, and the main electrical system will work at 36V rather than 12V. In practice this is about as high as system voltage can be taken without needing more expensive features like double insulation, demanded by safety regulations for any direct current over 50V.

The greater power produced by 42V alternators

*Opposite: This prototype unit by Siemens is typical of the flywheel-integrated electrical machines of the next generation, which will serve as starter motors, alternators, drive 'boost' units and possibly also to smooth operation of the running engine by countering cyclic torque variation. Every big 'first tier' supplier to the motor industry has a development programme for a machine of this kind, usually intended to operate with a 36V electrical system. (Siemens)*

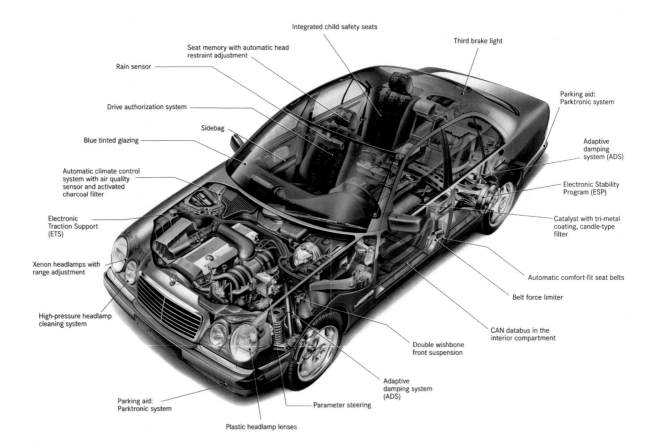

Integrated child safety seats

Third brake light

Seat memory with automatic head restraint adjustment

Parking aid: Parktronic system

Rain sensor

Drive authorization system

Adaptive damping system (ADS)

Sidebag

Blue tinted glazing

Electronic Stability Program (ESP)

Automatic climate control system with air quality sensor and activated charcoal filter

Catalyst with tri-metal coating, candle-type filter

Electronic Traction Support (ETS)

Xenon headlamps with range adjustment

Automatic comfort-fit seat belts

Belt force limiter

High-pressure headlamp cleaning system

CAN databus in the interior compartment

Double wishbone front suspension

Parking aid: Parktronic system

Adaptive damping system (ADS)

Parameter steering

Plastic headlamp lenses

will at last make practical ideas which engineers have wanted to try for some time. In earlier chapters we have talked about electric power steering, all-electric brake-by-wire, and the 'camless engine' with each valve individually electrically operated. But we are also talking, for example, about electrically driven air conditioning compressors, perhaps even electrically driven superchargers, to say nothing of an even wider range of power-hungry luxury items. Further demands will come from electrically heated catalysts or plasma-discharge exhaust aftertreatment, and engineers are even looking at things like electrically driven engine-coolant pumps.

Inevitably, there are some worries associated with a higher voltage. The worst is that the filament of a conventional 36V lamp bulb would be too flimsy to survive: the higher the voltage, the thinner the filament, and the more vulnerable it is to shock and vibration. For a time, 36V electrical systems will need to offer a stepped-down 12V supply for lighting (and perhaps some other) purposes. But we are already moving towards a world of HID headlamps and solid-state (LED) or discharge (neon) auxiliary lamps.

Renault, one of the vehicle manufacturers pushing hardest for 36V, reckons that by 2007 new cars will be all-36V and the existing 12V standard will effectively be dead.

On the power side of 36V system development, the three key elements are the 42V alternator itself, the battery, and the power distribution system. The alternator might adopt the general layout of existing 14V units, but its belt drive would need to handle the higher power involved – a toothed belt drive would probably be essential. As a result, by far the most interest seems to have switched to the idea of a 'toroidal' generator sandwiched between the engine and the transmission, built into the flywheel and forming a significant part of its mass. In effect this involves taking the existing alternator and redesigning all its components to make a unit which is very narrow, front to rear, but of much larger diameter. The combination of higher voltage and the new layout mean that such alternators will be far more efficient than existing ones – it will take relatively less engine power to provide the necessary electrical power.

*Opposite: This ghosted drawing of the Mercedes E-class shows the wide range of technologies which are now regarded as more or less* *essential in any up-market car if it is to be competitive – and more features are being added to the list all the time.* (Mercedes)

The toroid-in-flywheel design has many other potential advantages. Not only does it do away with the need for a belt drive; by reversing the alternator operation, the unit can be made to act as an extremely powerful and efficient starter motor, able to provide extremely fast and virtually silent engine starting. This in turn makes automatic start-stop operation in heavy traffic a practical proposition. Yet another advantage is that with suitable electronic control, the unit can act as a damper to reduce the cyclic torque variation of 4-cylinder engines, adding

or subtracting torque through the cycle, making them feel much smoother; the unit can also damp driveline torsional vibration, to smooth the effect of an abrupt power change or gearshift.

In addition, the motor can be used to add to the power of the internal-combustion engine for a short time, when climbing a steep hill or for faster overtaking. The engine itself can thus be made smaller and lighter, a direct energy-saving gain which can be supplemented by the potential ability of the

*Below: Renault says it is enthusiastic about the idea of building an electric motor/generator into the engine flywheel, to serve not only as the starter motor and* *power generator but also to smooth engine operation, to 'regenerate' power from the transmission, and to boost engine output when needed.* (Renault)

system to exercise 'energy management' to minimise losses especially during engine or mechanical braking – since in generator mode, the toroidal unit can recover energy from the transmission on the overrun and when travelling downhill. However, genuinely hybrid operation, with features such as starting from rest in electric mode, and the ability to select electric mode for continuous zero emission operation in restricted areas, needs more power than a 36V motor-generator can deliver. In such hybrid vehicles the unit would need to work at traction-motor voltages (90V and upwards) with the ability to deliver stepped-down voltages for general systems use.

Such is the promise of 42V motor-generators that it is easy to forget about the battery, but a 36V electrical systems demands 36V batteries. This might involve no more than a design change, because all batteries of

whatever voltage consist of a suitable number of individual cells. However, advanced functions such as quasi-hybrid operation, together with the need to cater for higher power outputs (including operation of the air conditioning and other functions when the engine is not running) are encouraging engineers to take advanced battery concepts, especially the nickel-metal hydride and lithium-polymer types, very seriously. Apart from this move to high energy-density concepts, two other trends can be seen in modern battery development. One is the 'intelligent battery' capable of managing and shutting down loads for the sake of safety and to preserve sufficient charge for engine restarting in all circumstances. The other is the relatively small, permanently charged battery needed as a backup for 'X-by-wire' control systems to guard against main power supply failure.

The adoption of 36V also brings benefits where the wiring loom is concerned. The higher voltage means that the same electrical power can be carried through thinner wires, which will allow wiring looms to be made slimmer and lighter if conventional designs

*At a technical seminar in 2000, BMW identified all these technologies as keys to increasing overall vehicle efficiency. New construction techniques and electronic systems figure strongly. (BMW)*

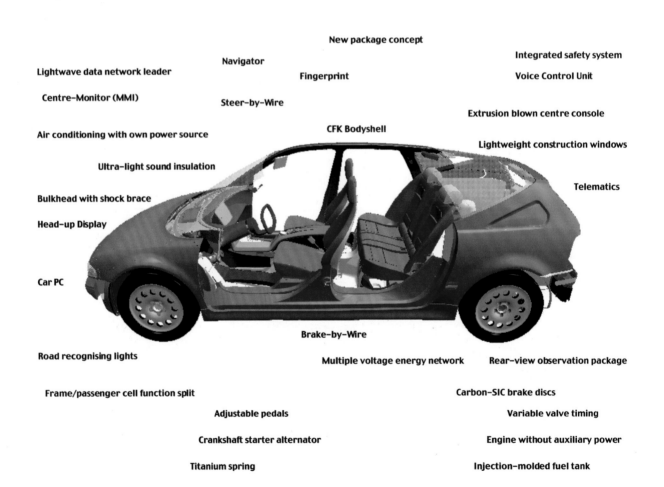

New package concept

Navigator

Integrated safety system

Lightwave data network leader

Fingerprint

Voice Control Unit

Centre–Monitor (MMI)

Steer–by–Wire

Extrusion blown centre console

Air conditioning with own power source

CFK Bodyshell

Lightweight construction windows

Ultra–light sound insulation

Telematics

Bulkhead with shock brace

Head–up Display

Car PC

Brake–by–Wire

Road recognising lights

Multiple voltage energy network

Rear–view observation package

Frame/passenger cell function split

Carbon–SIC brake discs

Adjustable pedals

Variable valve timing

Crankshaft starter alternator

Engine without auxiliary power

Titanium spring

Injection–molded fuel tank

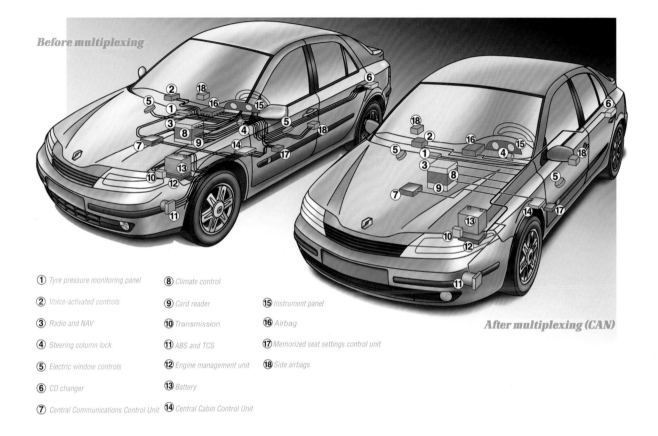

**Before multiplexing**

**After multiplexing (CAN)**

① Tyre pressure monitoring panel ⑧ Climate control

② Voice-activated controls ⑨ Card reader ⑮ Instrument panel

③ Radio and NAV ⑩ Transmission ⑯ Airbag

④ Steering column lock ⑪ ABS and TCS ⑰ Memorized seat settings control unit

⑤ Electric window controls ⑫ Engine management unit ⑱ Side airbags

⑥ CD changer ⑬ Battery

⑦ Central Communications Control Unit ⑭ Central Cabin Control Unit

remain in use. However, many systems specialists are now convinced that the future lies in a power 'ring main' – or a small number of rings, one for each main area of the vehicle – with the power take-off for each operating unit switched by a separate, multiplexed control circuit – which brings us to the second main area of electrical system development, that of power distribution and control generally.

*For the Laguna II, Renault turned to multiplexing as a means of reducing the sheer weight and volume of a car which not only employed a lot of new technology but was also 'future-proofed' through being able to accept systems* *as they became available. This drawing shows clearly the advantages of multiplexing. The counter-argument is that a considerable investment in technology is needed in order to make multiplexing work.* (Renault)

# Advanced **electrical control**

As already pointed out, when the first electrical systems were added to vehicles, power supply and control were combined in the simplest possible way, without distinguishing between them. A power lead, interrupted by a manually operated switch, ran from the battery to the component, which was earthed to the vehicle body. When the switch was made, power flowed and the component operated.

This approach worked perfectly well for at least half a century. Then the snags began to appear. First, the wiring around the instrument panel and steering column area housing the manual switches became

bulky and complex. Next, the wiring runs into the doors began to need special attention as electric window lifts, power door mirrors, door-mounted safety lights and central locking became popular. Even earlier than this, it became necessary to design the manual switches in high-power systems to accept high currents without overheating – or to use relays so that the switch only had to handle a fraction of the full current. Relays actually represented the first step along the way to separation of power supply and control signal. Eventually, luxury-class cars needed enough relays to make it worth housing them in a special box in the engine compartment, usually together with the fuses.

While any separation of power supply and control is a step in the right direction, it is only a beginning.

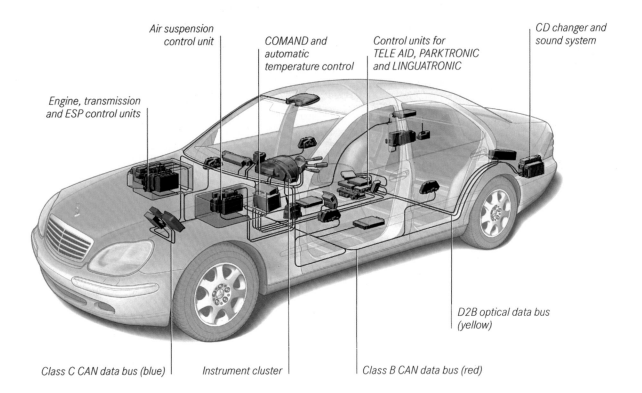

Air suspension
control unit

COMAND and
automatic
temperature control

Control units for
TELE AID, PARKTRONIC
and LINGUATRONIC

CD changer and
sound system

Engine, transmission
and ESP control units

D2B optical data bus
(yellow)

Class C CAN data bus (blue)

Instrument cluster

Class B CAN data bus (red)

*So much information must be passed around a large luxury car these days that communications and data handling must be fully engineered as systems in their own right. Possibly the best example of all is the Mercedes S-class seen here, which has three separate high-capacity networks distributing information according to purpose.* (DaimlerChrysler)

For instance, one possible approach to the door problem might have been to bridge the hinge with a wiring bundle consisting of a single high-capacity power cable and a number of low-current control cables running to relays inside the doors, but this raises the spectre of relays failing through repeated door-slamming. Instead, door electrics provided the entry point for multiplexing, a technology which allows not only the separation of the power and control functions, but also the simplification of control wiring to a single conductor carrying coded control signals for many different components, telling each one whether it should be switched on or off. In theory, multiplexing means the electrical system needs only two wires, one for the power supply and the other for signalling. Not only is this one stage beyond a relay-based system in which the control system remains a mass of individual wires (smaller, lighter, low-current wires, true); multiplex signals are well suited to 'solid-state' electronic power switching, so the fragility of mechanical relays is avoided too. A drawback is that each manual (or automatic) control switch, as well as each component, needs a small electronic module either to generate or to receive a specific instruction, and this adds to the cost of the system.

In addition, any multiplex system needs a 'communications protocol' – a common language shared by every multiplexed unit in the car (and preferably by every car from that manufacturer, and even more preferably by every car from any manufacturer). An industry-wide standard is still a long way off, but there are some widely accepted standards such as CAN (controller area network) and LAN (local area network). A closely argued point here is that some systems need far greater capacity for passing information than others, and it would be wasteful to use a high-capacity, high-technology system (which might well use an optical cable rather than an electrical conductor to carry its signals) for a low-requirement system. It would, in effect, be like installing a high-quality ISDN telecommunications line to your home and then using it only for normal telephone conversation.

ELECTRIC POWER

Some challenges remain in the perfection of multiplexing technology, and especially in ensuring that systems are flexible both in production (allowing a single system to be used in vehicles equipped to different standards) and in the aftermarket. Delphi has shown a system equipped with two types of interface – depending on whether or not the additional component has in-built 'intelligence' – and allowing the component to be installed on the same 'plug and play' basis now familiar in personal computer systems.

As for optical fibre, it is often seen as the 'ultimate' signal transmission medium, enabling small and ultra-light fibres to carry information at a far higher rate than any electrical conductor of comparable size. Optical fibre has the further advantage of being proof against electromagnetic interference, which has become a far greater worry in recent years. One factor which seems to be holding back the widespread use of optical fibres is the cost and reliability of electrical-to-optical converters, needed at each end of the optical-fibre run, and (yet again) a protracted debate over operating protocols. Fibres will certainly be used on a larger scale where the high-speed interchange of information is vital, for instance in the 'integrated safety systems' now being proposed by Delphi among others.

# 26 Systems for comfort and convenience

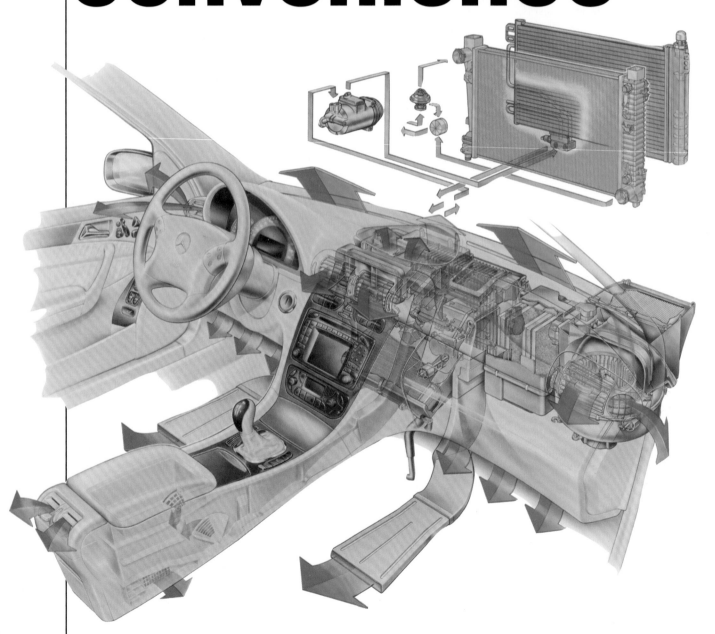

One of the vitally important yet often overlooked areas of vehicle engineering is that of comfort and convenience. Fundamentally it involves taking care of everything car occupants need to travel comfortably as well as safely (see Chapter 23) and efficiently (Chapter 24).

The most fundamental need of any car occupant is to be comfortably seated, which calls for properly distributed support across the area of the cushion and in the backrest. The problem here is that car seats need to cater for people of many different sizes, and in the case of the driver, must allow the creation of a sitting position which gives a good working relationship with the steering wheel and the pedals. In practice, it is easiest to achieve this when the driving position is relatively upright – more like a dining chair than a deckchair. When the driving position is semi-reclining, as in most low-slung sports cars, an adjustable steering wheel position (or in rare cases, a reach-adjustable pedal cluster) is essential for the accommodation of a wide range of driver sizes. Where an upright driving position can be achieved it brings two further advantages: better driver visibility, and easier entry to and exit from the seat and the cabin without effort, contortion or loss of dignity. All these things help to explain why so many drivers, and especially perhaps small women drivers, feel so much at ease when driving SUVs or 'people carriers'. To some extent, therefore, the search for a good driving position is a conflict between basic car design, which sees reduced frontal area and a low centre of gravity as desirable, and ergonomics which dictates that the driver should sit upright with as high an eye-line as practicable.

While cars have always had seats, and some seats have always been more comfortable than others, proper car heating is a more recent invention. Today it is taken for granted, but even in the late 1950s it was possible to buy cars in which the heater was an optional extra. It was later still before heating systems as we know them today, with airmix temperature control, quiet fans and user-selected heat distribution, became familiar. Properly planned ventilation with positive but controlled through-flow came later still, during the 1960s. Air conditioning, the ultimate refinement, had been widely adopted in the USA during the 1980s but is still winning its mass market in Europe.

Under the general heading of 'security and convenience' come a number of features which are now seen as desirable or even essential, but which would have astonished the car designers of the 1940s. We now take it for granted that any new car will include systems that make it more difficult for even a skilled thief to steal, for example. The sheer convenience of central locking and electric windows is something few drivers want to do without once they have become used to them. The list of such features is being added to all the time, and it is difficult to see quite where it may stop. After all, many people today spend as much time in their cars as they do sitting in their living rooms; why should the car interior be any less comfortable or spacious than the living room?

## Seating

The design of a seat and of a driving position is normally centred around the '50th percentile male' – the man who represents, in terms of height, weight, reach, leg length and so on, the mid-point of the entire male population which might be seen as potential customers. From that starting point, designers then try to accommodate the needs of occupants from the 10th to 90th percentile male. It follows, in theory and in practice, that very small women drivers potentially face the most extreme problems where the seat itself is concerned, while males above the 90th percentile may suffer problems of limited space – especially headroom – rather than with the seat as such. To a large extent, problems of sitting position can be overcome if enough adjustment for height and reach is provided, but sheer lack of space is a fundamental issue.

*Opposite: Modern heating, ventilation and air conditioning (HVAC) systems are extremely complex, and their integration into the car has to be considered at the earliest design stage. This diagram shows the system installed in the Mercedes C-class, introduced in 2000. Note the number of separate feeds for warm or cooled air, to the back seats as well as in the front. (Mercedes)*

Almost all passenger car front seats now offer adjustment of fore-and-aft position and of the backrest angle to the vertical. As already pointed out, the more reclined the driving position, the greater the range of fore-and-aft movement needed to cater for a given range of driver sizes. When adjustable backrests were first introduced, they were thought of mainly as providing a 'sleeper' position, especially for the passenger. Today backrest angle adjustment is commonly misused by drivers, especially large drivers, to overcome other ergonomic deficiencies: the greater the reclining angle, the greater the headroom (at whatever cost to an ergonomically correct driving position), while altering the angle at intervals will change the pressure distribution beneath the body and stave off the discomfort resulting from an unsuitable cushion.

Especially for semi-reclined driving positions, the steering wheel also needs to adjust fore-and-aft to enable drivers of different leg length to achieve an equally comfortable reach to the wheel. Vertical wheel adjustment may also help by creating sufficient rim clearance above the thighs of large occupants, while dropping the wheel clear of the field of view of small ones. In practice, vertical adjustment of the steering wheel – which is more easily and cheaply achieved – is found more often than adjustment for reach.

In 4-seat cars with only one door per side, the front seats must also fold or slide forward to permit access to the back seats. It is now common to find the front seat sliding to the forward end of its adjustment as the backrest folds forward, with 'position memory' provision in the mechanism to ensure that the seat afterwards returns to its original position rather than remaining fully forward.

In mid-range and luxury cars extra adjustments are provided for the driver's seat. The most common extra adjustment is seat height, but there are many seats which also provide adjustment of cushion tilt angle and the amount of lumbar support. Height adjustment is useful to both very small and very large drivers for achieving an adequate view; in 2000 Volvo showed a safety concept car in which a driver's eye height sensor and automatic seat height adjustment meant that all drivers were seated with their eyes at the right height for optimum visibility. Cushion tilt adjustment enables drivers to avoid slipping forward into an uncomfortable and unsound sitting position and, like backrest angle adjustment but more effectively, can shift the support pressure pattern to postpone the onset of permanent discomfort. To be really effective, lumbar support needs to be adjustable for height as well as firmness. Too much support at the wrong height can be as bad as a general lack of support.

The most common form of seat structure remains a tubular steel frame with either wire springing or a pressed steel cushion pan, with interior steel-sprung or polyurethane foam cushioning. Cushion pan design now often takes account of the danger of occupants 'submarining' beneath the lap-straps of their safety belt in frontal impacts, and incorporate some kind of hump to reduce this risk. Safety legislation now means the seat floor mountings must be strong enough to prevent the seat from tearing free during an impact, while the front seat 'hinge' between cushion and backrest must resist the impact of a back seat passenger being thrown forward: failure in this case is bad for both the back and front seat occupants. Most modern cars now attach the inboard safety belt buckle to the seat rather than the floor for improved harness geometry, and some high-line seats also have the inertia reel and shoulder guide built-in, removing safety-belt loads from the centre pillar at the expense

of greater structural weight in the seat itself. This arrangement is essential in 'pillarless coupé' body designs.

Despite the effect on both the cost and weight of vehicles, power operation of seats became more popular during the 1990s. It is now quite common to find front seats with power-operated adjustment for fore-and-aft reach, backrest angle, head restraint height, cushion tilt and seat height. More front seats are also provided with electric cushion heating, with suitable safeguards, while power-operated steering wheel position adjustment is an accepted luxury feature. Such adjustments may be accompanied by driving position memory, in which a number of preset seat and steering wheel position adjustments can be stored in a power operation system control processor, enabling the driver to select 'personally' correct settings when entering the vehicle. At the top end of the market, other functions such as power-operated door mirror positioning and even preferred radio station selection can be added to this automatic setting-up process.

# HVAC (heating, ventilation and air conditioning)

Because car users now expect such high levels of comfort, heating and ventilation systems have become more complicated and powerful. Airmix heaters, blending separate streams of hot and cold air, have been the industry standard because they respond more quickly to temperature selection. Large, low-noise, multi-speed fans have replaced ram-effect air intakes, the idea being to reduce changes in system performance with speed. Thermostatic control of cabin temperature, with electronically controlled automatic operation of system blending valves is increasingly common. Meanwhile engineers have taken a greater interest in reducing unwanted (and often powerful) solar heating through the windows and especially the windscreen, using tinted glass and even reflective metallised coatings. At the other temperature extreme, a few luxury cars are now equipped with double-glazed side windows.

Even the smallest cars tend now to be equipped with heating and ventilation systems which would once have been considered expensive. A typical minimum specification consists of an airmix heater assembly, multi-speed, low-noise centrifugal fan, face-level and front footwell vents, and supplementary dashboard-level outlets for demisting the side windows. Common additional features include an airflow-recirculating mode to prevent the entry of traffic fumes when stuck in congestion, and additional ducting to feed warm air to the back seats.

Regulation is mainly a question of valve design, especially of the unit which mixes fresh ambient air (or cooled air from the air-conditioning radiator) with hot air from the heater matrix, together with the valves which distribute the resulting mix within the cabin. The need for rapid engine warm-up from a cold start causes one or two problems. For emission-control purposes, the engine itself should warm up as quickly as possible, but the process may be slowed if available heat is immediately fed to the cabin. Because it is desirable to clear mist and ice from windows as quickly as possible to ensure driver visibility, the long-established electrically heated rear window has now been joined by the electrically heated windscreen, using much finer heating elements which are virtually invisible so long as the eye is focused at a greater distance. Electric demisting is not only quick and effective, but actually helps the engine to warm up faster by imposing an additional load.

Another problem which has recently emerged is that of the extremely low amount of heat rejected at light load by the new generation of highly efficient direct-injection diesel engines. Normally, the output of the cabin heating system is a function of heater matrix size and of the coolant flow capacity of the heater circuit; but even when fully warmed through, these high-efficiency diesels can fail to produce sufficient heat to maintain a cabin interior at a comfortable level in sub-zero ambient temperatures. Proposals for overcoming this problem have included auxiliary heater burners, and the use of heat rejected from water-cooled alternators. It has also been suggested that cars might be equipped with a system to use remaining engine heat to warm the cabin interior after the engine has been switched off, until either the coolant temperature or the battery voltage reaches a certain level.

A further refinement of the heating system, recently introduced by Renault in its current Espace, is to split the conventional single heater unit, complete with heater matrix, heater fan and distribution valve block (and the air-conditioning evaporator when fitted) into two smaller units, one on each side of the vehicle. Renault says that although this approach is slightly more expensive, the two smaller units are easier to install, reducing the length of the bulkhead area and thus increasing the crushable structure length to improve passive safety, while also allowing the front seat occupants each to have control of their own footwell temperature.

In the Arctic temperatures of the Scandinavian market, many cars are fitted with electric heaters plumbed into the coolant circuit or the sump, and plugged into domestic power sockets or even into sockets provided at public parking places. Devices also exist to cool down the cabin in hot climates when the engine is not running. In the early 1990s, the Mazda 929 was offered with the option of a ventilation fan whose electric motor was powered from roof-mounted solar cells. Any spare output was used to top up the battery charge. Mazda claimed its tests showed that the interior temperature of a vehicle left in hot sun could reach 75°C; the automatic ventilation system reduced this to 60°C, enabling the air-conditioning system to achieve a comfortable cabin temperature 30% quicker once the engine was restarted. Similar systems have since appeared on other production cars and on many concept cars.

It is now almost standard practice to provide some form of filtering in the ventilation system air intake. Given careful design, such units can be highly effective. Volkswagen for example claims the unit offered in the Golf removes at least 50% of all airborne particles, and up to 99% of any pollen present. Some manufacturers also use an activated-charcoal bed as part of the filter system, to trap pollutants and odours.

The considerable majority of cars sold in North America and Japan are now fitted with air conditioning, and the proportion of European cars equipped with HVAC systems is now rising steeply. More and more such systems are electronically controlled, using a cabin temperature sensor (and often more than one) to hold the user-selected cabin temperature. Additional features can include a cold-air feed to the glovebox or other compartment, to allow the storage of cool drinks in hot weather. Some systems now offer 'dual-zone' capability, enabling front seat occupants to select different temperatures. In a few cases, this ability extends to maintaining a third selected temperature in the back seat area.

There is a growing interest in reducing the energy consumption of air-conditioning systems, which can be responsible for significant parasitic losses, reducing performance and increasing fuel consumption. The latest air-conditioning compressors use variable-angle swashplate drives, matching the compressor stroke – and thus the power consumption – to the needs of the system. There has also been extensive development, especially in Japan, of electrically driven compressors, originally to serve the climate-control needs of electric vehicles. The primary advantage of electric drive is the energy efficiency resulting from strictly 'on demand' operation, but further advantages include easier interfacing with an electronic control system, and freedom of installation, avoiding the requirement for a bulky and carefully aligned belt-drive from the crankshaft.

All current air-conditioning systems use one of the family of refrigerants developed to replace the CFCs which served as the working fluid until the early 1990s, when they were shown to have a serious effect on the ozone layer of the atmosphere if they were released. Most manufacturers have developed programmes to retrieve and safely dispose of CFCs from older models, during service or at disposal, without releasing the harmful refrigerant into the atmosphere.

# Security and convenience features

One strong technical trend of recent years has been the adoption of power operation for equipment which used to be manually operated. Power-operated seat, steering column, mirror, and safety-belt height adjustment has already been mentioned. Other such items include window, sunroof and radio aerial operation, as well as the central locking of doors, luggage compartment and fuel-filler cover. Many of these items have spread to all but the cheapest 'entry level' models.

Power operation itself is not enough. Further improvements are still sought. For example, power-operated windows have become faster and quieter, and often now include pinch-detection devices to stall an operating motor if a rising window happens to trap fingers. Developments have also included 'one-touch' operation, usually only of the driver's window.

Similar developments have been applied to central-locking systems. These are usually now provided with remote-control operation, and with 'afterthought' provision for the closing of power-operated windows and sunroof if these have been left open. There has been a move away from the infra-red remote operation of early systems, to radio-frequency operation which is effective at greater ranges and can be more effectively encoded to guard against 'grabbing' by scanner units.

Vehicle security is fast becoming a design aspect in its own right. Most developed car markets have seen a steep increase in vehicle-related crime, and the motor industry is now showing greater interest in more secure locking systems and in alarm systems.

Where both remote-control central locking and an alarm system are fitted, it has become standard

*Opposite: An interesting feature of Renault's Laguna II, launched in 2000, is the keyless entry system via which the car recognises its driver by sensing the presence of a 'card' that he or she carries. So long as the card is close, the car will unlock at the first touch on a door handle. The card also acts as the 'ignition key' when inserted in a slot in the dashboard. Naturally, the system is heavily dependent on advanced electronics for its proper operation.*
*(Renault)*

practice to arm and disarm it via operation of the remote control switch. The days when 'casual' thieves could enter a locked car with zero or minimum damage are running out: locks and locking mechanism linkages are increasingly being equipped with features to make it more difficult to force an entry to a vehicle other than by breaking glass. Deadlocking systems are a deterrent even in this case, because the doors cannot be opened without the key (or correct remote-control transmitter) even from inside the car.

The technology of protection against driving away appears to be changing. The conventional approach – and a legal requirement in most markets – is to lock the steering column so that the car cannot be steered. This is not always effective, although it remains a valuable protection against the casual thief. Modern electronic engine-management systems now make it possible to prevent the engine being started without a correct entry to the computer. It is thus no longer possible to start engines by 'hot wiring' under the bonnet to bypass the ignition lock.

A new feature which combines convenience and security is 'keyless entry', offered by Renault in its Laguna II, launched in 2000. The driver carries a 'smart card' which is remotely recognised by the vehicle as the driver approaches; the central locking system then unlatches the driver's door as soon as the handle is lifted. Inside the Laguna, the driver then inserts the same card into a slot in the dashboard, to release the engine immobiliser. The engine can then be started with a simple push-button. To leave the car secure, the driver needs only push the button again, remove the card from its slot, get out, shut the door and walk away. As soon as the card is out of detection range, everything is locked.

Exactly how such systems work depends on the detail of the security requirement. In some markets, for example, customers worry about violent thieves crouching out of sight below the sill on the passenger side, waiting to jump in as soon as a central-locking system unlocks all the doors. In such markets, only the driver's door is unlocked to begin with. Also, as an alternative to an easily recognised 'smart card', some systems suppliers offer a personal 'identifier'

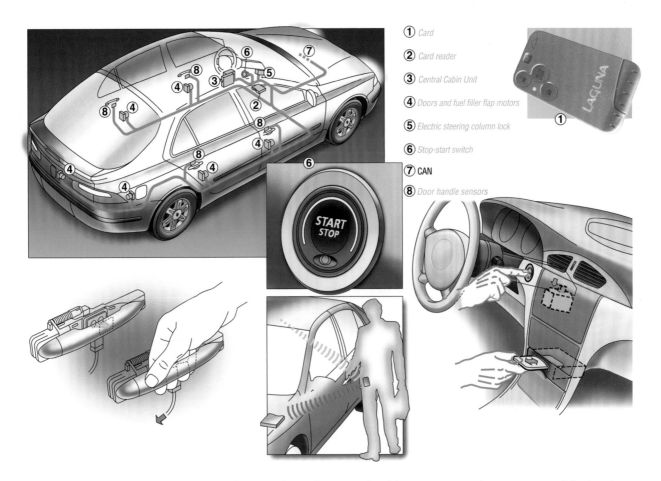

① Card
② Card reader
③ Central Cabin Unit
④ Doors and fuel filler flap motors
⑤ Electric steering column lock
⑥ Stop-start switch
⑦ CAN
⑧ Door handle sensors

which can be housed within any of a number of personal effects to conceal its function if lost or stolen.

Systems have also been created in which stolen vehicles may be 'tagged' by means of a small, hidden signal transmitter. These schemes have enjoyed considerable success in the recovery of high-value vehicles, but their cost and the potential load on the infrastructure has so far been a deterrent to their more general employment. This may change with the introduction of GPS-based technology and system automation.

# Index